Culture-specific Language Styles

D0726611

Leeds Metropolitan University

17 0362227 8

Child Language and Child Development: Multilingual-Multicultural Perspectives

Series Editor: Professor Li Wei, *University of Newcastle- upon-Tyne, UK*
Editorial Advisors: Professor Gina Conti-Ramsden, *University of Manchester, UK*
Professor Kevin Durkin, *The University of Western Australia*
Professor Susan Ervin-Tripp, *University of California, Berkeley, USA*
Professor Jean Berko Gleason, *Boston University, USA*
Professor Brian MacWhinney, *Carnegie Mellon University, USA*

Children are brought up in diverse yet specific cultural environments; they are engaged from birth in socially meaningful and appropriate activities; their development is affected by an array of social forces. This book series is a response to the need for a comprehensive and interdisciplinary documentation of up-to-date research on child language and child development from a multilingual and multicultural perspective. Publications from the series will cover language development of bilingual and multilingual children, acquisition of languages other than English, cultural variations in child rearing practices, cognitive development of children in multicultural environments, speech and language disorders in bilingual children and children speaking languages other than English, and education and healthcare for children speaking non-standard or non-native varieties of English. The series will be of particular interests to linguists, psychologists, speech and language therapists, and teachers, as well as to other practitioners and professionals working with children of multilingual and multicultural backgrounds.

Other Books in the Series
Language and Literacy in Bilingual Children
  D. Kimbrough Oller and Rebecca E. Eilers (eds)

Other Books of Interest
The Care and Education of Young Bilinguals: An Introduction to Professionals
  Colin Baker
Child-Rearing in Ethnic Minorities
  J.S. Dosanjh and Paul A.S. Ghuman
Cross-linguistic Influence in Third Language Acquisition
  J. Cenoz, B. Hufeisen and U. Jessner (eds)
Dyslexia: A Parents' and Teachers' Guide
  Trevor Payne and Elizabeth Turner
Foundations of Bilingual Education and Bilingualism
  Colin Baker
Encyclopedia of Bilingualism and Bilingual Education
  Colin Baker and Sylvia Prys Jones
Multicultural Children in the Early Years
  P. Woods, M. Boyle and N. Hubbard
Working with Bilingual Children
  M.K. Verma, K.P. Corrigan and S. Firth (eds)
Young Bilingual Children in Nursery School
  Linda Thompson

Please contact us for the latest book information:
Multilingual Matters , Frankfurt Lodge, Clevedon Hall,
Victoria Road, Clevedon, BS21 7HH, England
http://www.multilingual-matters.com

CHILD LANGUAGE AND CHILD DEVELOPMENT 1
Series Editor: Li Wei

Culture-specific Language Styles

The Development of Oral Narrative and Literacy

Masahiko Minami

MULTILINGUAL MATTERS LTD
Clevedon • Buffalo • Toronto • Sydney

For my wife, Hitomi, and our children, Tomoko, Noritaka and Kaori

Library of Congress Cataloging in Publication Data
Minami, Masahiko
Culture-specific Language Styles: The Development of Oral Narrative and
Literacy/Masahiko Minami
Child Language and Child Development: 1
Includes bibliographical references and index
1. Language acquisition. 2. Discourse analysis, Narrative. Japanese language–
Acquistion. 4. Mother and child. 5. Language and culture. 6. Literacy.
I. Title. II. Series.
P118.M55 2002
401'.93–dc21   2001044535

British Library Cataloguing in Publication Data
A catalogue entry for this book is available from the British Library.

ISBN 1-85359-574-8 (hbk)
ISBN 1-85359-573-X (pbk)

Multilingual Matters Ltd
UK: Frankfurt Lodge, Clevedon Hall, Victoria Road, Clevedon BS21 7HH.
USA: UTP, 2250 Military Road, Tonawanda, NY 14150, USA.
Canada: UTP, 5201 Dufferin Street, North York, Ontario M3H 5T8, Canada.
Australia: Footprint Books, Unit 4/92a Mona Vale Road, Mona Vale, NSW 2103, Australia.

Typeset by Florence Production Ltd.
Printed and bound in Great Britain by the Cromwell Press Ltd.

Contents

Preface

Language is a crucial universal form of human symbolic behavior. At the same time, language is a manifestation of the culture where it is spoken. Communication skills are one of the most important tools in our lives, and are essential for the development, maintenance, and transmission of culture from one generation to the next. The relationship between language and culture, however, is sometimes complicated. The United States, for example, is becoming increasingly pluralistic and multicultural. To understand the challenges in this cultural shift, we need to examine cross-cultural issues in children's narrative development.

This study is concerned with the discipline of interactional sociolinguistics. One way of defining the discipline is to study speakers' socially motivated linguistic choices. My research also concerns the relationship between linguistic forms and their functions in the development of children's narrative discourse, under specific cultural influences as well as developmental constraints. Aiming to facilitate cross-cultural understanding, this book is roughly divided into two sections. Section I focuses on an analysis of the personal narratives told by Japanese preschool children. Section II focuses on mother–child narrative discourse in Japan and North America, using categories of meaning that emerge from the data.

The results of Section I indicate that Japanese children tend to tell concise stories that are cohesive collections of several personal experiences. This succinct narrative style exhibited by Japanese children shows a remarkable contrast to the narrative style of North American children, which is typically a lengthy story detailing a single experience that often revolves around the solution of some problem. I have found that the simplicity of the Japanese children's style may strike Americans as 'boring,' 'unimaginative' or 'in need of special education,' unless such characteristics are pointed out and related to the Japanese cultural value of avoiding verbosity.

The results of Section II indicate: (1) English-speaking North American mothers allow their young children to take long monologic turns, ask their children many questions about the content of the monologue, and offer positive evaluation of the narrative; (2) Japanese mothers, on the other hand, paying close attention to their children's narratives, facilitate frequent turn exchanges and offer few evaluative comments. I therefore conclude that, from early childhood on, children become accustomed to culturally valued narrative discourse skills through interactions with their mothers. In terms of models of human development, however, rather than placing too much emphasis on cultural transmission models, my research focuses on sociocultural models that conceptualize parent and child as interactive partners in the creation of cultural meanings. The link between maternal narrative elicitation strategies and children's developing narrative skill is then demonstrated. In addition, Section II of my book will illuminate the degree to which sociocultural specificity and relativism attend narrative discourse practice. I also discuss issues related to emergent literacy as an extension of mother–child conversational interactions separately in Section II.

The material in this book may also be of interest to those who engage in the study of child language and child development. Developmental psycholinguists have argued that many clues to language development – literacy development in particular – can be identified in the conversational exchanges between mothers and their young children. Becoming literate is thus known as a process that begins long before schooling takes place, and parents' interaction with their children has an important influence on their children's language development. Transcription samples in this book provide valuable and richly illustrative descriptions of the coding systems used for analyzing the data collected.

I also believe that this research has great relevance to relations between individuals growing up with widely divergent sociocultural backgrounds, such as Japanese and Americans. First, the study addresses critical issues in the field of education, particularly in the sense that cross-cultural studies greatly help teachers working with students from other cultures. As a result of the rapid social diversification arising in large part from the increase in immigration from Asian countries such as China, Korea and Japan, early childhood education is playing an increasingly important role in the schools in the United States. In spite of the fact that educational settings are becoming increasingly multicultural, particularly in urban areas in the United States, people often assess other cultures through their own cultural lens and thus can easily be misled by ill conceived stereotypes. For example, an American teacher who comes from the cultural mainstream may not understand that the background culture of Japanese students relies on 'communicative compression,' and may also not understand how it affects students' expression. Therefore, I think it important to emphasize that cross-cultural studies hold significant meaning for education, and that the results of this research can serve as a document for teachers and administrators who may have difficulty understanding students from different cultural backgrounds.

Second, the stronger the political and economic relationship between the East and the West (e.g. between the United States and Japan), the more opportunities peoples of different countries with different cultures will have for contact and interaction. While misunderstandings based on cultural differences sometimes take place, this study suggests that such cultural differences not only in business but also in school settings have their origins in the differences in early mother–child interactions at home.

Thus, this book, I believe, can make a significant contribution to cross-cultural understanding. As I stated above, because the book deals with important issues of cultural diversity in terms of narrative development, it will be very useful to people living in modern societies that are becoming increasingly multicultural and multilingual. In this sense, the book further pertains not only to first-language acquisition but eventually to the instruction of second- or foreign-language learners as well. It is my hope that, particularly in the field of child language and development, my research can provide a basis for reducing cultural stereotypes and improving cross-cultural understanding.

Acknowledgments

I am indebted to the many people who have supported this work and provided me with invaluable support along the way. I wish to express my special thanks to the mothers and children who participated in this research project and generously gave their time for the interviews, and the preschool teachers and personnel in Japan who allowed me to observe classrooms and helped make the necessary arrangements. Most of the analysis, with the exception of Chapter 8, was done as part of my work toward a doctorate in developmental psychology at Harvard University. I owe a tremendous debt to the people who taught me there, and would like to thank in particular Catherine Snow and Lowry Hemphill. I am indebted to Terry Tivnan for statistical assistance. I was particularly fortunate to have the great privilege to work with Allyssa McCabe on some of this material.

The issues discussed in this book have been at the center of my attention for the last several years. During that time, some of the material in this book has appeared in various preliminary forms in other places. The ideas behind Chapter 2 first took shape when I edited a book entitled *Language Issues in Literacy and Bilingual/Multicultural Education*, which was published by the *Harvard Educational Review* in 1991. A slightly different version of the analysis that constitutes a portion of Chapter 4 was published as 'Japanese Preschool Children's Narrative Development,' *First Language* (1996), 16, pp. 339–363. Chapter 5 is a revision of material that originally appeared in 'Japanese Preschool Children's and Adults' Narrative Discourse Competence and Narrative Structure,' *Journal of Narrative and Life History* (1996), 6, pp. 349–373. Chapter 6 contains an analysis of texts that I also discussed in 'Maternal Styles of Narrative Elicitation and the Development of Children's Narrative Skill: A Study on Parental Scaffolding,' *Narrative Inquiry* (2001), 11, pp. 55–80. Chapter 7 reworks and integrates material that has appeared in a number of different places: 'English and Japanese: A Cross-Cultural Comparison of Parental Styles of Narrative Elicitation,' *Issues in Applied Linguistics* (1994), 5, pp. 383–407, 'Long Conversational Turns or Frequent Turn Exchanges: Cross-Cultural Comparison of Parental Narrative Elicitation,' *Journal of Asian Pacific Communication* (1995), 6, pp. 213–230, and 'Cultural Constructions of Meaning: Cross-Cultural Comparisons of Mother–child Conversations About the Past,' *Problem of Meaning: Behavioral and Cognitive Perspectives* edited by C. Mandell and A. McCabe (1997), pp. 297–345. 'Styles of Parent–Child Book-Reading in Japanese Families,' a paper that discusses issues contained in, and related to, Chapter 8 has been published in *Research on Child Language Acquisition: Proceedings of the 8th Conference of the International Association for the Study of Child Language* edited by M. Almgren, A. Barreña, M. Ezeizabarrena, I. Idiazabal and B. MacWhinney (2001), pp. 483–503. I have received many comments on the above mentioned papers, and I have tried to incorporate my responses to them in various parts of this book.

I wish to thank Professor Li Wei, General Editor of this new book series *Child Language and Child Development: Cross-Linguistic and Cross-Cultural Perspectives*, for allowing me the opportunity to transform collections of my research into a book. For help with the final preparation of the manuscript, I also thank Karen Oakley and Gary Bottone.

My greatest acknowledgment goes to my wife, Hitomi, for her love, support, patience and encouragement. Particularly, because without her support in the data collection and transcription, this study would not have been completed. I thank my children, Tomoko, Noritaka and Kaori, my parents and all of my relatives and friends for their encouragement. The research reported in this book was made possible through the dissertation support fund from the Harvard Graduate School of Education, and a travel and research grant from the Harvard University Office of International Education/Harvard Institute for International Development, San Francisco State University Research and Professional Development Support Fund. Transcriptions were made possible through an American Psychological Association Dissertation Research Award. The final preparation of the manuscript was assisted through a Presidential Award for Professional Development of Faculty from San Francisco State University.

Masahiko Minami

Chapter 1
Introduction

The Problems

In any society, a child's life is driven in part by particular models of what parents believe to be the 'good life' and the 'ideal individual.' Culture has a variety of implications in this respect. To begin with, culture is defined as consisting of a set of attitudes, beliefs, customs and values shared by a group of people, communicated from one generation to the next via language or some other means of communication (Fischer & Lazerson, 1984; Matsumoto, 2000; Super & Harkness, 1980). This definition suggests that culture is learned behavior, shaping attitudes and encouraging some types of behaviors more than others. Conversely, newborn babies have no culture; as they grow, they gradually acquire a particular set of behavioral patterns that are appropriate for their culture. In this way, culturally distinct parental goals and plans for child development are implemented in a wide variety of forms. Children from different cultures develop differently according to the cultural standards endorsed by the adults around them. Thus, the process of parents' socializing their children following specific cultural norms and, in turn, children's learning culturally appropriate behaviors is what socialization is all about.

This book focuses on language socialization; by acquiring linguistic knowledge, which is immersed in sociocultural knowledge, children become socialized through language. In fact, language socialization is defined by Ochs (1996) as 'the process whereby children and other novices are socialized through language, part of such socialization being a socialization to use language meaningfully, appropriately, and effectively' (p. 408). Because 'part of acquiring language is the acquisition of the social meaning of linguistic structures' (Ochs, 1986, p. 7), in this book culture is considered in relation to linguistic/discursive phenomena.

In divergent cultural settings, we can indeed observe dissimilarities in parental expectations and in communicative styles, and, accordingly, examining various aspects of children's pragmatic and sociolinguistic development becomes imperative. That is, cross-cultural differences in socialization often become discernible when observing that children in different cultures have to become competent in the appropriate pragmatic use of their language, as well as the grammar and vocabulary. In this way, the acquisition of a culture-specific communicative style – i.e. linguistic knowledge plus knowledge of the social rules of language use known as communicative competence (Hymes, 1974a) – plays a signifi-cant role in the process of language acquisition and the development of language skills, such as the choice of topics, rules of turn taking, modes of storytelling and rules of politeness (Heath, 1982, 1983, 1986). As adults, however, most of the pragmatic rules are so culturally ingrained that we are not even aware that we are following certain systematic rules.

Children learn grammatical patterns during the course of face-to-face interaction; interaction is viewed as a crucible that forges knowledge of the language that children are expected to acquire. Narrative is typically considered a text in which the narrator relates a series of events – either real or fictive – in the order in which they happened.[1] Furthermore, narratives are a communicatively driven form of discourse in that indi-viduals tell stories to one another and not to themselves (Stavans, 1996).[2] For the purpose of investigating cross-cultural differences, parent–child interactions, especially their narrative interactions as connected and extended discourse, provide good examples. To begin with, conversa-tion between parents, particularly mothers, and their young children forms the context in which narrative discourse abilities typically emerge. Snow and Goldfield (1981) present ways in which, through book-reading interactions with adults, young children learn what questions to ask and what responses to provide; for instance, illustrating that particular aspects of language use that parents emphasize will be eventually adopted by children, these researchers documented one child's sponta-neously supplying information that his mother had previously inquired about, over several sessions of reading the same book. This methodology focusing on narrative can be applied to language acquisition, particu-larly the foundation of communicative competence (Hymes, 1974a), with reference to mother–child interactions.

Furthermore, through conversational interactions, parents transmit to their young children not only language-specific representational forms and rules but also culture-specific interaction styles, such as culturally nurtured canonical narrative discourse patterns. Bruner (1990) specifically hypothesizes that (1) at an early stage of development, the child, inter-acting with the caregiver, enters into the world of meaning construction, and (2) the meaning creation process in narrative discourse is closely related to specific forms of cultural representation. Following his hypoth-esis, we will be able to claim that while people from virtually all cultures tell stories, at the same time, they shape culturally canonical forms of narrative, narrative thinking, and interpretations through social interac-tions. Thus, as Bruner puts it, 'Narrative structure is even inherent in the praxis of social interaction before it achieves linguistic expression' (p. 77) and 'four-year-olds may not know much about the culture, but they know what's canonical and are eager to provide a tale to account for what is not' (pp. 82–83).

Cross-cultural comparison of narrative productions has been addressed in previous studies. For example, Au (1993) describes 'talk story,' an important speech event for Hawaiian children in their local speech communities. 'During talk story children present rambling narratives about their personal experiences, usually enhanced with humor, jokes and teasing. The main characteristic of talk story is joint performance, or cooperative production of responses by two or more speakers' (Au, 1993, p. 113). Along similar lines, from her observation of 'sharing time' classes, Michaels (1981, 1991) draws the distinction between the ways that African American and European American children describe past events in their narratives. Further examining the same data as Michaels used, Gee (1985, 1986a, 1989a, 1989b, 1991b) illustrates differences in narrative between an African American girl and a European American girl; he categorizes the former as an oral-strategy (or poetic) narrative and the latter as a literate-strategy (or prosaic) narrative. It is thus critical to consider cultural differences in the ways in which children structure their oral personal narratives.

Despite widespread interest in emerging narrative discourse compe-tence, we lack information on how young children acquire culture-specific forms of narrative. To begin with, although research focusing on cross-cultural comparison of narrative studies already exists, much of that re-search addresses cultural differences within the United States. Furthermore, data from cultures using languages other than English are very limited, except for a small number of studies such as Hymes's (1981, 1982, 1985, 1990) work with Native Americans and Schieffelin and her colleagues' (Ochs & Schieffelin, 1984; Schieffelin, 1986, 1990; Schieffelin & Eisenberg, 1984) investigation of the language acquisition and socialization process of the Kaluli of Papua New Guinea. We know next to nothing about how these different styles are acquired in other countries and other languages.

The Theoretical Framework: Research Questions

In an effort to understand children's acquisition of pragmatic and socio-linguistic functions, this book examines how culturally specific aspects of young Japanese children's narrative discourse skills develop and eventually lead to literacy. As mentioned above, although previous anthropological studies have argued that different cultures adopt different approaches in talking with children about past events, there has been relatively little investigation into cross-cultural issues in narrative discourse development.

Likewise, in spite of the fact that research focusing on Japanese conversation already exists, there is little or no work on young children's personal narratives; moreover, virtually no extended analyses of narrative discourse in the context of mother–child interactions are at present available. Previous researchers (e.g. LoCastro, 1987; Maynard, 1989; White, 1989; Yamada, 1992) have described a variety of characteristic features of Japanese conversational discourse, such as back-channel utterances, brief vocalization of acknowledgment like *un* ('yeah,' 'uh huh'). Introducing the notion of 'sync talk,' Hayashi (1988) sheds light on collaborative message as well as discourse construction by Japanese speakers. Maynard (1989) and Yamada (1992) claim that spoken Japanese is produced in smaller units than traditional grammatical constructs, such as a sentence or a clause. Analyzing narrative segments, Maynard (1993) further identifies a variety of Japanese linguistic devices and manipulative strategies that essentially convey a subjective emotion as well as an individual's shared feelings with others. Although these studies analyzed naturally occurring conversations and/or narrative discourse, their data represent adult–adult interaction. Their studies do not address the issue of how the origins of narrative discourse style can be traced back to conversations between parents and children. In reviewing the previous work in this area, therefore, it is clear that past research on this topic has substantial shortcomings.

Designed to address a gap that currently exists in this body of research, this book examines Japanese preschool children's personal narratives in the context of parent–child interaction. The major goal of the book is to enable readers to be fully aware of the relationship between oral language skills and literacy, more specifically, of the interactive nature of language development and the development of literacy skills in a particular sociocultural context. The book will, I believe, provide those who are interested in narrative – oral personal narratives in particular – with the background necessary to understand the essentials of narrative discourse development, which may relate to the development of literacy in later years. The book also dispels many myths and misconceptions, such that Japanese speakers are reticent or reluctant to talk. It is therefore designed to give readers suggestions for becoming more efficient in understanding culture-specific language styles. This book, which aligns with interactional sociolinguistics, explores parent–child interactions and examines the relationships between language and culture, and between language and context. In it, I try to answer the following overall research questions:

(1) How do young Japanese children develop narrative structure?
(2) How do Japanese parents guide their children in the acquisition of culture-specific styles of narrative?
(3) As a possible continuum between language development and the development of literacy skills, what kinds of verbal interactions take place between parents and their children in order to facilitate emergent literacy?

Question 1 above is closely related to the studies conducted by Minami (1990) and Minami and McCabe (1991). These studies have found that Japanese elementary school children tend to speak succinctly about collections of experiences rather than at length about any one experience in particular. Consider the following narrative produced by an eight-year, four-month-old boy Shun. [Note: (1) The narrative is analyzed, using a version of hierarchical verse/stanza analysis (Gee, 1985; Hymes, 1981), which I will describe in Chapter 4 of this book; (2) A stanza, which has a unitary perspective in terms of time, location and character, is considered a thematically constant unit.]

Example 1.1 Shun's monologic narrative
Stanza A: [First shot]
(a) *saisho wa ne,*   1
    'As for the first (shot), you know,'
(b) *Ehime no toki ni yatte ne,*   2
    '(I) got (it) at Ehime, you know,'
(c) *itakatta sugoku,*   3
    '(It) hurt a lot.'

Stanza B: [Second shot]
(d) *nikaime wa ne,*   4
    'As for the second (shot), you know,'
(e) *itai omoi ne,*   5
    '(it would) hurt, you know,'
    wakatteta kara ne,   6
    '(I) knew, you know,'
(f) *maa ne,*   7

'Well, you know,'
   maa maa itaku nakatta kedo ne,   8
   '(it) didn't hurt so much, you know.'

Stanza C: [The other shots]
(g) *sono tsugi mo mata on'naji.*   9
     'The next (one) didn't hurt so much, either.'
(h) *ichiban saigo wa ne,*   10
     'As for the last (one), you know,'
(i) *zenzen itaku nakatta.*   11
     '(it) didn't hurt at all.'

To non-Japanese ears, this story might sound to consist of three short, separate narratives, none of which is fully developed. We can notice, however, that there is a nice progression from the first shot (Stanza A) that must have surprised the boy and was painful, to the second one (Stanza B) that did not seem so bad, and to the third and the last one (Stanza C) that did not hurt at all. Thus, this narrative includes cohesive collections of several experiences that the boy had. Furthermore, injuries are contrasted to each other (using *wa*, which carries a contrastive meaning, as explained later in Chapter 5), and each injury is described in an elegantly succinct three-verse form. Because of the nature of the Japanese language, the speaker/narrator omits pronouns, copulas and other linguistic devices (shown in parentheses) that help the listener to easily identify and empathize with the speaker/narrator (for more details about the Japanese language, see Chapter 2).

Similarly, a seven-year, ten-month-old girl Sayaka juxtaposed three different types of injuries across sections: (1) an injury in kindergarten, (2) a fall off an iron bar, and (3) two hernia operations. [Note: A section is a larger topic/thematic unit than a stanza.]

Example 1.2 Sayaka's monologic narrative
SECTION I: [Injury in kindergarten]

Stanza A: [Got hurt in kindergarten]
(a) *yoochien no koro,*   1
     'When (I was) in kindergarten,'
(b) *ashi o jitensha de hasande,*
     '(I) got (my) leg caught in a bicycle, and'   2
(c) *koko, koko kitte.*   3
     '(I) got a cut here.'

Stanza B: [Aftermath of injury]
(d) *gibusu shiteta, ikkagetsu kurai.*   4
     '(I) wore a cast for about a month.'
(e) *isshuukan kurai yasunde,*   5

   '(I) took a rest for about a week, and'
(f) *mata itta.*   6
   'And (I) went back again.'

SECTION II: [An iron bar]
Stanza C: [Fell off an iron bar]
(a) *koko kitta no.*   7
   '(I) had a cut here.'
(b) *tetsuboo kara ochite.*   8
   '(I) fell off an iron bar, and'
(c) *un, kuchi ga futatsu ni natchatta.*   9
   'yes, (I) had two mouths.'

SECTION III: [Hernia operations]
Stanza D: [The first operation]
(a) *unto, nanka umaretsuki,*   10
   'Um, well, (I) was born with (a) hernia,'
     da tte.   11
     'I heard.'
(b) *katappo wa,*   12
   'As for the one hernia,'
(c) *chitchai akachan no koro ni,*   13
   'when (I) was a little baby,'
(d) *nyuuin shite,*   14
   '(I) was hospitalized, and'
(e) *kitta no.*   15
   '(I) got an operation.'

Stanza E: [The second operation]
(f) *katappo ga kitte nakatta kara,*   16
   'Because (I) didn't have an operation for the other one,'
(g) *ichinen-sei no hajime goro ni,*   17
   'as an early first grader,'
     nyuuin shite,   18
     '(I) was hospitalized, and'
(h) *kitta no.*   19
   '(I) got an operation.'

As can be seen in Examples 1.1 and 1.2, stanzas mostly consist of three verses (which are basically defined as single clauses). We also notice that Stanza A in Example 1.1 and Stanzas A and C in Example 1.2 each consist of an orientation (i.e. the setting or context of a narrative), an action (i.e. a specific event or action), and an outcome (i.e. the result of a specific action). Minami (1990) and Minami and McCabe (1991) concluded that this three-verse, orientation-act-outcome pattern seems to represent the canonical pattern among Japanese elementary school children's oral personal narratives. Additionally, verse (c) in Stanza C (Example 1.2) shows

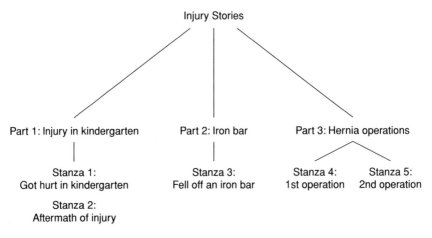

Figure 1.1 Graph of Sayaka's story structures in verse/stanza analysis

that Sayaka, pointing at her chin, meant that the wound was cut open as if it were also a mouth. Japanese listeners may feel that her use of this metaphor is somewhat humorous, but at the same time can easily imagine how severe and painful her injury was, and thus deeply empathize with her. Finally, Sayaka not only juxtaposed three different types of injuries across sections, but in Section III, after her orientative comments that served as background information, she also juxtaposed her hernia operations chronologically across stanzas. Figure 1.1 illustrates Sayaka's story structures. Minami (1990) and Minami and McCabe (1991) thus also concluded that, in addition to the three-verse, orientation-act-outcome pattern, a presentation of multiple experiences – isolated but related incidents – across sections and/or stanzas is another feature of Japanese elementary school children's oral personal narratives. Moreover, the combination of these multiple life experiences are shaped into a whole unified story in Japanese elementary school children's narratives.

To summarize the above results, it can be said that, despite follow-up questions that encouraged them to talk about one personal narrative at length, Japanese elementary school children generally present free-standing collections of several experiences. These features are, as a matter of fact, in striking contrast to data gathered in a study of European American children, who talked at length about one particular experience at a time (Peterson & McCabe, 1983). Minami (1990) and Minami and McCabe (1991) have further found that the number of experiences that the Japanese children presented ranged from two to four. Question 1 raised above is an extension of this line of past research, and this book examines whether a tendency in narratives told by young Japanese preschool children is similar to that observed in previous studies.

With regard to questions two and three, if we hypothesize that the course of development is continuous and each individual is located at a single point along the developmental continuum, then, we can assume that the origins of the kinds of Japanese elementary school children's narrative patterning previously described can be traced back to conversations between parents and children in earlier years in their homes. That is, I believe that through dialogic narrative discourse such as dinnertable conversations, Japanese mothers' style of interviewing children about past events would form a template for Japanese children's narrative form. Bruner (1983) claims that 'by using language first for limited ends the child comes finally to recognize its more powerful, productive uses' (p. 7). As already stated, Bruner (1990) thus emphasizes that understanding specific properties of a narrative is important because, when we look at narrative components, we see how, in the process of interacting with others, the narrator constructs his or her logic. Applying this social interaction paradigm across cultures, the primary agent of cultural transmission, usually the mother, provides the child with particular narrative styles. Previous studies (e.g. Bruner, 1977, 1990; Bruner & Lucariello, 1989; Nelson, 1989) of children's early social interactions have identified two major hypotheses: (1) There are culture-specific patterns of social interactions in narrative production; and (2) A particular caregiver's narrative style shapes the child's narrative style, contributing to differences in mothers' and children's styles within a given culture. To put it in another way, individual differences in interaction style will be observed within a particular culture, but at the same time, adult narrative preferences are culturally determined. Questions two and three, therefore, investigate how young Japanese children interact with their mothers and, further, what kinds of culture-specific patterns of communication are involved in mother–child interactions.

This book offers a unique approach to the topic of narrative and literacy development and adds a significant cross-cultural dimension. The link between narrating and being literate is emphasized throughout the book; in order for children to be considered literate, scholars such as Bruner (1986) believe that narrative is primary. In other words, narrative, as the first extended discourse to which young children gain access, is considered a prerequisite for literacy. In addition to the link between narrative and literacy, as this book will later reveal, exploring the form of Japanese parent–child interactions in the production of culture-specific personal narratives and book-reading activities is informative as well as important for better cross-cultural understanding.

The Structure of the Book

Brief overall organization

With an aim to facilitate cross-cultural understanding, the book is divided into five major parts with nine chapters. Part 1, which is composed of three chapters (Chapters 1–3), provides a theoretical and ethnographic background to the analytic chapters (Chapters 4–7). Chapters 4 and 5, which make up Part 2, deal with analyses of the personal narratives told by Japanese preschool children and adults. Part 3 (Chapters 6 and 7) studies mother–child narrative discourse interactions not only in Japan but also in North America, using categories of meaning that emerge from the data. Part 4, which includes only one chapter (Chapter 8), is a continuation of mother–child interactions but examines the relationship between sociocultural background and young Japanese children's development of literacy (through book-reading activities). The chapter thus makes the move from oral narrative (i.e. orality) to literacy. Following the fourth part is the concluding chapter (Chapter 9), which summarizes the current research findings, revisit the issues raised in previous chapters and discusses areas of future research. Each part, I believe, provides an enriching framework for consideration of many important issues in relation to sociocultural contexts in narrative discourse and emergent literacy.

Detailed organization of the book

As described above, this book examines developmental and cross-cultural aspects of children's narration. To be more specific, whereas Chapter 1 lays out the themes, goals and procedures of the book, Chapter 2 extensively reviews the relevant literature on language socialization and its impact on narrative discourse, with particular emphasis on cross-cultural differences. Thus, Chapter 2 demonstrates how the research questions presented above conceptualize the role of language socialization in relation to narrative discourse acquisition within a particular culture. Chapter 3 discusses methodology and other surrounding issues, such as the transcription system; it first describes the settings in which the data were collected, and then outlines the overall research methods. The chapter also examines the relationship between Japanese oral discourse style and literacy practices.

The main body of the book, Chapters 4–7, presents a detailed discussion of narrative development, monologic narratives first, followed by dialogic narratives (i.e. mother–child interactions). The main focus of Chapters 4 and 5 is, as the first goal of this book, to study the emergence of a culture-specific narrative style in Japanese children. Chapter 4, in detailing the research design for analyzing children's narrative structure, statistically analyzes monologic narrative production based on the establishment of the coding rules for the analysis of Japanese narratives. Chapter 5 then offers both qualitative and quantitative support for the results obtained from the statistical analysis in order to further deepen the understanding of monologic narrative. Specifically, through the presentation of particular narrative examples, the chapter illustrates similarities and differences between children's early narrative production and adults' fully developed production techniques.

The second goal of this book is to examine how Japanese parents guide their children in the acquisition of culture-specific styles of narrative; i.e. face-to-face conversational interaction is the focal point of investigation. Chapter 6 discusses the research design and procedure for analyzing Japanese mother–child interactions. It explores the relationship between maternal styles of narrative elicitation and children's developing narrative skill. To complement this work and to support generalization about the culture-specific nature of both caregivers' practices and children's emerging narrative structure, Chapter 7 further reports cross-cultural comparisons of maternal narrative elicitation patterns. To compare the Japanese data with data in other languages, such as English, we need to develop categories applicable to both languages (Minami & McCabe, 1995); otherwise, we might have no basis for comparison. The coding scheme used in Chapters 6 and 7, I believe, will satisfy such requirements.

The third goal of this book is to describe ways in which children learn early in their homes to internalize what they may expect in the classroom. Chapter 8 compares children's use of speech in face-to-face interaction with their mothers during book-reading activities at home. The chapter thus examines emergent literacy practices in Japanese homes from the perspective of social interaction and discusses the home–school continuum in language socialization.

Finally, Chapter 9 completes the goals of this book: to untangle the relationships among the emergence of monologic narrative skills, dialogic mother–child interactions and emergent literacy within the framework of extended narrative discourse. The chapter then discusses the educational significance and implications of the results obtained in this book and suggests directions for future research.

Notes

1. Narrative is generally defined as the manner of talking about a series of logically and chronologically related events (Ervin-Tripp & Küntay, 1997; Labov, 1972). A common guiding framework, however, is absent; a narrative that contains only a single event or which skips around in time is even possible (McCabe, 1997). [See Chapter 2 for more information.]
2. In this book, I basically adopt Hicks's (1994) definition of 'narrative discourse' in which 'there is some reference to temporally or thematically connected events' (p. 217).

Chapter 2
Literature Review

Narrative is defined as a form of extended discourse in which at least two different events are described so that a variety of relationships between them, such as temporal, causal and contrastive ones, become explicit. In Chapter 1, I laid out the plan of the book and set it in the context of my previous work on narrative discourse analysis (Minami, 1990; Minami & McCabe, 1991). In this chapter, mainly focusing on child language research, I first present an overview of the classic theoretical approaches to language studies, connecting two different disciplines of linguistics – generative grammar (and universalism), represented by Chomsky (1965), and sociolinguistic studies (and relativism to a certain extent), represented by such scholars as Gumperz (1981), Hymes (1974a) and Labov (1972). In so doing, I describe the nature of Chomskyan linguistics and its complex relationship to sociolinguistics, mainly through Hymes's invention of the term 'communicative competence.' I then focus on sociocultural aspects, discussing language acquisition and socialization in a variety of settings, such as Japanese society. As the literature review progresses, I increasingly make explicit my position as a social interactionist who believes that the child is not only under the influence of the environment but simultaneously acts upon and even creates the environment to a certain extent. This assumption is based on the social interaction paradigm advocated by Vygotsky (1978) and Bruner (1977). I also make clear my position as a new environmentalist in emphasizing the critical issue of cross-cultural differences; for instance, there are substantial cross-cultural differences in which children structure their narratives.

Language Acquisition

The Chomskyan revolution and its influence on language studies

In the 1950s most explanations of child development were dominated by behaviorist interpretations. The behaviorist dominance was especially true in Western societies in general, and the United States in particular.[1] Behaviorists, who are also called learning theorists or environmentalists, viewed the environment as molding the child; according to them, learning changes the child's behavior and advances his or her development. Because behaviorists considered the environment more influential in directing behavior than anything else, their claim did not stop at the level of discussing general cognitive skills. As can be seen in the expression of 'verbal behavior' (Skinner, 1957), they further regarded that children learn language in the same way that they learn other types of behavior. Skinner (1957), as the foremost proponent of learning theory, suggested that language is a special case of behavior and that language development is largely determined by training based on trial and error, and not by maturation (i.e. acquiring a language is a matter of establishing a connection between a set of stimuli and a verbal response).

Chomsky (1959), however, criticized the behaviorist approach represented by Skinner (1957) who claimed that language learning is based upon experience. Instead, according to Chomsky, because patterns of language development are similar across different languages and cultures, the environment plays a minor role in the maturation of language. Chomsky (1965) thus emphasized that humans have a biological endowment, which he called a language acquisition device (LAD), that enables us to discover the framework of principles and elements common to attainable human languages. The LAD contains fundamental knowledge about the basic nature and structure of human language, which is termed universal grammar (UG). Although grammatical rules of sentence structure are limited, no one could exhaustively list all the potentially acceptable sentences; thus, triggered by input, this internalized system of rules can generate an infinite number of grammatical sentences. Believing in a self-charged 'bioprogram' whereby language acquisition is autonomous, Chomsky (1985) writes:

> UG consists of various subsystems of principles; it has the modular structure that we regularly discover in investigation of cognitive systems. Many of these principles are associated with parameters that must be fixed by experience. The parameters must have the

property that they can be fixed by quite simple evidence, because this is what is available to the child; the value of the head parameter, for example, can be determined from such sentences as *John saw Bill* (versus *John Bill saw*).[2] Once the values of the parameters are set, the whole system is operative. (p. 146)

Chomsky (1985) thus hypothesizes that, in their language acquisition process, children move from the initial state of language faculty to the steady state, as if by simply flipping a series of switches. This parameter setting is considered to be set at a very early age through prosodic cues; i.e. infants find important clues to the basic configuration of their language in the prosodic characteristics of the speech they hear (Mazuka, 1998; Morgan & Demuth, 1996).

The linguistic revolution originated by Chomsky has exerted an enormous influence on contemporary child language studies, particularly research into children's acquisition of syntax, for almost four decades (e.g. Slobin, 1985; Wanner & Gleitman, 1982). Brown and Bellugi (1964), for example, stress the rule-governed nature of language acquisition. If the behaviorist theory, which believes that children's speech is not rule-governed but shaped by the contingencies, were applied to language acquisition, it would be assumed that child behavior is reinforced by a caretaker's approval and self-satisfaction only when the child follows the caretaker's lead. Brown and Bellugi, while acknowledging the significant influence of environmental or parental interactions (e.g. mothers modify their speech to their children by simplifying, repeating and paraphrasing), emphasized that the process of language acquisition cannot be explained by the behavioristic stimulus-response-reinforcement system alone. Rather, Brown and Bellugi feel that the child's inductive processing aids language acquisition. They thus pay particular attention to three processes that characterize the child's acquisition of syntactic structures. Analyzing toddlers' language acquisition, Brown and Bellugi conclude that mother–child interaction, which is a cycle of imitations, reductions and expansions, helps the child's inductive processing of the latent structure and rules of the target language.

Likewise, C. Chomsky (1969, 1972) examined elementary school children's language development and found a relationship to reading. With a particular emphasis on the innate mechanism for language learning, C. Chomsky suggests that this natural process of children's language development continues actively into their elementary school years. According to her, the degree of sophistication in language acquisition is reflected in the ability to understand grammatically complex sentences, such as 'John told Bill to leave' versus 'John promised Bill to leave.' Further, despite diverse individual differences (Nelson, 1981), particularly in terms of the rate of development, all children construct implicit grammatical rules and pass through a developmental sequence of linguistic stages.

Language as a socioculturally mediated product: Foundation of communicative competence

Examining the development of children's pragmatic ability is critical in order to understand language acquisition. As described above, the linguistic revolution initiated by Chomsky in the late 1950s (Chomsky, 1957) brought with it the importance of conceptualizing links between the role of language and the human mind, i.e. humans have some universal and innate ability to learn language. The corrective emphasis on biology, however, is an oversimplification just as extreme as the Skinnerian one, though on the opposite end of the nature–nurture continuum. That is, in addition to the inborn capacity to analyze the underlying rule-governed nature of the target language, serious consideration should be paid to early socialization, in order to explain the linguistic competence that young children acquire and develop. As Snow and Ferguson (1977) suggest, parents play a far more important role in their children's language acquisition than simply modeling the language and providing input for an LAD.

Generative grammar, represented by Chomsky, was challenged by sociolinguists who argued the relevance of variability in childhood environments and language use outcomes in other societies and cultures. Chomsky (1965), adopting the *langue-parole* distinction originally proposed by Saussure (1959), presented the dichotomy of competence (i.e. a person's internalized grammar of a language) and performance (i.e. the actual use of language in concrete situations). Challenging this dichotomy of competence and performance, Hymes (1974a), an advocate of the ethnography of communication, introduced the concept of 'communicative competence,' the ability not only to apply the grammatical rules of a language in order to construct a grammatically correct sentence, but also to know when, where, and with whom to use these correct sentences in a given sociocultural situation. Criticizing Chomsky's definition of 'competence' (which is simply defined as a fluent native speaker's knowledge of grammaticality), and instead emphasizing the importance of socioculturally shared knowledge and cognitive abilities, Hymes (1974a) states:

Chomsky's redefinition of linguistic goals appears, then, a half-way house. The term 'competence' promises more than it in fact contains. It is restricted to knowledge, and, within knowledge, to knowledge of grammar. Thus, it leaves other aspects of speakers' tacit knowledge and ability in confusion, thrown together under a largely unexamined concept of 'performance.' (pp. 92–93)

To draw an example from politeness, imagine a situation in which you ask a person living on the same street for a ride home. It goes without saying that you make a request differently, depending on a variety of factors such as age, sex, social hierarchy, personal relationships and the like. The expression of communicative intents, however, might also differ cross-culturally. In some cultures using indirect requests might be a societal norm, such as 'I was wondering if you would be able to give me a ride on your way home,' whereas in other cultures such convoluted communicative strategies are simply dismissed. Thus, it would be interesting to understand how children acquire culturally appropriate communicative strategies in the process of language development.

Hymes claims that Chomsky's dichotomy of competence and performance is too narrowly defined and therefore misleading. Hymes instead suggests that, contrary to the nativist/innatist position that tends to disregard sociocultural differences, these differences do affect the process of language acquisition at a variety of levels. Further, Gumperz (1981) clarifies the definition of 'communicative competence' as 'the knowledge of linguistic and related communicative conventions that speakers must have to initiate and sustain conventional involvement' (p. 325). Thus, whereas Chomsky focuses on the universal nature of language acquisition, Hymes and Gumperz stress characteristic features of the outcome of language acquisition in a specific sociocultural context. To illustrate the difference between these two positions, for example, in the nativists' idea, children in Japan learn to speak Japanese, whereas children in the United States learn to speak English; but the environmental input is minimal. In contrast, Hymes and Gumperz contend that language is largely shaped by culture-specific experiences and beliefs.

Like Hymes, Labov (1972), in his study of performance, has shifted a paradigm from isolated linguistic form (i.e. syntax or the grammatical sentences of a language) to linguistic form in human context, and analyzed the sequential use of language (i.e. discourse). Specifically, Labov (1972) studied the structure of African American Vernacular English (AAVE) narratives. To demonstrate that nonstandard dialects are highly structured systems, Labov took a very unique approach. In interviewing inner-city youth he used so-called 'danger-of-death' prompts, such as, 'Were you ever in a situation where you were in serious danger of being killed?' (1972, p. 363) to elicit narratives. And he described how narrators incorporate life-threatening events into their personal histories.

Labov and his colleagues define narrative technically as 'one method of recapitulating past experience by matching a verbal sequence of clauses to the sequence of events which (it is inferred) actually occurred' (Labov, 1972, pp. 359–360; Labov et al., 1968, p. 287; Labov & Waletzky, 1967, p. 20). Following Labov and Waletzky's (1967) argument, the smallest unit of linguistic expression that defines the function of narrative should be the independent, temporally ordered clause, because a temporal sequence of such narrative clauses constitutes the backbone of a narrative.

According to Labov (1972), furthermore, a fully formed oral narrative consists of a six-part structure: abstracts (i.e. summaries of the whole narrative at its outset), orientations (i.e. statements that provide the setting or context of a narrative), complicating actions (i.e. specific events), evaluations (i.e. statements that tell the listener what to think about a person, place, thing, event or more globally, the entire experience described in a narrative telling), resolutions (i.e. what finally happened) and codas (i.e. formalized endings of a narrative). Labov and his followers claim that stories of personal experience provide the simplest, but most fundamental narrative structures. By using this analysis, these researchers present the linguistic techniques and devices employed to evaluate experience within the speaker's particular cultural set, such as AAVE, and examine the basic structure of narrative within a particular culture. Overall, Labov and his colleagues' major contribution to the field was that they identified a delimited set of recurrent patterns. Although these researchers suggest that structural components in story/narrative are universal, they also stress that some linguistic variables among them are under the great influence of sociocultural variation, including not simply the sociolinguistic environment but also the wider cultural setting.

Bernstein (1971), an English sociologist, interprets competence-performance in a more sociocultural way. According to him, 'competence refers to the child's tacit understanding of the rule system,' but 'performance relates to the essentially social use to which the rule system is put' (p. 173). Bernstein thus reframes performance by collapsing Chomsky's notion of 'performance' and Hymes's conception of 'communicative competence.'

Bernstein (1971) further claims that there is substantial evidence suggesting effects of sociocultural variables; for example, working-class and middle-class people use different linguistic codes. Bernstein examined why children from working-class families could not keep up academically in school settings. According to Bernstein, middle-class speakers in England employ an *elaborated code* that facilitates the verbal elaboration of subjective intent, whereas working-class speakers, to a greater or lesser degree, employ a *restricted code*, a speech mode in which it is unnecessary for the speaker verbally to elaborate subjective intent. Bernstein's notion of codes, however, has been criticized because they fail to acknowledge an overriding concern with collaborative message as well as discourse construction by working-class speakers; for instance, working-class speakers are more likely to use affective nonreasoning strategies (Hemphill, 1989). Furthermore, because his conception has often been regarded as a 'verbal-deficit' theory and confused with social class, it has tended to be misused, especially in the United States (Brandt, 1990), where it was employed as a mechanism to explain the academic failure of children of linguistically nonmainstream backgrounds (including children from working-class homes).[3]

As researchers have tried to understand the acquisition of communicative competence, and narrative discourse competence specifically, they have explored a wider range of paradigms and drawn on diverse disciplines. Use of the Labovian six-part analysis of the oral narrative of personal experience (Labov, 1972), in particular, reveals an increasing sensitivity to the sociolinguistic or sociocultural environment as an important element in understanding the acquisition of this competence (for more detailed information about Labov's analysis, see Chapter 4).

Language Socialization

Language socialization in diverse cultural contexts

Language can be thought of as both a manifestation and product of a culture. One of the major issues in developmental psychology in general and language development in particular is: 'Which plays a more critical role, heredity or environment?' People have asked this question for years (e.g. Jensen, 1969). The discussion in this chapter so far has been, at least in part, related to this old nature-nurture issue. Imagine, for instance, Japanese-American toddlers who are genetically Japanese but being raised in American environment culturally. If hereditary factors are predominant in determining human behavior, the Japanese-American toddlers should behave like the Japanese. If environmental factors play a more critical role, on the other hand, the young children should be more like the Americans. Conducting this line of research, Caudill and Frost (1974) found that the Japanese–American infants behaved more like the American infants from other races. Their finding seems to suggest that environmental factors are the crucial contributor to determine the individual's behavior.

The issue, in reality, is not so simple, however. Culture consists of many complicated factors. Consider, for instance, US society, which sociologists have long described as a melting pot in which a variety of cultural experiences and background merge into something entirely new. According to Matsumoto (2000), culture can be defined as:

> a dynamic system of rules, explicit and implicit, established by groups in order to ensure their survival, involving attitudes, values, beliefs, norms, and behaviors, shared by a group but harbored differently by each specific unit within the group, communicated across generations, relatively stable but with the potential to change across time. (p. 24)

The above definition illustrates the nature of 'cultural psychology', the central tenet of which rests on the 'constructivist' conception of meaning, stipulating that social interactions are culturally constrained. That is, in different cultures, children's lives are shaped in different ways according to their parents' models and expectations of what the children's development should be. According to specific cultural norms, distinct goals and plans for child development are implemented in a wide variety of ways. Parents, especially mothers, in each culture socialize their children differently. Through the process of socialization, children acquire the ability to recognize and interpret the variety of activities that take place in their socioculturally specific environments. Thus, children growing up in different cultures have particular experiences through which they develop diverse expectations, preferences and even beliefs.

As discussed earlier, Hymes (1974a) stresses that, from early childhood on, children in different cultural settings learn the appropriate social use of their language, as well as its grammar and vocabulary. The acquisition of culture-specific communicative competence thus plays a critical role in the process of language acquisition and the development of narrative discourse skills. Miller (1982), for instance, describes a variety of culture-specific routinized interactions between mothers and their children in South Baltimore, and calls such interactions 'direct interaction,' which includes: (1) directing the children to speak appropriately (e.g. 'please,' 'excuse me,' and 'thank you'); (2) conversing with dolls appropriately; (3) rhyming, singing and playing verbal games; (4) using correct grammar, pronunciation, and intonation; and (5) counting, reciting the alphabet, and identifying the colors. The primary intent of Miller's (1982) study is to suggest that children from lower-class families in South Baltimore are being taught distinct styles of language and that they are not, therefore, linguistically deprived. [Note: Recall Bernstein's (1971) verbal-deficit theory introduced in this chapter, which, either implicitly or explicitly, condemns children's environmental, sociocultural and linguistic background for their failure in the classroom context.]

Mothers use a variety of socialization strategies to familiarize their children to culturally distinct patterns of communication, such as modeling, direct instruction, and play routines. Miller's study adds to a host of research demonstrating that different cultures have different priorities with respect to caring for, socializing, and educating young children. In different sociocultural settings, we can perceive differences in parental expectations and their resultant differing communicative styles (e.g. Heath, 1983). According to Hymes (1982), among the Chinook and some other Native American tribes, newborn babies were believed not to be babbling but to be speaking a special language that they shared with the spirits. Ochs and Schieffelin (1984) claim that 'what a child says and how she or he says it will be influenced by local cultural processes, in addition to biological and social processes that have universal scope' (p. 277). These researchers delineate characteristic features of the outcome of language acquisition in specific sociocultural contexts. Thus, while accepting Chomsky's (1965) notion of a highly abstract core of structures that is applicable to any language, these researchers put particular emphasis on the influence of environmental and sociocultural factors. The following remarks by Schieffelin and Ochs (1996) are clearly consonant with Hymes's notion of 'communicative competence' and aptly address a multilayered set of socioculturally based perspectives:

> First, the process of acquiring language is deeply affected by the process of becoming a competent member of a society, and second, the process of becoming a competent member of society is realized to a large extent through language, by acquiring knowledge of its functions, social distribution, and interpretations in and across socially defined situations. This is largely achieved through participation in exchanges of language in particular social situations. From this perspective, language is seen as a source for children to acquire the ways and world views of their culture. (p. 252)

The above remarks on language socialization point to the primacy of the social nature of language. Through different processes, from a very early age children are socialized into culturally specific modes of organizing knowledge, thought, and communicative style. Language acquisition, which includes mastery of communicative competence, and socialization are, therefore, two sides of the same coin.

Through investigation of the language acquisition and socialization process of the Kaluli in the highlands of Papua New Guinea, Ochs and Schieffelin (1984), Schieffelin and Eisenberg (1984), and Schieffelin (1986, 1990) find another example of how language is strongly dependent on social patterns. According to these researchers, Kaluli mothers do not believe that baby-babbling is language, and instead claim that language begins at the time when the child uses two critical words, 'mother' and 'breast.' More important, Kaluli mothers believe that children need carefully controlled, explicit instruction not only at the sentence level but also at the level of discourse, such as conversational skills. For instance, Kaluli mothers do not recast their children's utterances or engage in other modifications of their own language to fit the linguistic ability of the young child. [Note: 'Recasting' means adult response to a child's utterance in which the grammar is rephrased or corrected, while the message content is maintained.] Instead, children are expected to adapt to adult situations. During the first eighteen months or so, very little sustained dyadic verbal exchange takes place between adult and infant. The infant is only minimally treated as an addressee, and not treated as a communicative partner in dyadic exchanges.

The Kaluli attitude toward child language development shows a remarkable contrast to that of the European American middle-class mother who, from birth on, typically accommodates situations to the child. Kaluli mothers consider finely tuned child-directed speech (i.e. the special speech register used when talking to children, sometimes called 'CDS' in short or 'motherese') inappropriate; instead, they train their children to imitate adult forms of speech. The European American middle-class mother treats her young child not only as an addressee in social interaction, but also as a communicative partner whose unintentional vocalizations or movements can be treated as 'turns' (Snow, 1977) (note that, here, conversation is seen as a sequence of conversational turns). Such mothers simplify their speech to match more closely what they consider to be the communicative competence of the young child (Snow, 1972, 1977, 1983, 1986, 1989a, 1989b; Snow & Goldfield, 1981; Snow & Ninio, 1986). We should bear in mind, however, that, because differing environmental and sociocultural factors are operating in the European American middle-class and Kaluli speech communities, the communicative competence required for each community is consequently different. Therefore, arguing whether finely tuned child-directed speech and recasts contribute universally to an 'optimal course of language development' is not relevant.

Japanese language socialization

Socialization experienced in childhood prepares an individual to live in an adult society that reflects a culturally specific ethos or emotional climate. To further develop the discussion about language socialization in the previous section, we must be sensitive to cross-cultural differences. A set of similar sociocultural features might exist among Westernized or industrial societies; likewise, a different set of similarities might exist among non-Westernized or non-industrial societies. Taken together, certain contrasting features might be identified between Westernized and non-Westernized (or industrial and non-industrial) societies. This dichotomy, however, is simplistic at best and distorts the complex reality at worst. Westernized or industrial societies should not be lumped together in one category; neither should non-Westernized or non-industrial societies.

Japanese children are trained differently from both the American and Kaluli children described in the previous section. For example, despite the fact that both Japanese and American children in general live in similar industrial societies and in this sense experience no major economic differences, these two nations differ greatly in their cultural beliefs of how to care for, socialize and educate young children. The guiding principle of the Japanese can be characterized as social relativism, within which the individual is defined by the reference groups to which he or she belongs, including household, residential area, school attended or place of employment (Lebra, 1976). Although social relativism is characterized as relational and interpersonal, it does not necessarily imply that the Japanese do not possess the notion of independence or individualism (Holloway & Minami, 1996). Rather, as Maynard (1993) aptly summarizes, they have traditionally defined each individual, and his or her function, 'on the basis of the human relationships within the society of which he or she is a part' (p. 16); each individual is thus allowed to enjoy individualism and independence within a certain framework of group. According to Lebra (1976), on the other hand, American culture is characterized by the ethos dominated by the pursuit of individual autonomy and self-interest. Furthermore, although in Western cultures individualism is generally connected with creativity, it is somewhat difficult for an individual to nourish a Western sense of active individuality on Japanese soil, where Confucian beliefs have a strong influence; instead of using the term 'social relativism,' therefore, Miyanaga (1991) calls the Japanese type of individualism 'passive individualism.' In either case, in order to maintain good relationships in Japanese society, each individual is expected to follow a quasi-parent–child relationship and to be sensitive to the cues given by other members in the so-called family.

These differences are also reflected in differences in educational philosophies (Stevenson *et al.*, 1986; Stevenson *et al.*, 1990; Stigler & Perry, 1988). American educators tend to think that individual children are inherently unique in their limitations, and thus education appropriate for one child may not be appropriate for another (see a middle-class European-American's evaluation of Japanese children in Chapter 9). Westerners thus tend to rely on *nativism*. On the other hand, Japanese educators and parents are more comfortable in the belief that learning results less from native, inborn ability and more from experience gained through diligent practice. Thus, the Japanese educational philosophy is predicated upon *empiricism*.

As a reflection of these dissimilarities, we can easily imagine that, from early childhood or even toddlerhood on, Japanese children are trained differently from their American counterparts. For example, whereas in the United States peer relations are conceptualized primarily as dyadic, in Japan the primary goal of parents (and teachers as well) is to encourage children to function harmoniously within the group; i.e. getting along with others is sometimes considered more important than ability. Along similar lines, in the United States, primary focus is placed on verbal interaction between teachers and children; verbal expressiveness is thus considered a vehicle for social and emotional development, as well as a precursor to literacy and other academic skills. In contrast, Japanese express a preference for verbal restraint rather than effusiveness (Lebra, 1976). This orientation is reflected in child-care settings, where there is correspondingly less emphasis on encouraging verbalization from children (Shigaki, 1987).

Because a child must learn to speak a particular language with its culture-specific representational forms and rules of use, language practice is one aspect of early socialization that may reflect cultural differences. Caudill and his followers (e.g. Caudill & Schooler, 1973; Caudill & Weinstein, 1973) focused their research especially on the role of maternal communication with children. Caudill and Schooler (1973) found that American children, at ages two-and-a-half and six years, used verbal expression to communicate positive as well as negative emotions more frequently than did Japanese children of the corresponding ages. Also, Caudill and Weinstein (1969) found that Japanese middle-class mothers talked far less frequently to their toddlers than did American middle-class mothers. Caudill's cultural transmission model tends to assume that cultural norms affect parental behavior, which in turn exerts a (primarily unidirectional) influence on the child (Holloway & Minami, 1996). The model proposed by Caudill thus assumes that dissimilarities in the behavior of children in these two cultures result from cultural differences in their mothers' behavior (Schooler, 1996). In a characteristically individualistic society such as the United States, an individual should be verbally assertive, whereas in a characteristically group-oriented society such as Japan, an individual should be verbally restrained. Following Caudill's *cultural transmission* model, therefore, the direction of language development in a given culture would depend on understanding how the adults who are representing a specific culture use language.

Correspondingly, there are differences in the ways in which parents ascribe intentionality to their children's early utterances. A study of verbal exchanges between Japanese and US mothers and their three-month-old infants (Toda *et al.*, 1990) found that US mothers used more information-oriented speech (i.e. fully propositional sentences used in adult conversations) than did Japanese mothers; in contrast, in comparison to US mothers, Japanese mothers rarely used grammatically complete utterances, and spoke to their young infants in a more affect-salient manner (e.g. nonsense words, onomatopoeia and songlike-utterances).[4] Bornstein *et al.* (1990) studied Japanese and US mothers and their five-month-old infants and found that US infants are more active than Japanese infants in many ways, including motor behavior and positive vocalization. Interestingly, these researchers found that in comparison to Japanese mothers, US mothers made more referential statements and more frequently encouraged their babies to initiate physical exploration of their environment (e.g. attending to properties, objects and events around them) (Bornstein *et al.*, 1990). In contrast, Japanese mothers tended to promote their children's visual attention to their environments rather than facilitation of children's vocalization (Bornstein *et al.*, 1992) [e.g. Japanese mothers verbally encouraged infants to look at something in their environment more frequently than US mothers, such as *un, ano inu kawaii ne* ('yes, that dog is pretty, isn't it?')]. Thus, the results obtained from three- and five-month-old infants and their mothers already show significant differences between the two cultures. The results further illustrate that the two cultures evidently operate with different underlying belief systems and values about parenting.

Differences in mother–infant interactions in earlier years relate to differences in later years. US 13-month-old toddlers tend to be more advanced in language production and reception than Japanese toddlers of the same age (Tamis-LeMonda *et al.*, 1992).[5] Further comparing maternal speech to five- and 13-month-old infants in Argentina, France, Japan and the United States, Bornstein *et al.* (1992) found that while affect-oriented speech appeared across these four different cultures, Japanese mothers were the most frequent users of affect-salient speech; this finding is in line with the characteristic aspect identified when Japanese babies are three months old (i.e. Japanese mothers of three-month-olds were more affect-oriented than US mothers, using nonsense and onomatopoeic sounds). These findings moreover provide empirical support for the claim that, as far as Japanese mothers are concerned, the primary goal in early child rearing is to empathize (*'omoiyar-u,'* the verb form of *'omoiyari,'* which will be explained soon) with their children's needs and wants, and that, in contrast, Western cultures favor information-oriented speech and speech patterns that are characteristic of adult-adult conversation. In other words, to borrow Baumrind's (1971) typologies to describe parental discipline practices, US middle-class mothers seem to represent the authoritative parenting style, which emphasizes verbal give-and-take, whereas Japanese mothers appear to represent the permissive parenting style, which emphasizes warmth while allowing children to monitor their own activities as much as possible.

The term 'enculturation' refers to 'the acquisition of cultural representations, including representations of self, by the human organism' (LeVine, 1990, p. 99). The studies described above suggest that, from an early age on, Japanese children go through the enculturation process of *omoiyari* (empathy), which is embedded in the larger context of Japanese culture (Azuma, 1986; Clancy, 1986; Doi, 1973; Lebra, 1976; Shigaki, 1987). Furthermore, this enculturation continues into the school setting, and, in this sense, children's homes and the school constitute a continuum. For instance, Japanese preschool teachers do not intervene in the interactions between children, nor do they criticize individual children; they assume that other children will help a child in need (Lanham & Garrick, 1996; Lewis, 1991; Tobin *et al.*, 1989). As Clancy (1986) argues, a Japanese individual who is truly empathic does not rely on explicit verbal cues to understand someone's wishes because these should be intuited through more subtle cues of gesture and tone. The above-mentioned elliptical, affect-oriented style favored by Japanese mothers, therefore, illustrates that they are sensitive to their children, and it also helps their children acquire and develop this subtle communicative style at home

(Azuma, 1986; Shigaki, 1987), which might be necessary even in the school setting.

Enculturation, the process by which young children learn and adopt the ways and manners of their culture, is apparently related to strategies for controlling children's behavior. According to Hess *et al.* (1980), for example, in comparison to US mothers, Japanese adults, particularly mothers, tend to think that in the preschool period of development children mature emotionally and learn to be polite and obedient. In this way, Japanese mothers believe that even preschool children should be capable of reading the minds of others and putting themselves in another person's position in order to understand that person's feelings. Japanese mothers, however, do not fall into Baumrind's (1971) category of authoritarian parenting style, which values unquestioning obedience. As Clancy (1985, 1986) reports, as a control strategy, Japanese mothers appeal to the feelings of others and even of inanimate objects, such as 'This broccoli wants to be eaten so badly.' From an early age on, therefore, children go through the process of empathy training highly valued in Japanese society. The Japanese language has an expression *ishin denshin*, which, literally meaning 'I understand instinctively what you have in mind,' emphasizes the existence of a sort of mental telepathy between individuals. Verbosity is traditionally frowned upon, and proverbs like 'Silence is golden,' 'Still waters run deep' and 'The mouth is the source of misfortune' are favorably used. In Japanese society, mothers, as primary caregivers, thus induct their children into a subtle interactive communicative style.

Issues of ambiguity

Although speech acts are claimed to share some universal features (Brown & Levinson, 1987), they vary cross-culturally as well as cross-linguistically (Matsumoto, 1993). As previously discussed in Bernstein's theory of codes, the issue of ambiguous oral discourse as contrasted with literate discourse has received a great deal of attention in the United States (Cazden *et al.*, 1985). Michaels and Collins (1984), for example, report that African American children who are accustomed to disambiguating pronouns in oral narrative discourse by means of prosody (largely depending on intonation contours such as vowel elongation) are predicted by teachers to produce ambiguous, poorly written narratives. Philips (1972, 1982) describes how, because of differences in unconscious interactional norms, the verbal as well as nonverbal communicative style of Native American students caused conflicts and misunderstandings in interactions with Anglo teachers. Scollon and Scollon (1981) likewise observed that their two-year-old daughter Rachel, who could not read or write, was on her way to the literacy necessary later in the Western school setting. In contrast, the way a ten-year-old Athabaskan (or Athapaskan) girl in Alaska talked or wrote, despite its being grammatical, was regarded as oral and non-literate; her style, which was ambiguous, was considered to be inappropriate according to the Western norm of literacy. In US society, unfortunately, such ambiguity tends to be confounded with failure to acquire literacy and further connected with social class, with little consideration of cultural differences. Therefore, in US society, an oral style tends to be considered ambiguous and characterized negatively, whereas a literate style is likely to be regarded as being explicit and characterized positively.

These issues of ambiguity, explicitness, and social class, however, must be understood and qualified as relevant to orality and literacy in the highly heterogeneous US society. As Gee (1986b) argues, however, 'the oral/literate contrast makes little sense because many social groups, even in high-technology societies, fall into such mixed categories as residual orality' (p. 737). This argument by Gee corresponds to Heath's (1983) statement that 'the traditional oral-literate dichotomy does not capture the ways other cultural patterns in each community affect the uses of oral and written language' (p. 344) as well as to Hymes's (1974b) view that 'it is impossible to generalize validly about 'oral' vs. 'literate' cultures as uniform types' (p. 54).

As a matter of fact, when considering a different society, it becomes clear that an understanding of these issues involves a different constellation of orality and literacy. Following Hall (1976), a high-context communication refers to 'one in which most of the information is either in the physical context or internalized in person, while very little is coded, explicit, transmitted part of the message'; on the other hand, low-context communication means 'the mass of the information is vested in the explicit code' (p. 79). Hall considers context as a continuum, with high context on one end and low context on the other; cultural groups are situated at a variety of points along this continuum. According to Hall, Western cultures tend to be situated on the low context end of the continuum, whereas Asians tend to fall on the other end. We can see that the idea stated by Hall is similar to Bernstein's notion of codes, because high context cultures rely less on explicit, spoken language in order to transmit thoughts and messages; rather, they rely on the interpersonal relationships and the history of previous discussions. Hall (1989) writes:

> In sharp contrast, high context peoples like the Pueblo, many of Africa's indigenous cultures, the Japanese, and apparently the Russians . . . inhabit a 'sea of information' that is widely shared. . . . The 'sea of information' group lives in a unified, very high context world in which all or most of the parts interrelate. (p. 39)

As mentioned above, the Japanese language is a highly contextualized language; the speaker must be fully aware of (1) whether the relationship with the listener is intimate, or (2) whether the communication is impersonal. Certainly, sources of diversity within Japanese society should be recognized. Given the presence of Korean and Chinese minorities in Japan, the portrayal of monolithic collectivism within a framework of a homogeneous society is too simplistic a notion to capture real Japanese society. In a relatively homogeneous society like Japan, however, even if what the speaker talks about is not explicit but ambiguous, the similarity of background allows for more accurate inferences on the part of the listener (at least Japanese people believe so). As Azuma (1986) aptly mentions, 'In contrast to the West, where it is the sender's responsibility to produce a coherent, clear, and intelligible message, in Japan, it is the receiver's responsibility to make sense out of the message' (p. 9). This Japanese belief that the burden is always on the listener/reader and not on the speaker/writer is cultivated by the previously mentioned *omoiyari* (empathy) training. Ambiguous utterances may result in successful communication in Japan because interlocutors believe that they have the shared experience necessary to make sense out of the ambiguous uses of the language (Donahue, 1998). In Japan, as opposed to the United States, for instance, ambiguous communication can and does play a different role in the interface of orality and literacy. It is thus critical to examine how the language used in a society reflects widely accepted social norms and, conversely, how the social norms shape the language use.

Note, however, that not only in the East but also in the West the ambiguous mode of communication is acceptable in poetry. In an interview with Ekbert Faas (1978), the poet Gary Snyder said that he 'closes a poem where he feels it is developed enough for the reader to be able to carry it.' Scollon and Scollon (1981), referring to this same interview and finding similarities between Snyder's remarks and Athabaskan verse, claim that 'this reticence, this attitude of not telling the reader but rather leading the reader to undertake his own work of understanding is characteristic of the best in human communication' (p. 127).

Having lived in Japan for several years with his Japanese wife, Snyder has been influenced by Japanese culture. In the above-mentioned interview

(Faas, 1978) he actually refers to the lifestyle of the *haiku* poet Basho, who, according to Snyder, reflects a particular Japanese cultural aspect of Zen Buddhism. As a matter of fact, one poetic form that is the focus of interest in this book is *haiku*, which is explained later in Chapters 3 and 9. Considering *haiku* as a reflection of the narrative discourse pattern prevalent among Japanese, I will first discuss the origin and development of *haiku* in Chapter 3, and then compare the patterns observed in *haiku* with my narrative discourse analysis in Chapter 9.

Subtlety and ambiguity in the Japanese language

The Japanese language is a potentially rich area for linguistic study; subtlety and ambiguity are also found in the structure of the language itself. Typologically, Japanese is an Altaic language, in marked contrast to English or other Indo-European languages (Kuno, 1973). For example, Japanese is an SOV language, namely, a language in which the basic word order of transitive sentences is that of subject–object–verb. Japanese is also an agglutinative language (e.g. the verb root is followed by a series of affixes, adjusted by voicing assimilation to fit the root and other affixes) (Yamada, 1992). Moreover, whereas the use of determiners is generally obligatory with nominals (at least singular ones) in English, no such functional category exists in Japanese (Shibatani, 1990). Also, in contrast to English, which is a right-branching (RB), head-initial (HI) language, Japanese is a left-branching (LB), head-final (HF) language. For example, whereas in English a preposition is a head of the phrase (e.g. '**in** San Francisco'), an equivalent particle appears at the end of the phrase in Japanese (e.g. '*San Francisco de/ni*'). Thus, Japanese is characterized 'postpositional' as opposed to 'prepositional' (Kuno, 1973). Unlike English, moreover, in Japanese all case relationships can be represented by postpositional markers, such as the following:

kinoo	*watashi*	*wa*	*Fisherman's Wharf*	*e*	*ikimashita.*
yesterday	I	[T]	Fisherman's Wharf	to	went

'I went **to** Fisherman's Wharf yesterday.'

dare	*ga*	*kinoo*	*Stanford*	*de*	*hanashi*	*o*	*shimashita*	*ka?*
who	[S]	yesterday	Stanford	at	talk	[O]	gave	[I]

'Who gave a talk **at** Stanford University yesterday?'

(*Note*: [I] stands for an interrogative particle; [O] is an object case marker; [S] stands for the subject marker; and [T] stands for the topic marker.)

While the use of these case markers is sometimes optional (e.g. *kinoo watashi ø Fisherman's Wharf e ikimashita* or even *kinoo watashi ø Fisherman's*

Wharf ø ikimashita: 'I went to Fisherman's Wharf yesterday'), as seen in these two examples, two different types of particles mark the subject of a sentence for different purposes (the thematic/topic marker *wa* as opposed to the subject marker *ga*; for more detailed discussion see Chapter 5).

As Clancy (1986) points out, if we do not take intonation contour into consideration, because negation appears as a verb suffix that comes at the very end of a sentence, the speaker can negate a sentence at the final moment, inferring the listener's reaction (e.g. *'Fisherman's Wharf e itta to omou'* ('[I] think [she] went to Fisherman's Wharf') as opposed to *'Fisherman's Wharf e itta to omowa **nai**'* ('[I] do not think [she] went to Fisherman's Wharf')).

This is generally true of other cases, as well. For example, neither a syntactic nor a morphological cue is available to distinguish the difference between a head-final NP with a relative clause (e.g. *basu ni notta kodomo* [*basu* = 'bus,' *ni* = object marker, *notta* = 'took,' *kodomo* = 'child']: 'the child who took a bus') and a simple sentence (e.g. *basu ni notta*: 'ø took a bus'), except for the availability of the information after the verb. Therefore, the listener cannot identify whether the sentence he or she hears is a relative clause or not, until the head NP becomes available at the very end (Yamashita *et al.*, 1993). Overall, we need to consider the impact of distinctive features of a particular language (e.g. word order, branching directions, and occurrences of empty categories) not only on how the speaker produces that language but also on how the listener processes what he or she hears.

Moreover, because Japanese has case markers, unlike English, a relatively free word order is allowed. For example, while they are both acceptable, a sentence with right dislocation, *'anata ni ookiku natte hoshii mon, okaasan wa'* ('ø wants you to grow up a big boy, mom'), is sometimes used instead of *'okaasan wa anata ni ookiku natte hoshii mon'* ('Mom wants you to grow up a big boy'). Thus, case marking and word-order flexibility are the norm in Japanese. [For more detailed discussion see Chapter 5. However, it should be noted that English does have some case markers. For instance, even when an object case marker is not attached to pronouns, they are in many cases case-marked pronouns (e.g. The girl saved *us*. This tie becomes *him*).]

To make matters more complicated, however, in naturally occurring Japanese discourse, case markers are occasionally omitted (e.g. *'anata ookiku natte hoshii mon, okaasan'*: 'ø wants you to grow up a big boy, mom'); the subject and/or object can be omitted as well, e.g. *'ookiku natte hoshii mon'*: '(I) want (you) to grow up a big boy.' In other words, zero forms (ø) can be prevalently used when a character has been established not only in a preceding clause but also in the context; there is no need to use a full nominal expression or a pronoun. When telling narratives, for example, Japanese narrators tend to opt for dispensing with nominal references to entities that they assume to be in the focus of listeners' consciousness (Downing, 1980). Unfortunately, however, these ellipses consequently result in considerable ambiguity. In addition to flexible word order, therefore, as Clancy (1980, 1992) and Hinds (1984) argue, the rare use of pronominal references further spurs ambiguity in Japanese. Although no causal relationships between some syntactic features and particular cultural aspects are implied, the above-mentioned syntactic features of the Japanese language are well-suited for implementing a subtle communicative style.[6]

In terms of communicative styles within and across cultures, it is, of course, true that one can find individual differences; for instance, some Japanese children talk a lot, and some American children talk little. As cultural anthropologists claim (Whiting & Edwards, 1988), however, in spite of these individual differences, closer observation reveals behavioral similarities for children of a given age in each cultural setting. Rather than species-specific characteristics claimed by Chomsky (1965) (i.e. similarities across people who speak different languages in different cultures and societies), or person-specific variations (i.e. individual differences), finding such population-specific characteristics is necessary for understanding what culture-specific socialization is all about (LeVine, 1990). One thus may assume that children in one culture share many of their language skills with one another; they acquire a culture-specific model of communicative competence from different types of social experiences and characteristics of their social patterns.

In summary, the Japanese language offers an interesting case study for crosslinguistic as well as cross-cultural analysis. In addition to the syntactic differences, referential strategies, such as the low frequency of pronouns and the extensive use of nominal ellipsis, make the study of the acquisition of Japanese unique and of great potential interest for those who do research in crosslinguistic studies Furthermore, cross-cultural studies suggest that different patterns of social interactions are being used in different environments. This claim is especially true regarding language socialization, which is the critical area of socialization for the propagation of culture-specific communicative or narrative discourse competence.

The Social Interaction Approach

A theoretical background

In this section, I will discuss the social interaction approach based on sociocognitive theory. Like Piagetian theory (e.g. Piaget, 1959), sociocognitive theory regards language development as part of more general cognitive development, focusing on the acquisition of higher-order intellectual skills (e.g. Vygotsky, 1978). In contrast to Piagetian theory, however, the central tenet of sociocognitive theory is the foundational role of interaction in cognitive and language development. In this sense, sociocognitive theory is highly compatible with language socialization studies (e.g. Schieffelin & Ochs, 1986), which I have described previously.

Blum-Kulka (1997) defines pragmatic socialization as the process in which 'children become socialized to local cultural rules regulating conversation, such as the choice of topics, rules of turn-taking, modes of storytelling and rules of politeness' (p. 12). Many language rules that children learn from early childhood are inseparable from social conventions. Even in the first year of his or her life, the baby learns the rules of turn-taking through interactions with his or her mother; the mother says something, then the baby vocalizes, then the mother speaks again, and again the baby vocalizes. Over the years the child gradually learns a variety of conversational skills, such as opening and shifting topics, holding the floor, and distributing turns of talk (Ninio & Snow, 1996). It is thus important to study how children develop communicative abilities so that they become able to cope with particular situations and perform social-communicative acts effectively. However, as the distinction between psychology and linguistics is not always clear, the boundaries between developmental pragmatics and other domains, such as various types of cognitive and social skills, are incapable of precise definition. In fact, children's capability increases, enabling them to generate and integrate a variety of linguistic components, such as syntactic, semantic, pragmatic and lexical, and these components are further connected with children's growing social-cognitive competence.

Studies of language development and narrative discourse analysis have increasingly focused on communicative social interactions in the earliest stages of children's speech patterns. Because there are remarkably wide individual differences (Nelson, 1981) as well as cultural differences (Schieffelin & Ochs, 1986), those researchers who base their theories on the empiricist, interactionist paradigm have come to conceptualize: (1) individuals and society construct one another through social interaction; and (2) children are not passive beneficiaries of their environments but active agents in their own socialization throughout life. Elementary school children, for instance, likely socialize their parents through experiences at school. The progress in this viewpoint is predicated on the theory that individuals and society construct one another through social interaction (Ochs, 1986).

Vygotsky's (1978) ideas, which represent the sociocognitive theory, form a basis for the view of language as a socioculturally mediated product. For instance, Vygotsky hypothesizes that children learn from other people, and particularly that children's problem-solving skills, which include language, first develop through social interactions with more capable members of society – adults and peers – and then become internalized after long practice. Specifically, he interprets the acquisition of children's cognitive skills in terms of the 'zone of proximal development.' For Vygotsky, the zone of proximal development is determined by the relationship between the following two types of children's problem-solving behaviors: (1) the behaviors when children solve a problem by interacting with adults who can provide them with some guidance, such as structuring the problem, solving part of the problem, or providing suggestions (i.e. interpsychological behavior corresponding to the potential level of development); and (2) the behaviors when children can solve the problem by themselves (i.e. intrapsychological behavior in accordance with the actual level of development). As the child matures, the relationship between interpsychological and intrapsychological behaviors changes for a given task, so that children gradually come to solve on their own problems that previously they could solve only partially, or not at all, except through interpersonal supportive interactions provided by adults.

The zone of proximal development is thus a construct that helps explain how interaction contributes to children's development. Through the process of social interaction, adults provide children with the tools to establish complex series of actions in problem-solving situations. Because the process of social interaction takes place before children have the mental capacities to take appropriate actions to solve the problem on their own, adults need to regulate children's actions. Through the process of interaction, these regulatory behaviors taken by adults gradually become part of the children's own behavior. The relationship between cognitive development and social interaction, particularly early social interactions between children and more mature members of society, can be summarized by Vygotsky's claim that all higher mental functions appear twice in development: (1) first as social or interpsychological functions during interactions with other social agents, and

(2) only later, through the internalization of social-interactive processes, as individualized or intrapsychological functions.

Lave (1991) emphasizes learning within several 'apprenticeship' situations, such as those experienced by Mayan midwives in the Yucatan, supermarket butchers in an on-site training program and Alcoholics Anonymous groups. Because she claims that learning occurs within what she calls 'communities of practice,' she situates learning in a particular pattern of social participation; that is, a person moves from being a peripheral participant to a full participant in the sociocultural practices of the community in which he or she lives. Lave's emphasis on 'apprenticeship' is thus synonymous with social interaction. In this regard, Lave and Wenger (1991) state:

> Children are, after all, quintessentially legitimate peripheral participants in adult social worlds. But various forms of apprenticeship seemed to capture very well our interest in learning in situated ways – in the transformative possibilities of being and becoming complex, full cultural-historical participants in the world – and it would be difficult to think of a more apt range of social practices for this purpose. (p. 32)

Thus, development takes place within the context of meaningful social interactions in which adults guide and scaffold children's participation in socioculturally appropriate ways.[7]

When applied to the use of language, the social interaction paradigm suggests a culturally ideal adult-child relationship, as seen in the Japanese proverb 'Birth is much, but breeding is more' (which clearly takes sides with empiricism rather than nativism). In terms of first-language acquisition, for example, children acquire their first language through interactions with more competent members, usually mothers (e.g. Snow, 1977, 1983, 1986). In other words, an adult assists a young child in accomplishing what the child is not able to accomplish on his or her own. This type of relationship, however, should not be hypothesized to be a one-way interaction in which only one party is always influencing the other (i.e. unidirectional). Instead, children and their environments need to be conceptualized as a dynamic system in which they actively interact with and influence each other (i.e. bi-directional).[8] Even infants and small children are influential in socializing other members of their family as well as their peers. For instance, later-born children are said to tend to be slower in language development than first-born children perhaps because the existence of siblings causes parents' attitudinal changes, such as shortening of conversation directed at later-born children, and because siblings are not as good language models for later-born children as parents (Ochs, 1986). Similarly, it is easy to imagine that children socialize their peers into gender-specific modes of action and communication that they have acquired through social interactions such as game situations (Cook-Gumperz, 1992). It is also possible to assume that the links between gender and linguistic practices are culturally constructed (Borker, 1980) and, more importantly, developed through early social interactions (Gal, 1992). Unlike the cultural transmission paradigm represented by Caudill (Caudill & Schooler, 1973; Caudill & Weinstein, 1969), therefore, the social interaction paradigm rejects the unidirectional notion that parents pass along cultural formulas to their children; instead, it tries to depict how children's active processing of information results in both the reproduction of culture and the production of new elements.

In summary, as I wrote at the beginning of this section, the social interaction approach based on sociocognitive theory, which investigates higher level critical-thinking skills, and language socialization studies are compatible; in fact, language socialization studies have often examined pragmatic development within the framework of the zone of proximal development. In this regard, Kasper (2000) writes:

> Language socialization studies frequently engage sociocognitive theory. Even though language socialization and sociocognitive theory pursue different epistemological goals, their ontological stance is highly compatible. In both approaches, the acquisition of language and culture and the development of cognition critically depend on social interaction in concrete sociohistorical contexts. Both emphasize the role of expert members to guide novices in their accomplishment of tasks that they would be unable to complete on their own. Both reject a view of cognition that considers knowledge and learning (predominantly or exclusively) as an individual's intrapsychological representation and processes, arguing instead that knowledge, including knowledge of language, is not only transmitted but created through concrete interaction and therefore properly viewed as interpsychologically distributed and constructed. (p. 5)

Narrative Discourse Analysis

Within the social interaction paradigm

Storytelling is an interactive social act that occurs in culture-specific patterns; within the social interactionist paradigm, current research investigates the extent to which children's personal narratives are influenced and constructed through social interactions. This paradigm maintains that talking about past events or experiences first takes place in interactive contexts, and that social support facilitates the development of talking about the past (Sachs, 1979, 1982). Inspired by Vygotsky's (1978) zone of proximal development, Bruner (1977, 1983) maintains that, for learning to take place, children must have opportunities for cooperative verbal and nonverbal interactions with adults. He uses the term 'scaffolding' to describe these adult-child interactions, which are initially scripted and played by adults, who then involve children taking an increasingly major role in creating and performing the joint script. Bruner's notion of scaffolding, therefore, encompasses a variety of parental supports for language development in the young child. More specifically, the joint construction of stories by preschool children and adults (including joint book-reading activities) is an important context in which adults provide guidance and support to children in the process of narrative construction and comprehension. Through interaction, therefore, young children begin to understand the structures of narratives and, moreover, the processes involved in constructing meaning.

Further hypothesizing that in telling a story the child has to learn from adults the so-called dual landscape of narrative, Bruner (1986) explains:

> One is the landscape of action, where the constituents are the arguments of action: agent, intention or goal, situation, instrument, something corresponding to a 'story grammar.' The other landscape is the landscape of consciousness: what those involved in the action know, think, or feel, or do not know, think, or feel. (p. 14)

In other words, the landscape of action is a canvas on which the narrator paints the world of action in the story. The landscape of consciousness, on the other hand, describes 'how the world is perceived or felt by various members of the cast of characters, each from their own perspective' (Feldman *et al.*, 1990, p. 2). Developmentally, the child's acquisition of these two vehicles for thought and language production is crucial to understanding his or her progress in narrative production because, as Hudelson (1994) puts it, 'Narrative appears to be a fundamental process of the human mind, a basic way of making sense of the world' (p. 142).

The development of narrative has been studied extensively, in part because (1) narrative is considered to constitute a universal, basic mode of thought, and (2) untangling the intricate relationship between narrative and cognition is a meaningful endeavor. While narrative development orchestrates cognitive and linguistic dimensions across cultures and languages (Berman & Slobin, 1994), because the nature of the mind is simultaneously constrained by a specific culture and society, the concept of the dual landscape of narrative is also socioculturally constrained. Accordingly, studies of early stages of narrative discourse (e.g. Bruner, 1990; Nelson, 1989) have identified two major assumptions: (1) there are culture-specific patterns of social interactions in narrative production; and (2) a particular caregiver's narrative style shapes – and is sometimes shaped by – the child's narrative style, contributing to differences in mothers' and children's styles within a given culture.

Because mothers provide linguistic modeling in a variety ways, mothers are crucial agents of language socialization, including narrative development. A number of researchers (e.g. Eisenberg, 1985; Hudson, 1990, 1993; Ninio & Snow, 1996; Sachs, 1979, 1982; Snow & Goldfield, 1981) have proposed the intriguing possibility that the way in which adults initially structure conversations about past experiences affects the way in which children come to think about the past and themselves. Provided that the child later internalizes the particular narrative structure supplied by the mother, we may be able to assume that while different roles or slots may be allowed for adult and child participants, the child's style for talking about past events corresponds to the mother's style for talking about the past. Thus, a mother's initial narrative style would hypothetically predict her child's later narrative style. Fivush (1991), for example, proposes that those mothers who provide temporally complex and informationally dense narratives early in development have children who produce temporally complex and informationally dense narratives later in development (e.g. those mothers who ask for background information early in development have children who provide elaborated accounts about settings later).

Likewise, McCabe and Peterson (1991), in studying English-speaking North American mother–child discourse interactions, found that stylistic differences between parents also affect children's later narrative style. Parents of English-speaking, North American children recorded conversations about past events when their children were between the ages of two and six. Additionally, their children were interviewed at regular intervals by a researcher who provided minimal support while the children narrated past events. Some parents encouraged their children to expand upon the topic extensively, whereas others rapidly shifted topics of conversation with their two- and three-year-old children. By the end of four years, the children also differed from each other. Some children told lengthy narratives that built up to a high point, evaluatively dwelt on it, and then resolved it. Other children struggled to tell a story consisting of more than one event. A finding of most interest was that those parents who ranked highest in the frequency of topic-extension for their two- to three-year-old children were the same parents who had children ranking highest in terms of well-formed English narratives when the children were older. Furthermore, if mothers habitually asked their children to describe people, places, and things involved in some event, the children later on told stories that focused on orientation at the expense of plot. In contrast, if mothers habitually asked their children about what happened next, the children later on told stories with well-developed plots (McCabe & Peterson, 1990; Peterson & McCabe, 1992). Thus, McCabe and Peterson focused on how parental narrative elicitation style affects children's narrative style and content within one particular culture.

In narrative contexts, therefore, children's speech is guided and scaffolded by mothers who initiate and elicit the children's contributions about past experiences. Moreover, the view that parental talk provides a verbal framework for children's representations of past events implies that early social interactions shape young children's narratives into culturally preferred patterns. [Note, however, that I hypothesize two-way (i.e. bi-directional) interaction, which differs from the one-way (i.e. uni-directional) interaction emphasized in a cultural transmission model, as I have repeatedly stressed in this chapter.]

Analyzing narrative structure

Narrative is a superordinate term that includes a variety of forms, such as a script (i.e. what usually happens rather than a specific incident) and a personal event narrative (Ninio & Snow, 1996). Hudson and Shapiro (1991) emphasize the importance of children's early acquisition of script narratives; by age three, the majority of children will learn to be able to report what happens in familiar events, such as getting dressed in the morning and eating at a fast-food restaurant. If we hypothesize that scripts are a prerequisite to the emergence of real stories, we will need to understand how narrators (children and adults alike), as products of a particular culture, structure narratives as an orderly flow of information that makes sense to the listener.

Cultural learning is, in a sense, imitative learning, which is a very powerful tool for language development, as reviewed above. Investigating how children make generalizations, then, is a worthy endeavor, i.e. to borrow Piagetian terminology (Piaget, 1952), how, through imitation, children assimilate new information into productive schemes (i.e. organized patterns of thought and behavior) and schematize it. By early elementary school, children become proficient in telling stories conforming to culturally specific schemata for storytelling (Berman & Slobin, 1994). Children, in other words, acquire culture-specific ways of thinking for speaking.

Understanding cultural specificity, then, should mean accepting cross-cultural differences. At times, however, culture acts as a filter. The notion of the cultural filter indicates that when not only narrating events but also interpreting narrative events, we perceive them in a certain way from a certain angle. Narratives are seemingly everywhere. There is no reason to doubt that all of us have stories to tell. Wherever you go, you will probably find that narratives perform a variety of functions in human interaction. Even if the act of telling narratives is universal, however, how to tell and interpret stories should be regarded as a culturally deep-rooted activity.

It is thus critical to realize that there are substantial cross-cultural differences in narrative structure. As reviewed previously, language is not simply responsive to social activity, but language *is* social activity (Hymes, 1974a). More specifically, because narrative is a socioculturally situated activity, a specific narrative discourse style not only reflects the language socialization process, but it also represents a fundamental structure that has been socioculturally cultivated. Through cross-cultural comparison of narrative structure, therefore, we can see differences in social activities in different cultures.

Verse/stanza analysis

Many methods are available for analyzing narrative structure (McCabe & Peterson, 1991; Peterson and McCabe, 1983). Among them, a model called verse analysis was invented by Hymes (1981, 1990) to interpret Native American narratives; a version of it was later called stanza analysis by Gee (1985) in his application of the analysis to children's speeches in a particular elementary school setting. Chinookan and some other Native American narratives, according to Hymes, consist of hierarchical components that construct organized and rhetorically coherent underlying patterns. The most subordinate unit of the narrative is an intonational unit defined as the line. Some intonational units are called verses and have sentence-like contours. Oral narrative is an organization of lines, thematically grouped into verses, each of which is generally a simple sentence or clause. Verses, which serve as building blocks of a narrative, are grouped into stanzas, and stanzas into further larger units, such as scenes and acts. [Note that there are five different levels of hierarchical units, as Masuda (1999) proposes in his Quint-patterning Principle.

For more information, see Chapter 4.] Boundaries between units at all levels usually involve changes of location, speaker, or main character and often the presence of an initial marker, such as *now* at the beginning of a line (Hymes, 1985) and 'well' and 'and' at the beginning of a verse (Hymes, 1985, 1996). Using verse analysis, Hymes (1982) claimed that many Native American languages, such as Chinookan and Zunni, maintain culture-specific patterns of narrative structure and that the succession is normally of three or five units. For instance, Hymes (1981) identified a culture-specific representation of narrative construction, specifically a rhetorical configuration of Onset-Ongoing-Outcome.

Chafe (1977) expressed a similar idea by using such terms as schematization, framing and categorization. The theory advocated by Chafe views the cognitive comprehension of real-life situations in terms of story schemas (i.e. structures in semantic memory that specify the general arrangement or flow of information in storytelling). As a component of the frame, Chafe (1980) proposed the notion of 'idea unit.' Because the narrator verbalizes only one new concept at a time, spontaneous spoken language is produced in an idea unit. In other words, 'idea units,' which are defined as a series of brief spurts, are 'tone units' that correspond to the narrator's cognitive chunking of words. Chafe (1993) later divided idea units further into 'accent units' and 'intonation units.' Each segment of speech that ends in a terminal contour is identified as an intonation unit, whereas 'an accent unit consists of the word containing the primary accent plus whatever other words belong to the same constituent as that word' (p. 36), thus representing a single idea that is 'the domain of activation in consciousness' (p. 41).

In the example that follows, I apply Chafe's model to data that I collected (Minami & McCabe, 1995). I asked a Japanese mother of a five-year-old girl to tape-record their conversations about past experiences (for more details, see Chapters 6 and 7). The contexts are the mother and her child's recollections of their visit to an aquarium and observation of a rather dramatic scene. The numbers to the right refer to the minimum unit, which corresponds to Chafe's accent unit, and the accent units numbered 1 to 6 constitute intonation units.

Example 2.1 Yumiko (a girl aged 5;6) and her mother's interaction

Yumiko:	*sore ga **ne***	1
	'That one, you know,'	
	(Mother: *un*)	
	'uh huh'	
	*chitcha na sakana o **ne***	2
	'a small fish, you know,'	

(**Mother:**   *un*)
       'uh huh'

baku tte   3
'gulp'
   ano ne   4
   'um, you know,'
     baku tte ne   5
     'gulp, you know,'
       tabeta yo.   6
       'ate.'

Mother: *honto.*
       'Really.'
Yumiko: *un.*
       'Yes.'
Mother: *sonna no mita no.*
       '(You) saw such a thing.'
       hee, sugoi.
       'Wow, awful.'

Units of speech on the mother's part could be the brief 'uh-huh's' acknowledgment that signals her willingness for the child's narrative production to continue. More important, this instance, which reveals how the preschooler verbalized her possibly traumatic experience, is particularly useful to identify how cognitive processes are working during the narrative production (see also the micro-level narrative discourse analysis sections in Chapters 6 and 7). In this way, the above narrative exemplifies Chafe's two units of analysis:

> 'Accent units verbalize single ideas that are the domain of activation in consciousness. It is accent units that are the loci of the new, accessible, and given information. Intonation units, consisting of one or more accent units, verbalize clusters of such ideas.' (Chafe, 1993, p. 41)

Building upon the work of Hymes and of Chafe, Gee (1985, 1989a) formulated the notion of stanza as an ideal structure containing lines, each of which is generally a simple clause and corresponds to the idea unit, which, following Chafe (1980), is marked by a single intonation contour. A stanza consists of a group of lines representing a 'thematically constant unit' (Gee, 1986a, p. 403) that simultaneously stands as a contrast to prior units by virtue of incorporating a 'change of character, event, location, time, or narrative function' (Gee, 1989a, p. 289). Using this version of stanza analysis, Gee (1991b) illustrated the distinction between the ways that African Americans and European Americans describe past events in their narratives. Note that, as already described in Chapter 1, Gee categorized the former as an oral-strategy (or poetic) narrative and the latter as a literate-strategy (or prosaic) narrative.

Both verse and stanza analysis are now widely accepted as effective means of analyzing narrative structure (Hicks, 1990; Mishler, 1990, 1991, 1995). As Hicks (1990) states, 'An analysis based upon lines and stanzas enables one to address sociocultural differences in how children themat- ically and structurally organize their narrative settings' (p. 28). Furthermore, commenting on Gee's stanza analysis, Mishler (1990) argues that, in stanza analysis, 'the technical devices that make it work are clearly defined and visible; the underlying structure is specified; and his interpretation is tied directly to the data' (p. 431).

More important, these analyses have been applied successfully to nar- ratives from various cultures and have revealed culture-specific narrative patterns. For example, although Hawai'i Creole English has been consid- ered baffling, odd and unintelligible and thus concluded to be a form of restructured Standard English, Masuda (1995) identified rule-governed structures in narratives told by Hawai'i Creole English speakers: first, the inclination to versify exists, and second, the phenomenon of repetition or reiteration is prevalent in Hawai'i Creole English narratives.

In many ways, verse/stanza analysis, which is based upon lines, verses and stanzas, has helped crystallize culturally specific types of cognitive framing. The analysis has specifically enabled us to address sociocul- tural distinctiveness in how narrators from different backgrounds thematically and structurally organize their narratives.

High point analysis

As was mentioned previously, another method to analyze narrative structure is Labovian high point analysis, which assumes that a coherent personal narrative is organized around a high point, the point of the narrative (e.g. Labov, 1972; Labov & Waletzky, 1967; McCabe & Peterson, 1991; Peterson & McCabe, 1983). According to high point analysis, a good story begins by providing the listener with a stage setting, the orientation about place (where), time (when), characters (whom) and what the narrator is going to talk about; then, the story builds up to a crisis (high) point and suspends the action at this point, where its impor- tance is highlighted; finally, the narrator resolves this crisis. In other words, a story revolves around complicating actions or problems that need to be resolved. A good narrative, therefore, is organized around one or more points stressed by the narrator, with an emphasis on two important functions: (1) the referential function, which conveys infor- mation about the events and characters, such as what happened to whom;[9] and (2) the affective or evaluative function, which conveys to the interlocutor the narrator's attitude toward the events of the narrative or the event's significance to the narrator. Thus, a narrative not only retains the temporal ordering of the past event or experience, but it also evaluates that event or experience, suggesting its point or significance.

What makes a good narrative?

There are many ways to tell a story. It seems clear, however, that whether a narrative is good or bad depends on whether or not the listener can comprehend the narrative. No one considers a narrative good if he or she cannot comprehend it. To begin with, to be accepted by the listener, the narrator must demonstrate what Hymes (1974a) calls communicative competence. Moreover, our processing of a story is governed by a story schema – what we expect to happen in that story (i.e. cognitive structures for comprehension). The notion of schema is associated with Bartlett's (1932) early work, in which he attempted to reveal that remembering is not simple reproductive processing of a story, but that it rather represents the listener's reconstructing process based on an overall impression of the story. Furthermore, individual memory affects accuracy and expression (Clark, 1994). In the past, some researchers (e.g. Tulving, 1972) emphasized that episodic memory, which is considered one type of long-term memory (one of the components of human information processing), keeps a record of an individual's personal experiences and events that are specific to a time and a place. Sypher *et al.* (1994), however, argue that even if information is understood and stored in long-term memory, it is not always available. Rather, these researchers stress the constructive and reconstructive nature of memory. Sypher *et al.* (1994) write:

> We depart from earlier views of memory that suggested that memories of the past are safely stored and can be retrieved when necessary minus any trace of decay. We treat long-term memory as selective, in that we tend to recall only a subset of experiences. We also argue that at any given time we might recall things differently in that we constantly reinterpret our past. (p. 53)

Schank and Abelson's (1977) schema theory is also predicated on the notion of a script – a general description of what usually occurs in an event, such as going to a restaurant or going to a birthday party. Obviously, the notion of story schema is closely related to the underlying representation of narratives. Stein and Glenn (1979), proponents of episodic analysis, which treats narrative as organized information as purposive behavior, hypothesize the following: (1) 'incoming information is encoded in relationship to already existing psychological structures or patterns of information'; and (2) 'these existing structures determine the information encoded and inferences generated in the process of comprehension' (p. 115). Some researchers (e.g. Nelson, 1986, 1991; Nezworski *et al.*, 1982; Schank & Abelson, 1977) further claim that preschool children already represent stories, following general schemas/schemata (or general event knowledge) or scripts that guide story comprehension and production. Schank and Abelson (1977) thus claim that stories young children make up 'give a glimpse into the process of script generalization' (p. 227).

To make matters more complicated, however, a story schema – the underlying organizational paradigm for stories – seems culturally specific. In an exploration of cross-linguistic schema, Kaplan (1966) claimed the existence of culture-specific thought patterns. For example, the English pattern, which follows a direct and linear organization, is straight, whereas the Oriental pattern is indirect, forming a spiral circling around a point. Kintsch and Greene (1978), assuming the existence of culture-specific aids to story comprehension and reconstruction, selected a Native American story that was not in accordance with the Western norm of a good story. Conducting experiments on American college students, these researchers found that those American students had some difficulty in comprehending and reconstructing the Native American story. Similarly, according to Harris *et al.* (1988) report, foreign stories read to Americans were 'misremembered' to have been more like American stories.[10] Thus, there seems to exist a tendency that people forget less in stories taken from cultures that are similar to their own than in culturally dissimilar stories.

Not only in comprehension and recall, but also in production, we may assume that people from different cultures translate their knowledge and experience into narratives in culture-specific ways; we also assume, therefore, that different cultures have different ideas of what makes a story good. Using verse/stanza analysis, Minami and McCabe (1991, 1996) analyzed oral personal narratives told by Japanese elementary school children (aged five to nine) and found three distinctive features: (1) The narratives are exceptionally succinct; (2) they are usually free-standing collections of multiple experiences; and (3) stanzas almost always consist of three verses (which roughly correspond to three simple clauses) (for more information, see Examples 1.1 and 1.2 in Chapter 1).

To illustrate these various aspects, Minami and McCabe (1991) used Example 2.2, which was told by a seven-year, ten-month-old boy Yoshi, who lived both in Japan and in the United States. His injury stories, which are very brief, portray both the three-verse pattern and the presentation of multiple experiences.

Example 2.2   Yoshi's monologic narrative
Stanza A: [Abstract]
(a) *koronde,*   1
      '(I) fell down,'
(b) *koko o ookiku kega shitari,*   2
      '(I) got a big injury here,'
(c) *danboo ni butsukatte,*   3
      '(I) bumped into a heater,'
(d) *koko kega shita no.*   4
      '(I) got hurt here.'

Stanza B: [Injury in Japan]
(e) *saisho, koko wa ne,*   5
      'First, as for this one, you know,'
          nihon de ne,   6
          'in Japan, you know,'
              sunde ita toki ne,   7
              'When (I) lived, you know,'
(f) *da da da tte hashitte,*   8
      '(I) was dashing "dah, dah, dah,"'
          koronde,   9
          '(I) tumbled,'
(g) *kega shita.*   10
      '(I) got hurt.'

Stanza C: [Injury in the United States]
(h) *de, moo hitotsu wa ne,*   11
      'And, as for the other one, you know,'
(i) *asonde ite ne,*   12
      '(I) was playing, you know,'
          tsumazuite,   13
          '(I) stumbled,'
              danboo ni gachin te.   14
              '(I bumped) into a heater "bang."'
(j) *sorede ne,*   15
      'Then, you know,'
          koko kara chi ga poh poh tto.   16
          'from here, (it) bled "drip, drip."'

In Stanza A, Yoshi briefly talked about his injury in Japan, and then restarted to describe another injury he suffered in the United States in a more detailed manner. We can notice that this stanza departs from the three-verse pattern but that the stanza functions as an abstract of the two injuries to be described later in Stanzas B and C. According to Minami and McCabe (1991), this insertion of brief description of one experience is another feature of Japanese children's oral narratives.

The above-described features, according to Minami and McCabe (1991), furthermore, reflect the basic characteristics of *haiku*, a commonly practiced literary form that often combines poetry and narrative, and an ancient, but still widespread game called *karuta*, which also displays three lines of written discourse. Minami (1990) and Minami and McCabe (1991, 1996) suggest that these literacy games may explain both the extraordinary regularity of verses per stanza and the smooth acquisition of reading by a culture that practices restricted, ambiguous, oral-style narrative discourse.

Conclusions

To conclude Chapter 2, 'How do children learn to narrate?' is one of the questions posed in this book. Sometime during the second year of life – anywhere from 12 to 18 months – children begin to utter their first words. During the following four to five years, language acquisition and development occur quite rapidly. By the time children enter school, they seem to have mastered the major structural features of their language; for instance, they tell stories that conform to particular cultural schemata for storytelling. In fact, children seem to master nearly all of the linguistic features of the language to which they are exposed seemingly without specific instruction.

In this chapter, I first presented a historical overview of the field of language studies. The late-1950s witnessed a rapid development in child language studies, from the behaviorist theory of language put forth by Skinner to the Chomskyan revolution (Chomsky, 1957), which provided language researchers with new models to explore.[11] I then discussed developments in our understanding of how children learn to talk, with particular emphasis on the roles of innate, cognitive and social interactive factors in language development, as well as cross-cultural differences. I took this route of discussion because language production – not only at the syntactic level but also at the discourse level – is a combination of the nature of human thought and the structural properties peculiar to an individual's native language.

In this chapter, I have particularly focused on various aspects associated with pragmatic development, such as (1) the acquisition of culturally specific rules for using speech and (2) factors influencing language acquisition (e.g. the role of maternal input and scaffolding behavior). Toward the end of the chapter, I emphasized that narrative styles reflect the society and culture in which they are employed. Through narrative, an individual organizes his or her experience under the constraint of socio-cultural meanings; thus, narrative can be viewed as a microcosm of the individual mind, but more than that it reflects the larger social world. As Gee (1985) puts it, 'Just as the common core of human language is expressed differently in different languages, so the common core of communicative style is expressed differently in different cultures' (p. 11). Along the same lines, Cazden (1988) writes, 'Narratives are a universal meaning-making strategy, but there is no one way of transforming experience into a story' (p. 24). This trend in thinking is also advanced by Bruner (1990), who argues that meaning creation is tightly yoked to a specific style of cultural representation.

Furthermore, the development of children's personal narratives reflects not only their culture but also their age. As Eisenberg (1985) puts it, 'The ability to discuss and describe past events involves a number of cognitive, conversational, and linguistic skills not necessary when talking about objects and events that are visible when the conversation is taking place' (p. 177). To make matters more complicated, as previous research has revealed (e.g. Berman & Slobin, 1994; Nelson, 1989), cognitive, linguistic, conversational and social-interactional dimensions seem to take different courses in the process of language acquisition, and moreover, these factors interact in a complex fashion in narrative development. To better understand this complexity, when the social interactionist paradigm is applied to the study of narrative, the bulk of research in this area considers the caregiver, particularly the mother, to be the primary agent who provides a framework for the child to learn a particular narrative style.

Understanding how narrative develops is crucial because a specific narrative style not only reflects a fundamental structure that has been culturally nurtured, but also indicates a socialization process contributing to the formation of such cultural representation. Narratives enable individuals to make sense of their experiences in culturally satisfying ways. With these understandings as a basis, examining Japanese children's personal narratives in the context of mother–child interactions can offer important insights into the sociocultural basis for language acquisition.

Notes

1. To avoid misinterpretation, I add that although behaviorist theory was a dominant force in North American psychology, even in the 1950s competing forces were strong. That is, in addition to Skinner (1957), Staats and Staats (1957), for example, argued that many of the subtle nuances of word meaning are learned by the process of conditioning. In a larger view of child devel-

opment, however, the interactional approach (e.g. Hebb, 1953) stressed the need to describe fully the sequence of events leading to the normal appearance of a behavior. Likewise, the cognitive-developmental approach, represented by the Swiss scientist Piaget (1952), emphasized how thinking processes change as individuals develop through a series of stages.

2. Note that the English sentence 'John saw Bill' would be arranged as 'John Bill saw' in Japanese because the head of the verb phrase 'saw' comes at the end of the phrase. [See the discussion of branching directions and head directions later in this Chapter.] Additionally, it now seems to be more appropriate to replace the term 'modular' with 'domain-specific' (MacWhinney, 1999).

3. Conversely, Bernstein's (1971) theory of codes has been used to explain why some children do better than others in school (Torrance & Olson, 1985). The oral-literate dichotomy is considered dangerous because it is likely to be connected with the 'deficit hypothesis' that assumes that the parents in some sociocultural groups fall short of the skills necessary to promote their children's success at school. For example, examining the literacy programs to support low-income, minority and immigrant families, Auerbach (1989) warns that the so-called transmission of school practices model, which promotes parents' efforts toward school-like literacy practices in the home, function under the deficit hypothesis. Because this hypothesis, either implicitly or explicitly, condemns children's environmental, sociocultural, and/or linguistic background for their failure in the classroom context, it implies that the family, not the teacher, is responsible for providing adequate educational support. The oral-literate dichotomy has thus served as a basis for the match-mismatch formulation of literacy and its resulting deficit hypothesis.

4. Similar results were reported by Morikawa *et al.* (1988), who, like Toda *et al.* (1990), compared maternal speech to three-month-old infants for US and Japanese mother–child pairs. Morikawa, Shand and Kosawa found that Japanese mothers used indirect speech styles more frequently than did US mothers. Interestingly, according to these researchers, whereas US mothers produced a significant number of incomplete sentences, almost half of which served no communicative function, Japanese mothers used incomplete sentences with more functional purposes.

5. In their cross-sectional study, Fernald and Morikawa (1993) examined Japanese and US mothers' speech to six-, 12- and 19-month-old infants. These researchers found the following features: (1) Compared to Japanese mothers, US mothers labeled objects more often and more consistently. (2) On the other hand, Japanese mothers used objects to engage infants in social routines more frequently than did US mothers. More relevant here is that although based on maternal recount, Fernald and Morikawa report that US infants at 19 months had larger noun vocabularies than did their Japanese counterparts.

6. Obviously, the role of ambiguity in language occasionally presents problems for Japanese listeners. Even Japanese mothers in the sample collected for this book complained to their children about the use of ambiguous language. The practice of ambiguity, however, is more likely to present problems for listeners who are not full participants in Japanese culture, and hence are unable to make required inferences aptly.

7. Lave and Wenger's (1991) 'legitimate peripheral participation' resembles Rogoff's (1990) 'guided participation.' Following Rogoff *et al.* (1993), children's development is regarded as occurring 'through active participation in cultural systems of practice in which children, together with their caregivers and other companions, learn and extend the skills, values and knowledge of their community' (p. 1).

8. As seen later in Chapter 9, in Piaget's (1959) theory of cognitive development, language plays a relatively secondary role; instead, the sequence of more general development in cognition determines the sequence of language development (e.g. during the second year of life, children begin to use words in order to symbolize the world around them). Likewise, although Piaget has at times acknowledged social interaction as a possible factor in development, it is only secondary. On the other hand, combining many aspects of both the behaviorist and the linguistic positions (both are reviewed in this chapter), the social interaction approach shares with the behaviorists an emphasis on the role of the environment in terms of language development. Interactionists consider the functions of language in social communication to be important throughout the child's development. Thus, language acquisition is fundamentally embedded in the process of socialization. As Vygotsky (1978) argues, although language is a very special tool, it is at first only a tool for a young child's social interaction; as the child internalizes linguistic forms, the role of language changes from a social to a private one.

9. One referential component is 'complicating actions' – the sequence of specific, chronologically-ordered events comprising the experience. Another important referential component is orientation – information about people, place(s), time(s) and situation(s). These are discussed later in Chapter 4.

10. Here, I need to clarify a distinction in the study of narrative between story structure and content structure. The experiment of Harris *et al.* (1988) shows that foreign *content* schemas are less well remembered than familiar content schemas; for example, eating breakfast in a bar (really a pub) is a familiar schema in England but not in the United States. Harris *et al.* thus held story structure constant and varied content structure (i.e. content-focus). Kintsch and Greene (1978), on the other hand, varied story structure (i.e. structure-focus).

    Additionally, although I have primarily focused on form over content in my literature review, I certainly acknowledge the value of analyses that focus more on content for the questions that I am asking. That is, more content-based analyses can be found in studies such as Nelson (1989) and Nicolopoulou *et al.* (1994). In *Narratives from the Crib* (1989), Nelson and other researchers present an analysis of the sequentially organized narratives of a toddler, Emily, between the ages of 21 and 36 months, as well as her interactions with her parents. Particularly, these researchers examined Emily's construction of worldview, and analyzed her construction of self. Likewise, through a content-based analysis, Nicolopoulou *et al.* (1994) found that the stories told by four-year-old boys are systematically different from those told by girls of the same age.

11. Note that one recent theory is the emergentist approach (MacWhinney, 1999), which claims that domain-general cognitive mechanisms, such as working

memory, statistical learning and pressures on memory organization and retrieval, contribute to language acquisition, although an innate, domain-specific mechanism might allow the very initial emergence of language. More specifically, in this new framework, domain-general cognitive mechanisms work on environmental stimuli to render the complex and elegant structures that characterize language. Thus, the emergentist view is a constructivist one that emphasizes the interaction between the organism and the environment (i.e. children gradually learn through interacting with environmental factors such as parents' speech patterns). Despite the emergentist/constructivist approach, which seems applicable to any non-nativist approach (as long as 'emerging/developing' is seen as opposed to 'innate'), both nativist and empiricist approaches to the study of language acquisition will continue to co-exist.

Chapter 3
Research Design: Methodology and Basic Concepts

Chapter 2 traced the history of research on language acquisition and socialization, including Japanese language socialization. The chapter then described ways in which language acquisition and socialization, in the process of child development, relate to the level of extended spans of narrative discourse. This chapter is devoted to an explanation of methodology; i.e. I mainly explain the data collection procedure and transcription system with theoretical support before beginning the analysis in Chapter 4. At the end of Chapter 3, in order (1) to connect orality and literacy in Japanese society, and (2) to present the Japanese type of co-construction (e.g. the listener's anticipatory completions in response to the speaker's initial utterances), I also introduce the basic characteristics of *haiku* and *karuta*. I then discuss the relationship between the particular characteristics of these literary games and the Japanese narrative discourse style.

Type of Data Analyzed

'Yoochien,' Japanese preschool

The purpose of this book is to examine the relationship between linguistic forms and their functions in the development of Japanese *yoochien* (preschool) children's narrative discourse, under certain cultural influences as well as developmental constraints. Note that the term *yoochien* is often translated as 'kindergarten' but, unlike most kindergartens in the United States, *yoochien* is not part of the elementary school even if it is housed on the site of the elementary school. Preschool in Japan generally begins at age three or four and continues until age six, when children enter elementary school. In Japan, virtually all four-year-olds attend some form of preschool, either private or public. Historically, *yoochien* and *hoikuen* were developed for different purposes. *Yoochien*, under the auspices of the Ministry of Education, Science and Culture, was originally intended to serve children of mothers who were full-time homemakers; *yoochien* thus used to be an institution for middle-class families. On the other hand, *hoikuen*, operated by the Ministry of Health and Welfare, was originally set up to serve children of working mothers; *hoikuen* thus used to be associated with working-class families (Morigami, 1993). Because a great number of middle-class mothers are now employed at least part-time, however, the distinction between these two types of institutions is no longer associated with socioeconomic differences, and thus the boundaries cannot be sharply drawn (Boocock, 1989).

Some of the myths that surround Japanese education should be destroyed here. Newspapers and magazines outside Japan, particularly in the United States, sometimes report that Japanese preschools are 'examination-oriented' and 'Spartan in discipline' and that 'Japanese home training makes classroom discipline easy' (Peak, 1991, pp. 2–6). For example, a familiar perception of outsiders is that to ensure their future success and prosperity, two- and three-year-old Japanese children have to take an entrance examination or go through some type of selection process in order to enter a good nursery school, and, further, that Japanese mothers train their toddlers at home to attain this end. In this way, media reports often focus on the downward extension into the preschools of Japanese pressure to prepare for college entrance examinations. In reality, however, diversity among Japanese preschools exists; although some preschools certainly emphasize academic skills, there are some others that focus on group life and basic classroom routines and still some others that, at least superficially, resemble US play-oriented preschools (Holloway, 2000).

The question of what makes a good preschool depends on the values of particular cultures. A great number of Japanese preschools are in fact play-centered settings where little attention is paid to academic preparation (Peak, 1991). Furthermore, as discussed later in Chapter 5, the main role of the preschool is, unlike that of the home, to provide children with an environment where they can master the skills necessary for an individual to live in a group-oriented society (e.g. saying grace in unison before lunch under the direction of daily monitors). As a matter of fact, a survey of Japanese mothers of preschoolers revealed that virtually all ranked the experience of being in a group as the most important goal (Holloway & Minami, 1996). As Holloway (2000) describes, in other words, 'the preschool is a core institution in Japan, viewed as providing essential experiences that enable young children to obtain social and intellectual skills needed to function successfully in Japanese society' (p. 2).

Why study preschoolers?

The sample for this study includes 20 Japanese preschool children, half four years old and half five, and their mothers. Although the primary objective of this research was not to study gender differences, in order to offer a balanced sample, half of the children selected in each cohort were boys and half girls. Also, this balanced sample made it easier to match this Japanese-speaking group with another Japanese-speaking group in the United States (Minami, 1994, 1995, 1997; Minami & McCabe, 1993, 1995) and with the English-speaking group that McCabe and Peterson (1990, 1991) and Peterson and McCabe (1992) used in their studies (these groups will be described in detail later in Chapter 7).

More important, focusing on four- and five-year-olds reflects the age constraints that emerge from the analysis of young children's narratives. Primitive narratives can be identified very early in children's speech; children begin to talk about the past at the age of about 26 months (Sachs, 1979, 1982), but these early productions are short in any culture through the age of three and a half years (McCabe & Peterson, 1991). Three-year-olds' narratives are often simple two-event narratives, whereas four-year-olds' narratives are much more diverse (e.g. leapfrog narratives in which children give more than two events in a jumbled order, which makes it difficult for the listener to follow), and five-year-old English-speaking children tell lengthy, well-sequenced stories that end a little prematurely at the climax (often called end-at-the-high point narratives) (McCabe & Peterson, 1990; Peterson & McCabe, 1983). Thus, because preschool-age children can produce fairly complex narratives of several different kinds, we can claim that preschool is a period of extremely rapid development in the child's acquisition of narrative capacity.

Other factors also support the validity of studying preschool children's narratives. To begin with, storytelling involves a multitude of cognitive demands; during the preschool years a large number of cognitive abilities are rapidly developing, and some of them may affect children's narrative development, such as various metalinguistic abilities (i.e. the abilities to reflect upon and make judgments about particular aspects of language). The development of such metalinguistic abilities serves as a means to allow the child to deliver his or her images and impressions to others successfully and effectively, and metaphor is one of such metalinguistic abilities. Two-year-olds might pretend a broomstick were a horse, a push toy were a lawnmower or a soda bottle were a racing car. In such make-believe, two- or three-year-olds might be able to use one object to verbally symbolize another, but these symbolic thoughts (or representations) are limited in many ways. For example, although young children use metaphor, they have not yet become capable of using and interpreting other types of figurative language such as irony (Winner, 1988). On the other hand, four- and five-year-olds are capable of symbolizing their physiological conditions, such as 'I feel as if my mouth had been pasted up' after having bitten an astringent persimmon (a four-year-old) and 'I feel hot as if I were burning' (a five-year-old) after running and playing hard with a ball (Iwata, 1992). Moreover, they gradually become capable of employing and understanding irony. These metaphoric expressions might be culturally constrained, and the development of such metalinguistic abilities in earlier years further leads to later developmental stages of much more advanced, humorous (and emotive at times) metaphoric expressions, such as a seven-year-old child pointing to her chin and saying, 'I had two mouths,' meaning that an injury she had sustained by falling off an iron bar was cut open as if it were also a mouth (see Chapter 1).

Second, culture plays a major role in the form of children's narratives although, as discussed above, narrative development indicates regular age-related progresses, illustrating the importance of maturational factors. As previous studies (e.g. Cummings, 1980; Lewis, 1991; Peak, 1991) suggest, for instance, preschool is the period when Japanese children make a transition from the *amae* (undisciplined and indulgent)-based inside world to another world (i.e. preschool) where many children share one teacher and, moreover, where subordination of individual needs to collective goals is sometimes considered the dominant norm (for further discussion, see Chapter 5). To study preschoolers' narratives, therefore, both cognitive and cultural factors should be taken into consideration.

The difference in narrative development mentioned earlier can be further conceptualized by what Bruner (1986) calls the dual landscape of narrative: (1) the landscape of action, which relates to the external landscape of characters and the event in which the narrator takes part, and (2) the landscape of consciousness, which relates to the psychological landscape of the narrator's or the event characters' feelings, desires and emotional reactions (see Chapter 2). Astington (1990), emphasizing the importance of the young child's acquisition of these two landscapes of narrative, argues that 'this is what the four-year-old, but not the two-year-old, can achieve' (p. 153). As can be seen in this interpretation of the dual landscape of narrative, therefore, cognitive developmental stage is an important factor in deciding to focus on children aged four and five, an age when the children are old enough to convey both culture and perspective.

Descriptions of Woody City and Participants

Woody City

For the purpose of this study, narratives from middle-class Japanese mothers and their preschool children living in Japan were collected. I spent one entire summer in Culture Town, a newly-developed commuter/ bedroom community in a small inland basin city called Woody City in western Japan. Nestled among a range of low mountains, Woody City has 28,029 households with a registered population of 90,720 (3.24 people per household, as of 1 December, 1994). While old inhabitants of Woody City are mostly farmers, many residents who recently migrated to the city typically have white-collar jobs, commuting to a nearby metropolis. Family make-up is a noticeable aspect to distinguish newly migrated residents from old inhabitants. Extended families living together, which old inhabitants have in common, used to be the norm in Japan, particularly before World War II. According to Morioka (1986), the extended family used to be responsible for training and disciplining children so that they would be able to cope with the demands of adult life. Most households in Culture Town, however, consist of nuclear families, parents and their children. The number of people per household in Japan is 3.14 on average (Economic Planning Agency, 1990). In this demographic dimension, therefore, Woody City represents a typical Japanese suburban city.

Furthermore, a commuter train runs regularly between Woody City and the metropolis; it takes about one hour for a one-way journey. In Japan, the population concentration in metropolises is so dense that residential areas have been spreading out from metropolitan areas to the distant suburbs. Commuting time continues to increase; more than half the commuters in Japan travel more than one hour one-way to working places located in metropolises (Nittetsu Human Development, 1993). Due to the relatively high cost of local public bus transportation, many wives in Culture Town, most of whom are not employed full time outside the home, drive to the nearby station to send off their husbands early in the morning and welcome them late in the evening. In this sense too, Woody City – Culture Town in particular – is representative of a typical Japanese middle-class neighborhood.

Participants

Twenty preschool children living in Woody City participated in this study, along with their parents. All were middle-class children living in two-parent homes. These children consist of the following two age groups:

(1) Ten five-year-old middle-class Japanese children who were in five-year-old children's classrooms in preschool at the time of data collection (five boys and five girls; mean age = five years, three months).

(2) Ten four-year-old middle-class Japanese children who were in four-year-old children's classrooms in preschool at the time of data collection (five boys and five girls; mean age = four years, three months). None of these mother–child pairs had lived overseas at the time of data collection.

Of the 20 children, eight were first-born, nine were second-born, and the remaining three were third-born. Among the eight first-born children, three were only children at the time of data collection. All of the families were middle class as measured by the occupation and education of the father, and the education of the mother. Of the 20 fathers, 80% (16) had college degrees, two had graduated from professional school, and one had finished high school; one father had attended graduate school. Of the 20 mothers, 60% (12) had attended two-year (junior) college. One had attended professional school, two had finished high school only, and five mothers had four-year college degrees. Note that attending four-year colleges is a fairly recent trend for females. Because a large population of Japanese women used to attend two-year colleges rather than four-year institutions, up until recently such colleges have been considered the women's track in higher education in Japan (Fujimura-Fanselow, 1985).

Procedures for Data Collection

Data consisted of: (1) children's and their mothers' monologic narratives that were elicited by a neutral researcher, (2) mother–child interactions, with a particular focus on mothers' utterances when they verbally interacted with their children during narrative elicitation, and (3) mother–child interactions in the context of book-reading activities. All activities were tape-recorded and transcribed verbatim for coding. The specific procedures for the three types of activities that elicited narrative discourse and literacy practices of Japanese mothers and children follow:

(1a) Children's monologic narratives about past experiences elicited by a neutral researcher (for the analysis of children's monologic narrative structure).

(1b) Parents' monologic narratives about their own past experiences elicited by a neutral researcher (for the analysis of adults' monologic narrative structure).

(2) Parents' verbal interactions with their young children during narrative elicitation (for the analysis of maternal narrative elicitation strategies).
(3) Parents' book-reading styles and their young children's emergent literacy skills (for the analysis of parent–child book-reading).

Children's narrative structure

The first activity follows the Peterson and McCabe methodology (Peterson & McCabe, 1983) of eliciting natural, unmonitored, informal speech by using the so-called danger-of-death or scary event story originally developed in Labov's sociolinguistic research (Labov, 1972; Labov & Waletzky, 1967). Before eliciting narratives, rapport with the child was established through activities such as drawing pictures. Furthermore, in order to minimize the child's self-consciousness and not to influence his or her social behaviors, the conversations were recorded at the child's home or, if it was not available for some reason, the child's friend's home was used instead. In this sense, interactive interviewing – 'a conversational, open, or loosely structured mode, in which give and take is emphasized' (Modell & Brodsky, 1994, p. 142) – was conducted. Recording sessions were each half an hour long.

When the child was judged to be comfortable with the researcher, he or she was asked in their native language, Japanese, prompting questions related to injuries, in the manner developed by Peterson and McCabe (1983). This elicitation technique had previously been used with Japanese children (Minami, 1990; Minami & McCabe, 1991, 1996) and proved to be effective. Specifically, following a short prompt about an injury the researcher had suffered, the child was asked questions about personally experienced events: *'ima made ni kega shita koto aru?'* ('Have you ever gotten hurt?'), *'ima made ni chuusha shita koto aru?'* ('Did you ever get a shot?') or *'ima made ni hachi ni sasareta koto aru?'* ('Did you ever get stung by a bee?'). If the child said *'un/hai'* ('yes'), he or she was asked follow-up questions such as *'sore hanashite kureru?'* ('Would you tell me about it?'), for a more detailed account. Although such follow-up questions to children are not typical, neither are they unusual in Japanese discourse. To maintain conversational interaction and to further facilitate conversation, general subprompts (i.e. non-directive general cues) were also employed, such as *'un, un'* ('uh huh'), *'sorede/sorekara'* ('and/then'), *'motto hanashite kureru'* ('tell me more') or *'sorede doo natta no?'* ('then what happened?'), but no specific questions were asked, so that this narrative elicitation could allow for assessment of narrative skills in the absence of adult scaffolding. The interviewer avoided prompts that would lead to a particular pattern of narrative discourse. The narratives elicited from the children were thus relatively monologic in nature.

The above-described method had been extensively employed in eliciting narratives from Japanese elementary school children living in the Boston area (Minami, 1990; Minami & McCabe, 1991, 1996). For the research described in this book, the same method was applied to younger children. As McCabe and Peterson (1990) explain, injury is a topic that typically elicits extensive narrative production even from very introverted or young children; Minami (1990, 1996a, 1996b) and Minami and McCabe (1991, 1996) have proved that this technique works well for eliciting narratives from young Japanese children. The results of young Japanese children's past experiences are presented and discussed in Chapters 4 and 5.

Adults' narrative structure

Mothers' monologic narratives about their own past experiences were also collected. As with their children, an attempt was made to elicit monologic narratives from adult speakers. In the past, only a few narrative researchers have had adults perform the same task as children (e.g. Berman & Slobin, 1994; Scott, 1988). In terms of Japanese, the situation has been more or less the same; few studies have extensively examined adults' narrative style. Analyzing adults' narratives, however, is critical in that we can examine what linguistic devices and narrative strategies preschoolers have not yet been able to deploy in their narrative tellings, compared to adults. To examine the relative narrative competence of young children, adult narratives serve as a standard of comparison not only because they provide the universal or quasi-universal model of well-constructed, globally organized narratives, but also because they are considered the full-fledged or 'end-state' model within a particular culture. As Berman and Slobin (1994) and Scott (1988) also argue, therefore, including adults' narratives is advantageous in terms of measuring the relative narrative competence of young children. Unlike children, however, because parents were expected to express themselves with little difficulty, the injury story was not used as an elicitation technique. Instead, they were asked to talk about any experiences, such as their earliest memory. Additionally, when observing adults' narratives, we became aware that adult narrators shape their life stories through interactions with interviewers; adults' narratives illuminate the fact that life is full of interesting and sometimes even exciting twists and turns (see adult narratives in Chapters 5 and 9).

In addition to identifying what constitutes adult narrative competence in a given culture, this activity is also important for the following reasons: (1) it provides material to study the relationship between the mother's narrative style and the child's; and (2) to date, except for Maynard's (1993) work, few studies have been available that have extensively examined Japanese adults' narrative style. In other words, first, it is interesting to determine whether individual differences in narrative among Japanese mothers are reflected in differences among their children's (i.e. the effect of mothers' providing modeling). Second, the data from mothers are also important for demonstrating similarities among adult Japanese patterns of narratives.

In this session, in addition to providing monologic narratives, mothers were asked to fill out a questionnaire, which included parents' educational background and work as well as background information on the children (e.g. birth order). As seen previously in the description of the samples, knowing background information such as family make-up, parental occupations and education is important because of the possible influence of social class (i.e. Japanese parents of different socioeconomic status might guide their children in the acquisition of socioculturally specific styles of narrative). Along with young children's narratives of past experiences, the results of Japanese mothers' narratives of past experiences are presented and discussed in Chapters 4 and 5.

In both Chapters 4 and 5, children's narratives are followed by adults' for the following reasons: To begin with, one of the primary objectives of this project is to present the development of children's personal narratives, and thus examining adults' narratives is secondary. Second, although adult narratives are considered the culturally appropriate, full-fledged or 'endstate' model, children's narratives are not necessarily simplified versions of adults'. That is, as Cook-Gumperz and Green (1984) suggest, children may not simply model their own narratives based on those they hear from adults. Rather, from a very early age, children are sensitive to narrative structure (Stein, 1988), and around the age of four or five simple narrative structures emerge (Botvin & Sutton-Smith, 1977). As Applebee (1978) stresses, moreover, the simplicity of the narratives young children tell 'helps to highlight the principles which underlie their form' (p. 56). I thus believe that children's narratives are not simply modeled on the narratives they hear from adults, particularly mothers but that they simultaneously present universal patterns of narrative development. [Note: It might sound as if I were making jumps and flights in my argument, but Masuda (1999), as a matter of fact, even argues for a narrative discourse universal as Chomsky (1965) argued for a language (mainly syntactic) universal.] Finally, although having the adult model is important to identify what constitutes an adult level of narrative competence, adults' narratives, like children's, differ greatly in several aspects, such as the length of the narrative and the linguistic devices and strategies deployed; enormous individual differences among adults may reflect the cumulative influences of their experiential differences. For example, uses of syntactic constructions and levels of lexical register in narrative are affected by social experience. As Berman and Slobin (1994) and Scott (1988) argue, therefore, although including adults' narratives is advantageous in terms of measuring the relative narrative competence of young children, we cannot deny the possibility of having a wide range of adult standards.[1]

Parental styles of narrative elicitation

The purpose of this activity was to understand how mothers verbally interact with their young children during narrative elicitation. Mothers who participated in this project were supplied with tape recorders (unless they had one at home) and blank cassette tapes. They were asked to elicit interesting past events or experiences from their children in a relaxed and informal situation. In this way, mothers and their children were audio tape-recorded in their homes. Recall that, in the researcher's narrative elicitation described above, non-directive general cues were given and that narratives were thus elicited from the children without providing any scaffolding. In this mother–child conversational activity, on the other hand, mothers were expected to scaffold the narratives of their young children. In this project, following the methods McCabe and Peterson (1991) used in their studies, mothers are expected to ask their children to relate stories about personal experiences, about actual events that have happened in the past. However, mothers were also instructed to do this narrative elicitation activity as naturally and spontaneously as possible, as they ordinarily behave when they ask their children to talk about past events. In contrast to the adult interviewer's monologic narrative elicitation, therefore, this task is dialogic (or co-constructive) in nature and considered crucial to successful child narratives (Ninio & Snow, 1996). [Note: The talk of one party followed by the talk of another generally constitutes a turn (Goodwin, 1981), but co-construction means the talk that emerges through systematic processes of interaction in which recipients are very active co-participants. The issue of co-construction is one of the critical issues throughout the book, as can be seen not only in mother–child narrative interactions in Chapters 6 and 7 but also in *haiku* productions in this chapter and mother–child joint book-reading activities in Chapter 8.]

As described above, the task of parental verbal interaction with their young children during narrative elicitation can be defined as recounting a coherently organized personal narrative about a past event. Characterizing a child's narratives based on only one interaction, however, may lack reliability; for example, self-consciousness on the part of the child and even the mother may lead to potentially erroneous hasty generalizations. As Merriam (1988) argues, 'Reliability is problematic in the social sciences as a whole simply because human behavior is never static' (p. 170). To deal with this problem, mothers were asked to elicit narratives from their children about different occasions at different times. Following this instruction, some mothers scheduled one narrative interaction with their children right after coming home from preschool (or a day trip) and another narrative interaction at bedtime. By doing so, children recounted fortunate or unfortunate events from that day for the earlier narrative interaction, while they talked about events not only of that day but also of the distant past – or even described fantasies – for the later narrative interaction. The results of parental styles of narrative elicitation are presented and discussed in Chapters 6 and 7.

Styles of parent–child book-reading

The last activity connects two important or even parallel transitions in child development – (1) orality and literacy and (2) home and school – by examining the relationship between mothers' book-reading styles and their preschool children's emergent literacy skills. In addition to narrative elicitation activities, the mothers were also asked to look at a book brought by the researcher, *The Very Hungry Caterpillar* by Eric Carle (1969) and translated by Hisashi Mori into Japanese (Carle, 1976). This decision was made because developmental psychologists (e.g. McCabe & Peterson, 1991) argue that many clues to language development – literacy development in particular – can be identified in the conversational exchanges between mothers and their young children. In other words, becoming literate is a process that begins long before schooling takes place (Teale & Sulzby, 1986), and parents' interaction with their children has an important influence on their children's language development and acquisition of literacy skills. Particularly because children's oral language begins to blossom in the preschool years (Dickinson & McCabe, 1991), research on the effects of book-reading suggests its importance for preschoolers' literacy development (Beals *et al.*, 1994). To begin with, book-reading activities provide a beneficial learning environment for young children by familiarizing children with print (Sulzby, 1986). Book-reading practices also introduce children to ways of talking about books that they will encounter when they enter elementary school (Heath, 1983; Snow & Goldfield, 1981). Shared book-reading experiences are thus meaningful in terms of: (1) facilitating language development and emergent literacy; (2) encouraging the comprehension and interpretation of texts; and (3) teaching children how to participate in a range of discourse patterns that are expected in later school settings.

Cultural differences during the book-reading event have been addressed as well. Heath (1982, 1983, 1986), for example, states that children growing up in European American middle-class, European American working-class, and African American working-class families have different experiences with literacy and consequently develop different expectations concerning behavior and attitudes surrounding reading and writing events. According to Heath, whereas in mainstream (i.e. European American middle-class) homes mothers and their children negotiate story-reading through the scaffolding of mothers' questions and running commentaries, in European American working-class families children are allowed less interaction with regard to the content of the story. In African American working-class families there are few occasions for reading involving children. Heath concludes that each of their communicative styles reflects a unique culture-specific perspective toward socialization surrounding literacy. These findings therefore indicate that the culture of the home plays a significant role in affecting young children's socialization into language and literacy practices.

Another implication of such cultural differences relates to the importance of whether or not the language continuum from orality to literacy exists in children's homes. Following Olson (1977), the acquisition of literacy proceeds from context-dependent (i.e. contextualized), oral ways of thinking to the acquisition of context-free (i.e. decontextualized or self-contextualized), logical, message-focused skills, such as reasoning and problem-solving. Within Olson's framework, the acquisition of literacy might be equated with that of higher level critical-thinking skills, and the function of schooling is to make children's language skills increasingly explicit and decontextualized. What is emphasized here is the importance of the provision of decontextualized skills in preschool children's homes for later schooling (Snow *et al.*, 1994).

Because of different kinds of discourse contexts (i.e. narrating the contents of a story vs. narrating past experiences in a less structured setting), direct comparison will not be appropriate. Having had some exposure to storybooks, young children may be familiar with particular rhetorical forms of stories; it is therefore likely that they demonstrate more advanced skills in storybook narration. Conversely, because advanced skills may rarely appear in spontaneous speech, examining children's talking about the past may underestimate their age of acquisition of a variety of linguistic means and rhetorical devices. Yet, research into emergent reading among Japanese children is not only an interesting addition, it also plays a complementary role in understanding children's pragmatic development.

Styles of parent–child book-reading in Chapter 8 specifically focuses on the social supports for literacy development in Japanese homes. This decision was made because, although cross-cultural comparison of how books are read to young children exists, as can be seen above, much of that research addresses cultural differences in the United States. To fill a gap that currently exists in this body of research, therefore, Chapter 8 examines book-reading data collected from Japanese mothers and their preschool children.

Theoretical Framework and Data Analysis

The goal of this research as a whole is an in-depth data analysis that presents a portrait of the early social interactions that help children acquire communicative competence and thus become competent members of society. To interpret the data from Japanese mothers and children, just as multiple ways were used to collect data, multiple methods for data analysis are used. For example, the narrative study described in this book synthesizes the following two theoretical frameworks: (1) verse/stanza analysis (Gee, 1985; Hymes, 1981), and (2) high point analysis based on the Labovian approach (Labov, 1972, 1981; Labov *et al.*, 1968; Labov & Waletzky, 1967; Peterson & McCabe, 1983). [Note: Although Labov did not call his analysis high point analysis, because by age four or five North American children typically organize their stories around a major event (referred to as the high point), the analysis has conventionally been called high point analysis.] This synthesized analysis is further discussed in Chapters 4 and 5. In addition to this synthesized analysis and its coding schemes, a speech act coding system designed to assess mother–child conversational interactions in previous studies (e.g. McCabe & Peterson, 1991; Minami & McCabe, 1995) is also used for analyzing parental speech, which is presented and discussed in Chapters 6 and 7. Finally, shared book-reading activities between Japanese mothers and their children in Chapter 8 are analyzed using a modified version of *The Coding System for Home Bookreading*, which was originally developed by De Temple (1993) for analyzing mother–child book-reading practices in US society.

Preparation of Data

Over the past quarter century, interest in narrative discourse studies in the human sciences has grown significantly. We have accordingly witnessed a rapid growth in a variety of transcriptions and coding systems. Because narratives are invariably produced through conversational interactions, how to transcribe narratives and code them holds great significance. When tracing back studies of child language development, for instance, we can see that, in the late 1970s, Ochs (1979) emphasized transcription as theory. For example, she pointed out a potentially misleading impression in transcribing adult–child interactions. According to Ochs, because an adult is usually an initiator, in a vertically presented transcript, adult utterances tend to be above children's utterances, which may make it seem as if an adult were controlling a child's utterances. Ochs' arguments reveal that the transcription system, which should be as neutral as possible, actually plays a crucial role in analyzing data, particularly data related to narrative discourse development.

All the data included in this book were transcribed in accordance with the coding rules previously developed for Japanese data.[2] Specifically, the data were transcribed into computer files following the guidelines of Codes for the Human Analysis of Transcripts (CHAT) conventions for analysis by the Child Language Analysis (CLAN) software available through the Child Language Data Exchange System (CHILDES), an international network for analyzing language data (MacWhinney & Snow, 1985, 1990). [Note: CHILDES was originally developed by MacWhinney at Carnegie Mellon University and Snow at Harvard University to delineate the transcribing conventions and, moreover, to act as a repository for samples of children's language.] The transcription system developed for Japanese oral narratives was previously used for the data analysis of Minami (1994, 1995, 1996a, 1996b, 1997, 1998) and Minami and McCabe (1993, 1995) and has proved effective. The methods for analyzing the transcripts and coding schemes for monologic narrative structure are described in Chapter 4. Likewise, the methods for analyzing the transcripts and coding schemes for home book-reading are described in Chapter 8.

The Relationship Between Orality and Literacy

At the end of Chapter 3, tracing the history of Japan – particularly the history of Japanese literature – I present my view on the relationship between orality and literacy in Japanese society. In Chapter 2, I stated that narrative is a superordinate term that includes a variety of forms, ranging developmental psychology to literary studies. First, the widely known, three-line poetry form, *haiku*, belongs to literary studies but has a close relationship to Japanese discourse style. Second, its precursor *karuta* also displays three lines of verse. Here, delineating the orality-literacy continuum from a historical perspective, I present a preliminary argument of how these forms, which provide a route to literacy that is an alternative to the typical production of explicit, extended discourse seen in middle-class North American children, portray a discourse regulation mechanism for Japanese children's conversational narratives.

Overview: The history of *haiku*

The origin of *haiku*, a Japanese fixed-verse form of seventeen syllables with three lines in a five-seven-five pattern, dates back to ancient times (Yamada, 1956). The Manyoshu, the oldest existing anthology of poetry, was compiled in the eighth century. Although written in the letters that borrowed their pronunciations directly from Chinese characters, instead of the authentic Japanese letters that are employed together with Chinese characters nowadays, the Manyoshu is composed of about 4500 poems that form a Japanese tradition (Nittetsu Human Development, 1993).

Among a variety of types of poems collected in the Manyoshu, two types of poems apparently possess one characteristic feature observed in *haiku*, i.e. basic syllable patterns. These patterns break down into: (1) a 31 syllable verse form with five lines in a five-seven-five-seven-seven pattern, and (2) an arbitrary number of paired five-and-seven syllable-line verse form with two seven-syllable lines at the end. As a generic term, these two forms of poems were categorized as branches of *waka*, which literally means 'Japanese poems.' The former, shorter lyric poetry type specifically came to be called *tanka* ('short poem'), whereas the latter, longer verse form came to be called *chooka* ('long poem') (Sakurai, 1976). The order of patterning varies; according to Yasuda (1962), for instance, the Manyoshu had a five-seven syllable note, whereas the Kokinshu, an anthology of *waka* poetry complied in the year 905, had a seven-five syllable note. Considering the syllable pattern of five and seven, however, we can trace the origin of *haiku* to the ancient *waka*.

As mentioned above, the generic category of Japanese poetry, *waka*, had several variations such as *tanka* and *chooka*; but the shorter lyric poetry *tanka* gradually gained more popularity than *chooka* (Sakurai, 1976). Around the eighth century, *tanka* had already become the more predominant form, and even nowadays it is appreciated as a very popular verse form. The essence of *tanka* is the vivid expression contained in its 31 syllables; it is described as elegant and lilting (Yasuda, 1962). In *tanka*, the first three lines of five-seven-five syllables are *kami no ku* ('upper poem'), and the remaining two lines of seven-seven syllables are referred to as *shimo no ku* ('lower poem'). [Hereafter, according to general usage, I will use *tanka* and *waka* alternatively.]

In contrast to *tanka*, which stresses the beauty of life and nature and thus possesses a pure and noble character, *renga*, which literally means 'linked verse,' was originally vulgar and funny literature (Yamamoto, 1969). In *renga*, two or more people get together, and one of them composes and writes down a *kami no ku* ('upper poem'). Responding to the *kami no ku*, the other participant composes a *shimo no ku* ('lower poem'). In this way, a chain of poems can be linked, numbering up to around 100 altogether. Although a branch of *tanka*, *renga* was considered to be only a verse game and not serious literature, partly because it was developed by ordinary people living in villages, and not by noble court people (Yasuda, 1962).

As an interim verse form to *haiku*, and more important, as a verse form based on narrative, *renga* should not be overlooked, however. We should especially remember the fact that *renga* is based on a conversation between participants. Yamamoto (1969) explains that *renga* originated in a comic dialogue between a male group and a female group who, for a skit at a village festival, imitated the conversation between a god and a spirit. Thus, based on a conversational form, *renga* facilitated a close relationship among villagers. Conversely, *renga* could not be separated from the community; those who were engaged in composing *renga* lived ordinary lives. We can thus see in *renga* the wedding of narrative and poetry and of orality and literacy. Indeed, we may be able to claim that the early history of Japanese poetry itself was closely connected with oral narrative discourse.

Later a form appeared called *haikai*, which literally means 'funny' (Yasuda, 1962). *Renga* was developed by a person called Sogi (Saito, 1979) in the middle ages; it later came to be called *haikai-renga*. Later, Basho Matsuo, who lived in the late seventeenth century and called himself Basho, which means a Japanese banana plant, after the name of the hermitage where he lived (Asano, 1976), enhanced the value of *hokku* ('opening verse'), the opening seven-five-seven syllable lines of *haikai-renga*. By later generations, Matsuo was considered to have given autonomous life to *hokku* [as a matter of fact, in Western countries such as the United States or England, *haiku* was called *hokku* before World War II (Saito, 1979)]. In either case, it is true that Matsuo inspired an independent art form based on *hokku* and established *haikai* as an art form in which he dealt with life and nature, using aesthetic values such as the austere elegance called *wabi* and *sabi* (Isawa, 1984). [Note that *wabi* and *sabi* are nominalization of the adjectives *wabishii* ('lonely' as human being) and *sabishii* ('lonesome' in nature), respectively (Isawa, 1984).] As Yamamoto (1969) cautions, however, *haikai* was still an art form closely connected with the rural community; thus, it was not only colored by *wabi* and *sabi*, but it also retained a discourse character. This is evident when we see that Matsuo frequently referred to those who gathered for *haikai* as renjuu, which means 'linked people' (Murasawa, 1984; Shimizu, 1978).[3]

At the end of the nineteenth century, Shiki Masaoka claimed that only *hokku* ('opening verse') was worthy of being called literature, whereas *haikai-renga* was not.[4] Masaoka completely separated *hokku* from *haikai-renga* and came to use the word *haiku* in what he called the 'new form poetry movement' (Matsui, 1967). Up to today, however, *haiku* has retained a collective discourse character that has been derived from *haikai-renga*. When observing a variety of types of modern *haiku* movements, we can see several genres such as *daidokoro* ('kitchen')-*haiku* made by housewives (Shibata, 1984), or *ryooyoo* ('convalescence')-*haiku* by those who are receiving medical treatment (Murayama, 1984). In *haiku*, people describe events and feelings in their daily lives; thus, it is clear that *haiku* maintains the narrative aspects that were observed originally.

The term 'conversational aspects' rather than 'narrative aspects' might be considered more appropriate from the above examples. However, the following *haiku* that was made by Basho (Henderson, 1958) in 1686 and is still considered the best-known *haiku* in Japan, for example, illustrates a one-event narrative (my translation):

Example 3.1
   furu-ike ya   'An old pond';
   kawazu tobi-komu   'A frog jumps in,'
   mizu no oto   'Water-sound.'

Moreover, the following convalescence-*haiku* made by Sanpei Tamura (Murayama, 1984) after World War II strongly appeals to the reader's feelings as a one-event narrative (my translation):

Example 3.2

haru no yo no	'A spring night';
shibin oto o tatsu	'A bedpan makes sound,'
wabishisa yo	'Loneliness I feel.'

As seen above, the third line, 'loneliness I feel,' illustrates an evaluative coda (i.e. the evaluative sealing off of a narrative). Therefore, granted that the word 'narrative' is used somewhat loosely here, both *haiku* presented above have more narrative than conversational qualities.

Haiku as an illustration of Japanese discourse regulation mechanism

As seen in the previous section, evidence that *haiku* retains its discourse character is abundant. Other evidence is the inclusion of information regarding time, location and object, which correspond to orientations if we borrow Labov's (1972) terminology. As a literary feature of *haiku*, however, the inclusion of *kigo* (a word indicating season) is usually obligatory; *kigo* can sometimes refer to an animal as a character representing one of Japan's distinct four seasons. Unlike free discourse, in *haiku* it is impossible to depict an actual scene in detail due to the restriction to seventeen syllables. Consequently, abbreviating the essentials becomes necessary. The season word is an example of such abbreviation, and succeeds in evoking an image in the reader's mind. Citing Matsuo's work, which is still acclaimed as a masterpiece, Lee (1983) explains that *haiku* is composed of the three dimensions of location, object and time (Lee cites the translated version of the *haiku* in differently ordered lines; to be faithful to the original by Matsuo, however, I reordered the lines of the translated *haiku*):

Example 3.3

kare-eda ni	'On a withered bough,'	(Location)
karasu no tomari-keri	'A crow perched;'	(Object/Event)
aki no kure	'Autumn evening.'	(Time)

Time, location and object are crucial information for good narrative discourse in order for the listener to fully grasp what the poet/narrator intends to say. *Haiku* satisfies these pieces of essential information in a very compact and abbreviated form.

Considering the close relationship between *haiku* and narrative discourse, we should also not overlook the existence of *tsukeku* ('added verse'), which was originally *shimo no ku* ('lower poem') in *tanka* ('short poem'). The example below, which I translated into English, shows a *hokku* ('opening verse') by one of Matsuo's disciples, Boncho, and an *ageku* (which is 'responding verse,' but literally means 'raising verse'), one form of *tsukeku*, by Matsuo (Basho) himself, in response to the *hokku* (Yamashita, 1984). In other words, Basho's *tsukeku*, which corresponds to the listener's anticipatory completions in discourse, illustrates how storytelling organization accommodates more than one participant with access to the same event and, conversely, organizes an occasion in which there are more than one storyteller:

Example 3.4

Hokku (by Boncho):

ichinaka wa	'In the city,'	(Location)
mono no nioi ya	'The smell of things;'	(Object of deleted copula)
natsu no tsuki	'The summer moon.'	(Time)

Tsukeku (by Basho):

| *"atsushi atsushi" to* | ' "It's hot, it's hot" ' | |
| *kado kado no koe* | 'Voices at entrance gates.' | (Object of deleted copula) |

As we have seen previously, *haiku* dates back to the beginnings of Japanese history; in contrast to the oral lyric *waka*, *haiku* (then called *haikai*) was established as written literature (Yamamoto, 1969). In spite of such written literature, or rather because of the short five-seven-five syllable written literature, *haiku* has succeeded in avoiding excessive lyricism and describes things objectively and concisely. Furthermore, *haiku* was born from narrative practices among villagers and is still being practiced by people in general. *Haiku* is, in essence, sparse formalized written discourse for two or more parties; this characteristic is very different from poetry in the United States, where one person articulates his or her ideas for vast audiences or for very different people. Probably because the narrative features in *haiku* appeal to the Japanese, they still appreciate *haiku* and enjoy making *haiku* by themselves.

The three-line structure that characterizes *haiku* is frequently encountered by Japanese children as well. A private after-school program that has branches all over Japan subscribes to the idea that appreciating *haiku* raises preschool and elementary school children's language development and, more precisely, their metalinguistic awareness, i.e. knowledge about language or the ability to think about language (Tsubouchi, 1985; Kumon Education Institute, 1988). This after-school program thus encourages mothers to read a beautiful picture card on which a noted *haiku* is written to their children, until they have memorized it. This school also recommends that mothers read the first line so that children can recite the following lines. [Note: Similar three-line interaction styles are described in Chapter 8.]

This idea has its root in an old practice of card games played not only in the home but also everywhere in Japan. These card games, generally called *karuta*, a loan word, *carta*, from Portuguese (Hayashi, 1986), are similar in appearance to baseball cards but are played quite differently. One of the oldest such games is *hyakunin-isshu*, literally '100 *waka* poems,' with a five-seven-five-seven-seven pattern. These 100 *waka* poems, which date back to the seventh century, were gathered together into a whole in the thirteenth century (Ishida, 1984). To play the game, the cards on which only the latter two lines (i.e. the lower poem) of seven-seven sylla-bles are printed are laid face up. The players sit around these cards, listen to a person who is in charge of reading *waka* from the former three lines of five-seven-five syllables (i.e. the upper poem), and compete with each other by picking up the matching card. In order to win a game, people have to remember which of the upper poems read out matches one of the lower poems that are laid out.

Transmitting Japanese cultural traditions through card games shapes children's habitual way of using language from early childhood. Hayashi (1986) shows a set of old cards; for instance, one of the cards describes, in three lines like *haiku*, how courageously a *samurai* warrior hero in the thirteenth century fought against a giant flying squirrel. Especially in winter, one person reads and displays a card that has a three-line poem, proverb, or story. Children sit around a set of cards, each of which has the first letter (a symbol representing the first syllable) of a three-line poem, proverb, or story with a picture that depicts the content of three-line sayings. [Note that because of the Japanese syllabic systems, *hiragana* (i.e. the cursive form of Japanese syllabary) and *katakana* (i.e. the square form of the Japanese syllabary), the first letter has a one-vowel sound, often with a consonant before.] Children listen carefully and compete with each other to pick up the appropriate card. Similar but simpler cards are also available for young children. Therefore, *haiku* cards developed by the school mentioned above are based on the same traditional idea.

Even Japanese elementary school children who are studying overseas make *haiku* by themselves. The following are two pieces of *haiku*; one was written by an adult and used for raising children's meta-linguistic awareness (Kumon Education Institute, 1988), and the other one was written by a Japanese fourth-grader who lives in New York (Gakken, 1989) (note that I translated both *haiku* into English):

Example 3.5a

seppen o	'Snowflakes,'	(Object)
hoshi ga furashi nu	'Stars let them fall down;'	(Location)
kurisumasu	'Christmas.'	(Time)

Example 3.5b

samui kedo	'Although it is cold,'	(Time)
jiyuu no megami	'The Statue of Liberty'	(Object and Location)
senobi suru	'Stretches herself.'	(Event)

Probably everyone feels that the adult's poem is really poetic and sophisticated, whereas the child's is just cute or charming. But both pieces, in one way or another, symbolize inanimate objects. Of course, the Statue of Liberty is not necessarily considered as an inanimate object, because the Statue of Liberty is treated as 'she.' In Japanese, this personification of an inanimate object seems to be less poetic than in English; it is sometimes used even in daily conversations among Japanese people, especially among mothers who, providing children with explicit training in empathy, appeal to the feelings of inanimate objects (Clancy, 1985, 1986).

As a matter of fact, not only Japanese children but also children in public elementary schools in the United States have an opportunity to make *haiku*. But those children who learn to make *haiku* in US schools seem to learn personification of an inanimate object as a representation of poetic characteristics (Haley-James *et al.*, 1988). In US schools, in other words, *haiku*'s literary dimension is slightly exaggerated and, inversely, its narrative/discursive aspect is made light of. Some books/textbooks correctly explain that *haiku* consists of three lines (Norton, 1991), others, against the original norm, transform it into four lines; the famous Japanese *haiku* poet Buson Yosa's (Aso, 1959) rather unusual (in terms of syllables) *haiku*, 'Willow leaves have fallen/Spring water has dried up/Stranded stones here and there' (note a slash indicates a line break), is changed into 'Ah leafless willow . . ./Bending over/The dry pool/Of stranded boulders' (Houghton Mifflin, 1988).

Although it is probably true that both Japanese and North American children can appreciate *haiku* and learn to make it in order to raise their metalinguistic awareness, Japanese children may regard *haiku* more positively as a reflection of Japanese discourse regulation mechanism (i.e. short turns and co-construction). That is, 10,000,000 people make and appreciate *haiku* in Japan (Makimura, 1989); writing and reading *haiku* are so embedded in Japanese culture and society that Japanese children may have had considerable exposure to an oral discourse pattern similar to *haiku* and have acquired the habits of talking that resembles the *haiku* pattern. In Japan, schoolchildren are not necessarily formally instructed in written *haiku*, but because they are abundantly exposed to *haiku* in ordinary discourse situations, they require little instruction in order to compose it. *Haiku* and its precursor, *karuta*, may thus portray a discourse regulation mechanism for Japanese children and even adults. Thus, although the form of *haiku* is often taught in US classrooms and I assume that American children can appreciate *haiku*, it is introduced in a different way from the authentic one.

Kumon Education Institute (1989) presents the following two pieces of *haiku* that were made by second and third graders in Japan (my translation):

Example 3.6a   Second grader's *haiku*
kakekko de	'A foot-race,'
mune ga doki doki	'My heart is throbbing;'
tsugi wa boku	'Next is my turn.'

Example 3.6b   Third grader's *haiku*
akimatsuri	'An autumn festival,'
nigiyaka na oto	'Making a noise,'
tanoshi soo	'Everyone seems happy.'

The above *haiku* pieces, both based on customary autumn activities in Japan, sound as if they were part of ongoing conversation, and I thus hypothesize: (1) rather than a dichotomy, oral and written forms of narrative constitute a continuum, and (2) further, prose and poetry form a continuum or even merge in Japanese. If this is really the case, we may be able to assume that *haiku* reflects general discourse patterns among Japanese. Conversely, in ordinary discourse patterns such as personal accounts of particular situations, we may be able to observe a structure that is similar to *haiku*.

Proceeding with our discussion further, if we can prove that the Japanese (narrative) discourse style is illustrated in the *haiku* form, ambiguity in poetry contrasted with explicitness in expository style discussed in Chapter 2 will not hold, at least in the Japanese style of narrative. To put it in another way, as one of the aspects of decontextualization (or self-contextualization) typical of the literate orientation, past research (Cazden *et al.*, 1985; Hemphill, 1989; Michaels, 1981; Scollon & Scollon, 1981; Tannen, 1985) has revealed a higher degree of explicitness in European American middle-class children's discourse style, but ambiguous or restricted oral discourse style in working-class children's narratives in the United States. This type of social class differences might not hold in other cultures; in contrast to the previous findings, we may be able to find a different set of features in Japanese children's personal narratives.

Finally, recall that in Chapter 2, I stated the possibility of young children's emergent notion of scripts as generic, prototypical sequences of events anchored in mental schemata (i.e. memory structures that organize and preserve information relevant to some event). We can hypothesize that from early childhood on, Japanese children are exposed to a daily conversation style similar to *haiku* (or, more precisely, linked *renga*) in terms of the conciseness and frequent turn exchanges summarized as Japanese patterns of co-construction. Because a story schema serves as a shared mental representation that underlies how narratives are organized, it seems reasonable that children will eventually learn to tell narratives in a *haiku*-like manner.

Notes

1. When comparing narratives told by Japanese mothers, we can see that their narratives range from lengthy, elaborate and detailed narratives that provide the details of background information to very brief, concisely encapsulated and closely packaged narratives like young children's (for example, one mother's narrative is reminiscent of some of the preschool children's narratives). Thus, adults show considerable individual variation in the rhetorical choices, the linguistic devices and the strategies they use, as well as the length of the narrative.
2. There are basically two systems for Romanization: the Hepburn system devised in the nineteenth century by the American missionary James Curtis Hepburn (known as *Hebon-shiki* in Japan), which is based on phonetic notation, and *kunrei-siki*, which literally means the 'cabinet ordinance' system and is based on phonemic notation. Audiotapes were transcribed using the system devised by the author of this book, which generally corresponds to the *kunrei-siki*. The Hepburn style, however, is much easier to read than the *kunrei-siki*. For instance, those who prefer the Hepburn system to the *kunrei-siki* insist that signs on the street or at the railroad station (in Japan) be written in the Hepburn style. Although the preference for the Hepburn style over the *kunrei-siki* based on this reasoning has no logical foundations in terms of the Japanese language per se, for non-Japanese and/or those who are familiar with the English spelling system, all examples in the text of this book are represented by the Hepburn style.
3. It is interesting that the poet Gary Snyder (Faas, 1978), idealizing the relationship between a *haiku* teacher and his or her linked people, described that a teacher did not make his or her living by publishing *haiku* but functioned as a critic, receiving money by critiquing the work of his/her linked people. This relationship is sometimes criticized in Japan, however; some people ironically describe it as a wonderful necessary evil that tends to be misused and corrupted (Makimura, 1989).
4. The reader should bear in mind that Masaoka lived in the time when Japan was in the process of modernization, trying to catch up with Western industrial countries. In order to show that Japan traditionally possessed noble

literature comparable to that of Western countries, Masaoka reexamined Matsuo as a man of letters in Japan, and reached the conclusion that those who want to know Basho (Matsuo) as a man of letters should not appreciate him as a man who made *haikai* because *haikai* originally means 'funny' (Matsui, 1967).

Chapter 4
Monologic Narrative: Narrative Development

Preschool children's developing mastery of monologic narratives as a connected discourse form is the main topic of Chapters 4 and 5. In the past 20 years, a great deal has been written about narrative development, offering child language researchers an opportunity to study both universal and language-specific patterns of developing narrative structure. As Chomsky (1959) claims, unlike other animal species, human beings have a unique cognitive basis for language (i.e. universalistic). Yet, as children grow, they learn culturally appropriate communicative rules (i.e. particularistic). Although sounding a little like Skinner (1957) in terms of emphasizing reinforcement during language acquisition, when children are very young, these rules are constantly reinforced by enculturation agents, such as mothers. In fact, there are a variety of skills that preschool children must acquire in order to narrate on their own. Sustaining talk without a listener's extensive assistance, for instance, places unique demands on a speaker's communicative competence.

As stated above, narrative studies have emphasized the importance of both universal and cross-linguistic properties of narrative structure. This chapter particularly addresses the questions of: (1) How do Japanese four- and five-year-olds transform their experiences into narrative?; and (2) What developments are evident between these two age groups? The chapter specifically analyzes oral personal narratives of 20 middle-class Japanese preschoolers, half of them four years old and half five, and their mothers, using verse/stanza analysis and high point analysis. The patterning in stanzas reveals that compared to four-year-olds, five-year-olds have begun to use the form of adult-like narratives. High point analysis indicates that compared to four-year-olds, five-year-olds have begun to evaluate in the form of adult-like narratives. The results suggest that the preschool years, during which various narrative components evolve, represent a period of extremely rapid development in the child's acquisition of narrative capacity. The results also illustrate that from early childhood on, Japanese children learn the narrative mode of discourse valued by their mothers.

Narrative Development

Narrative is a term applied to a variety of discourse genres including personal narratives, scripts and fictional stories (Hudson & Shapiro, 1991). Since Labov and Waletzky (1967) hypothesized that fundamental narrative structures are to be found in oral versions of personal experience, conversational storytelling has received a great deal of attention. Labov and his colleagues (Labov *et al.*, 1968; Labov & Waletzky, 1967) collected narratives of ordinary people in their (extraordinary) everyday lives, and claimed that a fundamental concept of experientiality could be identified in conversational or spontaneous storytelling. According to Labov (1972), narrative is technically defined as a means of recapitulating past experience in an ordered set of clauses that matches the temporal sequence of the actual experience (see Chapter 2 for a review). The most basic requirement of a narrative is thus a recapitulation of chronologically sequenced events (Labov, 1972) or, more generally, some reference to temporally or thematically connected events (Hicks, 1994). [Note, however, that narratives containing only a single event, such as *haiku* (a traditional poem with a five-seven-five syllable structure reviewed in Chapter 3), are also possible (McCabe, 1991a, 1997).] Experiential narrative, following the Labovian methodology (Labov, 1972), relates to the function of tellability or reportability (i.e. worthiness of the story matter). Narrative correlates with human experientiality, and conversational narrative is situated at the core of narrativity.

In terms of narrative development, children's narrative structure moves from scriptlike accounts to specific recollections of real past events between the ages of two and three years (Eisenberg, 1985; Hudson & Shapiro, 1991). Narrative, which is the first extended discourse young children learn, is a natural mode for representing and remembering information. Developmentally, children begin to talk about the past at about two years of age (Eisenberg, 1985; Sachs, 1979, 1982). Although children's language development progresses toward extended narrative discourse, their early productions are brief through the age of three and a half years. Young children's narrative skills continue to develop throughout toddlerhood and the preschool years; particularly, preschool children are increasingly capable of structuring their oral personal narratives in a more refined and mature style.

Previous research has raised a wide range of issues in the areas of narrative development. Hudson and Shapiro (1991) claim that children's narratives reveal how children 'translate their knowledge into narratives' (p. 89). Hudson and Shapiro's (1991) work concerns how and what types of narrative develop at a specific age level of child development. Their study specifically examines how the conversational context influences the coherence of children's narratives; differences in situation might cause the same narrator to tell different types of narratives. Examining how the selection of the topic affects children's narrative production, Hudson and Shapiro illustrate how components of the narrative differ among children of different ages. Similarly, in her longitudinal study of three young children, Preece (1987) has found that preschoolers are capable of producing a striking variety of narrative forms, such as personal anecdotes, parodies, film retellings and fantasies; over half of their conversational narratives, however, concern real personal experiences.

As we have already seen in Chapter 2 and as we will see in greater detail later in Chapters 6 and 7, research on narrative discourse has also examined the role of social interaction in young children's language development and acquisition of narrative structure. This emphasis is based on Vygotsky's (1978) social interaction approach, which states that humans are fundamentally social and cultural beings and that, therefore, any cognitive skills have a social interactive origin. Moreover, the view that the caregiver's talk provides a verbal framework for children's representations of past events implies that early social interactions shape young children's narratives into culturally preferred patterns. For instance, in their longitudinal study of ten North American children, McCabe and Peterson (2000) found that the children's increasing skill at independently providing evaluative information was correlated with mothers' frequencies of prompting for and spontaneously providing evaluative information in their conversations with their children. These researchers interpreted this relationship according to Vygotskyan theories.

In this sense, it is also critical to consider cultural differences in how children structure their oral personal narratives. In other words, there are many ways to tell a story, and the development of children's personal narratives reflects not only their age but also their culture. For example, African American children tell a narrative consisting of a series of implicitly associated personal anecdotes (Michaels, 1981, 1991). Hawaiian children present 'talk story,' rambling personal narratives enhanced with humor, jokes and teasing in the form of joint performance, or cooperative production of responses by two or more speakers (Au, 1993).

As mentioned in Chapter 2, Japanese elementary school children tend to tell concise stories that are cohesive collections of several personal experiences (McCabe, 1997; Minami, 1990; Minami & McCabe, 1991, 1996). This succinct narrative style exhibited by Japanese children, which, at least superficially, resembles *haiku*, shows a remarkable contrast to European American children's narrative style, which is often a lengthy story that details a single experience and often revolves around the solution of some problem (Minami & McCabe, 1991). The central aim of this chapter is to explore whether the same tendency is observed in narratives told by Japanese mothers and their preschool children.

Chapter 4 analyzes monologic narrative production in Japanese and attempts to answer the following key questions:

(1) How do Japanese four- and five-year-olds transform their experiences into narrative? What do the differences between these two age groups tell us about their development?
(2) How do Japanese adults (i.e. mothers) transform their experiences into narrative? Are there any similarities and/or differences between adults' narrative style and children's narrative style?
(3) Is there any association between the mother's narrative style and her child's narrative style?

Understanding how narrative develops is crucial because a specific narrative style not only reflects a fundamental structure that has been culturally nurtured, but it also indicates a socialization process contributing to the formation of such cultural representation. With these findings as a basis, examining Japanese children's personal narratives can offer important insights into the sociocultural basis for language acquisition.

Methods

As explained in Chapter 3, narratives in the present study were elicited from children and their mothers, separately, in the manner developed by Peterson and McCabe (1983). Unlike the picture-book technique (e.g. Berman & Slobin, 1994), exactly the same stimuli were not given to each child; instead, the children were interviewed on a wide variety of experiences that they found meaningful. As has already been described in Chapter 3, when the child began to tell a narrative that had happened to him or her, only nonspecific social support was offered, such as such as *'un, un'* ('uh huh'), *'sorede/sorekara'* ('and/then'), *'motto hanashite kureru'* ('tell me more') or *'sorede doo natta no?'* ('then what happened?'). These responses are relatively neutral and simply serve as indications of the listener's interest in hearing whatever the child wants to narrate.

Narratives were transcribed and broken into utterances. Narrative structures were studied using slightly modified versions of the following two methods: (1) verse/stanza analysis as a structure-based analysis, and (2) Labov's (high point) analysis as a content-based analysis. Verse/stanza analysis has been applied productively to narratives from many cultures (e.g. Gee, 1985; Hymes, 1981). Utterances were also analyzed from the standpoint of high point analysis (e.g. Labov, 1972; Peterson & McCabe, 1983). That is, coding rules specifically developed for verse/stanza analysis and high point analysis of Japanese narratives (Minami, 1990, 1996a, 1996b; Minami & McCabe, 1991, 1996) were applied to monologic narratives produced by four- and five-year-olds and their mothers. As defined in this chapter, verse/stanza analysis and high point analysis can be effectively used to identify characteristics of Japanese narrative. The information we obtain by using these analyses can help answer the questions posed at the end of the previous section.

Synthesis of two types of analysis

From the diverse array of methods for analyzing narrative structure and content (see Bamberg, 1997c; Berman, 1995; McCabe & Peterson, 1991 and Peterson & McCabe, 1983, for a review), two different types of analyses were selected and synthesized. One is verse/stanza analysis (Gee, 1985; Hymes, 1981), which has been applied successfully to narratives from various cultures, and the other is high point analysis, based on the Labovian approach (Labov, 1972; Peterson & McCabe, 1983).

Rules of verse/stanza analysis in Japanese
To describe eight important factors in the ethnography of communication, Hymes (1972) used the letters of the term SPEAKING, i.e. Setting (components of act situation), Participants, Ends (goals and outcomes), Act (sequences), Key (the tone, manner, or spirit in which act is done), Instrumentalities (forms of speech), Norms and Genres. Oral narrative is an interesting area for those who are concerned with the ethnography of communication, and verse analysis is an effective tool to reveal patterns of oral narrative, through which we might be able to observe the above eight factors. The personal narratives were first coded into lines, verses, and stanzas based on coding schemes originally developed by Hymes (1981, 1982, 1985, 1990) and later extended by Gee (1985, 1986a, 1989a, 1991a, 1991b). Gee (1986a, p. 403) specifically hypothesizes the existence of the following units in any narrative performance:

(A) Idea units that converge on a unit called the *line*. Such units are relatively short and contain one piece of new, or better, focused, information. They will often, though not always, be clauses. The language will use whatever it uses to mark focused information to mark them (e.g. pitch glides), as well as junctural phenomena such as short pauses or hesitations.

(B) Lines will cluster into thematically constant units called *stanzas*. Stanzas will have a unitary perspective, not just in terms of larger elements like time, location, and character, but also in terms of a quite narrow topic or theme.

(C) Larger topic/thematic units called *sections*. Sections will be defined by a unitary perspective in terms of elements like location, time and character.

In the present study, as Masuda (1999) proposes in his Quint-patterning Principle, a narrative could be divided into a maximum of five different levels of hierarchical units. For instance, the most subordinate unit of the narrative is defined as lines, which correspond to what Chafe (1993) has termed 'accent units.' Lines are thematically grouped into verses (basically defined as single clauses), which, following Chafe's (1993) classification, are 'intonation units.' Verses are in turn grouped into stanzas, which are thematically constant units, and thus have a unitary perspective in terms of time, location, character and a rather narrow topic or theme. In adopting verse/stanza analysis for Japanese narratives, specific coding rules were formulated (Minami, 1990, 1996a, 1996b; Minami & McCabe, 1991). First, *ne* (*sa* or *na*, depending on the dialect) – the Japanese counterpart of the English 'you know,' 'OK?' or a tag question – functions as a pragmatic punctuation device in oral discourse (Okubo, 1959). Second, irrespective of conjunction type – whether it is a coordinate conjunction or a subordinate one – when a conjunction connects two clauses, each clause is considered an independent clause. These points are summarized in the following coding guidelines:

Rule 1 When Japanese *ne* ('you know') appears, it always signals the break between two lines. When *ne* comes at the end of one semantically complete statement, it also tends to signal the break between two verses.

Rule 2 Irrespective of conjunction type, a clause that is followed by (or follows) a conjunction forms one verse.[1]

Rule 3 A narrative consists of a maximum of five different levels. Among the five hierarchical levels of verse/stanza analysis, the basic level is the *stanza*, which is made up of the subordinate levels, *verse* and *line*; the stanzas can be grouped into the superordinate levels, *section* and possibly further into *apex*.

Rule 4 Number of experiences (coherent events distinct from other events in terms of space and time) is also determined independently of narrative form.

Following Labov's (Labov, 1972; Peterson & McCabe, 1983) definition of narrative, a narrative in this study was defined as two or more utterances that recount a specific past event. For this study, while only one prompt (i.e. earliest memory) was given to mothers, because plural short prompts were given to children in order to facilitate their narrative production, the longest narrative produced by each child was selected. This decision came from Peterson and McCabe's (1983) claim that because length is correlated with complexity, choosing the longest narrative produced by each child is appropriate for measuring his or her current level of narrative development.

Audiotapes were transcribed verbatim for coding in the format required for analysis using the Child Language Data Exchange System (i.e. CHILDES, MacWhinney & Snow, 1985, 1990). Japanese children's and their mothers' transcribed narratives were identified and coded in accordance with the above-described rules. Reliability was then estimated using the formula: (number of agreements divided by number of agreements + number of disagreements) × 100%. One person coded all the data, while another person independently coded eight full transcripts (i.e. four children's transcripts – two of each age – and four mothers' transcripts, thus 20% of the data). Rates of agreement for stanzas were estimated to be 100% for children's narratives and 96.15% for mothers' narratives.

Rules of Labov's (high point) analysis in Japanese

The second coding scheme focused on the content of each clause (which generally corresponds to a verse) in the personal narrative from the standpoint of Labovian methodology (Labov, 1972) [an adaptation of which was later used by Peterson and McCabe (1983) in their analysis of children's developing mastery of temporality and causality]. As discussed in Chapter 2, Labov and his colleagues (Labov *et al.*, 1967) elicited narratives from African American adolescents about a life-threatening experience, and presented linguistic techniques to evaluate the narration of experiences within African American Vernacular English (AAVE). Minami and McCabe (1991, 1993, 1995) have drawn from an adaptation of Labov's analysis called high point analysis (Peterson & McCabe, 1983) because of the central importance of ascertaining the emotional climax – high point – of the narrative.

The high point analysis coding scheme clarifies the role that each clause (or verse) plays in organizing a narrative. In the past, diverse units have been proposed by different scholars. To illustrate this point, Labov and Waletzky (1967) adopted the independent clause for their analytic unit. Some clauses play the role of descriptive 'orientation,' which is considered to 'set the stage for the narrated events,' whereas others are considered to function as 'evaluation,' 'actions,' and 'appendages.'

In addition, another two categories, 'reported speech' and 'psychological complements,' are introduced into the main (i.e. first-level) categories. 'Reported speech,' statements that report character speech by generally reproducing the speech performed, is included because it is considered linguistically marked recounting of a past speech event (Ely & McCabe, 1993), such as *'ano ne, 'chuusha shinai hito ehon yonde mattoite kudasai,' tte sensei itteta*' ('Well, you know, "Those who haven't gotten a shot, please read books while waiting," said the teacher'). As I will explain later in detail in Chapter 5, there are a variety of rhetorical strategies that the narrator deploys in order to involve the listener in the narrative. Reported speech, which Tannen (1986, 1989) calls 'a constructed dialogue,' is one of them and makes the narrative presentation, particularly the narrator's emotional state, vivid and thus includes a dramatic element.

'Psychological complements,' which express opinion, uncertainty, belief and impression (Deese, 1984), are also included to code such mental-state verbs as *omou* ('think'), *ki ga suru* ('feel'), *wakaru* ('know,' 'be sure'), *oboete iru* ('remember,' 'recollect') and *mitai* ('seem'). Maynard (2000) aptly points out that a Japanese individual cannot convey his or her feelings without using pathos-oriented (as opposed to logos) expressions, such as *to omoun desu* ('I think such and such') [note that *to* before *omoundesu* is the quotation-final particle *to*, which I will explain later in Chapter 5]. While complement clauses that express mental or inner states may increase with a child's age (Berman & Neeman, 1994), this category is primarily for adults' data and thus does not necessarily play a major role in the present analysis of preschool children's narrative development or at least in the analysis presented in this chapter (for further information, see Chapter 5).[2]

As briefly summarized above, therefore, clauses (or verses) produced by each participant were basically placed into one of the following six categories: action, orientation, evaluation, appendage, reported speech, and psychological complement. The focus in this chapter, however, is placed particularly on orientation, evaluation and action.

Orientation

In Labov's (1972) original analysis, orientation clauses acquaint the listener with who and what was involved in the event. Orientation clauses are not confined by any temporal juncture, and can range freely through the narrative sequence. They are therefore categorized as *free* narrative clauses (Labov *et al.*, 1968; Labov & Waletzky, 1967). In the present analysis, orientation clauses are statements in which the narrator digresses from the events of a narrative so that he or she can provide the listener with contextual embedding of the narrative, such as the setting, people, time, features of environment, conditions and ongoing behavior in the narrative. In Labov's analysis, because orientation clauses convey information about the characters and events in the narrative, they are also categorized as the referential function. Examples of this category would be: *'Tulip gumi no toki'* ('When [I] was in Tulip Class'); *'chiisai toki'* ('When [I] was small').

Evaluation

Another type of free narrative clauses is the evaluation clause, which provides the listener with emotional information about the narrative, such as what to think about a person: *'ma isogashikatta kara'* ('um, because [he] was busy'), place, thing, event or, more globally, the entire experience described: *'nakanakatta'* ('[I] didn't cry'); *'imademo sore ga fushigi nan desu kedo'* ('Even now that is strange, though'); *'soo yuu sabishii omoi shita tte yuu no ga tsuyoi desu ne, watashi wa'* ('I have very vivid memories of having been lonely'). Although both orientation and evaluation clauses are categorized as free narrative clauses, they function differently; whereas orientation functions as referential, evaluation functions as evaluative. Unlike orientation clauses, therefore, in Labov's categorization, evaluation is categorized as an affective (or evaluative) function; evaluation clauses inform the listener about why the narrator wants to tell the narrative.

Action

Specific actions, events or processes that take place are categorized as 'action': *'chuusha shita'* ('[I] got a shot'); *'makikomaretan desu ne, ashi o'* ('[I] was caught, you know, by the leg'). According to Labov's (1972) original definition, a narrative includes at least two sequentially ordered events; thus, actions are the only obligatory component of the narrative.

Furthermore, as opposed to *free* narrative clauses represented by orientation and evaluation clauses, because action clauses recapitulate a single event that took place at some discrete or restricted point in time, they are categorized as *restricted* narrative clauses (Labov, 1972; Peterson & McCabe, 1983). In other words, because restricted narrative clauses are temporally ordered, a change in their order will result in a change in the interpretation of the original semantic interpretation. [Note, however, that in another of Labov's categorization schemes, action clauses are categorized as the referential function just like orientation clauses. As a matter of fact, Labov and Waletsky's (1967) starting point was a distinction between these two essential functions of narrative: referential and affective (or evaluative).]

Along similar lines, Hopper and Thompson (1980) define foregrounding and backgrounding as follows:

> Users of a language are constantly required to design their utterances in accord with their own communicative goals and with their perception of their listeners' needs. Yet, in any speaking situation, some parts of what is said are more relevant than others. That part of a discourse which does not immediately and crucially contribute to the speaker's goal, but which merely assists, amplifies, or comments on it, is referred to as BACKGROUND. By contrast, the material which supplies the main points of the discourse is known as FOREGROUND. Linguistic features associated with the distinction between foreground and background are referred to as GROUNDING. (p. 280)

In the quotation above, the distinction between foregrounding (i.e. plot-advancing events/main line event clauses) and backgrounding (i.e. plot-motivating comments/contextualizing clauses) corresponds to Labov's restricted narrative clauses and free narrative clauses, respectively (see Table 4.1). With regard to this distinction, Peterson and McCabe (1991) state the following:

> Main line event clauses have been frequently described as the backbone or 'bare bones' of a narrative and describe what happened, whereas contextualizing clauses include identification of participants, setting, explanation, evaluation, and collateral information. (p. 30)

As Aksu-Koç and von Stutterheim (1994) explain, in other words, the central distinction between foregrounding and backgrounding is based on temporal categories. Foregrounded utterances refer to an event with temporal boundedness and thus play a major role in a shift-in-time

Table 4.1 Correspondence in narrative functions between Labov and Hopper and Thompson

Labov			Hopper & Thompson
Action	Referential	Restricted narrative clauses	Foreground
Orientation	Referential	Free narrative clauses	Background
Evaluation	Evaluative	Free narrative clauses	Background

relation; backgrounded utterances, in contrast, do not play an important role in advancing the temporal sequence (Aksu-Koç & von Stutterheim, 1994). An implication from this distinction in the context of narrative discourse development is that, as Berman (1994) emphasizes, 'the development of narrative abilities depends on the emergence of foreground/background distinctions' (p. 2).[3]

In addition to the above-mentioned main (i.e. first-level) categories, several subcategories (i.e. second-level categories) were also introduced. Appendages, for example, do not appear by themselves. Instead, they are a first-level category including narrative comments that appear either at the beginning (e.g. abstracts and attention-getting devices) or at the end of the main body of the narrative (e.g. codas). Abstracts, which function as a brief summary of the narrative as a whole or of its main point are added as a second-level category: *'anoo, onaji class no otoko no ko ga shinjattan desu'* ('um, a boy in the same class died'). Attention-getting devices also appear at the beginning of a narrative in order to attract the listener's attention: *'boku shitteru wa'* ('I know something'). Located at the end of narratives, codas include not only formalized endings of a narrative, such as *'oshimai'* ('that's it'), but also pragmatic endings of a narrative: *'moo nai'* ('[I] don't have any [more things to tell]').

Likewise, orientation, evaluation and action clauses are sometimes subordinate parts within other categories. For example, a narrative clause, *'**chotto dake** chi ga deta'* ('[I] bled **a little bit**'), describes a specific action that took place. At the same time, however, because the clause is accompanied by an evaluative tone, it is categorized as 'action with evaluation' In other words, the clause is classified as both 'action' and 'evaluation.'

Also, like the progressive verb form *be + V-ing* in English, the progressive form *V-te i* in Japanese represents ongoing actions, events or processes (Soga, 1983). Although past progressives may sometimes be used in straightforward event clauses, Peterson and McCabe (1983) consider past progressive verb forms to be a hybrid of orientation and complicating action. Following this line of categorization, clauses with progressive forms are considered to constitute actions with orientative information: *'jibun ni mukatte otomodachi ga 'ah' toka **i-tte i** ta'* ('Toward me, my friends were saying "uh" ').

'Outcome' is another subcategory. Minami and McCabe (1991, 1993) previously devised 'outcome,' which represents the result(s) of specific actions. This can be done evaluatively: *'dakara kowakattan da yo'* ('That's why [I] was scared'), or in terms of physical consequences: *'yoku nattan da yo'* ('[I] got all right'), or both: *'hone oretan da'* ('[I] got a broken bone'). As a cautionary note, however, without any specific actions, by definition there could be no outcome; in other words, while an action stands by itself, an outcome cannot.[4] As a natural consequence, unlike 'orientation' or simple 'evaluation,' outcome is not a free clause. Outcomes only follow actions and usually conclude stanzas. However, because this category primarily appears in children's data and not very often in adults' data, it does not play a major role in the present analysis.

Details of the coding rules for high point analysis in Japanese – the definitions and functions of each of the six main categories and nine subcategories, rules for coding, and examples – appear in Chapter 5 as well. There was one principal coder of the monologic narrative data, but eight full transcripts (i.e. four children's transcripts – two of each age – and four mothers' transcripts, thus 20% of the data) were independently coded by a second person. Inter-rater agreement on the category under which each verse falls was calculated. Cohen's kappa, an estimate of reliability that corrects for chance rates of agreement was 0.94, for the main categories (i.e. appendage, orientation, action, evaluation, reported speech, psychological complement) of the children's coding; for the subcategories (e.g. abstract, attention-getting device, coda, outcome) it was 0.89. Likewise, Cohen's kappa was 0.95 for the main categories of the adults' coding, and 0.79 for the subcategories. To describe the relative strength of agreement associated with kappa statistics, if the range is between 0.61 and 0.80, it is labeled 'substantial'; further, if the range of kappa is over 0.81, it is considered to represent 'almost perfect' agreement (Bakeman & Gottman, 1986; Landis & Koch, 1977). Therefore, except for one, which is still in the 'substantial' agreement range, all estimates of reliability fall into the range of 'almost perfect' agreement.

Synthesis of the two types of analysis

When we applied rules of verse/stanza analysis to one Japanese narrative, which was told by Tamotsu, a boy aged 4;7, the following organization is obtained. The basic-level category of verse/stanza analysis is *stanza*, whereas the subordinate-level categories are *verse* and *line*; the numbers to the right refer to the lines (the minimum unit) produced, and small letters (a–i) in parentheses indicate the beginning of each verse. Furthermore, as the superordinate-level category, closely related stanzas are grouped as a *section*. Verse/stanza analysis, therefore, displays a hierarchical structure, reflective of the experiences described in a narrative. High-point analysis coding is also provided; verses that fall into the categories of appendage, abstract, orientation, action, evaluation, outcome, and coda are indicated as APP, ABS, ORT, ACT, EVL, OUT and COD, respectively (for further information see Chapters 5 and 9). Note that each verse is not necessarily homogeneous in terms of high-point analysis categories; rather, mixed categories are prevalent.

Example 4.1 Tamotsu's monologic narrative
(Note: INT = interviewer)
SECTION I
Stanza A

(a) APP:ABS	*yoochien de koko ka **ne**,*	1
	'In preschool, here, you know,'	
	(INT: *un*)	
	'uh huh'	
	*koko toka **ne**,*	2
	'here, you know,'	
	(INT: *un*)	
	'uh huh'	
	koko toka kega shita no.	3
	'here (I) got hurt, you know.'	

Stanza B

(b) ORT:ACT	*uun to **ne**,*	4
	'Um, you know,'	
	(INT: *un*)	
	'uh huh'	
	ehtto, nanka Tamotsu otomodachi ni yuku toki ni,	5
	'um when I went to see a friend of mine,'	
(c) ACT:EVL	*koko dosun to kega shite.*	6
	'here, with a bump (I) got hurt.'	
	(INT: *un*)	
	'uh huh'	

SECTION II
Stanza C

(d) ORT:ACT	*koko ga **ne**,*	7
	'Here, you know,'	
	(INT: *un*)	
	'uh huh'	
	kanpu masatsu shiteru toki ni,	8
	'when (I) was taking a rubdown with a dry towel,'	

(e) ACT:ORT	*koo shite tara,*	9
	'when (I) was doing this,'	
	(INT: *un*)	
	'uh huh'	
(f) ACT:EVL	*chi ga de ta.*	10
(OUT)	'it bled.'	

Stanza D

(g) ACT	*un, sorede teepu hatta.*	11
	'Yes, (I) put a Band-Aid on.'	
(h) EVL	*uun, kutsushita ga,*	12
	'Um, (my) sock'	
	(INT: *un*)	
	'uh huh'	
	chi darake ni natta.	13
	'um (my) sock was full of blood.'	

Stanza E

| (i) APP:COD | *uun to moo nai.* | 14 |
| | 'Um, that's it.' | |

Data Analysis

Once all the transcripts had been coded and formatted, a series of Child Language Analysis (CLAN) computer programs were used to obtain frequencies of different codes, the total number of words, the number of different words, and the type-token ratio (i.e. the total number of different words divided by the total number of words; Templin, 1957). The results of these analyses are presented in the next section.

Results

Quantitative results

Using the previously mentioned coding rules, several principal characteristics of Japanese personal narratives were quantitatively analyzed.

Total number of words, total number of different words and type-token ratio in monologic narrative. Table 4.2 gives the means and standard deviations of the total number of words and the total number of different words used in each individual's monologic narrative. For the four-year-olds, the total number of words ranged from 31 to 129, and the total number of different words ranged from 19 to 65. For the five-year-olds, the total number of words ranged from 32 to 161, and the total number of different words ranged from 18 to 64. Additionally, similar type-token ratios (the total number of different words divided by the total number of words) of these two age groups indicate that the levels of lexical redundancy are almost identical. Neither gender nor age differences approached statistical significance in the three categories: (1) the total number of words, (2) the total number of different words, and (3) the type-token ratio. As far as these production variables are concerned, therefore, neither major developmental nor gender differences between four-year-olds and five-year-olds were observed.

Likewise, although a researcher elicited narratives from the children and adults, because turn-taking interaction between the narrator and the listener still took place, utterances over turns (i.e. the number of utterances produced by a speaker per turn) were examined. [As I explain later in Chapter 5, analyzing turn-taking interaction means that even a supposedly monologic narrative is co-constructed by the narrator and the listener, and is thus dialogic to some extent.] The four-year-olds' utterances over turns ranged from 1.00 to 2.25, whereas the five-year-olds' utterances over turns ranged from 1.00 to 1.80. Neither gender nor age difference approached statistical significance.

Narrative performance exhibited by the 20 mothers varied greatly. The total number of words ranged from 55 to 761; the total number of different words ranged from 35 to 211. The two children's groups were then compared with the adult group separately. Comparisons of mean scores by a t test showed that mothers' total number of words, $t(21)^5 = -7.62$, $p < 0.0001$, and total number of different words, $t(26) = -8.91$, $p < 0.0001$, were significantly higher than those used by four-year-olds. Also, mothers' total number of words, $t(24) = -7.35$, $p < 0.0001$, and total number of different words, $t(28) = -8.48$, $p < 0.0001$, were significantly higher than five-year-olds'. These results indicate that adult narrators used more words and a greater variety of words than young narrators. When considering stages of child development, these results are not surprising at all.

What attracts our attention, however, is that, in these two categories (i.e. the total number of words and the total number of different words), no significant associations were found between mothers and children. Pearson's product-moment correlation between mothers and children for the total number of words used was $r(18) = -0.019$. Likewise, the correlation between mothers and children for the total number of different words used was $r(18) = -0.097$. These results thus indicate that talkative mothers do not necessarily have talkative children, and that reticent mothers do not necessarily have reticent children.

Table 4.2 Means and standard deviations of total number of words, total number of different words, type-token ratio, utterances over turns and number of stories in monologic narrative production

Variable	Four-year-olds (n = 10)		Five-year-olds (n = 10)		Mothers (n = 20)	
	M	*SD*	*M*	*SD*	*M*	*SD*
Total number of words	75.90	31.77	75.60	47.80	384.35	175.28
Total number of different words	38.10	13.76	37.10	17.76	126.55	39.91
Type-token ratio	0.52	0.09	0.53	0.09	0.36	0.09
Utterances over turns	1.32	0.39	1.21	0.27	1.48	0.24
Number of stories	1.70	1.25	1.20	0.42	1.85	1.09

Note:
Total number of words:	Mothers > Four-year-olds	[$p < 0.0001$]
	Mothers > Five-year-olds	[$p < 0.0001$]
Total number of different words:	Mothers > Four-year-olds	[$p < 0.0001$]
	Mothers > Five-year-olds	[$p < 0.0001$]

Number of stories

In response to a prompt to talk about a time when they were injured, some children talked about more than one incident involving injury. For both four- and five-year-olds, the number of stories ranged from one to two, except for one four-year-old who provided five different experiences. Neither gender nor age differences approached statistical significance.

Mothers were prompted to talk about their earliest memory. Like children, the number of stories ranged from one to two, except for one mother who gave six different stories. No differences reached statistical significance either between adults and four-year-olds or between adults and five-year-olds.

Additionally, no significant association was found between the number of stories produced by the mother and the number of stories produced by her child. Like the results obtained from the total number of words and the number of different words, this result indicates that those mothers who produce many stories do not necessarily have children who tell many stories, and that those mothers who produce few stories do not necessarily have those children who do the same.

In summary, the results indicate that as far as vocabulary (i.e. the total number of words and the total number of different words) and the number of stories produced are concerned, the mother's narrative style does not necessarily predict her child's narrative style. In some respects, therefore, the results shown so far are not in line with the claims laid by Fivush (1991), McCabe and Peterson (1991) and Peterson and McCabe (1992) (which I described earlier in this chapter and Chapter 2).

Verse/stanza analysis

Structural patterns were examined using verse/stanza analysis. Overall, across the three groups, statistical analyses of the patterning in stanzas has yielded the following: (1) With regard to the proportion of three-verse stanzas, there were no differences between the groups of four-year-olds, five-year-olds, and adults (i.e. mothers); that is, the proportion of three-verse stanzas remains stable across the three groups. (2) Compared to four-year-olds, however, five-year-olds have begun to use the form of adult-like narratives. More detailed analyses are described below:

As can be seen in Figure 4.1, of the total 41 stanzas produced by the four-year-olds, two-verse and three-verse stanzas amount to 36.6% (15) and 29.3% (12), respectively. On the other hand, only 14.6% (6) of stanzas were longer than three verses. For individual four-year-olds, the average number of verses per stanza ranged from 1.8 to 4.5, and the number of stanzas produced ranged from 2 to 7.

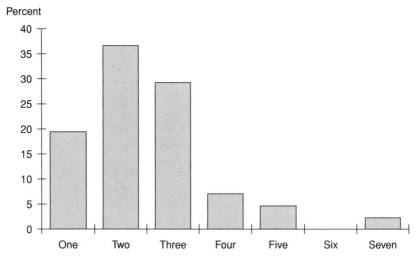

Figure 4.1 Histogram of verses per stanza (four-year-olds)

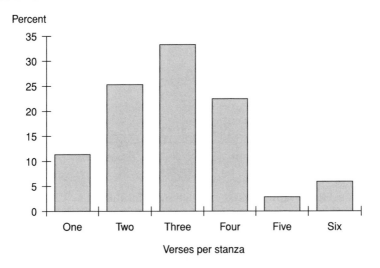

Figure 4.2 Histogram of verses per stanza (five-year-olds)

Similarly, as shown in Figure 4.2, of the total 36 stanzas produced by the five-year-olds, 25.0% (9) and 33.3% (12) were two-verse and three-verse stanzas, respectively. Unlike four-year-olds, however, over 30.6% (11) of the stanzas consisted of more than three verses. For individual five-year-olds, the average number of verses per stanza ranged from 2.0 to 4.5, and the number of stanzas produced ranged from 2 to 7.

The mothers presented a similar tendency in terms of verse/stanza structure. As Figure 4.3 illustrates, of the total 202 stanzas produced by the 20 mothers, two-verse and three-verse stanzas amount to 21.3% (43) and 28.2% (57), respectively; thus, almost half were two- or three-verse stanzas. At the same time, however, 42.6% (86) of the stanzas also consisted of more than three verses. The average number of verses per stanza produced by the mothers varied widely from 2.44 to 4.75; they also varied greatly in the production of the number of stanzas from 2 to 17. These figures illustrate that while some mothers produced lengthy oral narratives, others were reticent.

Table 4.3 gives the means and standard deviations of verse/stanza-related variables. Either in terms of average verses per stanza or the number of stanzas produced, no differences approached statistical significance between four-year-olds and five-year-olds. Each of these two age groups was then compared with the adult group (i.e. 20 mothers). In terms of the number of stanzas produced, four-year-olds are significantly less productive narrators than adults, $t(28) = -5.78$, $p < 0.0001$; likewise,

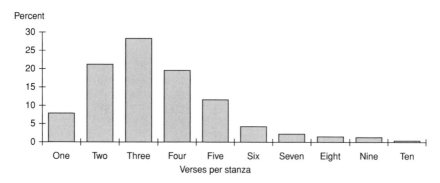

Figure 4.3 Histogram of verses per stanza (mothers)

five-year-olds are significantly less productive narrators than adults, $t(26) = -6.49$, $p < 0.0001$. In terms of average verses per stanza, however, while four-year-olds are significantly less productive narrators than adults, $t(28) = -3.09$, $p < 0.01$, the difference between five-year-olds ($M = 3.08$, $SD = 0.73$) and adults ($M = 3.49$, $SD = 0.63$) did not reach statistical significance. Although stanzas with four or more verses are the most common form produced by adults, as far as average verses per stanza are concerned, the narrative style exhibited by five-year-olds is similar to that of adults. In other words, both adults and five-year-olds produce approximately three verses per stanza on average.

Proportions of one-verse, two-verse, three-verse, and four- or more verse stanzas produced by each individual were calculated (for means and standard deviations, see Table 4.3). The box-plots shown in Figures 4.4, 4.5, 4.6 and 4.7 present the distributions of the three groups for one-verse, two-verse, three-verse, and four- or more verse stanzas, respectively.[6] Proportions of verses per stanza produced by adults show very different distributions from those by children, particularly four-year-olds. The proportion of one-verse stanzas ranged from 0 to 25; the proportion of two-verse stanzas ranged from 0 to 60; the proportion of three-verse stanzas ranged from 0 to 55.55; the proportion of four- or more verse stanzas ranged from 11.11 to 75. Thus, it seems that compared to four-year-olds, adults produced much larger proportions of four- or more verse stanzas.

With regard to these four categories – proportions of one-verse, two-verse, three-verse, and four- or more verse stanzas – four-year-olds and five-year-olds were compared. Although no differences approached statistical significance between four-year-olds and five-year-olds either in the proportion of one-verse stanzas or three-verse stanzas, marginal

Table 4.3 Means and standard deviations of verse/stanza related variables in monologic narrative production

Variable	Four-year-olds (n = 10)		Five-year-olds (n = 10)		Mothers (n = 20)	
	M	*SD*	*M*	*SD*	*M*	*SD*
Average number of verses per stanza	2.65	0.82	3.08	0.73	3.49	0.63
Number of stanzas	4.10	1.66	3.60	1.43	10.10	4.00
Percentage of one-verse stanzas	13.95	19.34	9.76	13.38	7.37	9.04
Percentage of two-verse stanzas	43.50	27.40	22.86	23.33	24.01	15.24
Percentage of three-verse stanzas	26.12	17.13	34.52	23.26	25.44	15.91
Percentage of four or more verse stanzas	16.43	20.80	32.86	22.62	43.18	18.04

differences were observed in the proportion of two-verse stanzas, $t(18) = -1.81$, $p = 0.09$, and in the proportion of four- or more verse stanzas, $t(18) = 1.69$, $p = 0.11$.[7] Thus, a smaller proportion of two-verse stanzas and, in contrast, a larger proportion of four- or more verse stanzas produced by five-year-olds might indicate that their narrative production is slightly longer than that of four-year-olds. A modest interpretation of these results is that five-year-olds are slightly more advanced narrators than four-year-olds. A bold interpretation, in contrast, is that five-year-olds are much more like adult narrators than four-year-olds.

The four-year-olds and the five-year-olds were each compared with the adult group (i.e. 20 mothers). In the proportion of three-verse stanzas, no differences approached statistical significance between the adult group and either one of the children's groups. Across the three groups, therefore, proportions of three-verse stanzas did not vary greatly. This result seems to indicate that the three-verse stanza is the canonical narrative form.

On the other hand, no differences were observed between five-year-olds and adults in any types of stanzas, although adults produced significantly larger proportions of four- or more verse stanzas than four-year-olds, $t(28) = -3.64$, $p < 0.01$. Although marginal, a difference was also observed between four-year-olds and adults in the proportion of two-verse stanzas, $t(12) = 2.09$, $p = 0.06$. Thus, as far as proportions of

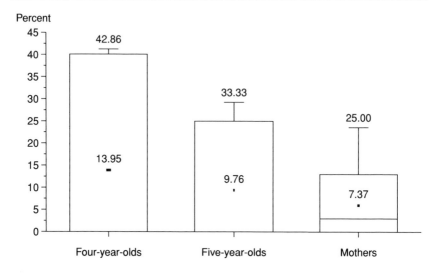

Figure 4.4 Means, medians, interquartile ranges, and extreme values for proportion of one-verse stanzas in the monologic narratives told by four-year-olds, five-year-olds and mothers.

Note: The box-plots in the figure are intended to make the patterns easier to follow; they provide a good deal of information on the distribution of subjects: the mean [plotted with a dot in the box], the median [the horizontal line across the box], the middle half of the data between the 25th and 75th percentiles [the outlined central box], the range of the main body of the data [the whiskers extending above the box]. Note that the median's horizontal line across the box is not visible for either four- or five-year-olds because the median, which is the middle attribute in the ranked distribution of observed attributes, is zero. As a matter of fact, more than half of each group's children (i.e. six of each group) did not produce one-verse stanzas.

stanza types are concerned, compared to four-year-olds, the narrative style exhibited by five-year-olds approaches that of adults. Therefore, we might be able to conclude that, compared to four-year-olds, five-year-olds' monologic narrative organization has moved in the direction of adult models.

High point analysis

As a content-based narrative analysis, narrative elements (i.e. action, orientation, evaluation, appendage and reported speech) were also examined (recall that the high-point analysis coding scheme clarifies the role that each verse plays in organizing a narrative). Proportions of these elements are shown in Table 4.4.[8] Overall, with regard to developmental

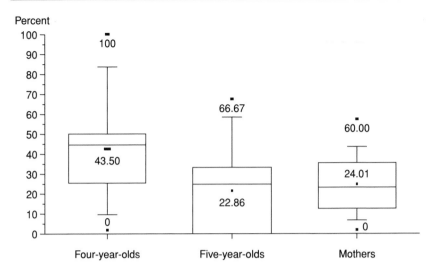

Figure 4.5 Means, medians, interquartile ranges, and extreme values for proportion of two-verse stanzas in the monologic narratives told by four-year-olds, five-year-olds, and mothers

Note: The box-plots in the figure are intended to make the patterns easier to follow; they provide a good deal of information on the distribution of subjects: the mean [plotted with a dot in the box], the median [the horizontal line across the box], the middle half of the data between the 25th and 75th%iles [the outlined central box], the range of the main body of the data [the whiskers extending above and below the box], and outliers [plotted with dots], which are 100 and 0 for four-year-olds, 66.67 for five-year-olds, and 60.00 and 0 for mothers.

differences among four-year-olds, five-year-olds and adults, high point analysis has revealed the following: (1) Compared to adults, young children emphasized a temporal sequence of action with less emphasis on non-sequential information, especially orientation. (2) Compared to four-year-olds, however, five-year-olds have begun to evaluate in the form of adult-like narratives. More detailed analyses are described below:

For the four-year-olds, the proportion of 'action' varied from 22.22 to 90%. The proportion of 'evaluation' also ranged widely from 0 to 76.92%. In contrast, the proportion of 'orientation' ranged from 10 to 33.33%, except for one child whose orientation elements constituted 77.78% of her narrative.

Wide variation was also observed among the five-year-olds. The proportion of 'action' ranged from 12.5 to 80%. The proportion of 'evaluation' also ranged widely from 10 to 84.21%. In contrast, the proportion

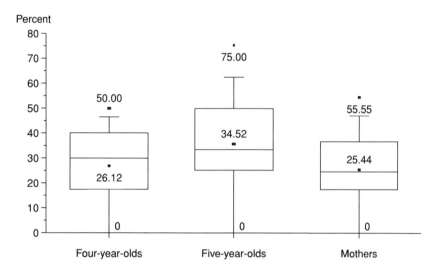

Figure 4.6 Means, medians, interquartile ranges, and extreme values for proportion of three-verse stanzas in the monologic narratives told by four-year-olds, five-year-olds and mothers

Note: The box-plots in the figure are intended to make the patterns easier to follow; they provide a good deal of information on the distribution of subjects: the mean [plotted with a dot in the box], the median [the horizontal line across the box], the middle half of the data between the 25th and 75th%iles [the outlined central box], the range of the main body of the data [the whiskers extending above and below the box], and outliers [plotted with dots], which are 50.00 and 0 for four-year-olds, 75.00 and 0 for five-year-olds and 55.55 and 0 for mothers.

of 'orientation' ranged from 7.14 to 40%. The proportion of 'action' was negatively (i.e. inversely) associated with the proportion of 'evaluation,' $r(18) = -.69, p < 0.001$. This inverse relationship indicates that (1) although a category of 'specific action with an evaluative comment' exists, it did not occur frequently; rather, many action statements and evaluation statements were provided separately, and (2) those five-year-olds who provided more action statements were likely to provide fewer evaluative comments, whereas those five-year-olds who provided fewer action statements were likely to provide more evaluative comments. [Note: Recall that action statements are categorized as the referential element and foreground information, whereas evaluative comments are categorized as the affective element and background information, according to Labov (1972) and Hopper and Thompson (1980), respectively.]

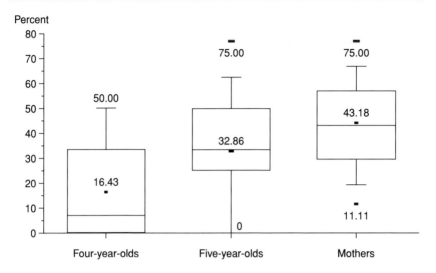

Figure 4.7 Means, medians, interquartile ranges, and extreme values for proportion of four- or more verse stanzas in the monologic narratives told by four-year-olds, five-year-olds and mothers

Note: The box-plots in the figure are intended to make the patterns easier to follow; they provide a good deal of information on the distribution of subjects: the mean [plotted with a dot in the box], the median [the horizontal line across the box], the middle half of the data between the 25th and 75th%iles [the outlined central box], the range of the main body of the data [the whiskers extending above and below the box], and outliers [plotted with dots], which are 50.00 for four-year-olds, 75.00 and 0 for five-year-olds and 75.00 and 11.11 for mothers.

For the 20 adults, the proportion of 'action' varied from 0 to 50%. The proportion of 'evaluation' was relatively high, ranging from 33.33 to 69.23, except for two adults whose evaluation elements were 18.18% and 25.58%, respectively. The proportion of 'orientation' ranged from 14.81 to 62.79%. The proportion of 'action' was negatively associated with the proportion of 'orientation,' $r(18) = -0.53$, $p < 0.001$, and marginally negatively associated with the proportion of 'evaluation,' $r(18) = -0.39$, $p < 0.09$. These inverse relationships indicate that (1) although there exist categories of 'specific action with an evaluative comment,' 'specific action with the progressive form (orientation),' and 'orientation with an action,' these categories did not occur frequently; rather, many action statements (which are sequential/foreground information) were provided separately from evaluation or orientation statements (which are non-sequential/

Table 4.4 Means and standard deviations of variables related to high point analysis (proportion)

Variable	Four-year-olds (n = 10)		Five-year-olds (n = 10)		Mothers (n = 20)	
	M	*SD*	*M*	*SD*	*M*	*SD*
Action	55.00	19.65	47.64	23.22	18.47	13.27
Orientation	26.87	20.03	23.67	10.90	38.87	14.18
Evaluation	33.39	22.08	41.24	25.25	46.73	13.15
Appendage	7.01	9.46	4.03	5.56	6.05	4.93
Reported speech	2.64	6.15	2.76	5.83	2.93	4.87

background information), and (2) those adults who provided more foreground information were likely to provide less background information, whereas those adults who provided less foreground information were likely to provide more background information.

No differences between four-year-olds and five-year-olds approached statistical significance in terms of action, evaluation or orientation. Each of these two age groups was then compared with the adult group (i.e. 20 mothers). The proportion of children's restricted narrative clauses (or foreground information) was substantially higher than that of adults'. That is, four-year-olds provided proportionately more action statements than adults, $t(28) = 6.04$, $p < 0.0001$; likewise, five-year-olds provided proportionately more action statements than adults, $t(12) = 3.68$, $p < 0.01$.

In complementary fashion, the proportion of the sum of evaluation and orientation clauses provided by adults was substantially higher than that of either one of the children's groups. That is, adults provided proportionately more free narrative clauses (or background information) than four-year-olds, $t(11) = 2.37$, $p < 0.05$. Also, adults produced proportionately more free narrative clauses than five-year-olds, $t(28) = 2.73$, $p < 0.05$.

The two components of free narrative clauses (or background information) were then examined separately, because, according to Labov and Waletzky (1967), while orientation serves the referential function, evaluation fulfills the affective or evaluative function. Although marginal, a difference was observed between four-year-olds and adults in the proportion of orientation statements, $t(28) = -1.90$, $p = 0.07$; likewise, five-year-olds provided proportionately fewer orientation statements than adults, $t(28) = -2.97$, $p < 0.01$.[9] As far as evaluation is concerned, however, compared to four-year-olds, five-year-olds' monologic narrative organization seems to move in the direction of adult models. Although four-year-olds gave proportionately fewer evaluation statements than adults, $t(28) = -2.08$, $p < 0.05$, the difference between five-year-olds and adults did not approach statistical significance.

Additionally, as far as the present data are concerned, the child's style of talking about past events did not correspond to the mother's style of talking about the past. Pearson's product-moment correlations between mothers and children for action, orientation and evaluation were $r(18) = 0.18$, $r(18) = 0.11$ and $r(18) = 0.26$, respectively. Thus, with regard to action, orientation, and evaluation, no significant associations were found between mothers and children. Individual differences in narrative components among Japanese mothers were not reflected in differences in narrative components among their children. These results therefore indicate that as far as these elements are concerned, the mother's narrative style does not predict her child's narrative style. Those mothers who give many action statements (i.e. who foreground such information) do not necessarily have children who give many action statements. Likewise, those mothers who provide many evaluation or orientation statements (i.e. who background such information) do not necessarily have children who provide many evaluation or orientation statements.

With regard to reported speech and appendages, no differences approached statistical significance between four-year-olds and five-year-olds. Likewise, no differences reached statistical significance between adults and either of the children's groups [ANOVAs run for reported speech and appendages revealed $F(2, 37) = 0.01$, $p = 0.99$ and $F(2, 37) = 0.57$, $p = 0.57$, respectively.] In the production of appendages, however, a gender difference was observed. Boys (four-year-olds and five-year-olds combined) produced 9.06% ($SD = 9.31$) on the average, while girls (four-year-olds and five-year-olds combined) produced 1.98% ($SD = 3.28$) on the average $t(11) = 2.26$, $p < 0.05$.[10]

Furthermore, the proportion of children's appendages was positively associated with the proportion of mothers' appendages, $r(18) = 0.48$, $p < 0.05$. This relationship suggests that those mothers who use many appendages have children who use many appendages. Also, children's gender was associated with the proportion of mothers' appendages, $r(18) = 0.66$, $p < 0.01$. Therefore, we can conclude that mothers of boys use more appendages than mothers of girls.[11]

Discussion

The ability to tell a coherent personal narrative is of critical importance in many aspects of an individual's life. Individuals of any age in any culture need this ability in order to communicate with everyone around them. Children in any culture need this ability in order to become accomplished narrators, listeners, readers and writers. The direction of narrative development, however, needs to be analyzed not only from the perspective of language universals but also from a language-specific point of view. The focus of this chapter has been the development of narrative form in young Japanese children. From a quantitative point of view, this section answers the initial questions posed at the outset of the chapter.

Narrative structure

Japanese children as well as adults seem to have a specific notion of what it means to stay on one topic. Earlier research (Minami, 1990; Minami & McCabe, 1991, 1996) identified that, despite follow-up questions that encouraged them to talk about one personal narrative at length, Japanese elementary school children spoke about free-standing collections of experiences rather than elaborating on any one experience in particular. Previous studies (McCabe, 1997; Minami, 1990; Minami & McCabe, 1991, 1996) have thus concluded that a presentation of multiple experiences seems to be characteristic of Japanese children's narratives. The present study identified a similar, though less prominent, tendency; one third (6) of the children talked about more than one time they were injured in one turn of talk. The difference in results between the present study and the previous one may be attributable to age difference; the present study examined preschool children, whereas the previous study focused on elementary school children. Supporting this interpretation, it is important to note that two thirds of the mothers (13) recalled more than one earliest memory. The difference between children and adults may be attributable to the linguistic/narrative competence that children at a certain developmental stage have at their disposal. A possible speculation is that the older an individual becomes, the more likely it is that he or she can tell about multiple experiences. [Note that a further examination of multiple stories will be given in Chapter 5.]

This study has shown that there are no significant differences between four-year-olds and five-year-olds with regard to the total number of words and number of different words used in each individual's narrative. That is, the degree of lexical redundancy of these two groups is almost identical. Moreover, there were no significant gender differences in these categories. As can be seen in individual differences in language acquisition in general (e.g. Goldfield & Snow, 1989), the findings in the present study seem to indicate that age or gender alone may not be good predictors of narrative development, probably because children develop at vastly different rates.

Age, however, does seem to be a factor in the specific area of stanza length. The patterning in stanzas, therefore, has proved to be not only an excellent tool to present how Japanese speakers turn their experiences into narrative, but also an excellent indicator to show what kinds of developmental changes take place among Japanese children aged four and five. With regard to the proportion of three-verse stanzas, there were no differences found between the two different age groups and the maternal group; although the proportion of four- or more verse stanzas is much more common than three-verse stanzas for adults, three-verse stanzas seem to be stable in terms of proportion. On the other hand, a smaller proportion of two-verse stanzas and, in contrast, a larger proportion of four- or more verse stanzas by five-year-olds, girls in particular, indicate that their stanzas are slightly longer than those of four-year-olds. Furthermore, although adults produce more four or more verse stanzas, no statistically significant differences were observed between five-year-olds and adults in any type of stanza. We can conclude that compared to four-year-olds, five-year-olds have begun to produce adult-like narratives.

As a content-based analysis, high point analysis has also proved to be an excellent indicator to show not only what kinds of similarities and/or differences exist between adults' narrative style and children's narrative style but also what kinds of developmental changes take place. The analysis has revealed that, compared to adults, among children's narratives the proportion of action clauses (i.e. restricted narrative clauses or foreground information) is high, while the proportion of free narrative clauses (i.e. background information) is relatively low. When telling a personal narrative, in addition to providing less information about the characters, the setting or the event, preschool children seem to pay less verbal attention to their own attitudes toward the event. In other words, compared to adults, young children emphasized a temporal sequence of action with less emphasis on non-sequential information, especially orientation. Although four-year-olds gave proportionately less evaluation than adults, no differences were observed between five-year-olds and adults. Therefore, while both four- and five-year-olds emphasize simple description of successive events, compared to four-year-olds, five-year-olds begin to evaluate at adult-like levels. The present study has revealed age-related differences between four-year-olds and five-year-olds, and more specifically, the transitional nature of five-year-olds; that is, five-year-olds try to express the meaning of the experiences that they had.

This result seems reasonable when considering what kinds of components are added and expanded in the process of narrative development. Following Labov (1972), referential and affective (or evaluative) elements are both indispensable for an ideal narrative. Action statements serve to move the plotline forward as it proceeds from orientation statements, whereas affective (or evaluative) statements convey the narrator's attitudes toward the narrative events. As Hopper (1979) defines it, foreground information refers to the parts of the narrative that relate a sequence of events with respect to a timeline thus constituting *skeletal structure* of the narrative, and, in contrast, background information refers to supportive narrative (e.g. orientation, which presents static descriptions of the scene, and evaluation, which describes the agent's motives) that does not itself narrate the main events. Thus, there is evidence that a relationship exists between an individual's age and the amount of background information he or she adds to the narrative. Moreover, as seen in the increased use of evaluation clauses with age, the older individuals become, the more non-sequential information they add to the narrative, in order to emphasize why they want to tell the narrative. The results obtained in the present study, in fact, confirm previous studies of different narrative genres (such as narratives based on wordless picture book, not about personal experiences, e.g. Berman & Slobin, 1994) which found that 'young children would focus mainly on description of events and activities, whereas older narrators would provide more background information relating to the attendant circumstances in which the unfolding plotline events are embedded' (p. 45).[12]

Although the proportion of appendages did not vary with age, two different types of gender differences were observed. Boys used more appendages than girls. Mothers of boys, furthermore, used more appendages than did mothers of girls. The use of appendages may make the narrative more explicit and even blunt and masculine.[13] When the mother told her own experiences (i.e. earliest memories), her child was asked to be with her, because her narrative might differ when she was with her child from when she was alone. Telling a narrative with her son might have thus influenced the mother's narrative style to take an explicit, masculine style.

Relationships between mother's narrative and child's narrative

Generally, differences in maternal behavior might explain some differences in the behavior of the children, but the findings in this chapter do not support this relationship. While analysis of appendages has indicated that the proportion of children's appendages was positively associated with the proportion of mothers' appendages, as far as the total number of different words, the number of different words and the number of stories were concerned, no such relationships were found. These results indicate that talkative mothers do not necessarily have talkative children, and that reticent mothers do not necessarily have reticent children. Likewise, no strong relationships were identified between mothers and their children with regard to action, orientation and evaluation statements. These results also indicate, for example, that those mothers who frequently give evaluation statements do not necessarily have children who give many evaluation statements. The contrast in results between appendages and these other narrative elements seems to indicate that the mother–child relationship in narrative style is rather complicated. That is, the narrative component skills might be modeled implicitly by the mother for her child, and, in that sense, the importance of parental modeling should not be underestimated. In some cases, however, this hypothesis was not necessarily supported. The results shown in this chapter illustrate that the child does not just imitate or reproduce his or her mother's style; modeling does not necessarily play an influential role in some areas of child development.

To conclude, from a statistical point of view, this chapter has tried to illustrate (1) in what areas young Japanese children's narrative development takes place, and (2) similarities and differences between adult narrative productions and children's early narrative productions. The chapter has also analyzed the relationship between linguistic forms and their functions in children's language/narrative development. With age, children change and develop in their capacity to provide non-sequential information, in order to produce full-fledged, rhetorically well-formed narratives, as most adult narrators do. Also, while the findings presented in this chapter, particularly the overuse of available devices (e.g. three-verse stanzas), might show some instances of a U-shaped pattern of development (Berman, 1994; Berman & Slobin, 1994; Strauss & Stavy, 1982),[14] preschool children seem to have understood what the canonical narrative form is, and they gradually try to tell narratives in culture-specific ways. Thus, the study illuminates the ages at which various narrative components develop; the preschool years clearly represent a period of extremely rapid development in the child's acquisition of narrative capacity. It also illustrates that from early childhood on, Japanese children learn the narrative style valued by their mothers for their future successful participation in the culture in which they live. To answer the same questions – what narrative components Japanese use for framing events – from different angles, then, the next chapter will turn to a more qualitative examination of Japanese monologic narratives.

Notes

1. Rule 2 may sound somewhat strange to English speakers. As Clancy (1985) explains, however, because Japanese is a head-final (HF) language [as opposed to English that is a head-initial (HI) language], 'conjunctions appear at the end of the first of two conjoined clauses, rather than at the beginning of the second, although the latter is an optional possibility' (p. 374). Japanese conjunctions are, in fact, divided into two types: clause-initial and clause-final conjunctions. Following Maynard's (1990, p. 187) categorization, clause-initial conjunctions include *soshite/sorede/de* ('and,' 'and then'), *sorekara* ('and then'), *shikashi* ('but,' 'however'), *demo* ('but,' 'though') and *dakara/desukara* ('so,' 'therefore'). On the other hand, *kedo/ga/noni* ('though,' 'although') and *node* ('because') appear at the end of a clause and are thus categorized as clause-final conjunctions. Furthermore, according to Maynard, some conjunctions such as *keredomo* ('but,' 'however,' 'though,' 'although') may appear in either a clause-initial position or a clause-final one.

2. Because 'psychological complements' syntactically appear in main/matrix clauses, they are included in the main (first-level) categories. Semantically, however, 'psychological complements' are additional, such as *'seishinteki ni mo fuan dattan da, to omoun desu kedo'* ('[I] was frustrated psychologically, [I] think'), and *'sono toki ni hajimete kurai shinu tte yuu ninshiki ga dekita gurai datta, to omoun desu'* ('At that time first, [I] formed the recognition that [human beings] die, [I] think': for this example, see Stanza G in Example 5.5). These examples might give an impression that psychological complements are not matrix clauses because they appear at the end of the sentences. However, in contrast to English, which is a right-branching (RB), head-initial (HI) language, Japanese is a left-branching (LB), head-final (HF) language (Kuno, 1973). Thus, psychological complements, which appear at the end of sentences, syntactically appear to be main/matrix clauses.

   Semantically, however, psychological complements do not function as main/matrix clauses; in much the same way as in English, psychological complements in Japanese serve as sentence adjuncts. Because of this complementary nature, therefore, clauses categorized as 'psychological complements' are not counted as independent verses in verse/stanza analysis.

   Although they are additional, a more important semantic function of psychological complements is that, like 'think' and 'feel' in English, the Japanese verb phrase *omou*, which is always preceded by the quotative *to*, suggests the narrator's modesty, an important aspect in Japanese culture. That is, not only in narrative contexts but also in discursive interactions in general, expressing one's feelings without these psychological complements is certainly possible, but human beings – or Japanese in particular – generally prefer avoiding direct assertions. Even when disagreeing with someone else, by adding these psychological complements one can make one's statement much more polite (Maynard, 1990). Psychological complements therefore play an important role in softening the message that the speaker wants to convey. Many languages have a great number of words and phrases that can be categorized as hedges (Brown & Levinson, 1987), but using hedges or hedge-like expressions effectively is particularly important in Japanese society where harmonious human relationships and social interactions are greatly valued (Lebra, 1976).

3. As a cautionary note, this relationship does not necessarily apply to other genres. Unlike personal narratives, in scripts 'the topic or *foreground* of the narrative is the general case, whereas episodic information is the *background* or commentary' (Hudson & Shapiro, 1991, p. 94).

   Additionally, although temporal sequence means the non-reversibility of two narrative clauses without alteration of the original semantic interpretation of the story, many orientation clauses can begin with markers of simultaneity or sequence and are marked for tense in relation to the main line event clauses (e.g. while I lay sleeping, a giant bat flew into the room). Using the term 'temporal sequence' may, at times, misstate what is characteristic of main line event clauses.

4. Although outcomes appear fairly regularly on their own in English-speaking children's narratives, particularly in preschoolers' narratives, in their story grammar analysis McConaughy *et al.* (1983) define 'outcomes' as 'events or states produced by a character's actions' (p. 386). Their notion of 'outcome' is regulated by certain rewrite rules that indicate 'how the grammar is used to describe the organization of story information in terms of an abstract hierarchical tree' (p. 387). The 'outcome' defined here shares certain aspects with the one defined by McConaughy *et al.* (1983).

5. As can be seen in this case, whenever the population variances are not assumed to be equal, the *t*-statistic based on unequal variances was used. When the variances of the two samples were quite different, therefore, this procedure reduced the degrees of freedom. This is why the degrees of freedom are sometimes different.

6. For four-year-olds, the proportion of one-verse stanzas to the total number of stanzas produced by an individual child ranged from 0 to 42.86%; the proportion of two-verse stanzas ranged from 0 to 100%; the proportion of three-verse stanzas ranged from 0 to 50%; and the proportion of four or more-verse stanzas ranged from 0 to 50%.

   Likewise, for five-year-olds, the proportion of one-verse stanzas ranged from 0 to 33.33%; the proportion of two-verse stanzas ranged from 0 to 66.67%; the proportion of three-verse stanzas ranged from 0 to 75%; and the proportion of four or more-verse stanzas ranged from 0 to 75%.

7. To test for the effect of group and gender, two-way (group × gender) analyses of variance were also conducted on these variables. ANOVA run for four-verse stanzas revealed that there was a marginal interaction effect of group and gender, $F(1, 16) = 4.18$, $p = 0.06$, as well as a marginal main effect of group, $F(1, 16) = 3.45$, $p = 0.08$. This interaction effect shows that the effect of 'group' differs by 'gender.' That is, five-year-old females ($M = 47.38$, $SD = 18.22$) gave proportionately more four or more-verse stanzas than did five-year-old males ($M = 18.33$, $SD = 17.08$); on the other hand, four-year-old males ($M = 20.00$, $SD = 21.73$) gave proportionately more four or more-verse stanzas than did four-year-old females. These results may indicate that developmental patterns differ by gender.

8. As was previously mentioned in the explanation of the coding rules, ignoring subcategories may result in gross simplification. For example, the narrative clause, *'hahaoya ni sugoku shikarareta'* ('[I] was **heavily** scolded by my mother') describes a specific action that took place. At the same time, however, because the clause is accompanied by an evaluative tone, it is categorized as 'action

with evaluation.' In other words, the clause is classified as both 'action' and 'evaluation.' As far as three major elements – action, orientation, and evaluation – are concerned, therefore, irrespective of the level of categorization (first level or second), whenever one of these variables appears, it is counted as one appearance. Therefore, because many comments are counted twice here, the proportions do not add up to 100%.

9. No differences approached statistical significance between four-year-olds and five-year-olds. This result nicely corresponds to the results reported by Peterson and McCabe (1983), who traced the development of orientation in the narratives of children between 3;6 and 9;6. According to these researchers, although older children provided more orientative comments, younger children provided the same number of orientation statements as older children, if length of the narrative was controlled for.

10. Using a two-sample t statistic, where the variance of each group is estimated separately, is appropriate whenever the population variances are not assumed to be equal, as is the case here.

11. Additionally, the proportion of mothers' action statements was positively associated with the proportion of children's appendages, $r(18) = 0.76$, $p < 0.0001$, suggesting that those mothers who give many action statements tend to have children who give many appendages. Furthermore, the proportion of mothers' action statements was marginally associated with children's gender, $r(18) = 0.41$, $p < 0.08$, implying that mothers of boys are more likely to provide action statements than mothers of girls.

12. Berman (1994) also states: 'In talking about what has happened, young children typically focus on events and activities, and pay minimal attention to motivational, evaluative, and other background elements' (p. 2).

13. The relationship between explicitness and masculinity seems to exist in the Japanese language. As Shibatani (1990) explains, females use more polite language than males; as can be seen in the use of the formal *mas(u)* style in *to omoimasu* ('[I] think') and *sumi masen* ('[I] am sorry.' 'Excuse me.' 'Thank you'), the politeness in females' speech is based on more frequent use of honorific forms, which may make their statement somewhat less explicit. [Note: *Sumi masen*, which is one of the apologetic expressions in Japanese, has multiple functions, such as (1) a request marker, (2) an attention-getting device, (3) a closing marker, (4) a regret marker, and (5) a gratitude marker (Kimura, 1994).] Conversely, males' speech sometimes lacks honorific forms, which may make their statements more explicit.

14. According to Berman and Slobin's (1994) explanation, children in the late preschool or early school-age period 'tend either to omit information that is necessary to the listener or to overuse available devices'; moreover, 'at the phase where children have just gained mastery of a particular system, they tend to use the relevant devices quite redundantly' (p. 609). Thus, U-shaped behavioral growth curves might explain the extraordinary regularity of verses per stanza demonstrated not only by the late preschool children in the present study but also by the early elementary school-aged children in Minami (1990) and Minami and McCabe (1991, 1993, 1995).

Chapter 5
Monologic Narrative Structure in Japanese

Language may be a uniquely human trait, but specific styles of communication are shaped by specific cultures and societies. Communication, in this sense, is a product of culture. The statistical analysis in Chapter 4 revealed some characteristic features of Japanese monologic narratives. With data on oral personal narratives told by Japanese preschoolers and adults, and with verse/stanza analysis (Gee, 1985; Hymes, 1981) and high point analysis based on the Labovian approach (Labov, 1972; Peterson & McCabe, 1983), it was discovered that children's and adults' narratives are similar in terms of structure in that they both tend to have three verses per stanza, and that children and adults tend to tell about multiple experiences. By contrast, there are some clear differences in terms of content and delivery. Whereas children tend to tell their stories in a sequential style, adults emphasize non-sequential information. Specifically, compared to children's narratives, adults' narratives place considerably more weight on background information, such as orientation and evaluation. This chapter tries to support the results obtained from the statistical analysis in Chapter 4 and further deepen the understanding of monologic narrative, specifically by illustrating similarities and differences between children's early narrative production and adults' full-fledged narrative production. The chapter further presents empirical evidence of Japanese preschool children's (1) narrative discourse competence and narrative structure and (2) rhetorical/expressive flexibility, compared to adults. The findings of this study strongly suggest that oral personal narratives told by Japanese preschoolers do not represent the final phase of development, particularly in terms of deploying effective linguistic devices and narrative strategies in order to express feelings and emotions. Rather, they still have a long way to go.

Narrative Discourse Competence and Narrative Structure

Narratives are tellings about past events not simple representations of memory. For instance, personal narratives, which involve a description of a past experience, are the primary means by which an individual makes sense of his or her experience. Furthermore, substantial cross-cultural differences have been identified in terms of narrative structure (McCabe, 1996). When telling narratives, Japanese narrators, for example, tend to opt for dispensing with nominal references to entities that they assume to be in the focus of listeners' consciousness (Downing, 1980). Although such ellipses potentially result in considerable ambiguity (Clancy, 1980, 1992; Hinds, 1984), a variety of emotive devices and manipulative strategies are deployed in Japanese narrative discourse, so that a narrator can convey his or her emotion to the listener successfully and effectively (Maynard, 1993).

Chapter 5 continues to analyze instances of Japanese oral personal narratives told by preschool children and adults, in order to detail the emergence of a culture-specific narrative style in Japanese children and to investigate differences between children's early narrative production and adults' narrative production. Specifically, this chapter discusses (1) what linguistic devices and narrative strategies young Japanese children already have at their disposal in their narrative tellings and (2) what narrative strategies they have yet to apply to their narrative tellings, compared to adult narrators. Through these comparisons, the chapter tries to answer a fundamental question of how, in narrative style, the sequence of clauses is organized in relation to the sequence of events that took place.

In terms of how adults deploy a variety of expressive options and rhetorical/linguistic devices to encode the narrator's perspective, this chapter also examines the effective use of proper verb-ending forms. Cognitive parameters relating to 'perspective taking' have received a great deal of attention in various fields. Frame theory (Chafe, 1977; Schank & Abelson, 1977) is based on the belief that human beings develop mental/cognitive frameworks to aid their comprehension of stories. Frame theory purports that the human mind, which generates narrative, is guided by the cognitive schema of governing the storing and retrieval of stories (Chafe, 1990). More specifically, the theory views the cognitive comprehension of real-life situations in terms of story schemas (i.e. structures in semantic memory that specify the general arrangement or flow of information in storytelling). As far as Japanese narratives are concerned, examining verb-ending forms gives an important clue to understanding the narrator's mental framework in general and his or her perspective in particular.

Furthermore, following a certain story schema, narrators may manipulate and construct their recollections; the act of telling stories is selective, constructive and reconstructive. Linguistic research concerning *point of view* has demonstrated that speakers take on particular points of view naturally (e.g. Bamberg, 1997a, 1997b). In the context of discourse, for example, Kuno (1987) proposed the notion of empathy perspective: the speaker represents his or her attitude toward event characters in different ways, as if changing camera angles. That is, the speaker has more than one way to express a certain event by identifying himself or herself with one of the event characters without altering the logical contents of the event. Kuno called this speaker's identification with the event participant 'empathy,' and the implication is that empathy plays a crucial role in constructing discourse.

Perspective taking is obviously not limited to individual speech acts. In the field of narrative, Bamberg (1997c) also proposed the notion of 'positioning,' in which he tried to see space, time and character as construction elements for discourse purposes, such as ' "my brother ran into my fist' versus 'I hit my brother with my fist" ' (p. 101). Therefore, as Stanzel (1984) claimed, one of the important psychological frames is the parameter of observational viewpoint (or perspective), although perspective taking emerges in various forms. For instance, in the teller mode a narrator relays the information, whereas in the reflector mode events appear to surface from the reflector character's perspective.

Although the above examples illustrate various roles of cognitive parameters relating to perspective taking, a more relevant issue in this chapter is how the adult narrator changes his or her position in relation to the listener and the narrative topic. When a narrator who has access to a certain distant topic tells a narrative about that topic, a triangular relationship emerges: the narrator, the narrative topic and the listener (Toolan, 1988) (see Figure 5.1). As the narrator is increasingly engrossed in the topic, he or she distances himself or herself from the listener; that is, a shift occurs from narrative external (i.e. a closer relation between the narrator and the listener rather than the relation between the narrator and the topic) to narrative internal (i.e. a closer relation between the narrator and the topic rather than the relation between the narrator and the listener) (see Figure 5.2). Focusing on external/internal perspective taking, Weist (1986) identified that a Polish narrator takes an external and an internal perspective on situations by distinguishing tense and aspect. As this chapter will reveal later, in the case of Japanese, by

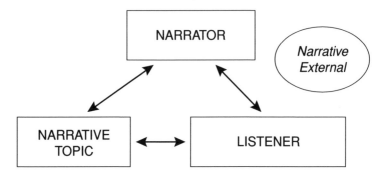

Figure 5.1 Triangular relationship between narrator, narrative topic, and listener: narrative external perspective taking [adapted from Toolan (1988)]

changing verb-ending forms, the narrator's perspective is explicitly woven into narrative accounts.

To summarize, this chapter has a threefold purpose: (1) to identify how Japanese preschoolers turn their experiences into narrative and to examine what developmental features are exhibited in their narratives, (2) to describe how Japanese adults turn their experiences into narrative and to show what the culturally appropriate full-fledged narrative looks like, and (3) to illustrate what similarities and differences exist between children's and adults' narratives. The chapter, which examines narrative devices developmentally as well as across ages, thus tries to approach the previously posed questions from a different angle:

(1) How do Japanese four- and five-year-olds transform their experiences into narrative? What do the differences between these two age groups tell us about their development?
(2) How do Japanese adults (i.e. mothers) transform their experiences into narrative? Are there any similarities and/or differences between adults' narrative style and children's narrative style?
(3) Are there any similarities between children's and adults' narratives? If there are, in what ways are they similar to each other?
(4) Are there any differences between children's and adults' narratives? If there are, in what ways are they different from each other? Also, what factors account for the differences: cognitive, linguistic or social-interactional (communicative) factors?

Briefly, in what follows, I will demonstrate the following: the data illustrate that adults make use of a richer range of expressive options than

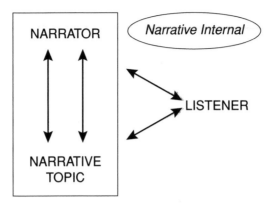

Figure 5.2 Triangular relationship between narrator, narrative topic, and listener: narrative internal perspective taking [adapted from Toolan (1988)]

children, and that adults employ a variety of linguistic means and rhetorical devices, such as the effective use of proper verb-ending forms, to encode the narrator's perspective. Children do not distinguish these subtleties.

Children's Narrative Structure

As mentioned previously, in this chapter I hope to show how a combination of quantitative and qualitative analysis enhances a basically quantitative presentation of language data. In the previous chapter verse/stanza analysis and high point analysis were introduced as effective vehicles for analyzing Japanese narratives. Both analyses have been applied to Example 5.1, from Ryota, a boy aged 3;8. His narrative was broken down into an aggregate of structural components. I argue that the basic-level category of verse/stanza analysis is stanza (see Coding Rule 3 of verse/stanza analysis in Chapter 4). Also, the subordinate-level categories are verse and line; the numbers to the right refer to the lines (the minimum unit) produced, and small letters (a–j) in parentheses indicate the beginning of each verse. Following Hymes (1982) and Gee (1991a, 1991b), furthermore, closely related stanzas are grouped as a section. Verse/stanza analysis reveals a hierarchical structure, reflective of the experiences described in a narrative.

Another method used to analyze narrative structure stems from Labov's (1972) seminal study of narrative syntax. Recall that Labov and his colleagues (Labov, 1972, 1981; Labov & Waletzky, 1967) claimed that oral versions of personal experience provide the simplest, but most fundamental narrative structures, and proposed a six-part structure of a fully formed oral narrative: abstract (i.e. summary at the beginning); orientation (which provides information about characters, setting, time and place); complicating action (which includes specific events and actions); evaluation (i.e. evaluative comments); resolution (i.e. final outcome of complicating actions) and Coda (i.e. formalized ending). Among these six components, orientation and evaluation, which are both categorized as free narrative clauses, and complicating action, which is categorized as restricted narrative clauses, are the three major narrative components required for a good narrative (Labov, 1972). Orientations provide attributes of people and objects, whereas evaluation refers to the subjective significance of an event for the narrator. Complicating actions lead up to a high point just before the resolution that completes the narrative. This method was later called high point analysis by Peterson and McCabe (1983) in their study of children's developmental transitions in producing narratives at different ages.

High-point analysis coding is informative in the ways in which it is used to code the content of those units identified by the use of verse/stanza analysis. For instance, at the beginning of his narrative, Ryota placed an appendage (APP), more specifically, an attention-getter (ATT) so that he could attract the listener's attention. Other verses that fall into the categories of action, orientation and evaluation are indicated as ACT, ORT and EVL, respectively. Additionally, to indicate the interviewer's utterances, INT is inserted in children's narratives. Notice that, despite frequent insertions of INT, compared to adults' narratives (which will be presented later), children's narratives have a more compact and easily observable structure.

Example 5.1 Ryota's monologic narrative
SECTION I
Stanza A

(a)	APP:ATT	*boku shitteru wa.*	1
		'I know (something).'	
(b)		*ano **ne**,*	2
		'well, you know,'	
		(INT: *un*)	
		'uh huh'	
	ORT	*sunaba de,*	3
		'in a sandbox,'	
(c)	ACT:EVL	***dokaan tte ne**,*	4
		'with a bang, you know,'	

	ano ne,			5
	'well, you know,'			
		(INT:	*un*)	
			'uh huh'	
	pataan tte ochite ne.			6
	'with a bang, (ø)[1] fell, you know.'			

SECTION II
Stanza B

(d)	*Mari chan ga ne,*			7
	'Mari, you know,'			
		(INT:	*un*)	
			'uh huh'	
	ano ne,			8
	'well, you know,'			
		(INT:	*un*)	
			'uh huh'	
ORT	*ato kooen de ne,*			9
	'besides, in the park, you know,'			
ACT	*ochitan.*			10
	'(ø) fell.'			
		(INT:	*sorede*)	
			'then'	
(e)	*un, ano ne,*			11
	'yes, you know,'			
		(INT:	*un*)	
	'uh huh'			
ORT	*buranko de ne,*			12
	'from a swing, you know,'			
ACT:EVL	*dokaan tte ochita.*			13
	'with a bang, (ø) fell.'			

Stanza C

(f) ACT	*un, sorede ne,*			14
	'yes, then, you know,'			
		(INT:	*un*)	
			'uh huh'	
	ano ne,			15
	'well you know,'			
	suberu to ne,			16
	'when (ø) slid, you know,'			
		(INT:	*un*)	
			'uh huh'	
(g) EVL	*juujuujuujuu tte.*			17
	'slip slip slip slip.'			
		(INT:	*sorede*)	
			'then'	

Stanza D

(h) ORT	*Mari chan wa ne,*			18

'Mari, you know,'

			(INT:	*un*)	
				'uh huh'	

              asoko no kooen de ne,   19

              'to that park, you know,'

			(INT:	*un*)	
				'uh huh'	

(i)   ACT   *buranko ittete ne,*   20

              '(ø) went to play a swing, you know,'

			(INT:	*un*)	
				'uh huh'	

(j)   ACT:EVL   *doboon tte ne,*   21

              'with a bang, you know,'

			(INT:	*un*)	
				'uh huh'	

              ochita no.   22

              '(ø) fell.'

Note: INT = interviewer

Acquisition of syntactic and pragmatic particles

Ryota's narrative in Example 5.1 indicates that he has mastered a variety of linguistic devices in his early stages of language acquisition. To begin with, different types of particles appear in his narrative: (1) a case particle *ga*, which marks the subject, appears in Line 7; (2) another case particle *wa*, which marks the topic or theme of a statement, appears in Line 18; (3) an interactional particle *ne* ('you know,' 'right?', 'don't you agree?', or a tag question), by which the narrator seeks the listener's acknowledgment and thus tries to establish rapport between the narrator and the listener, appears at many line-final as well as verse-final positions; and (4) the quotation-final particle *tte*, which is attached to an onomatopoeia, appears in Lines 4, 6, 13, 17 and 21. [Note: With regard to the quotation-final particle, recall a Japanese elementary school boy's narrative in Example 2.2 in Chapter 2.]

Telling multiple stories by effectively using case particles with different functions. In Example 5.1, when asked, 'Have you ever gotten hurt?' Ryota told two different injury stories: (1) his own injury in a nearby park (i.e. personal experience), and (2) his friend Mari's injury in the same park (i.e. someone else's experience that the narrator witnessed). Because the subject is omitted in Stanza A, who fell in a sandbox, making big sounds, is not clear (Lines 4–6). If Mari had fallen, what Ryota narrated in Stanza B would be a continuation of the story in Stanza A. However, because Ryota was asked by the interviewer whether he had gotten hurt, the subject of the narrative in Stanza A was clearly established as 'I' and thus omitted. In other words, because the character of the narrative had already been established and agreed upon by the narrator and the listener, the subject was not necessary. Therefore, Ryota was not remiss in failing to identify the subject of his utterances; he was responding according to culturally accepted practice of subject ellipsis (Clancy, 1980).

Although case markers are sometimes optional in Japanese, two different types of particles mark the subject of a sentence for different purposes. The subject on first mention (i.e. new information) is marked by the particle *ga* (subject marker),[2] whereas the subject that serves as the theme or topic of the sentence (i.e. old or given information) is marked by *wa* (thematic or topic marker) (Hinds, 1984; Kuno, 1973; Maynard, 1990).[3] Ryota's use of case marking presents further evidence that the main character of Stanza B is different from that of Stanza A. At the beginning of Stanza B (Verse (d), Line 6), Ryota introduced a proper noun, Mari (the name of a three-year, 11-month-old girl), to refer to the main character of the story. Moreover, although *ga* is sometimes used for a 'staging effect' (which is a metaphor of spotlighting a character, who has already been introduced, playing on the stage) (Maynard, 1997), it generally marks new information at any given point in narrative discourse, and thus labels the story in Stanza B as distinct from the story in Stanza A. In subsequent Verses (e) and (f) in Stanza C, the subjects are omitted because the main character Mari has already been introduced in the preceding Verse (d) and thus is established as old or given information.

Like English, in Japanese in order for the referent to serve as the theme or topic of a sentence, it should have already been introduced into the flow of information. Thus, by using the topic marker *wa*, the young narrator signaled that he would restate what had happened to his friend in the nearby park. Stanza D basically provides the same information as Stanza B. Ryota, once again, chose a proper noun to refer to the main character of his narrative. By using a nominal reference, he tried to make the main character of the story once again prominent. However, in contrast to Stanza B, in which Ryota chose the subject marker *ga* (to mark new information, Mari in this case), to begin Stanza D, Ryota chose the topic marker *wa* (Verse (h), Line 18), which is usually attached to mark old or given information, because in this stanza he continued to talk about what had happened to Mari.

The effective use of an interactional particle 'ne' to promote rapport between the narrator and the listener. Another noticeable aspect in

Ryota's narrative in Example 5.1 is frequent use of the particle *ne*. Minami (1990, 1994, 1996a, 1996b) and Minami and McCabe (1991, 1993, 1995) note that Japanese children use particles such as *ne* as a pragmatic punctuation device, signaling a break between two lines or, less regularly, between two verses. Similarly, Uchida (1986) maintains that Japanese children constantly use *ne* at the boundary of a grammatical unit, such as a sentence or a phrase boundary. Moreover, as 'you know' in English is used as an indicator of contextualization (Scollon & Scollon, 1981), in oral Japanese narrative discourse, *ne* is, in a sense, an attention-getting device. By uttering *ne*, the narrator waits for a brief acknowledgment from the listener,[4] such as 'uh huh.' Maynard (1989) states that 'storytelling is a joint activity between the storyteller and the story recipient,' and that 'the recipient plays an important role by co-authoring the text as well as by negotiating the meaning of Narrative Event' (p. 99). In this way, interlocutors establish and maintain a shared universe of discourse. Example 5.1 demonstrates how, through brief acknowledgment, even a supposedly monologic narrative is co-constructed by the young child and the listener, and is thus dialogic by nature.

Japanese *ne* does not always signal a break between verses, as stated previously in Coding Rule 1 for verse/stanza analysis (see Chapter 4). In Example 5.1, for instance, Verse (c) includes three *ne*s. The first two *ne*s each indicate a break between two lines, whereas the third one signals a break between verses because it follows the completion of a statement. Similarly, *ne*s that appear in Lines 16 and 20 demarcate Verses (f) and (i), respectively. Note that *ne*s that signal a break between verses come after a verb, whereas *ne*s that signal a break between lines do not come after a verb. Thus, spoken Japanese is produced in smaller units (Lines 1–22) than traditional grammatical ones, such as a sentence or a clause. Segmented by pragmatic markers, such as *ne* in '*dokaan tte ne*' ('with a bang, you know'), these smaller parts serve as units in Japanese oral narrative. [Note that the unit described here corresponds to what Maynard (1989) calls a pause-bounded phrasal unit. For more information, see Chapter 6.] The example above thus illustrates how preschool children construct narratives by using this pragmatic punctuation device at intersentential as well as intrasentential positions.

The effective use of the quotation-final particle 'tte' for both reported speech and onomatopoeia. Example 5.2, which is told by Sho, a boy aged 4;6, presents another interesting aspect, namely, that reported speech in Japanese is completed by simply adding the quotation-final particle *tte* at the end (but before the verb itta ['said']). Unlike English,

Japanese does not have an explicit grammatical distinction between direct and indirect speech. Also unlike English, in which indirect speech generally requires a rule for agreement of tense, Japanese does not require agreement of tense (Kuno, 1973). Compared to English, therefore, the grammar of quotation is much simpler in Japanese. In this example, Sho was prompted to talk about what had happened to him when getting a shot at the doctor's office. As can be seen from the high-point analysis coding, 'reported speech (RPT) with an explicit verb (EXP)' appears in Lines 10 and 11. In these lines, the quotation-final particle *tte* is morphological and is comparable to the line- and verse-final particle *ne*. The quotation-final particle *tte* can be also used to report examples of onomatopoeia, as seen in Example 5.1. Thus, the function of adding *tte* to reported speech is exactly the same as that of quoting onomatopoeia (i.e. citing speech and reporting sounds are accomplished by adding the same particle).

Example 5.2   Sho's monologic narrative
Stanza A

(a)		*ehtto **ne**,*			1
		'Um, you know,'			
			(INT:	*un)*	
				'uh huh'	
	ACT:EVL	*eh, naita.*			2
		'um, (ø) cried.'			
(b)		*uun ehtto **ne**,*			3
		'um, you know,'			
			(INT:	*un)*	
				'uh huh'	
	ACT:EVL	*dare ka Yamada Ryosuke kun to boku **wa** naita kedo **ne**,*			4
		'someone, Ryosuke Yamada and I cried, though, you know.'			
			(INT:	*un)*	
				'uh huh'	
(c)	EVL	*uun Haruki kun to **ne**,*			5
		'um, Haruki and, you know,'			
			(INT:	*un)*	
				'uh huh'	
		*ehtto **ne**,*			6
		'um, you know,'			
			(INT:	*un)*	
				'uh huh'	
		*dareka Yamada Nagao kun **wa** nakanakatta kedo,*			7
		'someone, Nagao Yamada didn't cry, though.'			
			(INT:	*un)*	
				'uh huh'	
(d)	ACT:EVL	*Shosuke kun to Yamada Ryosuke kun to boku **wa** naita.*			8
		'Shosuke and Ryosuke Yamada and I cried.'			

Stanza B
(e)   *ehtto ne,*   9
                             'um, you know,'
                                                        (INT: *un)*
                                                                'uh huh'
        RPT:EXP   *"itai,"*   10
                             ' "ouch," '
                             tte itta.   11
                             said (ø).'
(f)   ACT:EVL   *de, naita no.*   12
                            'and then (ø) cried.'
                                                        (INT: *so, sorede)*
                                                                'and then'

Stanza C
(g)   EVL   *demo ne,*   13
                            'but, you know,'
                                                        (INT: *un)*
                                                                'uh huh'
                            itai kedo ne,   14
                            'it hurt, though, you know.'
                                                        (INT: *un)*
                                                                'uh huh'
(h)   EVL   *hoochoo mitai.*   15
                            '(hurts) like a kitchen knife.'
(i)   EVL   *shinisoo datta.*   16
                            '(ø) was about to die.'
                                                        (INT: *honto)*
                                                                'really'
Stanza D
(j)   *ehtto ne,*   17
                            'um, you know,'
                                                        (INT: *un)*
                                                                'uh huh'
        ORT:EVL   *teppoo mitai datta kara ne,*   18
                                '(the syringe) looked like a pistol, you know,'
                                                        (INT: *un)*
                                                                'uh huh'
(k)   ACT:EVL   *konna ni marui non totte ne,*   19
                            '(the doctor) took out a round one like this, you know,'
                                                        (INT: *un)*
                                                                'uh huh'
(l)   *ehtto ne,*   20
                            'um, you know,'
                                                        (INT: *un)*
                                                                'uh huh'
        ACT   *nanka hikkurigaeshitotta marui no koo.*   21
                            '(the doctor) turned over a round one like this.'

(m)	*ano **ne**,*	22
	'um, you know,'	
ORT	*shiroi no.*	23
	'a white one.'	
	(INT: *honto*)	
	'really'	

Mastery of a special function of the case particle 'wa' at an early age. From the existence of a particular use of a case particle in Sho's narrative, it is evident that four-year-olds can plan ahead to tell multiple stories during the stage of narrative planning. Specifically, this is demonstrated in his mastery of an unusual usage of the case particle *wa*. Although, as previously explained, *wa* usually marks the topic or theme of a statement, two *wa*s that appear in this example serve a special function. Using *wa* in Lines 4 and 7, Sho introduced his friends for the first time. However, because he used a non-anaphoric reference *dareka* ('someone') at the beginning of each of these two lines, it is clear that the referents had not previously been introduced into the registry of the narrative discourse (this choice of word for first mention [*dareka*] is an example of Sho's sophisticated language use). As previously explained, the noun phrases on first mention are usually marked by *ga*. In Lines 4 and 7, however, Sho employed a special use of *wa*, which provides further evidence of his complex mastery of Japanese usage. That is, although the case particle *wa* is often considered a topic or thematic marker, Sho's uses of it in Lines 4 and 7 are not examples of topical or thematic marking. In this case, *wa* is used for contrastive purposes to indicate change of subject.[5] Verse (b) focuses on who cried when getting a shot; Verse (c), in contrast, tells the listener about who did not cry; and Verse (d) once again goes back to who cried. Unlike the use of *wa* as the thematic or topic marker, the contrastive use of *wa* is appropriate whether or not the referents have already been introduced into the present narrative discourse. As seen in this case, when the narrator introduces multiple topics or examples within a narrative, *wa* carries a contrastive meaning (also, recall Examples 1.1, 1.2 and 2.2 told by Japanese elementary school children in Chapters 1 and 2). Moreover, *ne* is an attention-getting device, and hence, when combined with the contrastive marker *wa*, it marks illocutionary force; that is, the combination of the syntactic particle *wa* and the pragmatic particle *ne* send a strong cue that the narrator is drawing attention to a contrasting pair.

Emphasis on Foreground Information

When a synthesis of verse/stanza analysis and high point analysis was applied to the narrative of Akio, a boy aged 5;4, the following organization was identified. Note that in addition to the first-level high-point analysis codes previously explained, two second-level codes appear in this example: coda (COD) and outcome (OUT).

Example 5.3   Akio's monologic narrative

Stanza A

(a)	ACT:ORT	*ano **ne**,*			1
		'Um, you know,'			
			(INT:	*un)*	
				'uh huh'	
		*supiido **dashite itara ne**,*			2
		'(I) was speeding, you know,'			
			(INT:	*un)*	
				'uh huh'	
(b)	ACT	*koronde,*			3
		'(I) fell,'			
(c)	ACT:OUT	*handoru magatte **ne**.*			4
		'the handlebars became bent, you know.'			

Stanza B

(d)	ACT	*odeko no byooin itte **ne**,*			5
		'(I) went to the forehead hospital,[6] you know,'			
(e)	ACT	*ano **ne**,*			6
		'um, you know,'			
			(INT:	*un sorede)*	
				'yeah, then'	
		*byooin itte **ne**,*			7
		'(I) went to the hospital, you know,'			
(f)	ACT	*sorede **ne**,*			8
		'then, you know,'			
			(INT:	*un)*	
				'uh huh'	
		*koko maite moratte **ne**,*			9
		'(I) had this (part) bandaged, you know,'			
			(INT:	*un)*	
				'uh huh'	
		odeko.			10
		'the forehead.'			
			(INT:	*un)*	
				'uh huh'	

Stanza C

(g)	ACT	*sorede **ne**,*		11
		'then, you know ,'		
		*ojiichan to obaachan ga **ne**,*		12
		'my grandpa and grandma, you know,'		
			(INT: *un*)	
			'uh huh'	
		arare o motte kite,		13
		'brought rice cake cubes,'		
(h)	ACT	*tabe te,*		14
		'(I) ate (those cakes),'		
(i)	EVL:OUT	*sorede **ne**,*		15
		'then, you know,'		
		daibu naotte kita.		16
		'(I) became very much okay.'		
			(INT: *ah honto,*	
			sorede)	
			'uh really,	
			then'	

Stanza D

(j)	APP:COD	*owari.*	17
		'that's it.'	

Verses (a-c) represent an 'action with orientation,' an 'action,' and an 'action with outcome,' respectively. Although Verse (a) is presented in the past progressive form *V-te i* (*dashi-te i* = be speeding) and thus provides the setting of the narrative (i.e. backgrounding), the verse still describes a specific action, 'speeding' (i.e. foregrounding).[7] Because Verse (c) describes a consequence of Verse (b), it is subcategorized as an outcome. At the same time, however, because Verse (c) is a specific event that took place ('the handlebars became bent') it should be categorized as an action. Therefore, the three verses in Stanza A describe a sequence of actions.

In this sense, because all components of stanza B represent an action sequence, they are similar to those of Stanza A. In Verse (f) Akio added information by placing a noun phrase (NP) *odeko* ('forehead') after the main verb, so that the listener could better understand where he had gotten injured. In Japanese, constituents that are placed after the main verb are typically described as 'afterthoughts.' The narrator adds on more specific information to the clause at the end, having belatedly realized that the listener will need more specific information to understand what the narrator has described (Clancy, 1985). This syntactic strategy can also be considered some type of right dislocation; that is, the narrator moves an NP from its position within a clause and leaves a pronoun copy of the NP in that position (Akmajian & Heny, 1980), *koko* ('this') in this case (Line 9). Adding further information after having completed an utterance thus helps the narrator increase his or her production in terms of the number of lines or even sometimes verses per stanza.

As can be seen in the presence of the subject marker *ga* in Line 12, because Stanza C introduces new characters (i.e. Akio's grandparents), the stanza is more complicated than the previous two stanzas. However, the omitted subject in the subsequent Verse (h) is the narrator himself. Furthermore, although Verse (i), *'sorede ne, daibu naotte kita'* ('then, you know, [ø] became very much okay'), serves an evaluative function, because it is subcategorized as an outcome, the function of the verse is somewhat different from a simple evaluation category. In other words, the events described in Verses (g) and (h) and Verse (i) represent a chronological sequence. Thus, Akio closely followed the temporal sequence of the events in Stanza C, too.

In Stanza D, Akio departed from the canonical three-verse pattern and concluded the story with a coda (*'owari'*: 'that's it'). To present his injury experience in this narrative, however, Akio mostly used three chrono-logical verses in a time sequence. In other words, although he chained events sequentially and structured his narrative causally, he did not necessarily elaborate on background information such as emotional states.

Example 5.4, which is told by Yuka, a girl aged 5;6, identifies the characteristic features of Japanese preschool children's narratives described in this section. First, as seen in Ryota's narrative in Example 5.1, Yuka talked about more than one time she was injured in one turn of talk: (1) a fall outside, and (2) a sore from a shoe. Second, the main theme of the narrative is described in a brief manner; that is, as was clearly seen in Akio's narrative, Yuka closely followed the temporal sequence of events without paying much attention to providing back-ground information, particularly her emotional states. Although Akio and Yuka share the chronological sequencing/chaining of narrative orga-nization (i.e. clear signs of a temporal organization), Akio's inclusion of actions by participants other than himself (i.e. his grandparents in Stanza C) as a subplot shows his sensitivity to narrative-setting as well as his ability to provide more elaborate temporal transitions summarized as referential elements, to borrow Labov's (1972) term. Yuka, on the other hand, fails to provide fully developed accounts in terms of temporal or causal interrelations. Akio's narrative, thus including more complex types of actions and relations, demonstrates the emergence of a richer time sequence.

Example 5.4   Yuka's monologic narrative
SECTION I
Stanza A

(a)	ACT:ORT	*hashittete.*	1
		'(I) was running.'	
(b)	ACT:OUT	*koronda.*	2
		'(I) fell.'	
(c)	ORT	*osoto de.*	3
		'(that happened) outside.'	

Stanza B

(d)	ACT:EVL	*chi deta.*	4
		'blood came out.'	
(e)	ACT	*teepu hatta.*	5
		'(I) put a Band-Aid on.'	

SECTION II
Stanza C

(f)	ORT	*chuookoen de ne,*	6
		'in the central park, you know,'	
(g)	ACT	*koko kutsuzure shita.*	7
		'(I) had a shoe sore.'	
(h)	ACT	*sorede, teepu hatta.*	8
		'then, (I) put a Band-Aid on.'	
(i)	EVL:OUT	*sorede moo naotta.*	9
		'then, (I) became all right.'	

Adults' Narrative Structure

Adult narratives

We now turn to an explanation of adult narrative style. The main aim of this section is to explore in detail what kinds of linguistic devices and strategies – free grammatical morphemes (functors, closed-class items), such as particles and connectives, as well as other lexical items – are deployed in adults' narratives in order to convey pertinent background information to the listener.[8] By studying the relationship between form and function in adult narratives, in this section I examine a range of examples of fully-fledged narratives. Example 5.5 is from Akira's mother. Like the children's narratives, if this narrative is arranged by grouping lines and verses thematically into collections of stanzas and sections, a distinctive form emerges from such interpretation. Although adults' narratives might not, in general, have the strong verse-like characteristics observed in young children's narratives, the inclination to versify still exists.

Example 5.5   A Japanese adult's (Akira's mother) monologic narrative
Stanza A
(a) EVL   *honto yuuto, anoo,*   1
                 'To tell the truth, well,'
                 anmari oboete nain desu, hotondo.   2
                 '(I) rarely remember anything.'
(b) ORT   *sorede, ehtto, oboeteru no ga shoogakkoo no ninensei gurai,*   3
                 'And, um, what (I) remember was when (I) was in second grade'
                 dattan desu kedo,   4
                 '(it) was, though.'
(c) APP:ABS   *anoo, onaji kurasu no otoko no ko ga,*   5
                 'Well, a boy in the same class,'
                 shinjattan desu.   6
                 'died.'
(d) EVL   **dakara**, *sono koto dake wa sugoku hakkiri oboete **masu** ne.* 7
                 'Therefore, (I) remember only that thing clearly, you know.'

Stanza B
(e) ORT:EVL   *anoo, warito kurasu no naka demo nantonaku hikarerutte yuu ka,* 8
                 'Well, in the class (he) was a boy to whom (I) was drawn for
                 some reason.'
(f) ORT:EVL   *anoo, ki ni naru sonzai no otoko no ko de.*   9
                 'Well, (he) was a kind of boy who was always on my mind.'

Stanza C
(g) ORT   *de, natsu yasumi ga owatte,*   10
                 'And the summer vacation was over.'
(h) ORT   *ehtto, shigyoo shiki **desu** ne,*   11
                 'Um, an opening ceremony, you know,'
(i) ACT   *ittara,*   12
                 '(I) went to (an opening ceremony).'
(j) ACT:ORT   *anoo, kyooshitsu e koo haitte yuki **mashitara**,*   13
                 'Well, (I) was entering the classroom like this.'
(k) ORT:EVL   *minna fudan to nan ka chigaun desu **ne**.*   14
                 '(I) felt something was strange about everyone, you know.'
(l) ORT:EVL   *yoosu ga nan ka zawa zawatto shite te.*   15
                 'The atmosphere was somewhat noisy.'

Stanza D
(m) ORT:EVL   *de, ikinari tomodachi ga,*   16
                 'And, suddenly, a friend of mine,'
                 *ehtto, ah, namae wasurete shimai **mashita** ne,*   17
                 'um, uh (the) name (of the boy who died) has escaped (my)
                 memory, you know.'
(n) RPT:EXP   *'dare sore kun ga,'*   18
                 ' "So-and-so," '
                 *"shinjattan **da yo**," tte.*   19
                 ' "died, I tell you," (said a friend of mine.)'
(o) RPT:IMP   *'hee' **tte**.*   20
                 ' "dear," (said I.)'

Stanza E

(p) EVL   *anoo, mada chiisakute,*   21
            'Well, because (I) was still small.'

(q) EVL   *soo yuu keiken wa hajimete **desu** shi **nee**.*   22
            '(I) had such an experience for the first time, you know.'

Stanza F

(r) ORT   *de, nan ka ehtto umi biraki ga hajimatta hi ni,*   23
            'And, um, on the first day of the season when the sea was
            open to the public,'

(s) RPT:IMP *"umi e tobikonde itte,"*   24
            ' "(He) jumped into the water"⁹ '

(t) RPT:IMP *anoo, "shinzoo mahi de,"*   25
            'Well, "because of heart failure," '

            *shinjattan **da yo**,"*   26
            ' "(he) died, I tell you," '

            toka itte.   27
            'said (a friend of mine).'

Stanza G

(u) EVL   *sono toki ni hajimete kurai shinutte yuu ninshiki ga,*   28
            'At that time first, the recognition that (human beings) die,'

            dekita gurai datta,   29
            '(I) formed,'

COM   *to omoun **desu**.*   30
            '(I) think.'

Stanza H

(v) EVL   *demo **yappari** sugoku, ah, shinjatta no kaa **to yuu** koto de,* 31
            'But, after all, the thing that "uh, (he) died," '

            *sugoku shokku o uke **mashita ne**.*   32
            'shocked (me) a lot, you know.'

(w) EVL   *sorede osooshiki ni itta hi no koto mo,*   33
            'And on the day when (I) went to the funeral service,'

            *hoka no koto wa zenzen oboete nain **desu** kedo,*   34
            '(I) don't remember, or anything else, though.'

(x) EVL   *anoo, sono koto wa hakkiri,*   35
            'Um, that incident clearly,'

            *oboete **masu ne**.*   36
            'remains in my memory, you know.'

Stanza I

(y) EVL   *ato yoochien no koto toka shoogakko ichinensei toka sannensei*
            *demo hotondo oboete nain **desu**.*   37
            '(I) rarely remember what happened when (I was) a
            preschooler, a first grader, or a third grader.'

(z) EVL   *sono koto dake gurai **desu ne**.*   38
            'Only that incident, you know.'

Stanza J
(aa) ORT:ACT *soo desu ne,*   39
              'Um, well, you know,'
              maa sono kyooshitsu ni patto haitte itta toki to.   40
              'when (I) was rushing into the classroom.'

Stanza K
(bb) ORT:ACT *ato osooshiki ni itta toki no.*   41
              'When (I) went to the funeral service.'
(cc) ORT:EVL *nan to naku bakuzen to shita,*   42
              'Somewhat a vague,'
              yoosu desu ne,   43
              'atmosphere, you know,'
              nanka,   44
              'somewhat.'
(dd) ORT:EVL *oozei minna narande te mitai na,*   45
              'Something like a lot of people were in line (at the funeral
              service)'
(ee) EVL   *sore dake desu ne.*   46
              'That's it, you know.'

Stanza L
(ff) APP:COD *ato tanoshii koto toka ne,*   47
              'Besides, something enjoyable, you know,'
              anmari nain desu yo.   48
              '(I) don't have, I tell you.'

The verb 'involve' comes from a Latin word 'involvere,' which means
'roll up' or 'wrap up.' [Note that, in this book, I use the expression 'wrap
up' as a metaphor in more than one way.] According to Caffi and Janney
(1994), linguists use the term 'involvement' in a variety of ways, with
reference to speakers': (1) *'inner states* as preconditions of interaction,' (2)
'emotive identifications with speech acts,' (3) *'uses of linguistic techniques and
strategies* as 'conventionalized ways of establishing rapport',' (4) intention
of *'overall rhetorical effects,* or senses of vividness evoked by strategic use of
narratives, reported speech, imagery, and so on,' (5) *'cognitive orientations
to shared discourse topics,'* and (6) 'metamessages of rapport, successful communication, shared feelings, etc., as means of enhancing social cohesion'
(p. 345). What is shared in the list above, as Caffi and Janney (1994) claim,
is the existence of 'a movement from an individual *psychological* orientation to an interpersonal *social* orientation, via *rhetoric-stylistic* orientation'
(p. 345). In what follows, I examine what kinds of linguistic means and
rhetorical devices adults deploy in narrative, for involvement purposes.
To comprehend a multilayered weave of human temporality, examining

such culture-specific or language-specific means and devices as involvement strategies is a rewarding endeavor in terms of understanding language development as life-long human development.

The use of causal connectives

A narrative connective *dakara* ('so,' 'therefore,' 'that's why') almost always appears when the narrator provides the listener with background information. Of the total 29 uses of *dakara* by adults, thirteen appeared at the stanza-initial position. In those cases, the narrative segments subsequent to *dakara* provide the listener with supplementary information. Another 11 appeared in the middle of a stanza, preceded by orientation or evaluation statement(s) or a combination of both. The remaining five appeared at the stanza-final position like the one that appears in Example 5.5 (Stanza A, Line 7: 'Therefore (*dakara*), [I] remember only that thing clearly, you know'). Here, *dakara* not only gives a conclusive tone to the stanza, but it also expresses the culturally shared assumption that what the narrator has briefly provided as an abstract (i.e. her classmate's death in Verse (c) in Stanza A) should be interpreted by the listener as a sufficient cause/explanation for a result/consequence (i.e. the narrator's clear memory of the incident in Verse (d) in Stanza A). In other words, by using *dakara*, the narrator conveys her personal position, attitude and, moreover, emotion toward the fact in a very brief way. I infer from her brevity that she assumes that the listener who is brought up in Japanese culture will naturally understand her strong emotional feelings and easily empathize with her.[10]

The use of adverbs

Like the examples of uses of *dakara*, the adverb *yappari* ('after all'), which appears at the beginning of Stanza H, adds the narrator's emotion and attitude (i.e. having been shocked) toward what she has previously narrated (i.e. her classmate's death). In Lines 31 and 32, *yappari* ('after all') refers back to the earlier description of her classmate's death. The adverb *yappari* therefore serves some kind of referential or anaphoric function in narrative.[11] Regardless of its anaphoric or non-anaphoric function, *yappari* triggers shared emotion between the narrator and listener. As the use of the connective *dakara* and the adverb *yappari* illuminate, the assumption of culturally shared emotion between the narrator and listener is particularly important for understanding Japanese personal narratives, adults' narratives in particular.

Two types of verbs in relation to narrative external/internal
perspective taking

Sophistication in adults' narrative, however, is most manifest in the manipulation of plain verb forms such as the copula *da*[12] (a linking verb like the English verb 'be') and formal *des(u)/mas(u)* verbal suffixes in Japanese. [Note that *des(u)* is the polite form of *da*.] Previous research (e.g. Mannari & Befu, 1991) has claimed that in Japanese society there is a distinction between 'insider' and 'outsider.' If a person the speaker addresses belongs to one of the speaker's circles, that person is an 'insider.' On the other hand, if the person is outside those circles, then the person is an 'outsider.' For example, someone's immediate inside circle is usually the family; a second inside circle might be the office circle or school classmates. This distinction is an integral part of the Japanese language as well (Niwa & Matsuda, 1964).[13] Ordinarily, the distinction between the *des(u)/mas(u)* forms and the plain forms is explained in terms of complex, culturally specific, elaborated rule systems for social exchange, which also involve asymmetries of power (e.g. teacher/student) (Bachnik, 1994). Japanese culture is sometimes described as a wrapping culture because of an association that gifts to outsiders should be wrapped; as Hendry (1995) argues, the Japanese language seems to represent a notion of wrapping. Whereas within the inner circle (e.g. family conversation) plain (or even informal/abrupt) styles such as *da* are regularly used, outside the inner circle the formal *des(u)/mas(u)* styles are preferred in order to maintain personal distance. When a Japanese speaker addresses an outsider, he or she uses the formal *des(u)/mas(u)* styles because the outsider is usually accorded a higher position than the speaker as a courtesy.

In the narrative context, moreover, the concept of 'inside' and 'outside' should be understood as a reflection of a narrator's conceptualization about the narrative event (Maynard, 1993). In Akira's mother's narrative (Example 5.5), the narrator mostly uses the formal *des(u)/mas(u)* styles, not only because the listener is outside of the narrator's circle, but also because the narrator is fully aware of the listener and addresses him directly (unfortunately, however, the verb style choice in Japanese is not evident in the English translation). In Stanza D, however, except for Line 17 (in which she said to the interviewer that the name of the boy who died in the sea escaped her memory), the narrator immediately reports what actually happened (i.e. her classmate's death in the sea), using the naked, abrupt *da* style within the reported speech followed by the quotation-final particle *tte* in Line 19, and how she responded to that news in a very brief but vivid way[14] (reported speech followed by the quotation-final particle *tte*) in Line 20. In other words, when narrating this stanza, she is not directly addressing the listener except for Line 17; instead, her perspective is always inside the narrative scene.[15] On the other hand, if she were to address the listener directly and thus take a narrative-external perspective, she would explicitly mark who performed the speech, by adding verbs with the formal *des(u)/mas(u)* styles, such as *'tomodachi ga ittan desu'* ('a friend of mine said') and *'watashi wa ii mashita'* ('I said') in Lines 19 and 20 respectively. Thus, as Maynard (1993) emphasizes, the verb style choice is reflective of the narrator's external or internal positioning in relation to the event that he or she is describing.

Likewise, the formal *des(u)/mas(u)* styles do not appear in Stanza F, where the narrator again takes the internal perspective when she repeats what had happened to the boy. Soon after that, however, she shifts her stance toward the narrative external perspective (Stanza G). In Line 31 at the beginning of Stanza H, furthermore, nominalization, which combines a clause (*'ah, shinjatta no kaa'*: 'uh, (he) died') and a noun (*koto*: 'the thing') by the quotative marker (*to yuu*), coupled with the formal *mas(u)* style in Line 32, clearly indicates some distance between the event (i.e. her classmate's death in the sea) and the narrator who is currently narrating the event. [Note: Nominalization is a device usually used to maintain a distance between the speaker and the listener (Brown & Levinson, 1987); in this case, however, it is used maintain a distance between the narrator and the event that he or she is narrating, signaling that the narrator is now taking a fairly objective stance toward the narrative event.] Toward the end of the narrative, the narrator takes an external rather than internal perspective. This distancing is a device that leads to the end of the story, and the narrator lets the listener know that she is closing her narrative.

To summarize, formal styles such as *des(u)* and *mas(u)* function not only as politeness markers but also as markers to show the narrator's perspective taking. As can be seen in studies on other languages (e.g. Toolan, 1988; Weist, 1986) Japanese narrative is not unusual, when it comes to the use of linguistic devices to represent external/internal perspective taking. In the case of Japanese narratives, however, when a situation is conceptualized from an external perspective, formal styles are salient (recall Figure 5.1); on the other hand, when conceptualized from an internal perspective, plain or even informal/abrupt styles such as *da* are prominent (recall Figure 5.2). More specifically, as if a camera lens zooms in on an object, as the narrator's perspective shifts toward narrative internal, the narrator tells the narrative without using the formal *des(u)/mas(u)* styles. Interestingly, this type of shift generally takes place in the middle of a stanza. Toward the end of a stanza, as if the camera lens zooms out of the focused object, the narrator likely becomes aware of the existence of something else, i.e. the listener, and addresses the listener directly; then, the narrator takes a narrative-external perspective or a more objective position, using the formal *des(u)/mas(u)* styles.[16] The choice of the verb-ending forms thus suggests the position that the narrator takes when telling a narrative.

Psychological Complements. As we studied in Chapter 4, Maynard (2000) argues out that a Japanese individual cannot convey his or her feelings without using pathos-oriented (as opposed to logos) expressions, such as *to omoun desu* ('I think such and such') [note that *to* before *omoundesu* is the quotation-final particle *to*, which is similar to *tte* in terms of function but more formal]. In Example 5.5, *omou* which appears at the stanza-final position (Stanza G, Line 30), does not simply report what the narrator thinks about the narrated event, but it also softens the severity of the narrator's statement while maintaining the narrator's emotions ('I formed, at that time, the recognition that human beings die').[17] Examples of other psychological complements found in the data are as follows:

Example 5.6
(a) *hontoo ni yoku asonda naa,*
     'Really, I played a lot,'
     to yuu ki ga shi masu ne.
     '(I) feel, you know.'
(b) *asobi ni itta,*
     '(I) went to play,'
     tte yu no o oboete imasu.
     '(I) remember.'
(c) *sore ga nan ka sugoku ne tanoshikatta,*
     'That was really fun,'
     yoo ni oboeteru.
     '(I) remember.'
(d) *ano nete ita koto,*
     'That (I) was sleeping,'
     ee, kioku shiterun desu.
     'Yes, (I) remember.'

These different psychological complements have in common that the narrator uses them in order to: (1) take account of the state of mind of the listener (in addition to that of the narrator himself or herself); (2) convey hedged performatives; and (3) modify the force of a speech act (Brown & Levinson, 1987).

Two types of interactional particles

The use of two interactional particles, (1) an assertive and/or emphatic particle *yo* similar to English expressions 'I tell you' and 'I'm sure' and (2) an agreement-seeking particle *ne* (or *nee* when elongated), also adds refinement to utterances in Japanese. From this contrast, we can easily infer that the speaker uses *yo* in order to deliver new information (which the speaker assumes that the listener does not have), whereas the speaker uses *ne* in order to convey old information (which the speaker assumes that the listener already has). [Recall the contrast between the subject marker *ga* to provide new information and the topic marker *wa* to refer to old information.]

In narrative contexts as well, although these particles both appear in the verse-final position in many cases,[18] their functions differ greatly. As seen in children's narratives, by uttering the sentence-final particle *ne* (or *nee*), the narrator seeks the listener's agreement, expresses the narrator's psychological and emotional dependence on the listener, and thus tries to establish narrator-listener rapport.[19] In other words, *ne* (or *nee*) appears only when the narrator is taking a narrative external position. [See Lines 7, 11, 14, 17, 22, 32, 36, 38, 39, 43, 46 and 47. In each case, *ne* or *nee* is used with the formal *des(u)/mas(u)* styles.] More specifically, in this example, *ne* or *nee* is used when the narrator provides background information (e.g. either orientation or evaluation or both), in order to negotiate the stance she is taking. Although not shown in the example, the listener, by showing brief vocal acknowledgments, signals that he shares common ground with the narrator (see the discussion of the reciprocal relationship between *amae* and *omoiyari* later). Thus, as seen in children's narratives, the interactional particle *ne* suggests that even a monologic narrative is dialogic by nature.

In contrast, *yo* is unidirectional: the speaker knows (1) something that the listener does not know or (2) that the listener has a different view. In Example 5.5, the narrator uses the other interactional particle *yo* not only when taking a narrative external position but also when taking a narrative internal position. That is, the narrator effectively uses *yo* right after the abrupt/informal *da* form when narrating the scene where her friend informed her, in an assertive and emphatic tone, of her classmate's sudden death (Lines 19 and 26, in which *yo* is used concretely to mark reported speech). In this way, although the particles *ne* and *yo* both illustrate the interactional nature of Japanese language, *ne* is interaction-focused, whereas *yo* is information-focused. Thus, these two types of particles function differently and enrich narratives in different ways.

Multiple stories, revisited

Although Example 5.5 is based on a single experience, two thirds of the adults' (13) narratives included more than one experience. In Stanza I (Lines 37 and 38) of Example 5.5, the narrator stated that all early memories except for her classmate's death had escaped her memory. As a matter of fact, however, she did not need to refer to whether she remembered other experiences; conversely, if she had remembered something else that was impressive, she might have narrated it in the interview. As the following example illustrates, adults used a variety of attention-getting devices as a prologue for another story:

Example 5.7   A Japanese adult's (Wakao's mother) monologic narrative
SECTION I
Stanza A
(a) APP:ATT   *uun, anoo, tanoshii taiken wa,*   1
              'Um, well, when (it) comes to happy experiences,'
(b) EVL   *watashi amari chiisai toki no koto oboete nain desu kedo ne.*   2
              'I do not remember much about (my) early childhood, though.'

Stanza B
(c) ORT:EVL   *anoo, taiku ga suki de,*   3
              'Um, (I) liked sports.'
(d) ORT:EVL   *hashiri ga sugoku tokui dattan de,*   4
              '(I) was very good at running.'
(e) ACT   *undookai no toki ni yoku hashitte.*   5
              'In track meets (I) ran well.'
(f) ACT:EVL   *ittoo ni nattan wa,*   6
              '(I) won the first place,'
(g) EVL   *yoku oboete run desu kedo.*   7
              '(I) remember well, though.'

Stanza C
(h) APP:COD   *sore gurai kana.*   8
              'Maybe, that's it,'
(i) ORT   *chiisai toki no omoide tte.*   9
              'when (it) comes to early childhood memory.'

SECTION II
Stanza D
(j) APP:ATT   *kowai taiken de hitotsu arun desu kedo.*   10
              'About scary experiences, (I) have one.'

Stanza E
(k) ORT   *watashi, ano, obaachan tachi to daikazoku de sunde mashite,*   11
              'I lived with my grandmother and other (relatives), with an extended family.'

(l) ORT	*watashi jishin mo yonin kyoodai de,*	12
	'And I am (one of) four brothers and sisters.'	
(m) ORT	*sorede sono toki, ehtto ojiichan obaachan mo sundetan **desu** kedo,*	13
	'And at that time, um, (I) lived with (my) grandfather and grandmother, though.'	

Stanza F

(n) ORT	*tochuu de watashi ga shoogakko no toki,*	14
	'While I was in elementary school,'	
(o) ORT	*nakunattan **desu** ne.*	15
	'(they) died, you know.'	
(p) ORT	*de, ojiichan obaachan ga neteta heya de watashi wa hitori de netetan **desu**.*	16
	'In the room where (my) grandfather and grandmother had slept, I slept.'	

Telling multiple stories in conjunction with the contrastive use of the case marker 'wa'

The narrator in this example uses an affective key (Ochs & Schieffelin, 1989) effectively; i.e. she uses an attention-getter as an appendage (Stanza A, Line 1), trying to involve the listener in a happy narrative that she is about to tell. More than that, the narrator had planned to tell multiple stories: *Wa* appears at the very beginning of the narrative (Stanza A, Line 1), and so it does not perform an anaphoric function in this instance. The narrator is using *wa* as a contrastive marker rather than a thematic or topic marker. In this way, it is clear that she had prepared to tell another story that would be in a striking contrast to the first happy experience. A second source of evidence that the narrator planned to tell another story can be seen in her narrative external positioning. The *des(u)* marking at the beginning of Section II indicates that she was fully aware of the audience and thus was taking a narrative external position.[20] Here, in contrast to the first happy story, the narrator tried to tell a scary story. Using an attention-getting device effectively, this adult narrator thus told about more than a single experience.

Results and Discussion

Narrative structure

Verse/stanza analysis

Verse/stanza analysis reveals a certain structural configuration shared by Japanese children and adults. Three-verse stanzas represent 29.3% (12) of the 41 stanzas produced by the four-year-olds and 33.3% (12) of the 36 stanzas produced by the five-year-olds. A similar tendency was identified among the adults; three-verse stanzas represent 28.2% (57) of the 202 stanzas produced in all. The four-year-olds and the five-year-olds were each compared with the adult group. As we have already seen in Chapter 4, in the proportion of three-verse stanzas, no differences approached statistical significance between the adults and either one of the children's groups (i.e. four- and five-year-olds). Across the three groups, proportions of three-verse stanzas did not differ greatly, and it is therefore concluded that three-verse stanzas seem to be stable in terms of proportion.

High point analysis

Although three-verse stanzas are predominant among adults and children alike and, in this sense, they are structurally similar to each other, high point analysis reveals that adult and children's three-verse stanzas are qualitatively different. Tables 5.1 and 5.2 present patterns of three-verse stanzas in four-year-olds' and five-year-olds' monologic narratives, respectively. Among the 12 three-verse stanzas produced by the four-year-olds, nine contain at least two action statements; an additional one includes one action statement. The remaining two consist of an appendage–appendage–appendage pattern and an evaluation–evaluation–evaluation pattern, respectively (see Table 5.1). All of the 12 three-verse stanzas produced by the five-year-olds include at least one action statement. Three show some kind of action-action-action pattern; seven have two action statements with the insertion of one *free* narrative clause at some point; and the remaining two include one action statement. Thus, most of the three-verse stanzas emphasize an action/temporal sequence and focus on foreground information (see Table 5.2).

Although a variety of three-verse patterns are theoretically possible, because orientative or evaluative *free* narrative clauses can be inserted anywhere in a sequence, the actual patterns observed were limited in type. That is, an orientation clause can range freely through the narrative sequence, without changing the fixed sequence of events. [For instance, see Stanza A of Yuka's narrative in Example 5.4, in which she could have inserted an orientation statement at the very beginning.] Likewise, an evaluation clause that provides the listener with the contextual significance can potentially be moved anywhere in the narrative. Regardless of where *free* narrative clauses are placed in a stanza, such as two two-action sequence patterns, 'ACT–ORT–ACT' and 'ORT–ACT–ACT,' they are considered to belong to essentially the same pattern. Tables 5.1 and 5.2, there-

Table 5.1 Patterns of three-verse stanzas in four-year-olds' monologic narratives

Pattern			Number	%
Three action-sequence pattern: Functions of				
1st verse	2nd verse	3rd verse		
ACT	ACT	ACT	2	
		Subtotal	2	16.7
Two action-sequence patterns: Functions of				
1st verse	2nd verse	3rd verse		
ACT:EVL	ACT	EVL	1	
ACT:EVL	EVL	ACT	1	
ACT	EVL	ACT:ORT	1	
EVL	ORT/ACT:EVL†	ACT	1	
ORT	ACT	ACT:EVL	1	
ORT:ACT	ACT	ACT:EVL	1	
ORT:ACT	ACT:ORT	ACT:EVL	1	
		Subtotal	7	58.3
Miscellaneous patterns: Functions of				
1st verse	2nd verse	3rd verse		
APP:ATT	ORT	ACT:EVL	1	
APP:ABS	APP:ABS	APP:ABS	1	
EVL	EVL	EVL	1	
		Subtotal	3	25.0
		Total	12	

† Note that in some cases two codes were simultaneously applied to one clause.

fore, indicate that three-verse stanzas with two-action sequence patterns are the most common forms produced by four- and five-year-olds.

Choice of emphasis on foreground information or background information

In contrast to children's narratives, in which descriptions of events are temporally sequenced and, moreover, causally connected (i.e. outcome), of the total 57 three-verse stanzas produced by the 20 mothers, only

Table 5.2 Patterns of three-verse stanzas in five-year-olds' monologic
narratives

Pattern			Number	%
Three action-sequence patterns:				
Functions of				
1st verse	2nd verse	3rd verse		
ACT	ACT	ACT	1	
ACT	ACT:OUT	ACT:EVL	1	
ACT:ORT	ACT	ACT:OUT	1	
		Subtotal	3	25.0
Two action-sequence patterns:				
Functions of				
1st verse	2nd verse	3rd verse		
ACT	ACT	EVL:OUT	1	
ACT:EVL	EVL	ACT:EVL	1	
EVL	ACT	ACT	1	
EVL	ACT:EVL	ACT	1	
ACT:ORT	ACT:OUT	ORT	1	
ORT	ACT:EVL	ACT:OUT	1	
ORT	ACT:ORT	ACT	1	
		Subtotal	7	58.3
Miscellaneous patterns:				
Functions of				
1st verse	2nd verse	3rd verse		
ORT	ACT	EVL	1	
ORT	ORT	ACT:EVL	1	
		Subtotal	2	16.7
		Total	12	

15.8% (9) include two action-sequence patterns. An additional seven
contain one action statement. None of the adults' three-verse stanzas,
however, show three action-sequence patterns (see Table 5.3). Instead,
66.7% (38) exclusively consist of *free* narrative clauses that focus on
background information. Therefore, although three-verse stanzas are
predominant among adults and children alike and, in this sense, they
are structurally similar to each other, adult and children's three-verse
stanzas are qualitatively different.

Similarities and/or differences between adult narrative productions and children's early narrative productions

Similarities between Adults' and Children's Narrative Devices and Strategies

Examples 5.1, 5.4 and 5.7 have shown that adults and preschool children alike tell narratives that include a collection of isolated, similar (or contrastive) events. In some aspects, moreover, even four- and five-year-olds deploy the same narrative devices and strategies as adults. Table 5.4 presents a list of the mean frequencies and the standard deviations of the linguistic items – morphological and lexical – examined in this chapter. Japanese narrators, regardless of their age, try to communicate by frequently using the interactional/rapport particle *ne* ('you know'). This particle probably emerges in early stages of language development and, moreover, comes to be used in the narrative context because of the mother's strong emphasis on a culturally preferred interactional style. That is, Japanese culture is characterized by interdependence, as seen in the reciprocal nature of *amae*, which means, following leading Japanese psychiatrist Takeo Doi's (1973) definition, the state of dependency on the indulgence or benevolence of another person, and *omoiyari*, an aspect describing consideration for others. Because people tend to attach a significant meaning to rapport and empathy in Japanese society – particularly because *amae* sometimes describes a child's feelings and behavior toward a parent – (Doi, 1973; Lebra, 1976), it is understandable that young children use the interactional/rapport particle in their early narrative production. Here, we also need to recognize the effect of maternal modeling (i.e. mothers provide their young children with linguistic modeling in a variety of ways).

The quantitative analysis in the previous chapter revealed that with regard to reported speech, four-year-olds, five-year-olds, and adults were equally competent in conveying reported speech. Examples 5.1, 5.2 and 5.5 in this chapter seem to support this statistical finding. The reason seems to be due in part to the relative simplicity of the formation of reported speech in Japanese (Clancy, 1985). As seen in the formation of onomatopoeias in Japanese (e.g. *dokaan tte*, which means 'with a bang'; also see Ryota's narrative in Example 5.1), simply adding the quotation-final particle *tte* makes reported speech (see Example 5.5); in other words, quoting onomatopoeias and reported speech forms a continuum in language acquisition in Japanese. As demonstrated by the example above, compared to English, which, in addition to rather complicated tense marking, has a grammatical distinction between direct and indirect

Table 5.3 Patterns of three-verse stanzas in mothers' monologic narratives

Pattern			Number	%
Two action-sequence patterns:				
Functions of				
1st verse	2nd verse	3rd verse		
ACT	ACT	ORT	2	
ACT	ACT:EVL	ORT	1	
ACT:EVL	ACT:EVL	ORT	1	
ACT	ORT	ACT	1	
ORT	ACT	ACT	2	
ORT/ACT:ORT†		ORT	ACT:ORT	1
EVL	ACT	ACT	1	
		Subtotal	9	15.8
Patterns consisting exclusively of free narrative clauses				
(background information):				
Functions of				
1st verse	2nd verse	3rd verse		
EVL	EVL	EVL	9	
EVL	ORT	EVL	5	
ORT	EVL	EVL	4	
ORT:EVL	EVL	EVL	2	
ORT	EVL	ORT	1	
ORT	ORT	EVL	2	
ORT:EVL	ORT	EVL	2	
ORT	ORT:EVL	EVL	1	
ORT	ORT	ORT	8	
ORT:EVL	ORT	ORT	1	
ORT	ORT	ORT:EVL	1	
ORT/ORT:EVL	ORT	ORT	1	
ORT	ORT/APP:ABS	EVL	1	
		Subtotal	38	66.7
Miscellaneous patterns:				
Functions of				
1st verse	2nd verse	3rd verse		
ACT:ORT	ORT:EVL	ORT	1	
EVL	EVL	ACT	1	
EVL	RPT:EXP	ACT	1	
ORT	EVL	ACT	1	

Table 5.3 (*cont.*)

ORT	EVL	ACT:ORT	1	
ORT:ACT	EVL	EVL	1	
ORT:EVL	ORT	ACT	1	
ORT	RPT:IMP	RPT:IMP	1	
ORT:EVL	RPT:EXP	RPT:IMP	1	
APP:ATT	EVL	EVL	1	
		Subtotal	10	17.5
		Total	57	

† Note that in some cases two codes were simultaneously applied to one clause.

speech, the formation of reported speech is relatively easy in Japanese. Thus, reported speech is used by young children in their narratives. Although Table 5.4 shows that adults use *tte* substantially more frequently than children,[21] this difference may be attributable to its broad use. That is, *tte* is used not only in reported speech and onomatopoeias but in other contexts as well. To form reported speech, children *do* use the quotation final particle *tte* that they have previously mastered to quote onomatopoeias in early language acquisition.

Likewise, children's narratives in this chapter support the claim that Japanese children generally master case particles relatively early (e.g. the thematic or topic marker *wa* and the subject marker *ga* at around two years of age, according to Clancy (1985)). Moreover, Sho's contrastive use of *wa* in Example 5.2 shows that four-year-olds can fully grasp the function of syntactic particles and are capable of extending the basic function to a rather sophisticated one. In other words, when considering his relative social inexperience, we might be amazed at such linguistic sophistication. Overall, therefore, early acquisition and deployment of the syntactic and pragmatic particles *wa*, *tte* and *ne* in young children's narratives seem to be based on linguistic and social-interactional factors.

Differences between adults' narrative and children's narrative

At the same time, however, many differences were observed between adults' narrative production and children's early narrative production.[22] The previous quantitative analysis reported that with regard to appendages, no differences approached statistical significance between four-year-olds, five-year-olds and adults. As seen in Example 5.7, however, compared to children, adults used a variety of attention-getting devices as a prologue for another story. In fact, because appendages are

Table 5.4 Mean frequencies and standard deviations of selected linguistic items in the monologic narrative context

	Four-year-olds (n = 10)		Five-year-olds (n = 10)		Mothers (n = 20)		F^a values for main effect of GROUP
	M	(SD)	M	(SD)	M	(SD)	
Particles							
ne	7.10	(5.65)	8.40	(7.85)	9.90	(6.46)	0.62
yo	0.20	(0.42)	0.00	(0.00)	2.90	(2.85)	9.36***
tte	0.90	(1.45)	0.80	(1.32)	8.00	(5.34)	16.41****
Connectives							
dakara	0.00	(0.00)	0.00	(0.00)	1.45	(1.73)	6.83**
datte	0.00	(0.00)	0.10	(0.32)	0.05	(0.22)	0.50
Adverb							
yappari	0.00	(0.00)	0.00	(0.00)	1.35	(2.01)	4.40*
Verbs							
des(u)/mas(u)	0.00	(0.00)	0.00	(0.00)	13.50	(8.24)	26.16****
da	0.20	(0.63)	0.00	(0.00)	3.00	(2.29)	15.05****

*$p < 0.05$; **$p < 0.01$; ***$p < 0.001$; ****$p < 0.0001$.
^{a}Degrees of freedom = 2, 37.

a composite first-level category including abstracts, attention-getting devices, and codas (see Chapter 4), the analysis of attention-getting devices alone reveals that in comparison to adults, children of both groups produced fewer attention-getting devices, $F(2, 37) = 6.25$, $p < 0.01$.[23]

Also, as seen in the previous chapter, the most noticeable difference between adults and children was observed in the proportions of foreground information (i.e. restricted narrative clauses) and background information (i.e. free narrative clauses). The examination of adults' narratives in this chapter has shown that the difference seems in part attributable to certain linguistic devices and manipulative strategies that encode the narrator's emotion. In children's personal narrative production, except for *ne*, they have not yet learned to deploy certain grammatical items (e.g. *dakara*, which means 'so, therefore, that's why'[24] and *yappari*, which means 'after all') that encode background information, evaluation in particular (see Table 5.4). The differences between adults and children then represent, as Berman and Slobin (1994) put it, how 'experiences are filtered – (a) through choice of perspective, and (b) through the set of options provided by the particular language – into verbalized events' (pp. 9, 611). Thus, although children seemed to be developing a sense of their voice and learning how to take audience into account when they were narrating, they did not seem to have mastered how to manipulate linguistic devices for the best effect.

Interestingly, studies on child language acquisition present seemingly contradictory evidence. Young children learn to put conjunctions to additional pragmatic use in discourse (Peterson & McCabe, 1991). Likewise, Japanese children begin to use connectives such as *dakara* ('so,' 'therefore,' 'that's why')[25] at about three years of age and the assertive and/or emphatic particle *yo* ('I tell you') and the formal *des(u)/mas(u)* styles even earlier at about two years (e.g. Clancy, 1985). These linguistic items are thus acquired at considerably younger ages than the preschool children in this sample. In the present study, however, the informal verb-ending style *da*[26] and the particle *yo*[27] each appear only twice in children's narratives,[28] and *yappari* ('after all') and *des(u)/mas(u)*[29] do not appear at all. Another connective *datte* ('but,' 'because'), which, like *dakara* ('so,' 'therefore,' 'that's why'), provides the listener with information, appears only once in children's narratives (Tomo, 5;6).[30] However, *dakara* does not appear at all in the children's monologic narratives. This difference seems to be due to the difference between the ordinary conversational context of childhood, which is often about the here-and-now, and the somewhat demanding task of telling a personal narrative. As Berman and Slobin (1994) claim, cognitively, young children 'cannot conceive of the full range of encodable perspectives,' and 'linguistically, they do not command the full range of formal devices' (p. 15).[31] Even if young Japanese children have cognitively learned and have command of these lexical items, they might use them only in set formulas or as unanalyzed units, such as *ohayoo gozai masu* ('Good morning'), *asobi mashoo* ('Let's play'), and *gochisoosama deshita* ('Thank you for a nice dish'). Young children, preschoolers in particular, are likely to use these words in formulaic speech patterns when participating in routinized interactions. However, when they talk about the past and produce personal narratives, because they have not fully mastered the social pragmatic functions or interactional dimensions of these words occurring in narrative, they might not be able to use them. For instance, because parents devote considerable effort to socializing their children in many politeness routines, by the time they learn how to speak, Japanese children have already received considerable input regarding polite language usage (Nakamura, 1996, 2000). Yet, unless they have fully grasped sociolinguistic features, such as how the *des(u)/mas(u)* styles function in relation to this societal concept of 'inside' and 'outside,' they may not freely use these verbs in their narratives.[32]

Likewise, the assertive and/or emphatic particle *yo* ('I tell you') is used only when the narrator provides the listener with new information or only when the narrator has better access to the information than the listener (Maynard, 1990, 1993). Such a social situation may not frequently occur in the relationship between the young child narrator and the adult listener. These considerations suggest that children's narrative development has to be a strongly interactive process, one which relies not only on specific cognitive and linguistic mechanisms, but also on the child's active participation in a narrative discourse environment attuned to the child's communicative needs.

When the concept of 'inside' and 'outside' is applied to the environment of preschool children, their inside circle is the family – the mother, in particular – and the second inner circle, although outside to some extent, is their preschool teacher and peers. Thus, even if preschool children have experienced a move from the *amae*-based inside world[33] (home where they are allowed or even expected to show regressive dependency and selfishness) to another world (preschool) and thus have some sense of insider–outsider distinction, they may still tend to consider their preschool teacher as an insider to them. They may tend to address their preschool teacher using an insider language that lacks the formal *des(u)/mas(u)* styles that represent social distance, power relationships or societal ranking. Benedict (1946) characterizes the life cycle typical of Japanese individuals as 'a great shallow U-curve'; i.e. babies and the elderly are allowed to enjoy a maximum freedom and indulgence.[34] Of course, preschool children are no longer babies, but they are considered to be young. Thus, in the Japanese preschool context, even if children address their teacher without the formal *des(u)/mas(u)* styles, they may be allowed to do so without being corrected. Moreover, because children are not usually placed in a higher position than adults, mothers and outsiders may not have the occasion to address children with the formal *des(u)/mas(u)* styles.[35]

As McCabe (1997) puts it, 'Narrative is a linguistic crossroads of culture, cognition, and emotion and serves the dual functions of sense-making and self-presentation' (p. 137). At the same time, however, cognitive, linguistic, and social-interactional dimensions may take different courses in the process of language acquisition. The present study shows that preschool children have not yet begun to deploy some linguistic or communicative devices and strategies, as well as rhetorical options, in their monologic narrative production, despite the fact that they have mastered those devices and strategies in early language acquisition. Some of the subtleties of Japanese narrative have yet to be learned by preschool-age children. Although the narrative patterns exhibited by Japanese preschoolers are arguably the ones out of which even more complex/sophisticated structures will be built, the simple narratives told by those children do not represent the final phase of development in terms of expressive options and rhetorical/linguistic devices. The findings thus indicate that unlike talking about the here-and-now, in the development of narrative skills four- and five-year-olds have a long way to go. Telling a narrative on their own does not seem to be an easy task for young children.

Conclusions

To conclude the two chapters that have examined Japanese monologic narratives, narrative is defined as a recounting of things that are both spatially and temporally distant. Among various types of narratives, personal narratives are categorized as descriptions of an individual's past experience in the sense that the accounts are reflective of the narrator's personal history. The widely accepted assumption is that because the human mind is guided by the schema of prepackaged expectations or interpretations, a narrative can be defined in terms of cognitive parameters (Fludernik, 1996). Imagine that a person who was involved in or witnessed a certain incident later recalls that incident during a conversation. An activity of this kind is regarded as telling an oral personal narrative. The narrative, however, is not generally a simple reproduction of the incident that the person experienced. Rather, according to discourse analysis in the Labovian tradition (Labov, 1972), narrators are expected to try to accomplish narrative tellability or reportability in order to avoid the listener's potential threatening of 'So what?'. We may therefore predict that the person will produce a narrative that is, more or less, organized, following a universal schema of beginning, a conflict, and a resolution, with some evaluative comments. In this sense, we might be able to claim that the basic processes of the human psyche are more or less universal.

In many cases, however, conversational storytelling includes other factors as well. To begin with, finding individual differences in narrative structure is not surprising. To make matters more complicated, because narratives are not only individual but also culturally influenced or even controlled affairs (Aksu-koç, 1996), people in different cultures make sense of their experience in differing ways (Gee, 1991a; Hymes, 1981; Michaels, 1991). In the study of story understanding, for example, Schank and Abelson (1977) characterized culture-specific expectations about a certain event as 'script.' Likewise, anthropological linguistics and sociolinguistics, which include what Hymes (1964) once called 'ethnographies of communication,' have been interested in identifying certain linguistic units that people in a particular society employ in the production of oral personal narratives (e.g. verse/stanza analysis). In addition to individual differences, therefore, we should conceptualize that narratives are organized within culturally specific frames.

Theories proposed by Hymes (1982) and Gee (1985) in part derive from the notion of psychological/cultural framing, in which the individual is assumed to develop mental/cognitive frameworks to aid his or her comprehension and production of stories under certain cultural constraints. Chapters 4 and 5 have attempted to apply this line of research in narrative analysis – Native American narratives studied by Hymes and African American Vernacular English (AAVE) by Gee – to Japanese oral personal narratives. In addition, in Chapter 5, I have examined language-specific narrative discourse markers as clues to a better understanding of cultural framing. The chapter has analyzed instances of personal narratives told by Japanese children and adults, detailing what linguistic devices and narrative strategies contribute to its culture-specific style.

More specifically, Chapter 5 has not only quantitatively but also qualitatively examined (1) Japanese children's development of narrative discourse competence and narrative structure and (2) the rhetorical/ expressive flexibility yet to be learned (compared with adult narrators). Structural aspects were studied using verse/stanza analysis and high point analysis, whereas rhetorical aspects were investigated by examining whether preschool children have a good command of certain linguistic devices and strategies when talking about personal experiences. Starting in childhood, children master the narrative skills expected in Japanese society. In addition to the morphologically easy items such as *tte* (for onomatopoeias and reported speech), children learn relatively easily to use the interactional/rapport particle *ne* in their narrative production. As Maynard (1989) puts it, 'the Japanese people are more preoccupied with using words in ways that contribute to empathy-building in conversation than they are with what propositional meaning the words themselves provide' (p. 219). Although frequency hypothesis (i.e. children's learning through imitation) does not always explain why children learn certain grammatical items earlier than others, the hypothesis seems to apply to this case; because mothers frequently use *ne* in their monologic narratives, we may be able to assume that mothers' frequent use of *ne* serves as a model for children's use of *ne*. That is, mothers, as primary agents of Japanese culture, seem to induct their children into a subtle interactive communicative style.

Previous studies (e.g. Clancy, 1985) have suggested that Japanese children begin to use the formal *des(u)/mas(u)* styles at about two years. In their monologic narratives, however, Japanese preschool children did not use *des(u)/mas(u)* styles at all. To begin with, because of their status in society (or simply because of their socially expected roles), children may not be rigidly required to use formal styles. As they become older and more attentive to adult formal speech, which is not necessarily addressed to them, and as they participate more actively in conversations with adults, particularly those who are outsiders to them, their experience with the formal *des(u)/mas(u)* styles may be extended to real social interactions and then appear in their narrative production. Thus, while some linguistic devices may appear early in development, it seems to take a considerable time span in order for the full range of adult usage of those devices to appear in narratives. Also, in order to use formal styles effectively in narrative, children may need to get more accustomed to the transition from home to school, a move from the *amae*-based inside world to some kind of outside world, where the meaning of life in a group (recall, for instance, Sho's narrative in Example 5.2) and a social hierarchy are emphasized. Overall, children need to acquire a wide array of optional linguistic devices; moreover, the range of functions served by such devices is elaborated and enriched across time and through experience. These findings therefore suggest that preschool-aged children still have a long way to go in the development of narrative skills.

The study on monologic narrative, which has mainly examined Japanese narrative discourse competence demonstrated by both children and adults, has presented at least two important implications. First, this study has revealed that there is a cross-linguistically common – possibly universal or quasi-universal – route of development for the creation of well-constructed narratives. Whereas children tend to tell their stories in a sequential style, adults emphasize non-sequential information; in particular, compared to children's narratives, adults' narratives place considerably more weight on feelings and emotions. As I previously suggested, we might be able to assume that the acquisition of a full range of narrative devices has a fairly lengthy developmental history. Second, the study has also revealed that speakers of a particular language – Japanese in this case – take a particular path of development, such as the acquisition of syntactic and pragmatic particles specific to their native language as well as the culturally preferred narrative structure. Preschool children seem to have already understood what the canonical narrative form is like (e.g. three-verse stanzas, telling multiple stories), and they gradually tell narratives in culture-specific ways, using language-specific means and devices. Through a study that focuses on culture-specific narrative structures, therefore, we can observe not only universal but also socioculturally and linguistically unique aspects of narrative.

Notes

1. As discussed in Chapter 2, in Japanese null subject pronouns (ø) are prevalent when a character has been established not only in a preceding clause but also in the context. In addition, the translation into English loses many characteristic features of the Japanese language, such as the verb-final word order, the uses of postpositional particles and null-pronouns, and the absence of indefinite and definite articles.
2. In other words, the use of *ga* on first mention creates a presupposition about the existence and specificity of a particular referent in narrative discourse.
3. Japanese is both 'topic-prominent' and 'subject-prominent,' in contrast to languages that are characterized as 'subject-prominent' languages (e.g. English) (Shibatani, 1990). Also, as explained in the text, the marking of case relationships is optional in Japanese. Furthermore, extensive ellipsis of case markers is grammatically acceptable and, moreover, sometimes pragmatically appropriate.
4. Although *un* ('uh huh') is often referred to as a 'back-channeling' response, use of the term 'back-channeling' is intentionally avoided. Although the term implies an unconditional signal to go on talking, some element of control is usually involved (see Chapter 6). Additionally, as can be seen in Example 5.1, monologic performances as well include a conversational partner who also uses *un*s ('uh huh') and *huun*s ('well').
5. The treatment of contrastive *wa* differs among linguists. Kuno (1973) claims that there are two distinct types of *wa*, the 'thematic/topic' one and the 'contrastive' one. Shibatani (1990), however, insists that 'one and the same *wa* has the effect of emphasizing the contrast when the discourse environment provides a background for contrast' (p. 265). Paying attention to a suprasegmental aspect in narrative discourse (i.e. prosodic cues in this case), Maynard (1990) gives further concrete explanations: 'when a *wa*-marked phrase together with *wa* is pronounced with phonological prominence, it implies contrast, regardless of whether the contrastive item is specified or not' (p. 58). However, given that the discussion of whether there exist two categorically different types of *wa* is beyond the scope of the present study, I do not argue this issue further.

6. This is a direct translation of the boy's way of describing the hospital (because his forehead was hurt by his fall from a bicycle, and he was treated at a hospital).
7. According to Hopper's (1979) distinction between foregrounding (i.e. main-line events or restricted narrative clauses) and backgrounding (i.e. commentary or free narrative clauses), the verbal aspect of foreground clauses tends to be perfective (e.g. completive or punctual), whereas that of back-ground clauses tends to be imperfective (e.g. progressive). As seen in the Coding Rules in Chapter 4, however, in the present study a clause that includes the imperfective aspect is considered to represent a hybrid of fore-grounding and backgrounding information.
8. Linguistic devices and strategies highlighted in this section were chosen because of my intuitive notion of their importance in narrative and/or because of their prominence in the literature; I was greatly inspired by Maynard's (1993) study on emotion for the writing of this section.
9. Although the literal translation of Line 24 is '(He) jumped into the sea,' because in English it might imply 'he committed suicide,' the translation has been changed.
10. The following narrative of autobiographical memory was told by Kana's mother who was in her forties (I also translated her narrative into English). In her narrative she uses the causal connective *dakara* ('therefore') effectively; *dakara*, as a matter of fact, appears at the beginning of a stanza):

> My mother had a quarrel. She ran away from home. Because of that, I lived with my grandmother, you know. And, speaking of a bath in those days, there used to be a public bath, you know. So, we went to a public bath. On our way back home from a public bath, my grandmother talked to a neighbor. 'My son's wife ran away from home. My son's wife is atrocious, I tell you,' said my grandmother. At that time, 'what a terrible thing my grandma is saying. She is speaking ill of my mom. What a repulsive wretch my grandma is!' I thought. I have a strong impression of this as a child, you know. This is a rather dismal memory as a child, you know. I wonder how old I was. My mother ran away from home very frequently. They had a quarrel very often. But because I remember this, I think I was probably a first or second grader, you know. *Therefore*, regarding that issue, you know, they often kept me awake very late in the evening. Because it was late in the evening, my grandma took me to a public bath. I took a bath, you know. The water was running from the back. That woke me with a start, you know.

11. However, *yappari* also appears without any anaphoric referent, such as '*otomodachi to yappari wakareru tte yuu no ga, ano tsurakute*' ('Separation from my friends, after all, was heartbreaking'). In this case, *yappari* itself does not convey very important information anaphorically; rather, it is used to appeal to the feelings of the listener, who, the narrator assumes, shares the same sociocultural background as the narrator and will thus understand the narrator's emotional state.
12. While there might be other opinions about the treatment of *da*, I follow Association for Japanese-Language Teaching (1984), Clancy (1985) and Shibatani (1990).

13. Three main types of characters are used for the writing of Japanese: *kanji* (Chinese characters), *hiragana* (the cursive phonetic syllabary), and *katakana* (the angular phonetic syllabary). As Gerbert (1993) points out, even the exclusive use of *katakana* for the spelling of loan words brought into Japanese from Western languages suggests the strength of the inside/outside distinction.

14. As Caffi and Janney (1994) argue, reported speech allows the narrator to express his or her emotional state vividly and thus works as a dramatic element. In one mother's narrative, as a matter of fact, she built up to an emotional high point by using reported speech.

15. To explain situations in which the speaker, not having to acknowledge any interpersonal relationship with the addressee, uses the plain copula *da*, Matsumoto (1993) mentions two different possibilities: (1) the relationship is intimate, and (2) the communication is impersonal. The use of *da* in relation to narrative-internal perspective taking roughly corresponds to the latter.

16. With regard to the position/location of the formal *des(u)*/*mas(u)* verb-ending forms, a quantitative examination of Japanese adult narratives was conducted. The verb position/location was judged to be either one of the following: (1) stanza initial, (2) stanza final and (3) stanza elsewhere. To examine possible differences in terms of the location/position, raw frequencies were then converted to proportional frequencies and compared across positions/locations. The formal *des(u)*/*mas(u)* verb-ending forms appeared more frequently at the end of stanzas ($M = 45.68$, $SD = 19.18$) than at the beginning ($M = 29.33$, $SD = 15.01$); they also appeared more frequently at the end of stanzas than somewhere else in the middle ($M = 4.99$, $SD = 17.77$). The statistical significance of the results was evaluated using a repeated-measures analysis of variance (ANOVA), with position/location as a within-subjects factor, for the variable of the formal *des(u)*/*mas(u)* verb-ending forms. The overall F test showed a significant difference $F(2, 38) = 5.24$, $p < 0.01$. Post-hoc tests indicated: (1) the formal *des(u)*/*mas(u)* verb-ending forms are more likely to appear at the end of stanzas than at the beginning, $F(1, 19) = 6.14$, $p < 0.03$; and (2) the formal *des(u)*/*mas(u)* verb-ending forms are also more likely to appear at the end of stanzas than somewhere else in the middle, $F(1, 19) = 7.49$, $p < 0.02$. Thus, the formal *des(u)*/*mas(u)* patterns are likely to appear stanza finally. [For further information, see Minami (1998).]

17. With regard to the location/position of psychological complements, a quantitative examination of Japanese adult narratives was conducted. To examine possible differences in terms of the location/position, raw frequencies were then converted to proportional frequencies and compared across positions/locations. Psychological complements appeared more frequently at the end of stanzas ($M = 71.60$, $SD = 33.20$) than at the beginning ($M = 7.14$, $SD = 19.30$); they also appeared more frequently at the end of stanzas than somewhere else in the middle ($M = 21.26$, $SD = 32.51$). The statistical significance of the results was evaluated using a repeated-measures analysis of variance (ANOVA), with position/location as a within-subjects factor, for the variable of psychological complements. The overall F test showed a significant difference $F(2, 26) = 12.70$, $p < 0.0001$. Post-hoc tests indicated: (1) psychological complements are more likely to appear at the end of stanzas than at the beginning, $F(1, 13) = 30.74$, $p < 0.0001$; and, also, (2) psychological complements are more likely to appear at the end of stanzas than

somewhere else in the middle, $F(1, 13) = 8.99$, $p < 0.02$. Therefore, psychological complements, such as *omou* ('think'), *ki ga suru* ('feel'), *wakaru* ('know,' 'be sure'), *oboete iru* ('remember,' 'recollect'), and *mitai* ('seem'), are identified as markers to wrap up a narrative stanza. [For further information, see Minami (1998).]

18. Strong correlations were found between the particle *ne* and the formal *des(u)/mas(u)* verb-ending styles, $r(18) = 0.86$, $p < 0.0001$, and between the particle *yo* and the formal *des(u)/mas(u)* verb-ending styles, $r(18) = 0.68$, $p < 0.001$. These results may suggest that unlike children, adults use these particles at the verse/clause-final position and not at the line-final position.

19. Recall that in Example 5.4, Yuka used *ne* to check whether the listener knows the park she was referring to (Line 6). Thus, interactional particles are not randomly distributed across types of narrative clauses.

20. Many adults' narratives indicate that even if they are taking a narrative internal position, at the end of the stanza they tend to resume a narrative external position (Minami, 1998). In Example 5.7, for instance, when narrating her experience in Stanza B, the narrator used informal endings, signaling that she was taking a narrative internal position. At the end of the stanza, however, she resumed using *des(u)*. Similarly, in another mother's narrative, the narrator used reported speech with informal endings, but at the end of the stanza, she returned to the formal *des(u)* style. Resuming the formal style at the end of the stanza thus reflects the narrator's psychological orientation: (1) the narrator tries to maintain personal distance with the listener; (2) at the same time, she is fully aware of the existence of the listener.

21. Bonferroni Post Hoc tests subsequent to the ANOVA showed that adults more frequently used *tte* than either one of the child groups.

22. Children were given prompting questions related to injuries, whereas mothers were asked to talk about their earliest memory. Some mothers, however, provided an injury story with many emotional descriptions. In Tamotsu's mother's narrative in Chapter 9 (Example 9.2), for example, the narrator vividly describes how she got injured when she was riding a bicycle with her father. Thus, although the issue of temporal distance – the recent past for children and the distant past for adults – may still remain, the genre is the same 'personal experiences.'

23. Frequencies were used for the analysis of attention-getting devices. Although proportions correct for differences in length and allow us to see differing relative emphasis on components of narration, because the overall proportion of attention-getting devices itself is very small, that measure may not be appropriate. A one-way analysis of variance (ANOVA) was performed on the variable, attention-getting devices, $F(2, 37) = 6.25$, $p < 0.01$. The ANOVA results were further analyzed in Bonferroni Post Hoc tests, which revealed that in comparison to adults, children of both groups used fewer attention-getting devices.

24. Bonferroni Post Hoc tests subsequent to the ANOVA showed that adults more frequently used *dakara* than either one of the children's groups.

25. In the coding rules of high point analysis, another connective *kara* is treated in a similar way to *dakara* because *dakara* is etymologically a combination of *da* and *kara* (Maynard, 1993). Although children use *kara*, compared to *dakara*, its function is limited. It neither provides supplementary information nor

expresses culturally shared assumptions. One child (Yuka, 5;6) did use *dakara*, which is the only use of *dakara* produced by children. Also, recall that for the present study, plural short prompts were given to children in order to facilitate their narrative production, and that the longest narrative produced by each child was selected. Unfortunately, because Yuka did not use *dakara* in the longest narrative, it is not included in Table 6.4.

26. Bonferroni Post Hoc tests subsequent to the ANOVA showed that adults more frequently used *da* than either one of the children's groups.
27. Bonferroni Post Hoc tests subsequent to the ANOVA showed that adults more frequently used *yo* than either one of the children's groups.
28. Some might argue that the copula *da* is used mostly by males and the final particle *yo* mostly by females. It is certainly true that *da* sounds somewhat blunt and masculine (Shibatani, 1990), while *yo* sounds somewhat feminine (Sakata, 1991). However, as seen in Table 5.4, adult females use *da* mostly followed by a psychological complement or the past-tense marker *ta*. Also, *yo* is used by males in conjunction with *da* (see Lines 19 and 26 in Example 5.5, in which the female narrator reports what her male classmate said).
29. Bonferroni Post Hoc tests subsequent to the ANOVA showed that adults more frequently used *des(u)/mas(u)* than either one of the children's groups.
30. According to Maynard (1993), although the narrator uses *dakara* when providing explanatory information from a somewhat neutral perspective, the narrator uses *datte* when he or she provides information in order to justify his or her position. Maynard (1993) further argues that '*datte* is often used by a child in an interaction with parents or people with whom the *amae* 'psychological and emotional dependence' relationship is established' (p. 115). I will discuss children's use of *datte* in the context of mother–child interaction in later chapters.
31. As can seen in Chapter 7, however, in dialogic or interactional narrative contexts, young children have command of a wider range of formal devices and lexical items.
32. As Berman (1994) explains, because children tend to perform better in some types of storytelling settings than in others, different tasks may elicit different kinds of narratives from young children. Shapiro and Hudson (1991) claim that 'preschoolers begin to distinguish stories from other narrative genres' (p. 961). For example, in Uchida's (1990) study using a wordless picture story, Mercer Mayer's *Frog, Where Are You?* (1969), a four-year, ten-month-old Japanese girl was able to take the two kinds of perspectives – narrative internal and external. Having had some exposure to storybooks, young children may be familiar with the rhetorical form of stories. Thus, the difference between these results may be explained in terms of genre.
33. Although Japanese discipline in the home is apparently permissive by American standards (Clancy, 1986; Peak, 1991), instances of harsh and authoritarian practices have also been described (e.g. Schoolland, 1990). The nature of behavioral control thus differs depending on the role, age and gender of the adult.
34. Western observers report that they were overwhelmed by the sheer noise level created by exuberant Japanese preschoolers (Lewis, 1984, 1991; Peak, 1989, 1991). To Americans, Japanese preschool teachers (elementary school

teachers as well) appear to value spontaneous rowdy play and make little demand for self-control (Lewis, 1984, 1991).

35. As a cautionary note, I certainly accept Cook's (1997) claim that mothers sometimes use the formal *des(u)/mas(u)* forms when they serve food, preside over household matters, teach social norms and scold their children. Parents use the formal styles because these activities are related to parents' social responsibility. Cook (2000) suggests that 'children's understanding of the *masu* form as a marker of the public self is crucial in interpreting this form as a marker of politeness later in their life, for politeness is an implicature that arises in certain social contexts in which display of the public self is expected' (p. 13). In this sense, Cook's distinction between 'public/social' and 'private' in terms of verb-ending patterns makes sense.

Chapter 6
Parental Narrative Elicitation Styles

Narrative is not only a general and spontaneous activity that one can observe in any culture, but it also shows culturally discrete patterns. Up to this point the main focus of this book has been detailing the emergence of a culture-specific narrative style in Japanese children. The previous two chapters, which have analyzed narratives through the lens of culture, identified certain narrative discourse patterns and linguistic devices that are socioculturally embedded. For instance, theories based on psychological/cultural framing such as verse/stanza analysis (Gee, 1991a; Hymes, 1990) have tried to explain the culture-specific cognitive comprehension and interpretation of spatially and temporally distant events in terms of hierarchical schemata; those theories, in fact, have contributed greatly to the study of the cultural diversity of narrative structure. Using both Labov's (1972) high point analysis and verse/ stanza analysis for Japanese, Chapter 5 has identified how certain narrative discourse patterns and linguistic devices contribute to the cultural framing of Japanese oral personal narratives. The findings reported in the previous chapters thus re-emphasize the importance of understanding narratives, oral personal narratives in particular, because they are reflective of human interactions that always take place in socioculturally specific contexts.

Whereas the previous two chapters have addressed young children's and adults' personal narratives, Chapter 6 looks at their narratives in the context of mother–child interactions. Here, I emphasize that narrative should be viewed as a dialogic mode of telling, or a jointly constructed narrative, rather than a monologic mode of telling. Specifically, I conceptualize a conversational narrative as a product that is jointly constructed and produced by the mother and child. The results demonstrate that from early childhood on, Japanese children learn the narrative style valued by their mothers. The chapter also illustrates the link between maternal narrative elicitation strategies and children's developing narrative skill; that is, Japanese mothers, scaffolding children's narratives, support their children's progressive contributions to the narrative task in a variety of ways in accordance with cultural requirements.

Parental Scaffolding

Studies on child language acquisition suggest that like children elsewhere, Japanese children acquire their language very early (Clancy, 1985). To account for how children acquire language, however, there has been considerable debate over the years and, consequently, competing theories have been proposed. One such theory that has attracted considerable attention is Pinker's (1984) language learnability theory, which proposed a model of 'semantic bootstrapping' in which children initially use a set of innate linguistic knowledge of ('linking') rules to map thematic roles such as agent and patient onto syntactic functions such as subject and object. In contrast, Bowerman's (1991) competing hypothesis suggests that knowledge of linking rules is learned on the basis of linguistic experience (e.g. with mothers). In either case, issues of maternal speech to young children are related to issues of the mechanisms underlying language acquisition, whether biological/innate or environmental, or even how these two factors interact and overlap with each other, as earlier discussed in Chapter 2.

Developmentally, the linguistic function changes from the sentential level to that of discourse. As early as 20 months, children begin to talk about past events, marking the beginning of narrative discourse production. Furthermore, the emergence of narrative development can be identified in spontaneous descriptions of past events that children produce in conversation. In this sense, language development includes a range of social interactions between an adult and a child in which the child performs narrative-telling activities, with a certain degree of adult assistance.

Since the 1960s evidence has been provided that maternal linguistic approaches influence the cognitive development of children (Azuma, 1996; Hess & Shipman, 1965). Scaffolding, which means the temporary support that parents or other adults give a child performing a task (Bruner, 1977, 1983), has attracted a great deal of attention. It is said that an inverse relationship exists between the child's current ability and the amount of support to be provided. The less ability a child has in performing a given task, the more direction the parent provides; in contrast, the more ability the child has, the less direction the parent provides. In this way, the more the child becomes able to perform, the less the parent helps. When the child performs a given task on his or her own, the parent takes away 'scaffolds' because they are no longer necessary.

Accordingly, recent studies of language acquisition and language development have focused not only on the structural aspects of children's narrative discourse (e.g. Peterson, 1990; Reilly, 1992), but also on the effect of maternal styles of talking with young children (e.g. McCabe & Peterson, 1991; Peterson & McCabe, 1992). Akatsuka and Clancy (1993) and Clancy (1999), for instance, suggest that language input from adult speakers, especially from mothers, is a crucial source of information for language acquisition and that children are sensitive to particular input patterns. According to these researchers, the roles that the mother plays in her child's language acquisition, in conjunction with the encoding of the speaker's (i.e. mother's) affective meanings, are considered important in light of the early emergence of certain types of sentences among Japanese children.

Likewise, Mayes and Ono (1993) claim that, in their research, a young Japanese child followed the pattern presented in the adult input when deciding what to mark with the Japanese case marker *ga* (which is used for both subject and object marking, such as '*dare ga* ['who' with a subject marker] *kore ga* ['this' with an object marker] *dekiru* ['can do'] *ka* [question] ' which means 'Who can do this?'). Mayes and Ono thus suggest that parental uses of *ga* markings are a highly significant predictor of the child's uses of the same particle and, therefore, claim that their findings provide strong evidence for the important role of adult input.

In narrative contexts in particular, children's speech is guided and scaffolded by mothers who elicit children's contributions about past experiences. There is substantial evidence that mothers play a critical role in shaping various aspects of their children's narrative discourse skills. Eisenberg (1985) examined the dialogic nature of conversations of young children with their mothers and identified three phases of development: '(a) dependency on adult participation; (b) the discussion of elements common to many instances of an event, rather than the unique occurrences of a specific event (i.e. dependence on a 'script' of the event); and (c) talk about unique occurrences, but difficulty in planning a lengthy discourse' (p. 177). Hudson (1990, 1993) studied the role of parent–child conversations in the development of young children's ability to talk about past events. Investigating the effects of maternal elicitation style, she emphasized the influence of repeatedly recounting events on the emergence and development of early autobiographical memory.

Other researchers have also emphasized maternal style differences in narrative elicitation, with a focus on the relationship between maternal behavior and subsequent child performance. McCabe and Peterson (1990, 1991, 2000) and Peterson and McCabe (1992) claim that stylistic differences between parents also affect children's later narrative style. As we have seen in detail in Chapters 2 and 4, according to these researchers, if mothers habitually ask their children to describe people, places and things involved in some event, the children later tell stories that focus on orientation at the expense of plot; in contrast, if mothers habitually ask their children about what happened next, the children later tell stories with well-developed plots (McCabe & Peterson, 1990; Peterson & McCabe, 1992).

Likewise, Fivush (1991) suggests that those mothers who use a more elaborated elicitation style early in development influence children to provide more elaborated accounts later in development. Additionally, Fivush and Fromhoff's (1988) 'elaborative' mothers, who provide a substantial amount of information, correspond to what Hudson (1993) calls 'high elaboration mothers'; Fivush and Fromhoff's 'repetitive' mothers, on the other hand, correspond to Hudson's 'low elaboration mothers.' Thus, the sorts of questions mothers ask during children's narratives predict the aspect of the narrative children will elaborate a couple of years later. For instance, mothers who ask for background information are likely to have children who emphasize setting, whereas mothers who ask for evaluation are likely to have children who emphasize perspective (McCabe & Peterson, 1991). More general assumptions behind these studies are: (1) There must be a positive relationship between maternal patterns of talking and children's cognitive attainment; and (2) the frequency with which children hear linguistic patterns in parental speech plays a crucial role in determining children's linguistic patterns.

In this way, the presence of distinctive maternal styles of narrative elicitation becomes important if we can relate them to children's narrative discourse skill. As can be seen in what Bruner (1977, 1983) termed 'scaffolding,' Vygotsky (1978) also suggested another important concept of the 'zone of proximal development,' the difference between the child's actual level of development (i.e. with no external guidance) and the level of performance that he or she achieves with the adult's support (i.e. with external guidance); thus, children's cognitive skills first develop through social interactions with more mature members of society and then become internalized after long practice. When applied to narrative contexts, the social interaction paradigm suggests that the ability to structure personal narratives develops through social interactions between children and adults, especially mothers.

In studying mother–child interactions in a given culture, it is easy to imagine that parents differ from one another in many ways when talking with their children. As we have observed in the studies described above, some parents extend one topic extensively, whereas others are more likely to shift topics of conversation with their children. In other words, parents differ in terms of what kinds of orientation and evaluation they both prompt for and model. The role of individual and cultural variation among mothers is important in early face-to-face interactions for children. Conversation analysis (e.g. Sacks *et al.*, 1978), for instance, provide systematic evidence for collaborative behaviors in communication processes. As Levinson (1983) puts it, 'face-to-face interaction is not only the context for language acquisition, but the only significant kind of language use in many of the world's communities' (pp. 43–44). In other words, because interlocutors create a joint reality, relationships between these two parties must be fully taken into consideration. Thus, because the mother is generally the primary individual interacting with her young child, the early conversational context for the child's narrative development is shaped by maternal questions and prompts.

As a natural extension of this assumption, the mother, either implicitly or explicitly, provides her child with culturally appropriate narrative forms. It can be hypothesized that through interactions with the mother, the child learns to tell his or her own stories using culture-specific representational forms and rules. In other words, it is assumed that as a result of early social interactions, young children's narratives are shaped into culturally preferred narrative patterns.

To summarize, personal narratives order experience by making sense of the general flow of events in a person's life. The origins of narrative style, however, can be traced back to conversations between parents and children (Sachs, 1979). The second goal of this book is thus to examine how Japanese parents guide their preschool children (four- and five-year-olds) in the acquisition of culture-specific styles of narrative. Monologic narrative, as discussed in Chapters 4 and 5, presents a more cognitive view of narrative development; dialogic narrative, as illustrated in the taped conversations between mother and child, being related to communicative competence, illustrates a more interactive view of narrative development. Specific research questions that can be posed in this context are as follows:

(1) What linguistic items (e.g. particles, adverbs, connectives and verbs) do mothers frequently use when eliciting narratives from their children?

(2) What, if any, differences in narrative elicitation styles are found between mothers of four-year-olds and mothers of five-year-olds?
(3) What, if any, differences in mothers' narrative elicitation styles are found to be used with boy children and girl children?
(4) What relationships are observed between maternal patterns of narrative elicitation and children's developing narrative skill?

The main purpose of this chapter is thus to explore the relationship between maternal styles of narrative elicitation and children's narrative development.

Once the relationship between parental elicitation strategies and children's narratives is identified, this chapter then investigates the extent to which children's personal narratives are influenced and constructed through social interactions. It specifically examines both micro- and macro-level aspects of parental styles of narrative elicitation. A speech act coding system, which was previously applied to analyze how speech acts are mapped onto dialogic narrative discourse in English (Dickinson, 1991; McCabe & Peterson, 1991), is also used to code maternal speech. This type of analysis and this coding system allow us to see how speech acts are mapped over turns in narrative discourse and can provide answers to the overall question of how Japanese parents guide their children in the acquisition of specific styles of narrative.

Method

Participants

The sample for the present study of parental narrative elicitation patterns is the same 20 Japanese preschool children, half aged four and half five, and their mothers who appeared in previous chapters. It should be remembered that, for each age cohort half of the children studied were boys and half were girls. Mothers who participated in this project were supplied with tape recorders and blank cassette tapes and asked to record at home occasions when their children liked to tell them 'stories about personal experience, about real events that have happened in the past' (McCabe & Peterson, 1991, p. 226). Mothers were asked to do so in as natural a way as possible, 'like you ordinarily behave when you ask your child to talk about past events' (McCabe & Peterson, 1991, p. 226). That is, mothers were asked to elicit interesting past events or experiences from their children, and no more specific instructions or requests were provided.

Of the tapes provided, 100% were returned to the researcher. Audiotapes were transcribed verbatim for coding in the format required for analysis using the Child Data Exchange system (MacWhinny & Snow, 1985, 1990). Some mother–child pairs, however, talked about more events than others. To establish a comparable data base, therefore, a decision was made to analyze only the initial three narrative productions by each mother–child pair. All the data used in this chapter (and Chapter 7 as well) are thus based on the initial three narrative productions from each mother–child pair.

Lexical Level Analysis

Total number of words, total number of different words, type-token ratio in dialogic narrative

Briefly, in what follows, I will describe age-related similarities and differences in mother–child narrative discourse interactions at the lexical level. For instance, I will illustrate age-related differences in mothers' narrative elicitation styles with regard to the quantity of words, which I consider an indication of the difference in parental scaffolding. More detailed analyses are described below:

Quantity and variety (children's patterns)

Table 6.1 presents the means and standard deviations of the total number of words and the total number of different words used in dialogic narrative interactions. For the four-year-olds, the total number of words ranged widely from 44 to 1114; the total number of different words ranged from 24 to 234. For the five-year-olds, the total number of words ranged from 123 to 493; the total number of different words ranged from 55 to 150. The larger numbers of the four-year-olds' total number of words and number of different words than those of the five-year-olds were attributable to one boy's (Tamotsu) and one girl's (Yumi) fairly long dialogic narrative productions. Similar type-token ratios (i.e. the total number of different words divided by the total number of words) of these two age groups, however, indicate that the levels of lexical redundancy are almost identical.

Neither gender nor age differences approached statistical significance for any of the three dependent variables, (1) the total number of words, (2) the total number of different words and (3) the type-token ratio. Interesting interactions between age and gender, however, emerged. In dialogic narrative, the four-year-old boys ($M = 500.00$, $SD = 381.90$) produced a larger total number of words than did the four-year-old girls ($M = 471.80$, $SD = 362.54$), while the four-year-old girls ($M = 139.00$, $SD = 57.83$) produced a larger number of different words than did the

Words

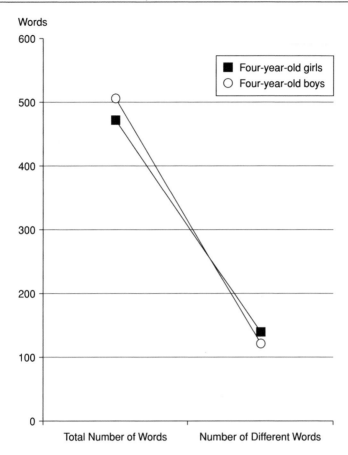

Figure 6.1 Total number of words and number of different words by child's age group and gender (four-year-olds)

four-year-old boys (*M* = 128.20, *SD* = 72.67) (see Figure 6.1). In contrast, the five-year-old girls produced both a larger total number of words (*M* = 368.40, *SD* = 112.93) and a larger number of different words (*M* = 128.40, *SD* = 31.00) than did the five-year-old boys (*M* = 218.00, *SD* = 83.91; *M* = 86.40, *SD* = 31.42) (see Figure 6.2).

Utterances over turns (i.e. the number of utterances produced by a speaker per turn) were also examined. The four-year-olds' utterances over turns ranged from 1.042 to 1.818, whereas the five-year-olds' utterances over turns ranged from 1.019 to 1.786. Although neither gender nor age difference reached statistical significance, the mean of the four-year-olds is slightly higher than that of the five-year-olds. Although the

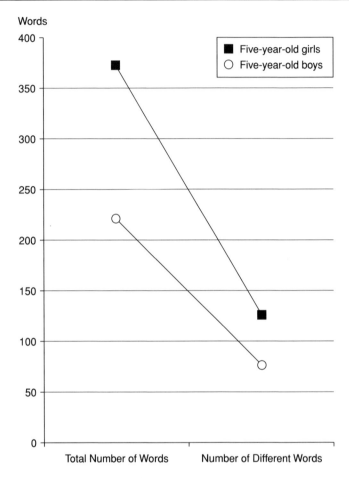

Figure 6.2 Total number of words and number of different words by child's age group and gender (five-year-olds).

development in this area looks as if it went in the opposite direction, there are two possible explanations. First, this age-related decline happened because one particular four-year-old's (Tamotsu) exceptionally high score on utterances over turns pulled up the mean of the four-year-olds' utterances over turns. Second and more important, because of the nature of Japanese type of interaction (i.e. co-constructed discourse, or frequent turn exchanges), the longer conversational turns (i.e. holding the floor for a longer period of time) does not necessarily serve as a good developmental indicator.

Table 6.1 Means and standard deviations of total number of words, total number of different words, type-token ratio and utterances over turns in dialogic narrative production

Variable	Four-year-olds (n = 10)		Five-year-olds (n = 10)		Mothers (n = 20)	
	M	SD	M	SD	M	SD
Total number of words	485.90	351.36	293.20	122.81	554.70	245.65
Total number of different words	133.60	62.18	107.40	36.82	140.20	39.66
Type-token ratio	0.33	0.10	0.38	0.06	0.27	0.05
Utterances over turns	1.30	0.23	1.19	0.22	1.66	0.32

Quantity and variety (maternal patterns)

Dialogic narrative performance exhibited by the 20 mothers also varied greatly. The total number of words ranged widely from 272 to 1012. The total number of different words ranged from 86 to 223. The mothers of four-year-olds produced a marginally larger total number of words ($M = 658.40$, $SD = 295.70$) than did the mothers of five-year-olds ($M = 451.00$, $SD = 126.73$), $F(1, 16) = 3.92$, $p = 0.065$. Although the difference is marginal, the result obtained here is considered important because it appears to indicate that the mothers of four-year-olds, regardless of the child's gender, felt more need to extend their children's narrative productions than did the mothers of five-year-olds.

Linguistic items

In Chapter 5, I examined linguistic items – morphological and lexical – used by the four- and five-year-olds and their mothers when they told monologic narratives, as effective strategies for involvement. The linguistic items used by the four- and five-year-olds in mother–child interactions exhibit both similarities to and differences from those that they used in their monologic narrative productions (see Table 6.2).

Similarities between monologic and dialogic narrative discourse

As explained in Chapter 5, *ne* ('you know') expresses the narrator's psychological and emotional dependence on the listener, and thus tries

to establish narrator-listener rapport or intersubjectivity, which Ninio
and Snow (1996) define as 'a state in which two or more persons share
a feeling of "togetherness"' (p. 23). The children frequently used the
rapport particle *ne* in both contexts (recall Ryota's narrative in Example
5.1). Like the results obtained from monologic narrative productions, the
difference in the use of *ne* between adults and children did not approach
statistical difference. Also, as previously seen in the children's monologic narratives, children did not use the adverb *yappari* ('after all,' 'as
expected') in mother–child interactions, either. As far as these linguistic
items are concerned, there is no obvious distinction between monologic
and dialogic narratives.

Differences between monologic and dialogic narrative discourse
    The distributions of other linguistic items in the dialogic narrative
context, however, are strikingly different from those in the monologic
narrative context. That is, what appeared to be differences between adults
and children in monologic narratives are no longer distinct in dialogic
narratives. The children used the assertive/emphatic particle *yo* ('I tell
you': e.g. *demo oborenakatta* ***yo***: 'But [I] wasn't drowned, I tell you') and
the quotation-final particle *tte* (e.g. *'itai itai'* ***tte*** *naiteta*: ' "[It] hurts, [it]
hurts," [I] was crying') more frequently in mother–child interactions. A
connective, *dakara* ('so,' 'therefore'), which did not appear at all in monologic narratives, was used by four children (e.g. ***dakara*** *kuroi no nutta*:
'That's why [I] painted [it] black'). Further, another connective, *datte*
('but,' 'because'), which appeared only once in monologic narratives,
was used by nine children (e.g. ***datte*** *obachan ga soo itta mon*: 'Because
a middle-aged woman [someone's mom in this case] said so'). Similarly,
the formal *des(u)/mas(u)* styles were used by five children,[1] although these
forms never appeared in their monologic narratives. Finally, the informal
verb-ending form *da*, which was used by only one child in monologic
narrative contexts, frequently appeared in mother–child interactions.
    In the past some studies (e.g. Phillips, 1973) explored whether there is
a difference in vocabulary choice between mothers' speech to children
and adults, i.e. whether mothers as adults speak to children in the same
way as they speak to other adults. In the present study, the linguistic items
used by the mothers in mother–child interactions also exhibit both similarities to and differences from those used in their monologic narrative
productions. Mothers frequently used the rapport particle *ne* ('you
know'), the assertive/emphatic particle *yo* ('I tell you'), and the quotation-
final particle *tte*, all of which they also used when talking about past
events on their own. Likewise, they used the informal/plain copula *da* in

Table 6.2 Mean frequencies and standard deviations of selected linguistic items in the context of mother–child interaction

	Four-year-olds		Five-year-olds		Mothers		F^a values for main effect of GROUP
	(n = 10)		*(n = 10)*		*(n = 20)*		
	M	*(SD)*	*M*	*(SD)*	*M*	*(SD)*	
Particles							
ne	22.40	(25.82)	18.80	(16.46)	11.45	(9.62)	1.64
yo	2.50	(2.22)	1.70	(3.16)	4.30	(4.64)	1.76
tte	7.80	(8.27)	4.60	(3.50)	5.80	(3.44)	1.03
Connectives							
dakara	1.10	(2.51)	0.10	(0.32)	0.10	(0.31)	2.33
datte	0.80	(0.92)	0.50	(0.71)	0.05	(0.22)	5.74**
Adverb							
yappari	0.00	(0.00)	0.00	(0.00)	0.05	(0.22)	0.49
Verbs							
des(u)/mas(u)	0.40	(0.52)	0.10	(0.32)	0.30	(0.66)	0.76
da	3.10	(4.25)	1.00	(1.41)	4.00	(3.96)	2.32

*$p < 0.05$; **$p < 0.01$
[a] Degrees of freedom = 2, 37.

both contexts. However, the connective *dakara* ('so,' 'therefore'), which was extensively used by some mothers in their monologic narratives, appeared only twice in the context of mother–child interactions. Also, the adverb *yappari* ('after all,' 'as expected'), which frequently appeared in mothers' monologic narratives, appeared only once in mother–child interactions. Moreover, the formal *des(u)/mas(u)* verb-ending forms, which all mothers frequently used in their monologic narratives, were used by only four mothers in the context of mother–child interactions.

Thus, the mothers' attitudes in interacting with their children were apparently different from their attitudes when they talked about their own personal experiences to an adult interviewer. Simply put, these attitudinal differences may be attributable to mothers' use of child-directed speech (i.e. form of speech used by adults to talk to young children). Socioculturally, however, these differences could be attributable to the fact that mothers are talking with their children, whom they consider immature group members. For instance, because the formal *des(u)/mas(u)* styles express the speaker's respect to the listener, mothers did not need to use such styles. In mother–child interactions, moreover, mothers did not use the connective *dakara* ('so,' 'therefore') and the adverb *yappari* ('after all,' 'as expected'). These two forms – connective and adverb, respectively – are based on the culturally shared assumption that what the narrator has stated is interpreted by the listener as 'a sufficient cause/explanation for a possible (or plausible) result/consequence' (Maynard, 1993, p. 97). Thus, mothers may frequently use these linguistic items when talking with adults who fully understand the culturally shared assumption, but may not necessarily do so when talking with their children. Obviously, part of the reason why mothers did not use these two forms is that they were eliciting narratives from their children and not narrating by themselves. To compare mothers' use of connectives in the two different settings (i.e. when talking with adults and when talking with children), therefore, it would be useful to collect narratives of mothers to their children.

The differences in monologic and dialogic narrative contexts may also suggest that four- and five-year-olds, to some extent, perceive the difference between 'inside' and 'outside,' which was discussed in the previous chapter, but in a different way than adults (i.e. mothers) do. Recall, for example, that in Table 5.4 in Chapter 5, the assertive and/or emphatic particle *yo* ('I tell you') appeared only twice when their past experiences were elicited by an outsider. As can be seen in Table 6.2, however, in mother–child interactions, the four-year-olds and five-year-olds used the particle 25 times and 17 times, respectively. The difference in the use of *yo* of these two settings can be explained as follows: The narrator uses the particle *yo* only when he or she provides the listener with new information or only when he or she has better access to the information than the listener (Maynard, 1990, 1993). Such a situation may not frequently occur when addressing an interviewer (i.e. outsider) because when the speaker addresses an outsider, the outsider is usually placed in a higher position than the speaker. On the other hand, the child may use *yo* when addressing the mother, who is an insider; unlike adults' notion that age relates to higher position, the child treats the mother as an equal partner in an inside circle. Likewise, a young child's attitudinal differences between monologic narratives (toward an outsider) and dialogic narratives (with an insider) are evident in other items, such as the more frequent use of the informal/plain *da* style in mother–child interactions.[2] Overall, whereas the mother considers her child an inferior insider, the child's overriding emphasis is on his or her mother as an intimate partner in an inside circle.

Further, dependence relates to the use of connectives. In mother–child interactions children used *datte* ('but,' 'because') subsequent to which they provided information in order to justify their position. A two-way (age group × gender) analysis of variance (ANOVA) accompanied by Bonferroni Post Hoc tests showed that although four-year-olds used *datte* significantly more frequently than adults, there was no statistically significant difference observed between five-year-olds and mothers. As Maynard (1993) argues, '*datte* is often used by a child in an interaction with parents or people with whom the *amae* 'psychological and emotional dependence' relationship is established' (p. 115). We may conclude that although four- and five-year-olds both use *datte* when talking with their mothers, because five-year-olds are more mature than four-year-olds, they less frequently underscore their psychological/emotional dependence on their mothers. Conversely, because four-year-olds are more likely to rely on their mothers emotionally as their intimate partner in an inside circle, they use *datte* very frequently. Overall, these results may suggest that although the genre – talking about past events – is the same, dialogic narrative productions in the context of mother–child interactions differ greatly from monologic narrative productions. Thus, differences of situation may cause the young narrator to employ very different linguistic devices in telling personal narratives. Even if he or she narrates the same story, we may observe that situational influences reshape the deployment of linguistic devices in many ways.

Micro-level Narrative Discourse Analysis

Narrative discourse devices

The purpose of this micro-level narrative discourse analysis is to provide detailed information regarding how discourse devices employed by Japanese mothers shape their children's narrative style. Specifically, this section discusses two major types of discourse devices: (1) the listener's *un* ('uh huh') in response to the narrator's *ne* ('you know') and (2) the listener's use of *huun* ('well').

Example 6.1 is from Sachi, a girl aged 5;9. Sachi and her mother are in the middle of a conversation about a birthday party held at preschool at which her teacher was costumed as a ghost. Some of the linguistic items that have been examined above appear in this example, such as the rapport particle *ne* ('you know') and the connective *datte* ('but,' 'because').

Example 6.1 Sachi and her mother's interaction
Mother: *tanjoobi kai de obake yashiki shite,*
               'At a birthday party, (you) played haunted house.'
Sachi: *ehtto ne,*
               'Um, you know,'

                                                  (**Mother**:   *un*)
                                                       'uh huh'

Sachi: *sensei uso tsuiten no.*
               'the teacher was a liar.'
               koo shite ne,
               '(She) did this, you know,'

                                                  (**Mother**:   *un*)
                                                       'uh huh'

Sachi: *sensei ga ne,*
               'the teacher, you know,'

                                                  (**Mother**:   *un*)
                                                       'uh huh'

Sachi: *omen kabutte,*
               'put on a mask,'
               koo shite ne,
               'and did this, you know,'

                                                  (**Mother**:   *un*)
                                                       'uh huh'

[. . .]

Sachi: *datte sensei ne,*
               'because the teacher, you know,'

                                              (**Mother**:   *un*)
                                                'uh huh'

Sachi: *Kumagumi san no heya e itta toki ne,*
               'when (we) went into the *Kumagumi* (the 'Bear' Class) room,
               you know,'

                                              (**Mother**:   *un*)
                                                'uh huh'

Sachi: *konna kao datta mon.*
               '(we found her face) was like this.'
                                              (**Mother**:   *ah so*)
                                                'uh really'

Sachi: *obake no kao datta mon.*
               '(Hers) was a spooky face.'
Mother: *obake no kao dattan.*
               '(Hers) was a spooky face.'
               hee!
               'Oh, my!'

The role of brief verbal acknowledgment

    Spoken Japanese, as explained in the analysis of monologic narratives
in Chapter 5, is often produced in smaller units than traditional grammatical ones, such as a sentence or a clause. These smaller units are

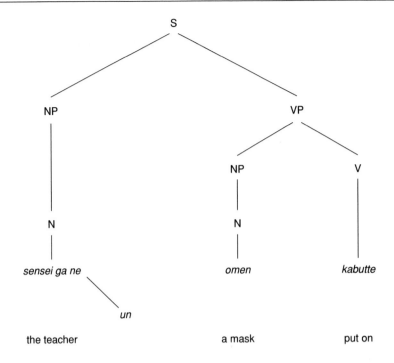

The teacher, you know, put on a mask.

Figure 6.3 Child's *ne* immediately followed by mother's *un*.

often marked by the particle *ne*, which serves as a contextualization device similar to 'you know' in English. Okubo (1959), for example, defines this type of *ne* as an indication that a child, pausing there, is searching for what to say next. The particle *ne* also serves as a marker of what Maynard (1989) calls a pause-bounded phrasal unit, which would correspond to what Chafe (1980) calls an 'idea unit' – a series of brief spurts in narrative discourse (for more information, see Chapter 2). As Sachi's narrative illustrates, segmented by sentence- or clause-final particles (e.g. *koo shite ne*, 'did this, you know') as well as particles within a sentence (e.g. *sensei ne*, 'the teacher, you know'), these smaller parts serve as units in oral Japanese discourse (see Figure 6.3).[3]

More importantly, as discussed in the previous chapter, because the particle *ne* is used as an attention-getting and, thus, contextualization device, it contributes to the harmonious mutual understanding that is highly valued in Japanese society. The effectiveness of *ne* in this regard is also evidenced in Example 6.1, in which, as one of the noticeable aspects, the mother contributes to the child's narrative construction by frequently showing brief acknowledgment *un* ('uh huh'). *Aizuchi*, which literally means 'alternate/mutual hammering' (or back-channeling, to borrow Yngve's (1970) term), describes a situation in which the listener gives responses that make a conversation go smoothly. By uttering *ne* ('you know'), the speaker may elicit the listener's brief verbal acknowledgment. [Note: In Japanese culture, using frequent back-channeling is considered to be polite because it is assumed to signal that the listener is paying attention to the speaker (Maynard, 1989; Yamada, 1992).] In return, the listener's frequent brief acknowledgment *un* is a discursive device that helps the narrator construct a sentence, thereby facilitating narration. Uchida (1986) has claimed that without listeners' proper brief acknowledgments, the storyteller would not be able to tell folktales rhythmically. As far as Japanese narrative is concerned, therefore, the story recipient's brief acknowledgments effectively signal that he or she shares common ground with the storyteller. In the context of mother–child interactions, we can further claim that the Japanese mother speaks few words and few utterances per turn, and instead, often simply shows attention, which, in fact, serves to divide the child's utterances into small units. Japanese narrative discourse is therefore, through attention-getting devices and brief acknowledgment, co-constructed by the child and the mother.

The role of prefacing 'huun'

A second discursive device used by many Japanese mothers to show attention is *huun* ('well'). In Japanese adult discourse, *huun* has been described as serving a prefacing function signaling the introduction of a new topic (Maynard, 1989; Yamada, 1992). The Japanese mother–child interaction, however, reveals that *huun* is more complicated than has originally been discussed, and that, instead, it has the following four different functions: (1) prefacing of topic-extension, (2) prefacing of topic-switch, (3) simple verbal acknowledgment and (4) brief acknowledgment accompanied by echoes (which are, by definition, the repetition of a word or word group immediately after hearing it by the interlocutor).

When a child talks about a particular incident, if the mother says, '*huun, sorekara*' ('Well. Then?') or more extensively '*huun, sorekara doo shita no?*' ('Well. Then, what did you do?'), the mother's use of *huun* prefaces her wish to extend the topic. Thus, this use of *huun* serves as prefacing of topic-extension. In each of the following examples, notice that, whether a leading question for the topic-extension takes the form of a wh- (i.e. open-ended) question or a yes-no (i.e. closed-ended) question, *huun* prefaces the topic-extension statement. That is, right after uttering *huun*, in order to extend a topic, Akira's mother uses a wh- question (Example 6.2a), but Kana's mother uses a yes/no question (Example 6.2b). Furthermore, in Ayaka's example below (Example 6.2c), she and her mother are talking about what happened at a Buddhist service for her late grandfather. The first *huun* is used to preface the mother's topic-extension statement; right after uttering *huun*, Ayaka's mother pushes her to elaborate on the same topic further. To achieve her intention, although Ayaka's mother used a general prompt, '*sorekara*' ('then') right after uttering *huun*, because Ayaka could not provide a satisfactory answer, her mother then gave a more specific, yes/no (closed-ended) question, *banana mo tabetan?* ('Did [you] eat a banana, too?'):

Example 6.2a Akira   (boy, age 4;6)
Mother: *watagashi oishi katta?*
             'Was the cotton candy good?'
Akira: *un.*
             'Yes.'
Mother: *huun.* [**prefacing of topic-extension**]
             'Well.'
             nan no aji shita?
             'What kind of taste did (it) have?'
Akira: *ehtto, watagashi no aji.*
             'Um, (it had a) cotton candy taste.'

Example 6.2b Kana   (girl, age 4;6)
Kana: *Ryota kun ga ne, mieta no.*
             '(I) saw Ryota.'
Mother: *huun.* [**prefacing of topic-extension**]
             'Well.'
             de, 'Ryota kun mo issho ni asobo,' tte ittan?
             'And did (you) say "Ryota, let's play together"?'

Example 6.2c Ayaka   (girl, age 5;3)
Ayaka: *ochagashi mitai na yatsu tabeta.*
             '(I) ate something that was like a tea cake.'
Mother: *honto.*
             'Really.'
             huun. [**prefacing of topic-extension**]
             'Well.'
             sorekara?
             'Then?'
Ayaka: *uun.*
             'Um.'
Mother: *banana mo tabetan?*

'Did (you) eat a banana, too?'

Ayaka: *un.*
'Yes.'

Mother: *ne.*
'You see.'

Ayaka: *un, tabeta.*
'Yes, (I) did eat (one).'

Mother: *oishikatta?*
'Did (it) taste good?'

Ayaka: *un.*
'Yes.'

Mother: *huun.* [prefacing of topic-switch]
'Well.'

kyoo wa nani shite asondetan?
'What (games) did (you) play today?'

In contrast to *huun* as prefacing of topic-extension, if the mother says, '*huun, hoka ni nani shita no kyoo yoochien de?*' ('Well. What else did you do in preschool today?'), the use of *huun* signals a preface to a new topic. In Ayaka's example above, in contrast to the first *huun*, which prefaces the mother's topic-extension statement, the second *huun* in Example 6.2c prefaces the topic-switch; this time, Ayaka's mother uses an open-ended question initiating a new topic. Likewise, in each of the following examples, *huun* prefaces a topic-switch statement. Notice how Ryota's mother changes the topic of conversation from playing the drum to riding a bicycle (Example 6.3a). Similarly, Sae's mother changes the topic from playing in the swimming pool to playing in the sea. 'Playing in the water' is shared in these two related topics (Example 6.3b):

Example 6.3a   Ryota (boy, age 3;8)

Mother: *taiko mo kirai?*
'Don't (you) like (to play the) drums, either?'

Ryota: *un.*[4]
'No.'

Mother: *huun.* [prefacing of topic-switch]
'Well.'

ah so, soshitara ne, konaida no ne jitensha de ippai hashitta de sho.
'Um, then, you know, last time (you) rode (your) bicycle a lot, didn't (you)?'

Ryota: *un.*
'Yes.'

Example 6.3b   Sae (girl, age 4;8)

Mother: *don nan shite asonda?*
'What did (you) enjoy doing (in the pool)?'

Sae: *oyoida.*

'(I) swam.'

Mother: *huun.* [**prefacing of topic-switch**]
'Well.'
umi itta tte itteta ne.
'(You) said (you) went to the sea, didn't (you)?'
umi tanoshi katta?
'Did (you) enjoy (playing in) the sea?'

Example 6.3c Sachi (girl, age 5;9)
Mother: *sorekara?*
'Then?'
nani mo nai?
'Nothing else?'
Sachi: *un.*
'No.'
Mother: *huun.* [**prefacing of topic-switch**]
'Well.'
sonnara ne, ehtto hora ano yoochien no otomari hoiku atta ja nai.
'Then (changing the topic), you know, um (you) had an overnight stay at school.'
Sachi: *un.*
'Yes.'

In the case of simple acknowledgment, if the mother says to the child '*huun,*' and the child then continues his or her story, it can be interpreted that the mother simply acknowledges what the child has said. The function of this *huun* is thus very similar to the function of the previously mentioned *un* ('uh huh'). In the second example below, for instance, Tamotsu and his mother are in the middle of discussion about what he bought as souvenirs when he went to an amusement park with his grandparents (Example 6.4b). When comparing Tamotsu's mother's *huun* and *un*, it is evident that they function in similar ways:

Example 6.4a Sho (boy, age 4;6)
Sho: *oneechan usagi san minakatta.*
'(My) older sister didn't go see the rabbits.'
Mother: *huun.* [**simple acknowledgment**]
'Well.'
Sho: *hitori de mita.*
'(I) went to see (the rabbits) by myself.'
Mother: *hitori de mita?*
'Did (you) go to see (the rabbits) all by yourself?'
Sho: *un.*
'Yes.'

Example 6.4b Tamotsu (boy, age 4;7)
Mother: *nani katta?*

'What did (you) buy?'
Tamotsu: *uun to, ne, Warabe chan no nee, ano Kitty no booshi no pinku no yatsu.*
'Um, you know, for Warabe (my younger sister), you know, that "Hello Kitty" hat, a pink one.'
Tamotsu kun wa Keroppy no mizuame man.
'For me, syrup in a *"Keroppy"* man bottle.'
Mother: *oishii?*
'Does (it) taste good?'
Tamotsu: *un.*
'Yes.'
oishi katta.
'(It) tasted good.'
Mother: *huun.* **[simple acknowledgment]**
'Well.'
Tamotsu: *de ne Tamotsu kun wa tameru yatsu aru de sho,*
'And, you know, (I got) a coin bank [or something to keep] for myself.'

                                            (Mother: *un*)
                                            'uh huh'

Example 6.4c Akio (boy, age 5;6)
Akio: *niwatori mo ita.*
'(I) saw chickens, too.'
Mother: *huun.* **[simple acknowledgment]**
'Well.'
Akio: *de ne gyuunyuu nonda.*
'And, you know, (I) drank some milk.'

In some cases, furthermore, the mother first echoes her child's utterances, either partially or entirely, and then says *huun*; soon after that, the child continues his or her story. The function of this *huun* is similar to that of simple acknowledgment *huun* because neither one plays the role of prefacing. Unlike simple acknowledgment *huun*, however, turn-taking interaction takes place in this case. Moreover, this type of *huun*, although an unplanned effort, more positively performs a topic-extension function (i.e. 'Well then .../Think about it ...') than does simple acknowledgment *huun*. In the first example below, Sho and his mother are talking about a trip to a nearby mountain (Example 6.5a). As a leading question, Sho's mother uses a closed-ended (i.e. yes/no) question, which, in reality, serves as a prompt for content information. That is, a simple 'yes' or 'no' is inadequate as an answer because she expects the child to mention who went to the hotel with them. Then, to draw expected answers, she repeatedly uses the brief acknowledgment *huun* after echoing what Sho has said.

Example 6.5a Sho (boy, age 4;6)
Mother: *Rokkoo san no hoteru oboeteru?*
'Do (you) remember the hotel at Mount Rokkoo?'
Sho: *Rokkoo san no hoteru?*
'The hotel at Mount Rokkoo?'
Mother: *un.*
'Yes.'
Mother: *dare to itta no?*
'Who did (we) go with?'
Sho: *wasureta.*
'(I) forgot.'
Mother: *wasuretan.*
'(You) forgot.'
***huun.* [brief acknowledgment after echo]**
'Well [Well then . . ./Think about it . . .]'
Sho: *ah, Ta kkun da.*
'Uh, (it must have) been Ta.'
Mother: *Ta kkun to issho ni ittan?*
'So Ta was with us?'
Mother: ***huun.* [brief acknowledgment after echo]**
'Well.'
Sho: *Ta kkun to boku to.*
'Ta and me.'

Example 6.5b Ayaka (girl, age 5;3)
Ayaka: *tsume dashiteta mon.*
'(The rabbit) bared her claws.'
Mother: *tsume dashiteta mon.*
'(The rabbit) bared her claws.'
***huun.* [brief acknowledgment after echo]**
'Well.'
Ayaka: *demo (unintelligible) itaku nai.*
'But (it) didn't hurt.'
Mother: *honto.*
'Really.'

As can be seen in these examples, *huun* indicates a certain mental transition. While uttering *huun*, the mother evidently decides whether to continue the current topic or terminate it and introduce a new one. In reference not only to *un* but also to *huun*, using the term 'back-channeling' has intentionally been avoided because this term implies an unconditional signal to go on talking. While sometimes *huun* is used by the mother to preface topic-extension, at other times *huun* is used by the mother to take the floor through topic-switch. Overall, we may be able to conclude that the more the mother uses this discourse device of prefacing of topic-extension, the further the child develops the topic.

Reliability

Using the categorization described above, all 105 maternal *huun* utterances were categorized independently by two raters.[5] Inter-rater agreement across the four categories resulted in a Cohen's kappa statistic of 0.97, representing 'almost perfect' agreement (Bakeman & Gottman, 1986; Landis & Koch, 1977).

Results

Similarities between mothers of four-year-olds and mothers of five-year-olds

Two types of discourse devices in Japanese were statistically analyzed, namely, the child's *ne* ('you know') immediately followed by the mother's *un* ('uh huh') and maternal *huun* ('well'). For the first discourse device (*ne* followed by *un*), I counted frequencies of the child's *ne* immediately followed by the mother's *un* and conducted a two-way (age group × gender) analysis of variance (ANOVA) on this frequency variable. This test revealed that there was no significant effect of age group or gender. As far as this variable is concerned, therefore, regardless of age and gender, Japanese mothers use the same strategy to support their children's narrative production.

Differences between mothers of four-year-olds and mothers of five-year-olds

For the second discourse device (the use of *huun*), I coded all maternal *huun* utterances in accordance with their function. I then conducted a multivariate analysis of variance (MANOVA) for the four dependent variables, (1) prefacing of topic-extension, (2) prefacing of topic-switch, (3) simple verbal acknowledgment and (4) brief acknowledgment accompanied by echoes. Although the results of the overall multivariate test did not approach statistical significance, a subsequent series of analyses of variance (ANOVA) accompanied by Bonferroni Post Hoc tests revealed the following: (1) As can be seen in Table 6.3a, there was a significant univariate effect of the age group on the 'maternal prefacing of topic-extension *huun*,' $F(1, 16) = 5.34$, $p < 0.05$. A Bonferroni Post Hoc test showed that mothers of four-year-olds used *huun* as prefacing of topic-extension more frequently than did mothers of five-year-olds.[6] (2) As seen in Table 6.3b, there was also a main univariate effect of gender on the 'maternal simple verbal acknowledgment *huun*,' $F(1, 16) = 4.57$, $p < 0.05$. A Bonferroni Post Hoc test revealed that mothers of boys more frequently used huun as simple verbal acknowledgment than did mothers of girls.[7]

Table 6.3a Mean frequencies and standard deviations of mothers'
'huun' (by age group)

	Mothers of four-year-olds		Mothers of five-year-olds		F^a values for main effect of AGE GROUP
	M	*(SD)*	*M*	*(SD)*	*GROUP*
Prefacing topic-extension	3.60	(2.67)	1.30	(1.57)	5.34*
Prefacing topic-switch	1.40	(1.17)	1.10	(1.52)	0.23
Simple acknowledgment	2.30	(3.09)	0.80	(1.55)	2.33
Brief acknowledgment after echo	0.60	(1.07)	0.30	(0.67)	0.67

*$p < 0.05$
a Degrees of freedom = 1, 16.

Table 6.3b Mean frequencies and standard deviations of mothers'
'huun' (by gender)

	Mothers of sons		Mothers of daughters		F^a values for main effect of GENDER
	M	*(SD)*	*M*	*(SD)*	
Prefacing topic-extension	2.70	(3.06)	2.20	(1.75)	0.25
Prefacing topic-switch	1.00	(1.33)	1.50	(1.35)	0.63
Simple acknowledgment	2.60	(3.20)	0.50	(0.71)	4.57*
Brief acknowledgment after echo	0.70	(1.06)	0.20	(0.63)	1.85

*$p < 0.05$.
a Degrees of freedom = 1, 16.

The first result indicates that compared to mothers of five-year-olds,
mothers of four-year-olds, regardless of the child's gender, were more
likely to give topic-extension prompts right after uttering *huun*. Mothers
of four-year-olds tried to facilitate narrative conversation, pushing for
more elaborated information of the same topic; consequently, with all

the *huun*s, they support their children's narrative building. Thus, there is a distinct age-related decline in the use of prefacing of topic-extension *huun*. As previously seen in Examples 6.2a, b and c, right after uttering *huun*, mothers tried to push their children to elaborate on the same topic further, using both closed-ended and open-ended questions (in many cases, mothers moved on to closed-ended questions when their children's responses to open-ended questions were not satisfactory). Therefore, frequent use of *huun* for this purpose by the mothers of four-year-olds probably reflects that they felt more need to extend their children's story than did the mothers of five-year-olds. This result also seems to correspond to the previously reported finding (in this chapter) that the total number of words produced by the mothers of four-year-olds in mother–child interactions is larger than that of the mothers of five-year-olds.

The second result indicates that compared to mothers of daughters, mothers of sons, regardless of the child's age, were more likely to simply acknowledge their sons' talk. This difference might be attributable to the difference in interactional style between boys and girls; boys' conversational interval might be longer than that of girls, so that mothers of sons might have tended to use *huun* as a filler. Thus, the difference might be nothing but a reflection of mothers' concern that boys are slower than girls in language development.

Although the above explanation probably holds, another possible reason for this difference is that the boys were more reticent than girls, and thus mothers needed to facilitate their sons' talk more. Recall that although not approaching statistical significance, in mother–child interactions the four-year-old boys produced a smaller number of different words than did four-year-old girls. Recall also that in mother–child interactions five-year-old boys produced both a smaller total number of words and a smaller number of different words than did five-year-old girls. Thus, although the result may not imply that mothers' strategy to encourage children's narrative production has backfired, more use of simple acknowledgment *huun* by mothers of boys seems related to the results previously presented in this chapter.

Macro-level Narrative Discourse Analysis

So far this chapter has focused on the functions of the two major types of discourse devices, *'un'* ('uh huh') and *'huun'* ('well'). The macro-level narrative discourse analysis then examines overall maternal narrative elicitation patterns.

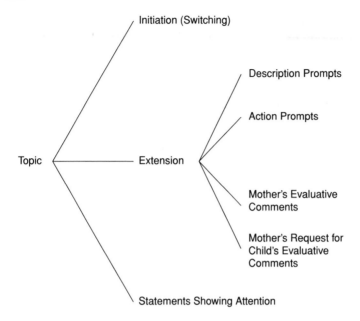

Figure 6.4 Coding system

Coding rules

Transcripts of all parents' speech were scored according to a specific speech act coding system, which was originally developed by Dickinson (1991) and McCabe and Peterson (1991). By using this coding scheme as a basis, Minami (1994, 1995) and Minami and McCabe (1993, 1995) have devised coding rules that are also applicable cross-linguistically, particularly to Japanese data.

Figure 6.4 gives a visual representation of coding rules for parental speech; transcripts of all parents' speech were scored according to these coding rules. Parental utterances were coded as one of three types: (I) topic-initiation (or topic-switch), (II) topic-extension and (III) conversational strategies that simply show attention, such as *'un'* ('uh huh') and *'huun'* ('well'). Utterances categorized as topic-extension were further categorized into: (A) descriptive statements that describe or request description of a scene, a condition or a state, (B) statements about or requests for actions that, accompanied by an action verb, describe a specific action, (C) the mother's evaluative comments and (D) the mother's request for child's evaluative comments.[8] Detailed guidelines for these categorizations are explained below:

(I) Topic-initiation (switching)
(1) Open-ended questions initiating a new topic (e.g. *'kyoo yoochien de nani shita no?'*: 'What did [you] do in preschool today?').
(2) Closed-ended questions initiating a new topic (e.g. *'suuji awase yatta?'*: 'Did [you] play matching numbers?').
(3) Statements initiating a new topic (e.g. *'kono mae Disneyland e itta de sho.'*: 'The other day [we] went to Disneyland.').
(II) Topic-extension
(4) Open-ended questions extending topics (e.g. *'nani ga ichiban suki datta?'*: 'What did [you] like best?').
(5) Closed-ended questions extending topics (e.g. *'tanoshi katta?'*: 'Did [you] enjoy it?').
(6) Statements extending a topic (e.g. *'nani ka itteta de sho.'*: '[You] were saying something.').
(7) Clarifying questions (e.g. *'nani?'*: 'what?').
(8) Clarifying questions that were partial echoes (e.g. *'dare ga chuu shite kuretan?'*: 'Who kissed [you]?' after the child said, *'chuu chuu chutte yatte.'*: 'Kiss, kiss, kissed [me].').
(9) Echoes (e.g. *'shiranakatta no.'*: '[You] didn't know' after the child said, *'shiranakatta.'*: '[I] didn't know.').
(III) *Other conversational strategies*
(10) Statements showing attention, such as brief acknowledgment (e.g. *'un.'*: 'Yes.') and prefacing utterances (e.g. *'huun.'*: 'Well.').[9]

Speech patterns that are categorized into topic-extension are further categorized into:

(A) Descriptive statements (which describe or request description of a scene, a condition, or a state)
'ato, Momotaro no hon mo atta de sho.': 'Besides, there was a book about the Peach Boy.'
'denki ga tsuiteta ne.': 'The lights were on, you know.'
'jibun de unten suru kuruma?': 'Is (it) a car that you can drive yourself?'
(B) Statements about or requests for information about actions (which, accompanied by an action verb, describe a specific action)
'janken de saisho kimeta.': 'First, (we) decided by using the scissors, paper, and rock game.' [= First, we decided it by a coin toss.]
'banana mo tabetan.': '(You) also ate a banana.'
'umi ni ittetan?': 'Did (you) go to the sea?'
'Yuki chan ga arattan.': 'Yuki washed.'
'nan te kaita no Yukari chan wa typewriter de?': 'What did (you) write on the typewriter, Yukari?'

(C) Mother's evaluative comments
　　'*sore ii ne.*': 'That's good, you know.'
　　'*Aki chan chiisa katta mon ne.*': 'Because (you) were small, Aki, you
　　know.'
　　'*uso.*': 'That's not true.'
(D) Mother's request for child's evaluative comments
　　'*sore doo omou?*': 'What do (you) think about it?'
　　'*u chan no doko ga kawaii no?*': 'What is cute about the bunny?'
　　'*oishi kattan?*': 'Did (it) taste good?'

The above evaluative comments – (C) mother's own and (D) mother's
request for child's evaluative comments – were judged according to the
following criteria, which are a revised version of the categories that
Peterson and McCabe (1983) originally devised.

(1) High degree of stress and emphasis
　　'**sugoku** kirei na e ga **ippai** kakete atta.': 'There were **a lot of very**
　　beautiful pictures hanging (on the wall).'
(2) Exclamation
　　'*hee!*': 'Oh, my!' '*ge!*': 'Dear!'
(3) Repetition
　　'**mada mada** natsu yasumi dakara ne.': 'Because (you) are **still still** in
　　the summer vacation, you know.'
(4) Compulsion
　　'*ikanai to **ikenakatta**.*': '(I) **had to** go.'
(5) Similes and metaphors
　　'*kuchi ga futatsu ni nattchatta.*': '(I) had two mouths.' [= My lip was
　　split in two. See Example 1.2 in Chapter 1.]
(6) Attention getter
　　'*chotto kiite!*': 'Now listen!'
(7) Words per se (words that connote particular judgmental meanings,
　　such as 'pretty' and 'awful')
　　'**warui** koto shitan?': 'Did (you) do a **bad** thing?'
(8) Negatives and modified negatives
　　'*omoku **nai** yo **zenzen**.*': '(It) is **not** heavy **at all**, I tell you.'
(9) Intentions, desires, hopes, guesses, and predictions
　　'*video ippai miyoo.*': 'Let's watch a lot of videos.'
(10) Causal inquiries and explanations
　　'*nande oboreta no?*': 'What do (you) mean (you almost) drowned?'
　　'*toomorokoshi tabeta kara ne.*': 'Because (I) ate corn, you know.'
(11) Objective judgments
　　'*sensei wa yorokondeta?*': 'Was the teacher glad?'

(12) Subjective judgment to evaluate the events (the narrator's own
     opinions about matters that are disputable/questionable)
     'oneechan ijiwaru shita.': '(My) sister did something mean to (me).'
(13) Fact per se (judgment is included in stating a fact)
     'hitori de dekita?': 'Could (you) do it by yourself?'
(14) Internal emotional states
     'omoshirokatta.': '(I) enjoyed it.'

As seen above, some evaluative comments can be brought under two
or more of the above-mentioned subcategories. For example, the statement **'mada mada** *natsu yasumi dakara ne'* ('Because [you] are **still still**
in the summer vacation, you know'), which is cited in (3) above, is a
combination of repetition and a causal explanation.

Also, in some cases, action statements and descriptive statements are
accompanied by evaluative comments. As was mentioned previously in
Chapter 2, in Labov and Waletzky's (1967) framework, narrative serves
two functions: one is referential and the other is evaluative. For example,
the statement *'sugoku kirei na e ga ippai kakete atta'* ('There were a lot of
very beautiful pictures being hung') can be considered a descriptive
statement (and thus referential). Likewise, the statement *'warui koto
shitan?'* ('Did [you] do a bad thing?') can come under the category of
action statements (also referential). However, because evaluative
comments are clearly included in these maternal utterances, they are
both judged to fall under the category of 'evaluative comments.'
Therefore, there is an overriding principle that evaluative comments
precede descriptive statements or statements about actions.

Once all the transcripts were coded, a series of Computerized Language
Analysis (CLAN) programs were employed to analyze frequencies of
different parental speech patterns.

Reliability

There was one principal coder of the dialogic narrative data, but four
full transcripts (i.e. 20%) were randomly selected and coded by a second
person. Intercoder reliability was 0.97 for the first level (topic-initiation,
topic-extension, and statements showing attention) and 0.87 for the
second level (statements about or requests for descriptions, statements
about or requests for actions, mother's evaluative comments, and
mother's request for child's evaluative comments). One person coded
the remaining conversations.

Table 6.4 Mean frequencies and percentages (standard deviations) of mothers' prompts to children about past events

	Mothers of four-year-olds		Mothers of five-year-olds		F^a values for main effect of AGE GROUP
	M	(SD)	M	(SD)	
Requests for descriptions					
Frequencies	19.10	(8.94)	15.00	(7.35)	1.2
Percentages	13.36%	(3.46)	14.72%	(4.83)	0.53
Requests for actions					
Frequencies	28.80	(15.59)	23.50	(10.01)	0.76
Percentages	20.23%	(8.89)	24.30%	(11.27)	0.78
Requests for evaluations					
Frequencies	32.00	(13.24)	16.50	(7.88)	10.37**
Percentages	24.64%	(10.49)	17.18%	(8.30)	3.56†
Evaluations by mother herself					
Frequencies	22.70	(14.61)	15.40	(10.34)	1.50
Percentages	14.96%	(6.12)	14.69%	(6.62)	0.01
Statements showing attention					
Frequencies	36.20	(31.46)	27.10	(20.85)	0.56
Percentages	24.22%	(17.36)	26.18%	(19.15)	0.06
Initiation					
Frequencies	3.00	(0.00)	2.80	(0.63)	1.00
Percentages	2.59%	(1.46)	2.93%	(1.00)	0.37

$\dagger p < 0.10$; $^*p < 0.05$; $^{**}p < 0.01$.
[a] Degrees of freedom = 1, 16.

Results

For each category of parental speech, the total frequency of such speech was counted; the proportional frequency was also calculated by dividing the total frequency of each category by the total number of utterances that the mother produced. First, raw frequencies were analyzed because they represent the impact that loquaciousness might have on children's narration (e.g. Hoff-Ginsberg, 1992; McCabe & Peterson, 1991; Reese *et al.*, 1992). Second, proportional frequencies were used because they correct for differences in length and allow us to see differing relative emphasis on components of narration. To test for the effect of age group and gender, multivariate analyses of variance (MANOVA) were conducted for the major coding categories: (1) maternal requests for descriptions, actions, and evaluations, (2) maternal evaluations, (3) statements showing attention and (4) initiation.

With regard to frequencies, although the results of the overall multivariate test did not approach statistical significance, a subsequent series of univariate analyses of variance (ANOVA) accompanied by Bonferroni Post Hoc tests revealed the following: There was a significant univariate effect of the age group on maternal requests for child's evaluative comments, $F(1, 16) = 10.37$, $p < 0.01$ (see Table 6.4). A Bonferroni Post Hoc test showed that mothers of four-year-olds requested evaluation from their children more frequently than did mothers of five-year-olds.[10]

In terms of proportions, there was a marginal effect of the age group, Wilks' lambda = 0.48, approximate $F(5, 12) = 2.57$, $p = 0.08$. As can be seen Table 6.4, the effect of the age group was largely attributable to a marginal effect on maternal requests for child's evaluative comments, $F(1, 16) = 3.56$, $p < 0.08$. Although a Bonferroni Post Hoc test did not reach statistical significance, the mothers of four-year-olds requested proportionately more evaluation ($M = 26.44$, $SD = 10.49$) than did the mothers of five-year-olds ($M = 17.18$, $SD = 8.30$).

Likewise, although the results of the overall multivariate test did not approach statistical significance, there was a marginal univariate effect of gender on maternal requests for child's evaluative comments, $F(1, 16) = 4.37$, $p = 0.053$. Although a Bonferroni Post Hoc test did not reach statistical significance, the mothers of sons requested proportionately more evaluation ($M = 25.05$, $SD = 9.28$) than did the mothers of daughters ($M = 16.77$, $SD = 9.26$).

Relationship Between Maternal Narrative Elicitation Patterns and Children's Developing Narrative Skills

This section examines the relationship between maternal narrative elicitation styles (i.e. dialogic narratives or scaffolded narratives with the mother) and children's developing narrative skill as observed when a researcher elicited narratives from the children *without scaffolding* (i.e. monologic narratives or minimally scaffolded narratives with the interviewer).

Table 6.5 displays correlations between equivalent (and related) measures in the two different narrative activities, monologic narratives

Table 6.5 Correlations between children's performance measures in two different narrative activities (four-year-olds and five-year-olds combined)

	DUOT	MNDW	MTNW	DNDW	DTNW
MUOT	0.46*	0.17	0.22	0.17	0.11
DUOT		0.41†	0.43*	0.57**	0.62**
MNDW			0.95****	0.41†	0.44*
MTNW				0.33	0.38†
DNDW					0.94****

†$p < 0.10$; *$p < 0.05$; **$p < 0.01$; ***$p < 0.001$; ****$p < 0.0001$.

MUOT: Utterances over turns in monologic narrative
DUOT: Utterances over turns in dialogic narrative
MNDW: Number of different words used in monologic narrative
MTNW: Total number of words used in monologic narrative
DNDW: Number of different words used in dialogic narrative
DTNW: Total number of words used in dialogic narrative

Note: Dialogic = with the mother, with scaffolding. Monologic = with the researcher, with minimal scaffolding.

and dialogic narratives (four-year-olds and five-year-olds combined). A pattern of positive correlations emerges between equivalent measures in the two different activities: (1) *quantity and variety* – the greater the number and variety of words the child used when interacting with his or her mother, the more words and greater variety of words he or she would use when constructing narratives alone; (2) *duration* – the longer the mother allowed her child to continue talking per turn during narrative elicitation, the longer the child would continue to talk during a monologic narrative, using a greater number and variety of words. Although not listed in the table, it seems that the longer the mother allows her child to continue to talk (i.e. utterances over turns) in mother–child interactions, the larger number of stanzas the child produces in the monologic narrative context, $r(18) = 0.67$, $p < 0.0001$. These data suggest a possible transfer from one context (mother–child interactions) to another (monologic narrative production).

How mothers verbally interact with their young children during narrative elicitation corresponds to the children's current level of narrative skills. Although marginal, maternal requests for actions during narrative elicitation were found to be inversely associated with children's action statements in their monologic narrative productions, $r(18) = -0.41$,

$p = 0.07$ (see Table 6.6). In other words, the fewer action statements the child provides when talking about past events on his or her own (i.e. monologic narrative), the more requests for actions the mother makes during narrative elicitation (i.e. dialogic narrative).[11] Furthermore, the more action statements the child provides when talking about past events on his or her own, the fewer requests for actions the mother makes during narrative elicitation. Although seemingly not supportive of a social interactionist point of view, this relationship is reasonable when considering the following: In mother–child interactions, the mother requested her child to talk about actions when she considered that her child gave insufficient action statements (although the mother's repeated prodding might also have squelched her child's initiative). When a researcher elicited narratives with minimal scaffolding, the child did not talk much about actions, either. The converse is also true. If the mother considered that her child had provided sufficient action statements during narrative elicitation (i.e. in the dialogic narrative context), she may not have felt the need to elicit more action statements. Because the child was relatively capable of providing action statements, when asked to talk about the past on his or her own (i.e. in the monologic narrative context), he or she also provided relatively sufficient action statements. Therefore, maternal narrative elicitation strategies predict children's developing narrative skill.

The assumption that maternal narrative elicitation styles reflect children's developing narrative skill nicely accounts for other results obtained in Chapter 4 (monologic narrative). Recall that in the micro-level narrative discourse analysis in this chapter, mothers of four-year-olds used *huun* ('well') as prefacing of topic-extension more frequently than did mothers of five-year-olds. In Chapter 4 a smaller proportion of two-verse stanzas and, in contrast, a larger proportion of four- or more verse stanzas by five-year-olds indicated that their narrative productions are slightly longer than those by four-year-olds. Compared to mothers of five-year-olds, then, the more frequent use of *huun* as prefacing of topic-extension by mothers of four-year-olds may reflect their concern that they need to develop and facilitate their children's narratives, staying on a topic they have selected.

Mothers of four-year-olds requested evaluation from their children more frequently than did mothers of five-year-olds (also recall a similar result reported in Note 8 of this chapter). Once again, the above-mentioned assumption nicely explains the relationship between maternal styles of narrative elicitation and children's developing narrative skill. In Chapter 4, high point analysis of monologic narratives indicated that four-year-olds gave proportionately less evaluation than adults, although

Table 6.6 Correlations between measures of two different narrative activities (maternal narrative elicitation patterns in mother–child interactions and children's monologic narrative production)

	MACT	MEVL	MCEVL	CACT	CEVL	CORT
MDES	−0.08	0.36	0.00	−0.06	0.18	0.29
MACT		−0.03	0.16	−0.41†	0.27	0.07
MEVL			−0.08	0.18	0.01	−0.10
MCEVL				−0.05	−0.03	0.20
CACT					−0.69**	−0.32
CEVL						−0.02

†$p < 0.10$; *$p < 0.05$; **$p < 0.01$.
MDES: Maternal requests for descriptions (dialogic)
MACT: Maternal requests for actions (dialogic)
MEVL: Evaluations by mother herself (dialogic)
MCEVL: Maternal requests for evaluations (dialogic)
CACT: Child's action statements (monologic)
CEVL: Child's evaluation statements (monologic)
CORT: Child's orientation statements (monologic)
Note: Dialogic = with the mother, with scaffolding. Monologic = with the researcher, with minimal scaffolding.

no differences in evaluation were observed between five-year-olds and adults. It would seem reasonable to conclude that when four-year-olds do not provide sufficient evaluative accounts in mother–child interactions, mothers would tend to emphasize requests for evaluations. In fact, they did so. Therefore, differences in elicitation style between mothers of four-year-olds and mothers of five-year-olds are differences in children's narrative skill related to age.

In connecting maternal narrative elicitation strategies with children's developing narrative skill, we can further explain why the differences in maternal requests for descriptions and actions between the mothers of four-year-olds and the mothers of five-year-olds did not approach statistical significance. When a researcher elicited narratives from the children with minimal scaffolding, both four- and five-year-olds could provide relatively adequate foreground information (i.e. actions), and, in fact, no difference was observed between these two age groups. In contrast to action statements that are categorized as referential (Labov & Waletzky, 1967), in the monologic narrative production task, although orientation is also considered referential, both age groups provided a relatively small number of orientation statements; however, like action statements, there was no difference in orientation statements between the two age groups. Thus, it seems reasonable to assume that, because the four- and five-year-olds provided similar numbers of action and orientation statements, which are both categorized as referential elements (Labov, 1972), not only in monologic narrative productions but also in mother–child interactions, the mothers of four-year-olds and the mothers of five-year-olds chose similar narrative elicitation styles.

Finally, in mother–child interactions, mothers of sons were found to request proportionately more evaluation than mothers of daughters. Although not significantly different, the results of high point analysis in Chapter 4 indicated that when asked to talk about past events on their own, boys gave proportionately less evaluation than did girls of the same age. That is, the mean of the proportion of evaluation (i.e. affective elements) of the five-year-old girls was 46.56 ($SD = 31.68$), whereas that of the five-year-old boys was 35.93 ($SD = 18.99$). Likewise, the mean of the proportion of evaluation of the four-year-old girls was 35.57 ($SD = 15.14$), whereas that of the four-year-old boys was 31.22 ($SD = 29.25$). What appears to be a difference between mothers of sons and mothers of daughters in narrative elicitation styles, in fact, reflects a difference in developing narrative skills between boys and girls.

Discussion

This analysis of how Japanese parents guide their children in the acquisition of narrative provides some answers to the initial questions posed at the outset of this chapter.

Linguistic items used by mothers during narrative elicitation

Mothers frequently used the rapport particle *ne*, the assertive/emphatic particle *yo*, and the quotation-final particle *tte* both when talking about past events on their own and when interacting with their children during narrative elicitation. In the context of mother–child interactions, however, mothers used some linguistic items very differently from their monologic narrative production. For example, when interacting with their children during narrative elicitation, mothers did not use linguistic items such as the formal *des(u)/mas(u)* verb-ending forms, the adverb *yappari* ('after all,' 'as expected'), and the connective *dakara* ('so,' 'therefore'). What mothers provided (and did not provide) in their narrative turns to scaffold their children's narratives seems to be reflected in the use of the linguistic items that children provided when telling narratives on their own.

Age differences

Compared to mothers of five-year-olds, mothers of four-year-olds more frequently used *huun* to preface topic-extension. In comparison to mothers of five-year-olds, mothers of four-year-olds also requested more evaluation from their children. These tendencies may reflect the fact that because four-year-olds often said *un* ('yes') or *uun* ('no') without saying any more, their mothers needed to appeal to topic-extension strategies or to draw some kinds of evaluative comments from them, such as in the example below, in which Akira (boy, age 4;6) and his mother are talking about catching goldfish in a local festival.

Example 6.6   Akira and his mothers interaction
Akira: *tsukamae tara, kawaisoo?*
             'Do (goldfish) feel sad when (they're) caught?'
Mother: *kawaisoo?*
             'do (they) feel sad?'
Akira: *un.*
             'Yes.'
Mother: *kawaisoo na no?*
             '(You wonder whether they) feel sad?'
Akira: *un.*
             'Yes.'
Mother: *huun.* [prefacing of topic-extension]
             'Well.'
             demo iru yo kingyo ie ni.
             'But (we have) goldfish at home.'

Although children are shown to come to internalize and gain performance competencies through mother–child interactions like the above (Vygotsky, 1978), children's attitudes obviously influence their mothers' strategies. For example, if children were not capable of providing sufficient evaluative comments by themselves, mothers would insist that their children provide more of them. If, on the other hand, children can provide relatively satisfactory evaluative comments, mothers do not need to ask their children to provide more. As I emphasized in Chapter 2, therefore, the mother's emphasis on requests for evaluations should be conceptualized as a product of a bi-directional interaction with the child rather than a unidirectional action.

Gender differences

Compared to mothers of daughters, mothers of sons, regardless of the child's age, more frequently used *huun* as simple verbal acknowledgment. Also, mothers requested proportionately more evaluation from sons than from daughters. This tendency seems reflective of Japanese mothers' concern that boys are usually slower than girls in language development. The tendency may also reflect Japanese folk psychology represented in old sayings such as 'Talkative males are embarrassing,' which not only emphasizes that boys should be reticent but also acknowledges the general tendency that boys are more reticent than girls.

Relationship between mother and child measures

Maternal styles of narrative elicitation affect their children's narrative techniques. For example, an inverse relationship was identified between the mother's requests for actions during narrative elicitation and the child's action statements in monologic narrative. Although this result appears counterintuitive, mothers have been found to scaffold children's narratives in ways that are consistent with the social interactionist paradigm in which language plays a social-communicative role (Bruner, 1977; Vygotsky, 1978). More specifically, mothers work on eliciting what is socioculturally desired but not present. That is, in mother–child interactions, unless the mother considers that her child gives sufficient action statements, she scaffolds her speech to her child by providing requests for actions. Overall, it seems clear that Japanese mothers simultaneously pay considerable attention to their children's narratives and support their children's progressive development of narrative skills.

Moreover, mothers' scaffolding strategies may not necessarily reflect children's failure to provide particular information. They may also be reflective of mothers' concern or culturally-based assumptions. Mothers were found to try to scaffold their son's talk by using *huun* as simple verbal acknowledgment and by requesting proportionately more evaluation. Although it is true that boys were less productive than girls during parental narrative elicitation, these mothers' attitudes may reflect mothers' concern (or culturally-based assumptions) that boys develop less quickly than girls. Thus, this chapter discusses how maternal elicitation strategies influence children's developing narrative skills and provides insights into mothers' concern about the development of their children's particular skills. To answer related questions from different angles, the next chapter will further focus on culture-specific patterns of social interactions.

Notes

1. Children not only used the *des(u)/mas(u)* styles in set formulas, such as *'ohayoo gozai masu tte yuu no wa ?'* ('How do [you say] *ohayoo gozai masu* [Good morning] [in English]?') and *'sumi masen, nemuri . . .'* ('Excuse me, but [I] am sleepy'). They also used these forms playfully when addressing

their parents, such as *'kore desu yo'* ('This is [it]'), *'shite ari maseen'* ('[I] didn't do any shopping [in the amusement park]') and *'kono pink non o yatte iki masu'* ('[I] do this pink one like this'). However, their use of the formal *des(u)/mas(u)* styles does not necessarily indicate that four- and five-year-olds are capable of encoding narrative external/internal positioning discussed in Chapter 5.

2. Recall the two different types of situations in which the speaker uses the plain copula *da* (Matsumoto, 1993) (see Note 15 in Chapter 5). In this case, *da* is used because the communication is impersonal (i.e. between insiders).

3. Note, however, that late preschool and early elementary school-aged children may be most extreme in adhering to using *ne*. As discussed in Chapter 4 (see Note 14), a U-shaped pattern of behavioral growth (Berman, 1994; Berman & Slobin, 1994; Strauss & Stavy, 1982) might explain the excessive use of the particle *ne*, particularly the clause-final one.

4. The use of *un* ('yes') in this case means 'no' in English. Whereas in English the speaker answers 'yes' or 'no' without regard to the form of the question, in Japanese the speaker usually answers 'yes' or 'no' in agreement with the literal meaning of the question. According to conventional grammar, therefore, Japanese *un* ('yes'), as an answer to a negative question, corresponds to English 'no.' As can be seen in Example 6.3a, in Japanese, in answering the question *'taiko mo kirai ?'* ('Don't [you] like [to play the] drums, either?'), because the child did not like to play the drums, he answered, *'un/hai'* ('What you said is correct'). If the child had liked to play the drums, on the other hand, then the answer would have been *'uun/iie'* ('What you said is not correct').

5. The function of *huun* was categorized by examining the subsequent mother's or child's response. The categorization of topic-extension applies, if the mother extends the topic subsequent to *huun*. Likewise, the topic-switch categorization applies, if the mother introduces an entirely new topic right after uttering *huun*. Simple acknowledgment applies, if the child still continues his or her talk right after *huun*. Finally, brief acknowledgment accompanied by echoes applies, if the child still continues his or her talk right after maternal echoes followed by *huun*. Thus, the function of *huun* was judged by looking at what comes after it.

6. The mothers of four-year-olds used *huun* as prefacing of topic-extension 3.60 times ($SD = 2.68$) on average, whereas the mothers of five-year-olds used *huun* for the same purpose 1.30 times ($SD = 1.57$) on average.

7. The mothers of boys used *huun* as simple verbal acknowledgment 2.60 times ($SD = 3.20$) on average, whereas the mothers of girls used *huun* for the same purpose 0.50 times ($SD = 0.71$) on average.

8. No significant associations were found between these four variables (this information is presented in Table 6.6). Although marginal, however, the mother's request for child's evaluative comments was negatively correlated with the age of the child, $r(18) = -0.38$, $p = 0.09$. This means that compared to mothers of five-year-olds, mothers of four-year-olds made more requests for evaluations during narrative elicitation (i.e. dialogic narrative).

9. Regardless of its type (prefacing of topic-extension, prefacing of topic-switch, simple verbal acknowledgment, or brief acknowledgment accompanied by echoes) *huun* itself serves to show attention, and thus all the prior categories are included here.

10. The mothers of four-year-olds requested evaluation from their children 32.00 times (*SD* = 13.24) on average, whereas the mothers of five-year-olds requested evaluation 16.50 times (*SD* = 7.88) on average.

11. The data in this study show that mothers are found to ask for information about action if it is missing, whereas it was earlier suggested in this study that mothers solicit evaluations when missing. This difference is probably attributable to the fact that the mother's action requests are individually tuned to her child but that, in contrast, evaluation requests are made across the board by mothers of four-year-olds, whether or not the child has already provided some evaluation.

Chapter 7

Cross-cultural Comparison of Parental Narrative Elicitation

Personal narratives not only involve a description of a past experience as a ubiquitous aspect of human behavior, but they simultaneously embody both developmentally and culturally specific modes of telling a story or recollection. Chapters 4 and 5 detailed the emergence of narrative styles in Japanese children; for instance, four- and five-year-old Japanese children tend to focus on action in their personal narratives, whereas Japanese adults focus on evaluation and orientation in similar circumstances. Complementing these findings regarding monologic narrative performances, Chapter 6 elaborated on how Japanese parents guide their children in the acquisition of narratives. Examination of mothers' scaffolding of dialogic narration with their children has revealed, for instance, that the mothers of four-year-olds asked their children for more evaluation than did the mothers of five-year-olds. Other scaffolding effects identified in the previous chapter include: the fewer action statements the child provided when talking about past events in monologue, the more requests for actions the mother made during dialogic narrative elicitation.

To complement this work and to support generalizations about the *culture-specific* nature of caregivers' practices, this chapter examines mother–child narrative discourse interactions from a cross-cultural perspective. By cross-cultural research, I mean the comparison of two or more cultures on some variable. For research to be cross-cultural, we must compare cross-cultural data with intracultural data. A study comparing Japanese and North American mother–child interactions in this chapter, therefore, should be based, to begin with, on the examination of how Japanese mothers interact with their children, which we saw in great detail in Chapter 6. Without taking such an action, we would not be able to see how Japanese mothers' interaction styles differ from those of North American counterparts. Conversely, it is only the difference between intracultural and cross-cultural studies that suggest what is unique about Japanese mother–child interactions.

By comparing Japanese and North American mother–child pairs, the chapter illustrates: (1) North American mothers allow their young children to take long monologic turns, ask their children many questions about the content of the monologue, and offer positive evaluation of the narrative. (2) On the other hand, Japanese mothers, whether living in Japan or the United States, paying close attention to their children's narratives, facilitate frequent turn exchanges and offer few evaluative comments. Focusing on mother–child interactions, I now investigate cross-cultural issues in narrative development.

Cross-cultural Differences in Parental Elicitation Patterns

Whorf (1956) hypothesized that the particular language one speaks affects the manner in which one perceives and thinks about the world; the Eskimo language is often used as a piece of evidence because it contains more words for snow than English does. According to Berman and Slobin (1994), some of the strongest evidence to support the Sapir–Whorf hypothesis comes from studies of typological narrative discourse analysis. Regardless of whether we accept the Sapir–Whorf hypothesis or not, it seems true that language (and narrative in particular) is a vehicle by which we bring our thoughts and meanings into order. In this sense, it might be better to express this idea in a converse way. That is, culture has a pervasive influence on language; for instance, culture affects pragmatics (e.g. the use of apologies, compliments). As Bloom (2000) aptly states, 'Language allows us to express our thought and understand those of others – to become full-fledged members of the human community.' (p. 259). Therefore, in strong terms, we might claim that, from early childhood on, through mother–child interactions, children acquire a specific worldview as they acquire language. Even in weaker terms, we might be able to maintain that, through narrative discourse interactions, the mother and the child negotiate the meaning of the actions around them and the child learns how to embed it in language.

As I described in Chapter 2, comparing behavioral patterns in different sociocultural settings has long been an important approach in the field of psychology. In terms of language acquisition, as I described in Chapter 2, people in different cultures have different beliefs about how children learn language. A good example to illustrate this difference is the Kaluli of Papua New Guinea who believe that carefully controlled, explicit instruction should be given to children not only in the forms of language but also in conversation skills (Ochs & Schieffelin, 1984). Kaluli mothers behave as if they were Skinnerians (Skinner, 1957), believing that children will not be able to learn language and conversational skills without explicit instructions. In terms of differences between Japan and North America, Shapiro and Fernald (1998) analyzed speech used by Anglo American and Japanese mothers in play with three-year-olds; these researchers found: (1) Anglo American mothers used more agentic utterances that highlighted interpersonal exchange; (2) Japanese mothers, on the other hand, tended to use more affirming utterances that emphasized shared experience.

Even within one culture, differing subcultures exist. In Chapter 2, I also reviewed Bernstein's (1971) theory of codes, which was developed in order to account for the social class differences in children's success and failure. According to Bernstein, different social groups have different linguistic orientations, which are mainly used by the family members as a way to control and regulate the behavior of other members in the family. The elaborated code, which is context independent or universalistic in meaning, is mainly deployed by members of middle-class families, whereas the restricted code, which is context dependent or particularistic in meaning, is more often used by working-class families. Furthermore, following Bernstein, both the elaborated and restricted codes are based on two distinct forms of appeal. The elaborated code is based on person centered (i.e. individuated) forms of appeal, whereas the restricted code is based on positional forms of appeal, i.e. appeals based on authority, status, and community norms. [Note, however, that Bernstein's theory has come in for a great deal of criticism, as mentioned in Chapter 2.] Thus, cultures differ in ways in which they behave toward children learning language.

In Chapter 6 of this book, analyzing monologic and dialogic relationships, I have documented the impact of maternal styles of interacting on children's narrative style within Japanese families: (1) the greater the number and variety of words the child used in dialogue, the more words and the more different words he or she used alone; (2) the longer the mother allowed her child to continue talking per turn during narrative elicitation, the longer the child would continue to talk during monologues. Taking one step further, in this chapter, I will investigate cross-cultural issues in narrative development and demonstrate that each individual culture adopts very different approaches in talking with children about past events. Specifically, I will compare: (1) Japanese-speaking mother–child pairs living in Japan, (2) Japanese-speaking mother–child pairs living in the United States and (3) English-speaking North American mother–child pairs.

This chapter tries to answer the overall question of how parents guide their children in the acquisition of culturally appropriate narrative discourse interactions. Specific research questions are as follows:

(1) What, if any, similarities and/or differences in narrative elicitation styles are found between mothers of four-year-olds in different cultures?
(2) What, if any, cross-cultural differences in narrative elicitation styles are found between mothers of four-year-old boys and mothers of four-year-old girls?
(3) What, if any, similarities and/or differences in narrative elicitation are found between mothers of five-year-olds in different cultures?
(4) What, if any, cross-cultural differences in narrative elicitation styles are found between mothers of five-year-old boys and mothers of five-year-old girls?

This chapter continues to explore both micro- and macro-level aspects of maternal narrative elicitation strategies. To delineate maternal strategies, I continue to use the same speech act coding system (Dickinson, 1991; Minami, 1994, 1995; Minami & McCabe, 1993, 1995) in order to examine cross-linguistically how speech acts are mapped over turns in narrative discourse.

Method

Participants

Chapter 7 consists of two studies: Study 1 compares (1) 10 middle-class Japanese four-year-olds and their mothers living in Japan (none of these mother–child pairs had experienced living overseas at the time of data collection) and (2) 10 English-speaking middle-class North American four-year-olds and their mothers. Similarly, Study 2 compares (1) 10 middle-class Japanese five-year-olds and their mothers living in Japan (none of these mother–child pairs had experienced living overseas at the time of data collection), (2) eight middle-class Japanese five-year-olds and their mothers living in the United States and (3) eight English-speaking middle-class North American five-year-olds and their mothers. All mothers agreed to interview their children about real past events at home.

Contrastive narrative discourse analysis

As seen above, this chapter compares the results from two different Japanese groups with a similar study of North American parent–child interactions. This chapter specifically compares the results obtained from the two Japanese groups' data – the Japanese mothers and their children who have appeared in previous chapters and Japanese mothers and their children who have lived in the United States (for two years on average) – with data collected from children of comparable ages by McCabe and Peterson (1990, 1991).

McCabe and Peterson (1990, 1991) conducted a longitudinal study of white, middle-class English-speaking North American children, along with their parents (all mothers in the North American group had attended college). This study began when the children were two years old and continued for six years.[1] Like the other study, in their study McCabe and Peterson asked parents to elicit narratives about real events from their children at home.

Examining Japanese children's personal narratives in the context of mother–child interactions has offered important insights into the cultural basis for language and narrative discourse acquisition. In light of this paradigm, furthermore, comparing Japanese mothers and English-speaking North American mothers is interesting in many respects. That is, by introducing the paradigm of mother–child interaction, I would like to conceptualize parent and child as interactive partners in the creation of sociocultural meanings. This is accomplished by introducing *contrastive narrative discourse analysis*, which, basically corresponding to the macro-level narrative discourse analysis introduced in Chapter 6, clearly identifies discourse style differences between Japanese mother–child pairs and English-speaking North American mother–child pairs. Moreover, *contrastive narrative discourse analysis* brings to light the underlying values that a society holds concerning the proper socialization of its members. Comparison of culturally distinct narrative discourse styles illustrates not only similarities but also differences in the processes whereby young children acquire the ability to recognize and interpret the sociocultural activities that are taking place in their socioculturally specific environments. The analysis thus highlights within-culture similarities and contrasts them to other societies, rather than looking at the role of individuals within a culture.

Although McCabe and Peterson's data provide a good sample to compare with the Japanese data in this study, a major difference exists. The present research is a cross-sectional study, whereas McCabe and

Peterson's research is a longitudinal one (they collected data from all 10 children at half-year intervals between the ages of three-and-a-half and six years). To cope with this potential methodological problem, the data were matched; the data of the group of Japanese-speaking four-year-olds are paired with the data of the English-speaking North American children when they were four years old, and the data of the group of 10 Japanese-speaking five-year-olds are also paired with the data of the English-speaking North American children recorded when they were five years old. [Note: Although McCabe and Peterson's longitudinal data include 10 children, because of some differences in narrative elicitation format, I used eight five-year-olds.]

Additionally, because another data set, which was collected from Japanese mother–child pairs living in the United States was available, it was also included for the present analysis. All the Japanese children in the United States had college-educated mothers and fathers who, with two exceptions, had attended graduate school. As described in Chapter 3, the Japanese mothers living in Japan are slightly different in educational status from the Japanese mothers living in the United States. Both Japanese groups included in the present study, however, are technically middle-class families; in this sense, equivalence in terms of socioeconomic status is maintained. [Note that more than 80% of Japanese consider themselves (and are considered) middle class although contemporary Japan might, in reality, include several middle classes (Tobin *et al.*, 1989).]

Each group is also balanced in terms of gender and the children's average age. Mothers were asked to tape-record conversations at home with their children, discussing past experiences in as natural a way as possible. Some mother–child pairs talked about more events than others. To establish a comparable data base, therefore, only the initial three narrative productions by each mother–child pair were analyzed.

Study 1

The purpose of Study 1 was to analyze conversations between mothers and their four-year-old children from two different groups in order to study culturally preferred narrative elicitation patterns. Earlier research (Minami, 1990; Minami & McCabe, 1991, 1996) found that Japanese elementary school children, despite follow-up questions that encouraged them to talk about one personal narrative at length, speak succinctly about collections of experiences rather than at length about any one experience in particular (see Examples 1.1. and 1.2 in Chapter 1 and Example 2.2 in Chapter 2). This succinct narrative style exhibited by

Japanese children shows a remarkable contrast to European American children's narrative style, which is typically a lengthy story detailing a single experience that often revolves around the solution of some problem (Minami & McCabe, 1991).

To identify the discourse patterns that may account for such differences in early mother–child interactions, Study One includes data from North American four-year-olds and their mothers collected by McCabe and Peterson (1990, 1991), in addition to the Japanese group that has been mentioned in previous chapters. The following two dialogues – one between a four-year-old Japanese boy, Sho, and his mother, and the other one between a four-year-old North American girl, Cara, and her mother – illustrate differences in maternal patterns of narrative elicitation:

Example 7.1—Sho and his mother's interaction
Mother: *ja Sho kun wa nani iro no densha ga yokatta ka na?*
'Then, Sho, what color train did (you) like best?'
Sho: *eh tto, reddo.*
'Um, red.'
Mother: *reddo?*
'Red?'
Sho: **datte ne,**
'because, you know,'

(**Mother:** *un*)
'uh huh'

Sho: *eh piano reenjaa ni noru mon.*
'Piano Ranger[2] rides (it).'
Mother: **huun. [prefacing of topic-extension]**
'Well.'
reddo no densha nanka notta koto aru?
'Have (you) ever ridden on a red train?'
Sho: *un.*
'Yes.'
Mother: *honto?*
'Really?'
Sho: *un.*
'Yes.'
Mother: **huun. [simple acknowledgment]**
'Well.'
Sho: *notta koto nai?*
'Didn't (you) ever ride (on a red train)?'
Mother: *nai **yo**, okaasan **wa**.*
'Mother certainly never did [I tell you].'
Sho: *boku aru.*
'(I) did.'
Mother: *hee.*
'Oh, my!'

Sho:	*un.*
	'Yes.'
Mother:	*doko iku toki ni notta no?*
	'Where did (you) go on (the red train)?'
Sho:	*aka chan no toki.*
	'(It was) when (I was) a baby.'
Mother:	*notte nai **yo**.*
	'(You) have never ridden (on a red train), really [I tell you].'
Sho:	*aka chan no toki,*
	'When (I was) a baby,'
	notta.
	'(I) rode (on a red train).'
Mother:	*notte nai **yo**.*
	'No, (you) didn't, really [I tell you].'
Sho:	*hitori de notta no.*
	'(I) rode (on it) by myself.'
Mother:	*hitori de aka chan no toki doo yatte noru no?*
	'How can a baby ride (on a train) by himself?'
Sho:	*eh tto **ne**,*
	'Um, you know,'

(Mother: *un*)
'uh huh'

Sho:	*eh tto,*
	'um,'
Mother:	*densha noru toki wa kippu ga iru no **yo**.*
	'For sure, (you) need a ticket to ride on a train [I tell you].'
Sho:	*un soo.*
	'Uh really.'

Example 7.2—Cara and her mother's interaction

Cara:	And you know what?
	We even saw a bear track.
Mother:	Bear tracks?
Cara:	Yeah.
Mother:	Out behind the children's center?
Cara:	Yes.
Mother:	What did they look like?
Cara:	Big hairy footprints.
Mother:	Who found those?
Cara:	I me Joey Nicholas.
Mother:	Ohhh.
Cara:	And Frazer.
Mother:	Did you follow the tracks?
Cara:	Yes.
Mother:	And what did you find?
Cara:	A bear!
Mother:	Where?
Cara:	In the field.
Mother:	And what was the bear doing in the field?

Cara:	It was eating our soup, our snack – honey and peanut butter.
Mother:	And what did you say to that bear when you found that bear in the field?
Cara:	Said "Go get your own honey."
Mother:	You wouldn't even share with the bear?
Cara:	I did.
Mother:	Was it a girl bear or a boy bear?
Cara:	A girl.
Mother:	Did you find out what her name was?
Cara:	Yes *(unintelligible)*.
Mother:	Pardon.
Cara:	*(unintelligible)*.
Mother:	Oh that's a nice name for a bear. Was she friendly?
Cara:	No.
Mother:	What did she do that wasn't friendly?
Cara:	Scratch us.
Mother:	Scratched you? Oh dear. Were you a bit scared?
Cara:	Me and Joey and Nick and Frazer.
Mother:	What did you and Joey and Nick do?
Cara:	Ran.
Mother:	Was there a teacher with you?
Cara:	Yes.
Mother:	Who went with you?
Cara:	Audrey.
Mother:	Audrey.
Cara:	For a bear hunt.
Mother:	Oh. Well, no wonder the bear wasn't friendly, if she thought you were hunting her.
Cara:	No. We weren't hunt. We were just looking for her.
Mother:	Oh, you weren't trying to kill her. Did you tell her that? And did she get more friendly then? No? What did she do?
Cara:	Still scratched. Eight times.
Mother:	And what did you do, after when she scratched you?
Cara:	I didn't. We looked all over the place for bears.
Mother:	You just kept looking for more bears? You didn't. Well, what about your scratches?
Cara:	We just went back to the children's center.

I'm just joking.
No bears live in St. John's right?
Mother: It's a good story though.

Encoding and decoding

Although as adults we do not consciously think about the communicative process, children need to learn various levels of linguistic rules, such as phonology, syntax and pragmatics, which is most relevant to the purpose of this book. One way of understanding the communication process is in light of encoding and decoding. To begin with, encoding means the process of turning a message into certain linguistic forms, such as word(s), phrase(s) or sentence(s). The individual who encodes and sends messages and meanings is an encoder. Decoding, on the other hand, refers to the process of trying to understand the meaning of word(s), phrase(s) or sentence(s) sent by the encoder. The individual who decodes the messages and meanings sent by the encoder is a decoder.

Obviously, culture has a pervasive and profound effect on the encoding and decoding process. Because many rules are transmitted and reinforced by enculturation agents such as mothers, as we grow, we need to be reminded about these rules less; more than that, we become able to use such rules without any conscious effort. As adults, as a result, we are well-versed in conducting culturally specific ways of communication. Viewing a communicative interaction process from encoding and decoding, therefore, we realize that we share a certain set of encoding and decoding rules with other individuals in our culture. In this process, in other words, we consequently develop a certain set of expectations about communication, which is related to the notion of schema that I explained in previous chapters.

Cultural specificity needs to be further substantiated, with regard Example 7.1. Within one culture, interlocutors share more or less the same ground rules. They encode and decode messages using the same cultural codes. That is, the sender (i.e. encoder) packages the message into a culturally specific set of signals and transmits them to the receiver (i.e. decoder). Because both encoder and decoder share more or less the same codes and rules of encoding and decoding, the encoder packages the messages and the decoder opens them, as if the two parties were engaged in wrapping and unwrapping messages in a box or a *furoshiki* (cloth wrapper) to borrow a traditional Japanese custom. Example 7.1 shows how a Japanese four-year-old and his mother, as an encoder and a decoder (or vice versa), use and interpret the linguistic items and discursive devices that were studied in previous chapters. To explain why he likes a red train, for instance, Sho uses *datte* ('but,' 'because') in Line 4, which a young child often uses in mother–child interactions because he or she can establish the recognized and favored *amae* relationship. Further, right after uttering *datte*, the child adds the rapport particle *ne*, which is immediately followed by the mother's brief acknowledgment *un* ('uh huh'), a sign of *omoiyari* (empathy) signaling that the decoder has interpreted the decoder's message without fail.

Grice's maxims

I also consider this type of verbal exchange very important to understand culturally meaningful contexts, particularly in light of the maxims of conversation originally established by the Western philosopher H.P. Grice (1975): (1) maxim of quantity (saying only as much as is necessary), (2) maxim of quality (saying only the truth), (3) maxim of relevance (saying only what is to the point) and (4) maxim of manner (saying perspicuously but unambiguously). The Gricean maxims identify general cooperative principles and have contributed to research on pragmatics (Sperber & Wilson, 1986). Interlocutors, as encoder and decoder, establish and maintain common ground in communication. In this case, as discussed in Chapter 6, the notion of grounding is evidenced in the brief acknowledgment *un* ('uh huh') through which the mother and the child construct common frameworks. That is, brief acknowledgments, which effectively signal that the receiver/decoder (i.e. the mother) shares the ground on which the sender/encoder (i.e. the child) is standing, serve as a contextualization cue. Brief but economical acknowledgments in this example, either implicitly or explicitly, enhance common ground in conversations; they also delineate the Gricean framework of maxims of quantity in a particular setting. Furthermore, in this example, the mother and the child, as an encoder and a decoder, try to construct mutually shared frameworks by negotiating the meaning of a past event through a kind of the *amae-omoiyari* exchange, which is, in fact, in line with the cooperative principles proposed by Grice (1975).

Communicative interactions, however, are never a one-way street, with one individual always encoding and transmitting messages and meanings and another individual always decoding those messages and meanings. Sho's mother's attitude is much more complex than the child originally anticipates. Her initial *huun* ('well') prefaces her leading question, '*reddo no densha ni notta koto aru?*' ('Have [you] ever ridden on a red train?'), which takes the form of a closed-ended (yes/no) question in Line 7. In fact, '*un*' ('yes') from the child is not the answer that the mother expects. Thus, although she utters the second *huun* as simple acknowledgment, later using the assertive/emphatic particle *yo* ('I tell you') and *wa* for a contrastive purpose (see Chapter 5), the mother says, '*nai yo okaasan wa*' ('Mother certainly never did [I tell you]') in Line 13.

The above action taken by the mother alludes to the fact that the child's memory of the past is false. The question that still remains, however, is whether the young child is capable of understanding the mother's complex logic or even her insinuations: namely, (1) the mother has not ridden on a red train; (2) a young child cannot ride on a train alone; and, therefore, (3) the child has not ridden on it either. Is the four-year-old capable of capturing this complex meaning attribution process? Is he able to deconstruct meanings into their components? If not, why doesn't the mother say outright (perspicuously, following the maxim of manner) that a baby cannot ride on a train by himself? The mother's utterance 'I haven't ridden on a red train' urges the use of implicatures to increase discourse tension, and the utterance can easily lose its meaning unless the implications are understood. Yet such an utterance provides the means for the kind of indirect talk that forces 'meaning performance' upon the listener. The answer seems to lie in the Japanese preference for self-control or self-attribution in meaning-making, which I will discuss later in detail.

Mothers provide a various types of support, such as conversational, historical, and psychological (Ninio & Snow, 1996). Although both Japanese and North American mothers in Examples 7.1 and 7.2 are similar in that they try to extend topics, they differ greatly in how and in what directions they extend her child's productions of the past. As we have studied, culture affects pragmatics, and these differences become clear when we examine conversations in light of the Gricean maxims (Grice, 1975). Sho's mother is particularly concerned about whether what her child has stated is true or not. Using the assertive/emphatic particle *yo*, she sticks to simple factual statement and tries to inform him that what he has stated is not true. Cara's mother's narrative elicitation stands in contrast to that of Sho's mother. Cara's mother allows her to take the floor for longer periods of time, and even encourages this by asking her many more descriptive questions than does Sho's mother, which in part represents the general Western value of independence and individual expression. For Cara's mother, even an imaginary bear must be described in terms of how friendly it was, what its name was and its gender. Further, Cara responds to her mother's request by describing the bear in detail. Moreover, unlike Sho's mother, Cara's mother does not provide brief vocalization of acknowledgment. Thus, North American mothers may encourage their children to provide an explicit context even if it is an imaginary story; in Japanese families, on the other hand, parent-controlled conversations and factual representation may be their linguistic norms. Both Japanese and North American mother–child interactions adhere to the maxim of relevance but in different ways. From early childhood on, therefore, children seem to be exposed to culturally valued narrative discourse skills through interactions with their mothers.

Parents' Styles and Children's Behavior

Although children come to internalize what is valued in their society and gain performance competencies through mother–child interactions, children's attitudes are obviously influenced by their mothers' narrative elicitation strategies. Over the years, developmental psychologists have studied different types of parenting techniques. Recall that in Chapter 2 I referred to Baumrind (1971), who has tried to identify the link between children's social competence and parental styles of child rearing. She maintains that parental 'firm control' promotes effective socialization of children, particularly children's internalization of values and meanings. If Baumrind's notion is applied to conversational contexts, we might be able to claim that mothers who give many evaluative comments try to promote their children's internalization of socially accepted values. This is tricky, however. Recall Akira and his mother's interaction in Example 6.6 in Chapter 6, in which, while talking about catching goldfishes in a local festival, the mother does not give any evaluative comments to her child; instead, she simply deploys topic-extension strategies and tries to draw some kinds of evaluative comments from him.

What is implied here is that although the influence of firm control might hold true in North American contexts, it might not be true in other cultures. Instead, whether exerting firm control is the most effective strategy in child rearing seems to be left to the discretion of an individual who lives in a specific culture. While North American mothers might regard giving evaluative comments as the best strategy, Japanese mothers may not consider it an effective way. As can be seen in Akira's mother's attitudes, Japanese mothers, who try to elicit evaluative comments from their children, can be regarded as giving them the least external control. Japanese mothers seem to believe that, without any external pressure, their children still can internalize *omoiyari* (empathy) [e.g. with goldfishes, in Example 6.6]. This explanation supports Lewis's (1995) and Vogel's (1979) general claim that Japanese adults – mothers and teachers alike – do not make explicit demands on children, who nevertheless internalize parental, group, and institutional values and meanings. In this regard, Peak (1991) writes:

> Japanese society eventually expects a high degree of self-control and suppression of personal desires and feelings in public social situations. But the wish to assume this control must be initiated and sustained by the child himself, or else, it is believed, the long-term effectiveness of the child's social adjustment will be impaired. (p. 85)

As far as child rearing is concerned, therefore, Japanese seem to believe that less salient external control will result in more internalization of socioculturally appropriate behavioral standards by the child. What is also important is that unlike the Western notion of individualism, the Japanese philosophy holds that an individual can only claim his or her meanings, which are inevitably related to his or her own will and personality, within the framework of groupism (or more precisely, social relativism as introduced in Chapter 2).

The discussion now turns to the question of whether the characteristic differences in these samples are true of other mother–child interactions.

Coding

Transcripts of all parents' speech were coded according to the speech act coding system introduced in Chapter 6.

Reliability

All transcripts were coded by an individual who is bilingual in Japanese and English. Two full transcripts of Japanese and two full transcripts of English were independently coded by individuals fluent in each of those languages, respectively. Cohen's kappa, an estimate of reliability that corrects for chance rates of agreement, was 0.97 for the first level (topic-initiation, topic-extension and statements showing attention) of the Japanese coding; it was 0.87 for the second level (descriptive statements, statements about actions, mother's evaluative comments and mother's request for child's evaluative comments). Likewise, Cohen's kappa was almost 1.00 for the first level of the English coding, and 0.88 for the second level. Thus, all estimates of reliability in this case fall into the range of 'almost perfect' agreement (Bakeman & Gottman, 1986; Landis & Koch, 1977).

Results

Maternal styles of narrative elicitation
In this analysis proportional frequencies were used; using raw frequencies was judged not to be appropriate for this case because the frequency of Japanese mothers' coded utterances ($M = 141.80$, $SD = 58.23$) was substantially higher than those of the North American mothers ($M = 58.10$, $SD = 26.12$), $t(18) = 4.17$, $p < 0.001$. To test for the effect of group and gender, multivariate analyses of variance (MANOVA) were conducted for the major coding categories: (1) maternal requests for descriptions, actions, and evaluations, (2) maternal evaluations, (3) statements showing attention and (4) initiation.

Table 7.1 Mean proportional frequencies (standard deviations) of mothers' prompts to children about past events (four-year-olds)

	Japanese mothers of four-year-olds		North American Mothers of four-year-olds		F^a values for main effect of GROUP
	M	**(SD)**	**M**	**(SD)**	
Requests for descriptions					
Percentages	13.36%	(3.46)	23.94%	(6.72)	18.54***
Requests for actions					
Percentages	20.23%	(8.89)	23.22%	(12.65)	0.36
Requests for evaluations					
Percentages	24.64%	(10.49)	14.00%	(9.82)	6.37*
Evaluations by mother herself					
Percentages	14.96%	(6.12)	23.14%	(12.51)	6.15*
Statements showing attention					
Percentages	24.22%	(17.36)	10.26%	(6.06)	5.35*
Initiation					
Percentages	2.59%	(1.46)	5.44%	(1.89)	15.54**

*$p < 0.05$; **$p < 0.01$; ***$p < 0.001$.
[a] Degrees of freedom = 1, 16.

There was a significant multivariate effect of group, Wilks' lambda = 0.48, approximate $F(5, 12) = 11.76$, $p < 0.001$. A subsequent series of analyses of variance (ANOVA) accompanied by Bonferroni Post Hoc tests were conducted. The effect of group was largely attributable to significant univariate effects on maternal requests for descriptions, $F(1, 16) = 18.54$, $p < 0.001$, maternal requests for evaluations, $F(1, 16) = 6.37$, $p < 0.05$, maternal evaluations, $F(1, 16) = 6.15$, $p < 0.05$, statements showing attention, $F(1, 16) = 5.35$, $p < 0.05$, and initiation, $F(1, 16) = 15.54$, $p < 0.01$.[3] As can be seen in Table 7.1, in comparison to the North American mothers ($M = 23.94$, $SD = 6.72$), the Japanese mothers requested proportionately less description ($M = 13.36$, $SD = 3.46$). In comparison to the North American mothers ($M = 14.00$, $SD = 9.82$), however, the Japanese

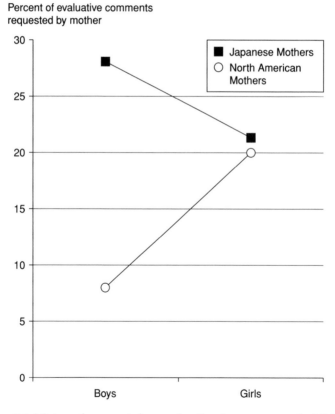

Figure 7.1 Maternal request for evaluation by group and child's gender (percentage)

mothers requested proportionately more evaluation from their children ($M = 24.64$, $SD = 10.49$). Furthermore, the Japanese mothers gave proportionately less evaluation ($M = 14.96$, $SD = 6.12$) and showed proportionately more attention ($M = 24.22$, $SD = 17.36$) than North American mothers ($M = 23.14$, $SD = 12.51$; $M = 10.26$, $SD = 6.06$).

There was, however, also a significant interaction effect of group and gender on the proportion of maternal requests for evaluations, $F(1, 16) = 4.58$, $p < 0.05$. As described above, compared to the Japanese mothers, the North American mothers requested proportionately less evaluation from their children. The North American mothers of sons, however, requested proportionately even less evaluation ($M = 8.27$, $SD = 4.09$) than did the North American mothers of daughters ($M = 19.73$, $SD = 10.88$). Furthermore, the mean percentage of the Japanese mothers who have sons ($M = 27.94$, $SD = 10.94$) is substantially higher than that of the Japanese mothers who have daughters ($M = 21.35$, $SD = 10.05$) (see Figure 7.1).

Although the results of the overall multivariate test did not approach statistical significance, there was a significant univariate effect of gender on maternal evaluations, $F(1, 16) = 8.34$, $p = 0.05$. A Bonferroni Post Hoc test revealed that mothers of sons gave proportionately more evaluation than did mothers of daughters. [Note: For the mothers of sons, the category of 'evaluations by the mother herself' accounts for 23.81% ($SD = 10.89$) of maternal narrative elicitation, whereas for the mothers of daughters the same category accounts for 14.29% ($SD = 7.90$).]

This effect of gender, however, differs by group; there was a significant interaction of group and gender on the proportion of maternal evaluations. That is, the proportionately higher level of maternal evaluation comes solely from the North American mothers. As seen in Figure 7.2, the difference in the mean percentage of the North American mothers who have sons ($M = 32.50$, $SD = 7.72$) and the North American mothers who have daughters ($M = 13.78$, $SD = 8.58$) is very pronounced, compared to the difference between the Japanese mothers who have sons ($M = 15.12$, $SD = 4.28$) and the Japanese mothers who have daughters ($M = 14.80$, $SD = 8.12$). Therefore, while the North American mothers of daughters gave proportionately similar evaluation to the Japanese mothers of sons and daughters, North American mothers of sons gave a substantially larger proportion of evaluation than any other (sub)group. [Note: The direction of mothers' giving evaluation to and requesting evaluation from their children might be confusing. Although, as we have seen, the North American mothers of sons requested proportionately less evaluation than did the North American mothers of daughters, they actually gave proportionately more evaluation.]

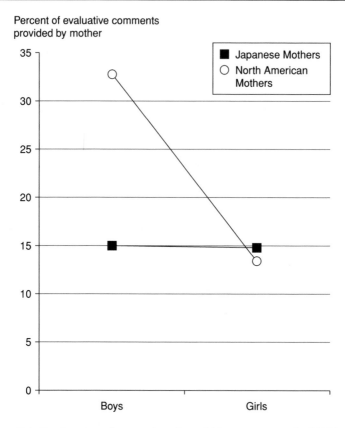

Figure 7.2 Evaluations by mother herself by group and child's gender (percentage)

Child's length of turns

In addition to the frequencies of the coded behaviors, the child's utterances over turns (i.e. the number of utterances produced by a speaker per turn) were examined. More specifically, in order to resolve issues of equivalence between the two languages (Japanese and English), the information unit[4] was used for segmenting narrative discourse. For example, aruite aruite ('[I] walked and walked') is simple repetition/emphasis of one particular action and thus one information unit, whereas te de totte aketa ('[I] grabbed [it] by hand and opened [it]') consists of two separate actions and is thus considered two pieces of information. In other words, the definition of 'utterance' in this study is equivalent to the information unit. By doing so, the same phenomena observed in two different language groups were

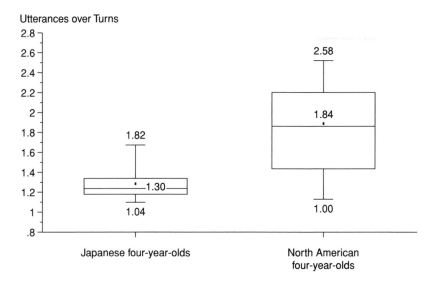

Figure 7.3 Children's ratio of utterances over turns

equated. Furthermore, a turn was defined in both Japanese and English data as statements occurring before a listener responded.

Japanese mothers effectively kept their children from talking at length by frequently showing attention (note that I have avoided using the term 'back-channeling' because it is usually considered to function as encouragement for the speaker to go on talking). At four years, Japanese children are producing approximately 1.30 utterances per turn on the average ($SD = 0.23$), whereas North American children are producing 1.84 utterances per turn on the average ($SD = 0.52$), $F(1, 16) = 8.30$, $p = 0.01$, (see Figure 7.3). Thus, while North American mothers allow their four-year-olds to take long monologic turns, and give many evaluative comments, Japanese mothers simultaneously pay considerable attention to their four-year-olds' narratives and facilitate frequent turn exchanges.

Summary and discussion

This section answers the first two questions posed at the outset of this chapter.

Cross-cultural similarities and differences

Both Japanese and North American English-speaking mothers support their four-year-olds' talk about the past by trying to extend the topic. Their guidance, however, ensures it taking the shape of narration valued by their culture. Specifically, comparison of mothers from the two cultures yielded the following salient contrasts: In comparison to the North American mothers of four-year-olds, the Japanese mothers of four-year-olds (1) requested proportionately less description from their children, (2) gave proportionately less evaluation, (3) requested proportionately more evaluation from their children and (4) showed proportionately more verbal attention.

The last finding shown above, for instance, supports previous researchers' (e.g. LoCastro, 1987; Maynard, 1989; White, 1989; Yamada, 1992) claim that Japanese speakers use verbal acknowledgment (which is usually called back-channeling) more frequently than English speakers. The result likewise corresponds to Hayashi's (1988) claim that Japanese speakers use 'sync talk' (which means overlapping speech) much more frequently than English speakers, in the sense that the use of frequent verbal attention by Japanese mothers thus supports a collaborative message as well as a discourse construction highly valued by Japanese speakers.

Connection between maternal patterns of narrative elicitation and children's narrative skill

In terms of the link between maternal narrative elicitation strategies and children's current narrative skill, we have obtained mixed results. That is, connecting maternal patterns of narrative elicitation with children's developing narrative skill, the assumption discussed in Chapter 6 (i.e. maternal narrative elicitation styles reflect children's developing narrative skill) cannot adequately explain these differences. When comparing cross-culturally and/or cross-linguistically, mothers' scaffolding strategies do not necessarily seem to reflect children's failure to provide particular information. In other words, because of cross-cultural differences, it is not clear that mothers are trying to elicit what is desired but not present. For example, even if Japanese mothers requested less description from their four-year-olds than did North American mothers, it would not necessarily mean that Japanese four-year-olds were capable of providing more descriptive statements than North American children of the same age. Assumptions that suggest a relationship between maternal narrative elicitation styles and children's developing narrative skill within the Japanese group do not seem to apply cross-culturally or cross-linguistically. Rather, maternal elicitation strategies could in part reflect mothers' desire to develop particular narrative skills in their children. Unfortunately, because monologic narrative data from the North American group are not available in this study, what is discussed here is still a matter of conjecture.

Yet, in some cases, the assumption of a connection between patterns of narrative elicitation and children's developing narrative skill still seems to apply. For instance, the Japanese mothers of four-year-olds resembled the North American mothers of four-year-olds in one way. The difference in requests for actions between the Japanese mothers of four-year-olds and the North American mothers of four-year-olds did not approach statistical significance. From one perspective, these results could be interpreted to support the notion of *skeletal structure* (Hopper, 1979) (i.e. as discussed in Chapter 4, providing foreground/sequential information, such as action statements, in narrative constitutes the *skeletal structure* of the narrative). It seems that compared to non-sequential/background information (e.g. orientation and evaluation clauses), the tendency to provide foregrounded/sequential accounts develops early both cross-culturally and cross-linguistically (Berman & Slobin, 1994). In other words, it is assumed that because both four-year-old groups provided relatively sufficient foreground information (i.e. actions), compared to other components such as background information, mothers did not necessarily need to support their children's further contributions, and thus no difference was observed in this aspect of maternal narrative elicitation.

Gender differences

In comparison to the North American mothers of daughters, the North American mothers of sons (1) gave proportionately more evaluation, but (2) requested proportionately less evaluation. By contrast, the Japanese mothers of sons requested proportionately more evaluation than did the Japanese mothers of daughters. The gender-of-child-differences must be treated carefully in terms of culture. There is a well-documented finding in North America that daughters are more likely than sons to participate in conversations (Reese & Fivush, 1993). As far as the North American data is concerned, therefore, the result obtained does not necessarily mean that because the boys participated in the narrative discourse interactions to a greater extent than their female counterparts, mothers did not request evaluation from their sons. As far as the Japanese data is concerned, however, the explanation seems different. Recall that in Chapter 6 the Japanese mothers of sons were found to request more evaluation than the mothers of daughters, and that this gender difference reflects a difference in developing narrative skills between boys and girls (i.e. girls are more capable of encoding evaluation in their monologic narratives than boys). It seems, therefore, that, regardless of the context (i.e. either monologic or dialogic), because boys are less capable of encoding evaluation than their female counterparts, the Japanese mothers requested much evaluation from their four-year-old sons.

To conclude Study 1, the direction of scaffolding seems different between these two culturally distinct groups. North American mothers help to mold a child's cognitive development by actively giving evaluations to a child who is almost ready to perform with a little help (i.e. particularly boys). On the other hand, Japanese mothers help to mold a child's cognitive development by actively facilitating frequent turn exchanges as well as by eliciting evaluations from a child who is not necessarily ready to perform even with parental support (i.e. particularly boys).

As I stated earlier in the qualitative study of this chapter, another implication is that investigation should be conducted into how the Japanese type of interaction is explained within the framework of the four Gricean conversational maxims (Grice, 1975), the general principles that are considered to underlie the efficient use of language. The maxim of quantity, for example, suggests that the utterances be only as informative as is required for the current purposes of the conversational exchange. Japanese mothers' brief interaction style seems to violate the maxim of quantity. The maxim of manner states that the contribution should be clear and unambiguous, not verbose and disorganized. As seen in Sho and his mother's interaction in Example 7.1, however, the mother's use of a great amount of insinuations seems to violate the maxim of manner as well. Thus, the Western formulation of rules for efficient speech should be treated carefully when they are applied to non-Western conversational discourse. Yet, another possible interpretation – at least from Japanese point of view – is: It is North American mothers who violate the conversational maxims, because they say more than necessary and are unnecessarily informative. Therefore, the interpretation of such Gricean maxims seems to be left to each culture's norms.

Study 2

The first section of Study 2 (the micro-level narrative discourse analysis) compares mothers from two different Japanese groups: (1) 10 middle-class Japanese five-year-olds and their mothers living in Japan (none of these mother–child pairs had experienced living overseas at the time of interview); and (2) 8 middle-class Japanese five-year-olds and their mothers living in the United States. The second section of Study 2, further including North American mother–child pairs, examines culturally preferred narrative elicitation patterns when children are five years old.

Total number of words, total number of different words, type-token ratio in dialogic narrative

Tables 7.2a and 7.2b present the means and standard deviations of the total number of words and the total number of different words used in dialogic narrative interactions. For the Japanese five-year-olds living in Japan, the total number of words ranged from 123 to 493, and the total number of different words ranged from 55 to 150. For the Japanese five-year-olds living in the United States, the total number of words ranged widely from 141 to 512, and the total number of different words ranged from 65 to 120.

Quantity (children's patterns)

Although no differences reached statistical significance between the two groups, there was a marginal effect of gender on the total number

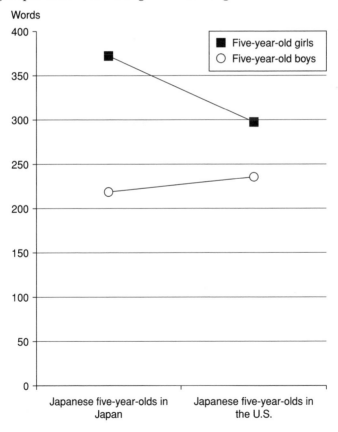

Figure 7.4 Total number of words by group and children's gender

of words, $F(1, 14) = 3.94$, $p = 0.067$. The Japanese five-year-old girls living in Japan produced a larger total number of words ($M = 368.40$, $SD = 112.93$) than did the Japanese five-year-old boys living in Japan ($M = 218.00$, $SD = 83.91$). Likewise, the five-year-old Japanese girls living in the United States produced a larger total number of words ($M = 299.75$, $SD = 159.49$) than did the five-year-old Japanese boys living in the United States ($M = 235.00$, $SD = 95.75$) (see Figure 7.4). As far as these samples are concerned, therefore, whether living in Japan or the United States, girls develop faster than boys in terms of quantity of words produced. Or simply, wherever they live, Japanese five-year-old girls are more talkative than Japanese five-year-old boys.

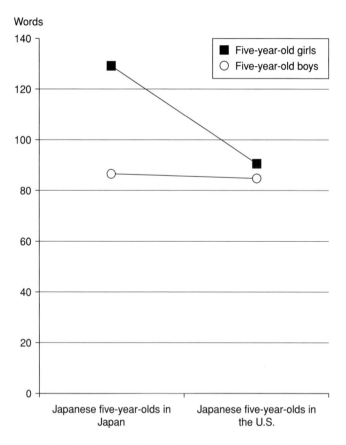

Figure 7.5 Number of different words by group and children's gender

Variety (children's patterns)

Although gender difference in the total number of different words did not approach statistical significance, $F(1, 14) = 3.05$, $p = 0.10$, the Japanese five-year-old girls living in Japan produced a larger number of different words ($M = 128.40$, $SD = 31.00$) than did the Japanese five-year-old boys living in Japan ($M = 86.40$, $SD = 31.42$). Also, the Japanese five-year-old girls living in the United States produced a larger number of different words ($M = 91.25$, $SD = 28.29$) than did the Japanese five-year-old boys living in the United States ($M = 85.00$, $SD = 23.58$) (see Figure 7.5). These results therefore suggest that not only in terms of quantity but also in terms of variety, whether living in Japan or the United States, five-year-

Table 7.2a Means and standard deviations of total number of words, total number of different words, type-token ratio in dialogic narrative production (children)

Variable	Japanese children in Japan (n = 10)		Japanese children in US (n = 8)	
	M	SD	M	SD
Total number of words	293.20	122.81	267.38	126.60
Total number of different words	107.40	36.82	88.13	24.34
Type-token ratio	0.38	0.06	0.36	0.07

Table 7.2b Means and standard deviations of total number of words, total number of different words in dialogic narrative production (mothers)

Variable	Japanese mothers in Japan (n = 10)		Japanese mothers in US (n = 8)	
	M	SD	M	SD
Total number of words	451.00	126.73	330.25	243.28
Total number of different words	127.70	29.44	111.13	59.03

old girls are more productive narrators than their male counterparts in mother–child interactions.

Maternal patterns

No differences approached statistical significance between Japanese mothers in Japan and Japanese mothers in the United States in these categories. These results suggest that, with regard to the quantity and variety of words, whether living in Japan or the United States, middle-class Japanese mothers behave in similar ways in mother–child interactions.

Linguistic items (parent data)

The linguistic items examined in Chapters 5 and 6 (mainly as means of involvement) were once again used in order to study differences between these two Japanese groups. Those items used by the mothers of both Japanese groups are very similar, except for the assertive/emphatic particle *yo* ('I tell you'), which the Japanese mothers living in Japan used more frequently ($M = 3.00$, $SD = 2.67$) than did the Japanese mothers living in the United States ($M = 0.75$, $SD = 0.71$), $t(11) = 2.56$, $p < 0.05$.[5] Because the use of *yo* indicates the speaker's exclusive accessibility to or sole possession of certain information, the speaker justifiably requests the listener's attention. The result obtained here, therefore, might indicate that Japanese mothers in Japan take more authoritarian roles than Japanese mothers living overseas, if we could apply Baumrind's (1971) typology (i.e. the 'authoritarian' child-rearing style, which emphasizes the values of control and obedience) to this data.

Whether living in Japan or the United States, however, Japanese mothers frequently used the rapport particle *ne* ('you know'). The frequent use of *ne* is considered to contribute to the harmonious mutual understanding that is highly valued in Japanese society, and this norm applies to Japanese living overseas. Thus, even if Japanese mothers live outside of Japan, they try to maintain the interaction style that is valued in their native culture.

Linguistic items (child data)

The linguistic items used by the five-year-olds of both Japanese groups are also similar except for the informal/plain verb-ending form *da*, which the Japanese children living in the United States ($M = 4.13$, $SD = 2.85$) used more frequently than did the Japanese children living in Japan ($M = 1.00$, $SD = 1.41$). This result might indicate either (1) the Japanese

Table 7.3 Mean frequencies and standard deviations of selected linguistic items in the context of mother–child interaction (mothers)

	Japanese mothers in Japan (n = 10)		Japanese mothers in the US (n = 8)		t^a values
	M	(SD)	M	(SD)	
Particles					
ne	11.90	(8.58)	7.13	(9.48)	−1.12
yo	3.00	(2.67)	0.75	(0.71)	−2.31*
tte	4.80	(2.20)	4.25	(5.37)	−0.30
Connectives					
dakara	0.00	(0.00)	0.38	(1.06)	1.13
Adverb					
yappari	0.10	(0.32)	0.25	(0.46)	0.82
Verbs					
des(u)/mas(u)	0.10	(0.32)	0.00	(0.00)	−0.89
da	4.10	(3.81)	5.13	(3.09)	0.62

*$p < 0.05$
[a] Degrees of freedom = 1, 16.

children living overseas were (or were allowed to be) more egalitarian and assertive than the Japanese children living in Japan; or simply (2) the Japanese children living overseas did not have many opportunities to learn to be polite in Japanese ways.

Some differences, however, emerged in relation to gender. There was a marginal effect of gender on the rapport particle *ne*, $F(1, 14) = 3.58$, $p < 0.08$. Although a Bonferroni Post Hoc test did not approach statistical significance, whether living in Japan or the United States, girls used *ne* more frequently ($M = 29.00$, $SD = 17.94$) than did boys ($M = 14.67$, $SD = 11.40$). Similarly, there was a marginal effect of gender on the quotation-final particle *tte*, $F(1, 14) = 3.53$, $p = 0.08$. Although a Bonferroni Post Hoc test did not reach statistical significance, whether living in Japan or the United States, girls used *tte* more frequently ($M = 5.67$, $SD = 4.15$) than did boys ($M = 2.67$, $SD = 2.92$).[6]

Brown (1996) suggests that, as far as Western societies are concerned, women have a more relational self, whereas men have a more individualistic self.[7] Following his assumption, because both *ne* and *tte* function affectively, we might be able to interpret the present finding as indicating:

Table 7.4a Mean frequencies and standard deviations of selected linguistic items in the context of mother–child interaction (children by location)

	Japanese five-year-olds in Japan		Japanese five-year-olds in US		F^a values for main effect of GROUP
	(n = 10)		(n = 8)		
	M	(SD)	M	(SD)	
Particles					
ne	18.80	(16.46)	25.63	(16.45)	0.89
yo	1.70	(3.16)	3.00	(2.00)	0.90
tte	4.60	(3.50)	3.63	(4.34)	0.32
Connectives					
dakara	0.10	(0.32)	0.38	(0.52)	3.04
datte	0.50	(0.71)	0.13	(0.35)	1.70
Adverb					
yappari	0.00	(0.00)	0.13	(0.35)	1.30
Verbs					
des(u)/mas(u)	0.10	(0.32)	0.00	(0.00)	0.78
da	1.00	(1.41)	4.13	(2.85)	9.44**

*$p < 0.05$;**$p < 0.01$
[a] Degrees of freedom = 1, 14.

(1) girls are more relational, whereas boys are more individualistic and autonomous; (2) the gender-related behavioral difference applies not only to the West but also to the East; and, moreover, (3) developmentally, a child's learning of gender role is evident in linguistic items used in mother–child interactions.

Verse/stanza analysis and high point analysis

In Chapters 4 and 5, a synthesis of two different types of analyses were applied to Japanese four- and five-year-olds' and their mothers' personal narratives, namely, verse/stanza analysis (Gee, 1985; Hymes, 1981), which has been applied successfully to narratives from various cultures, and high point analysis based on the Labovian tradition (Labov, 1972). In terms of function, verse/stanza analysis was used to break a

Table 7.4b Mean frequencies and standard deviations of selected linguistic items in the context of mother–child interaction (children by gender)

	Japanese five-year-olds boys (n = 9)		*Japanese five-year-olds girls* (n = 9)		*Fª values for main effect of GENDER*
	M	**(SD)**	**M**	**(SD)**	
Particles					
ne	14.67	(11.40)	29.00	(17.94)	3.58*
yo	2.33	(3.20)	2.22	(2.33)	0.001
tte	2.67	(2.92)	5.67	(4.15)	3.53*
Connectives					
dakara	0.11	(0.33)	0.33	(0.50)	3.04
datte	0.33	(0.50)	0.33	(0.71)	0.008
Adverb					
yappari	0.11	(0.33)	0.00	(0.00)	1.30
Verbs					
des(u)/mas(u)	0.00	(0.00)	0.11	(0.33)	0.78
da	1.78	(2.17)	3.00	(3.04)	1.70

*$p < 0.10$
ª Degrees of freedom = 1, 14.

narrative into units (i.e. structure-focus), whereas high point analysis was used to code the contents of those units (i.e. content-focus). As seen in Aya (a Japanese girl living in the United States, age 5;6) and her mother's co-constructed narrative (i.e. during maternal narrative elicitation) below, when a synthesis of verse/stanza analysis and high point analysis is applied to jointly produced narratives by Japanese children and their mothers living in the United States, a similar organization is obtained. Like personal narratives told by Japanese four- and five-year-olds in Japan, Aya's narrative account exemplifies an action sequence; that is, when her American peers drank Japanese wheat tea, the taste of which must have been strange to them, they said 'It's yucky.' Note that in this example, Aya and her mother use the quotation-final particle *tte*. Note also that in this example lines are indicated by the numbers to the right, and that small letters (a-g) in parentheses indicate the beginning of each verse.

Example 7.3   Aya and her mother's interaction
Aya: (a) **ACT**

ano ne,   1
'Um, you know,'
    minna ga hoshii tte itte ne,   2
    'all (the kids) said that they wanted (to try it), you know,'
                                          (**Mother**: *un*)
                                          'uh huh'
Aya: (b) **ACT**
de ne,   3
'But, you know,'
    nomuto ne,   4
    'when (they) drank (it), you know,'
(c) **ACT:OUT**
"yucky" *tte itteta.*   5
'(They) said "It's yucky." '
Mother: (d) **ACT:ORT**
miteru toki wa,   6
'When (they) were looking at (the wheat tea)'
(e) **ACT**
hoshii tte itte,   7
'(they) said that (they) wanted (to drink it),'
(f) **ACT**
sorede nondara.   8
'But then once (they) drank (it),'
(g) **ACT:OUT**
"yucky" *tte ittetan ne.*   9
'(They) said "It's yucky," is that it?'

Verses (a–c) produced by the child conform to the pattern of a three-verse action sequence, which was found typical among young Japanese children (see Chapter 5). The mother confirms what the child has narrated, using a similar action sequence. At the initial part of her turn, however, she scaffolds the orientation. That is, she clarifies the ongoing behavior of the narrative, narrating a clause representing a specific action with the progressive form *V-te (i)* (note that, as can be seen in Verse (d), in colloquial Japanese *i* is sometimes omitted). Thus, while the mother confirms what the child has narrated using a similar action-sequence pattern focusing on foreground information, in order to extend the topic, she also adds background information (i.e. orientation).

Micro-level narrative discourse analysis

Narrative discourse devices in Japanese

Like the micro-level narrative discourse analysis in the previous chapter, this section examines the two types of discourse devices: (1) the listener's *un* ('uh huh') in response to the narrator's *ne* ('you know') and (2) *huun* ('well'). By doing so, this section examines the impact of culture on maternal narrative elicitation styles.

Like Japanese mother–child pairs living in Japan, Japanese mother–child pairs living in the United States use four different types of *huun*: (1) prefacing of topic-extension, (2) prefacing of topic-switch, (3) simple verbal acknowledgment and (4) brief acknowledgment accompanied by echoes. Example 7.5, for instance, which is from Teru (a boy, age 5;1) and his mother, shows two opposing uses of *huun* as a means of extending or switching the conversation. The first *huun* comes right before the child's topic extension statement. Teru's mother's simple acknowledgment *huun* allows him to elaborate further on the same topic. The second *huun*, on the other hand, comes right before a topic-switch; this time, Teru's mother changes the topic of conversation from play to lunch.

Example 7.4—Prefacing of topic-extension
Satoshi (a Japanese boy in the US, age 5;3)
Mother: *huun* [**prefacing of topic-extension**]
　　　　'Well.'
　　　　ano sensei nante namae daroo?
　　　　'What is that teacher's name?'
Satoshi: *wakan nai.*
　　　　'(I) don't know.'

Example 7.5—Simple acknowledgment and Prefacing of topic-switch
Teru (a Japanese boy in the US, age 5;1)
Teru: *boku wa ne, zuuto ne, block atarashii block de ne,*
　　　　zuuto hikooki ne, ano ne, hikooki toka kuruma toka ne,
　　　　tsukutte asondeta.
　　　　'I was, you know, always, you know, playing with blocks, new blocks, you know, always making airplanes, you know, um you know, airplanes and cars.'
Mother: *huun.* [**simple acknowledgment**]
　　　　'Well.'
Teru: *ano zuuto otonashiku asonderu no boku wa.*
　　　　'Um, I am always playing quietly.'
Mother: *honto?*
　　　　'Really?'
Teru: *Yuri chan to Aki kun to boku.*
　　　　'Yuri and Aki and I.'

Mother: *huun.* **[prefacing of topic-switch]**
'Well.'
obentoo kinoo wa takusan nokoshite kita kedo, kyoo wa kirei ni tabeta ne.
'About yesterday's lunch, (you) left a lot, but today (you) ate it all,
didn't you?'
Teru: *un.*
'Yes.'
Mother: *ooku nakatta no?*
'It wasn't too much?'
Teru: *un.*
'No.'
Mother: *onigiri no hoo ga ii ne.*
'Rice balls are better (for lunch), aren't they?'
Teru: *un.*
'Yes.'
Mother: *onigiri no hoo ga tabeyasui de sho?*
'Rice balls are easier to eat, aren't they?'

Example 7.6   Brief acknowledgment accompanied by echoes
Kotaro (a Japanese boy in the US, age 5;9)
Mother: *doo yatte nagete ireru no?*
'How do (you) get (it) to go in when (you) throw (it)?'
Kotaro: *nagete ireru kedo, dechau.*
'I (try to) get (it) in but (it) comes back out.'
Mother: *dechau no.*
'(It) comes back out.'
huun. **[brief acknowledgment after echoes]**
'Well.'
Kotaro: *un.*
'Yes.'
takai tokoro ja nai yo.
'(It) is really not very high [I tell you].'

Results

Two types of discourse devices in Japanese were statistically analyzed,
namely, first, the child's *ne* ('you know') immediately followed by the
mother's *un* ('uh huh') and second, maternal prefacing *huun* ('well').
[Using the categorization described in the previous section, all maternal
huun utterances were categorized independently by two raters. Inter-
rater agreement across the four categories resulted in a Cohen's kappa
statistic of almost 1.00.] For the first, a two-way (group × gender) analysis
of variance (ANOVA) was conducted on the frequency variable of 'the
child's *ne* ('you know') immediately followed by the mother's *un* ('uh
huh').' This test revealed that there was no significant effect of group or
gender. As far as this variable is concerned, therefore, whether living in

Japan or the United States, Japanese mothers use the same strategy to support their children's narrative production. This result seems to suggest a strong influence of the native culture on adults.

An environmental effect (whether living in Japan or the United States), however, exists at the same time. For the second, a multivariate analysis of variance (MANOVA) was conducted for the four dependent variables, (1) prefacing of topic-extension, (2) prefacing of topic-switch, (3) simple verbal acknowledgment and (4) brief acknowledgment accompanied by echoes. There was a significant multivariate effect of group, Wilks' lambda = 3.58, approximate $F(4, 11) = 3.59, p < 0.05$. This effect was largely attributable to a significant effect on maternal prefacing of topic-extension *huun*, $F(1, 14) = 6.27$, $p < 0.05$. A Bonferroni Post Hoc test showed that Japanese mothers living in the United States more frequently used *huun* to preface topic-extension than did Japanese mothers living in Japan. As a matter of fact, the Japanese mothers living in the United States used *huun* to preface topic-extension 3.00 times ($SD = 1.31$) on average, whereas the Japanese mothers living in Japan used *huun* for the same purpose 1.30 times ($SD = 1.57$) on average. This result indicates that compared to Japanese mothers of five-year-olds living in Japan, Japanese mothers of five-year-olds living in the United States seem to be influenced by living in a talkative environment.

Table 7.5 Mean frequencies and standard deviations of mothers' 'Huun' (by group)

	Japanese mothers of five-year-olds in Japan		*Japanese mothers of five-year-olds in US*		*F^a values for main effect of GROUP*
	M	*(SD)*	*M*	*(SD)*	
Prefacing topic-extension	1.30	(1.57)	3.00	(1.31)	6.27*
Prefacing topic-switch	1.10	(1.52)	0.50	(0.53)	1.04
Simple acknowledgment	0.80	(1.55)	1.25	(1.98)	0.32
Brief acknowledgment after echo	0.30	(0.67)	0.13	(0.35)	0.40

*$p < 0.05$
[a] Degrees of freedom = 1, 14.

Macro-level Narrative Discourse Analysis

Coding

Transcripts of all parents' speech were coded according to the speech act coding scheme previously used.[8]

Results: Maternal styles of narrative elicitation

First, raw frequencies were analyzed because they represent the impact that great talkativeness might have on children's narration (e.g. Hoff-Ginsberg, 1992; McCabe & Peterson, 1991; Reese et al., 1992). In addition, proportional frequencies were used because they correct for differences in length and allow us to see differing relative emphasis on components of narration. To test for the effect of group and gender, multivariate analyses of variance (MANOVA) were conducted for the major coding categories: (1) maternal requests for descriptions, actions, and evaluations, (2) maternal evaluations, (3) statements showing attention and (4) initiation (see Table 7.6).

With regard to frequencies, there was a multivariate effect of group, Wilks' Lambda = 0.18, approximate $F(12, 30) = 3.39$, $p < 0.01$. Univariate ANOVAs were run for each of the dependent variables. The effect of group was largely attributable to a significant univariate effect on maternal statements showing attention, $F(2, 20) = 4.29$, $p < 0.05$. The results were further analyzed in Bonferroni Post Hoc tests, which revealed that mothers of both Japanese groups gave more verbal acknowledgment (i.e. statements showing attention) than did North American mothers (see Figure 7.6).[9] The effect of group was also attributable to a marginal univariate effect on evaluations by mother herself, $F(2, 20) = 2.98$, $p < 0.08$. Although Bonferroni Post Hoc tests did not show statistically significant differences among the three groups, compared to North American mothers, mothers of both Japanese groups gave less evaluation.

In terms of proportions, there was a significant multivariate effect of group, Wilks' lambda = 0.24, approximate $F(10, 32) = 3.36$, $p < 0.01$. Univariate ANOVAs were run for each of the dependent variables. The effect of group was largely attributable to significant effects on maternal requests for descriptions, $F(2, 20) = 3.82$, $p < 0.05$, maternal evaluations, $F(2, 20) = 9.13$, $p < 0.01$, and statements showing attention, $F(2, 20) = 6.32$, $p < 0.01$. The results were further analyzed in Bonferroni Post Hoc tests, which suggest the following: (1) In comparison to North American mothers, Japanese-speaking mothers in both groups gave proportionately less evaluation (see Figure 7.7).[10] (2) Mothers of both Japanese groups gave proportionately more verbal acknowledgment (i.e. statements showing

Table 7.6 Mean frequencies and percentages of mothers' prompts to children about past events (five-year-olds)

	Japanese mothers in Japan		*Japanese mothers in US*		*North American mothers*		*F^a values for main effect of GROUP*
	M	*(SD)*	*M*	*(SD)*	*M*	*(SD)*	
Requests for descriptions							
Frequencies	15.00	(7.35)	14.00	(7.89)	17.63	(15.00)	0.25
Percentages	14.72%	(4.83)	20.81%	(4.56)	18.90%	(5.38)	3.82*
Requests for actions							
Frequencies	23.50	(10.01)	15.50	(10.92)	17.88	(15.93)	0.95
Percentages	24.30%	(11.27)	22.68%	(6.57)	19.84%	(12.66)	0.37
Requests for evaluations							
Frequencies	16.50	(7.88)	8.75	(5.12)	21.38	(19.89)	2.04
Percentages	17.18%	(8.30)	14.24%	(8.98)	21.44%	(9.55)	1.40
Evaluations by mother herself							
Frequencies	15.40	(10.34)	7.75	(10.85)	28.25	(25.82)	2.98
Percentages	14.69%	(6.62)	8.85%	(7.39)	28.01%	(12.41)	9.13**
Statements showing attention							
Frequencies	27.10	(20.85)	17.50	(6.80)	7.50	(7.27)	4.29*
Percentages	26.18%	(19.16)	28.31%	(9.03)	8.46%	(4.17)	6.32**
Initiation							
Frequencies	2.80	(0.63)	2.75	(0.71)	2.38	(1.06)	0.65
Percentages	2.93%	(1.00)	5.11%	(2.08)	3.35%	(2.80)	2.71

*$p < 0.05$; **$p < 0.01$
[a] Degrees of freedom = 2, 20.

attention) than did North American mothers (see Figure 7.8).[11] (3) However, Japanese mothers living in the United States requested proportionately more description from their children than did Japanese mothers living in Japan.[12] Moreover, there was no statistically significant

Frequency

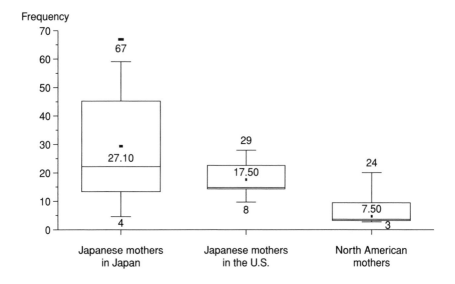

Figure 7.6 Distribution of maternal statements showing attention (frequency)

Percent

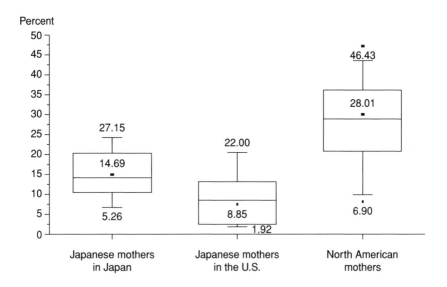

Figure 7.7 Distribution of mother's evaluative comments (percentage)

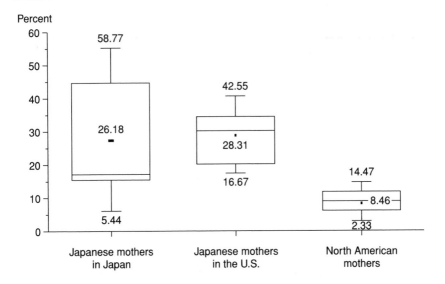

Figure 7.8 Distribution of maternal statements showing attention (percentage)

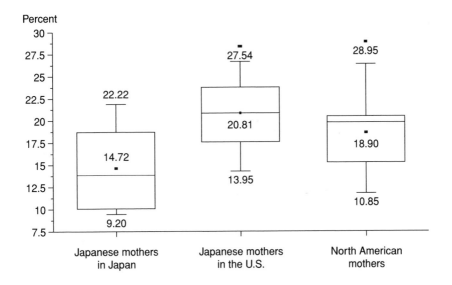

Figure 7.9 Distribution of maternal requests for descriptions

difference in the distribution of maternal requests for descriptions between Japanese mothers living in the United States and North American mothers (see Figure 7.9).

Results: Child's length of turns

In addition to the frequencies of the coded behaviors, I examined the child's production of information units, which I call 'utterances over turns' (i.e. the number of utterances produced by a speaker per turn) here. That is, I compared the length of turn in information units for Japanese children with that for North American children. For the five-year-old group, although males' utterances ($M = 2.33$, $SD = 1.04$) were slightly longer than females' ($M = 1.90$, $SD = 0.84$), North American children produced approximately 2.11 utterances per turn on the average ($SD = 0.90$). On the other hand, Japanese children living in Japan and the United States produced 1.19 utterances ($SD = 0.22$) and 1.24 utterances ($SD = 0.10$) respectively. Thus, Japanese-speaking children, whether living in Japan or the United States, produced about 1.22 utterances on the average.

A 3×2 (group × gender) analysis of variance (ANOVA) was performed on the variable, utterances over turns. This ANOVA accompanied by Bonferroni Post Hoc tests revealed that Japanese children, whether living in Japan or the United States, produced fewer utterances per turn than

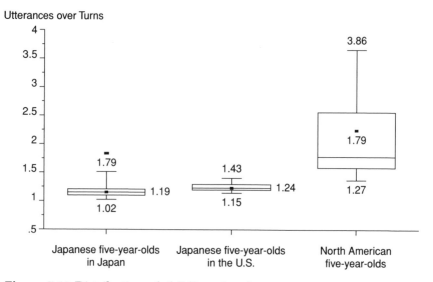

Figure 7.10 Distribution of child's ratio of utterances over turns

did North American children, $F(2, 20) = 7.76$, $p < 0.01$ (Figure 7.10). Thus, while North American mothers allow their five-year-olds to take long monologic turns, and give many evaluative comments, Japanese mothers, whether living in Japan or the US, simultaneously pay considerable attention to their five-year-olds' narratives and facilitate frequent turn exchanges.

Summary and discussion

Examining how parents guide their children in the acquisition of culture-specific styles of narrative, this section answers the last two questions posed at the outset of this chapter.

Cross-cultural similarities and differences

The micro-level narrative discourse analysis, in which mothers from the two different Japanese groups are compared, suggests that Japanese mothers in the United States were more likely to use a particular discourse device (*huun*: 'well') to preface topic-extension. As we have seen, the macro-level narrative discourse analysis, further including North American mother–child pairs, yielded salient differences: (1) In comparison to North American mothers, mothers of both Japanese groups gave proportionately less evaluation. (2) Both in terms of frequency and proportion, mothers of both Japanese groups gave more verbal acknowledgment than did North American mothers. (3) Japanese mothers in the United States, however, requested proportionately more description from their children than did Japanese mothers in Japan.

Similarities also emerged among the three groups. The difference in maternal requests for actions did not approach statistical significance. As discussed earlier in the analysis of four-year-olds, the result obtained here seems to support the claim that, compared to non-sequential information, the tendency to provide foreground (i.e. sequential) information such as action statements in narrative develops early cross-linguistically as well as cross-culturally (Berman & Slobin, 1994). Because five-year-olds provided relatively sufficient foreground information (i.e. actions), compared to other components such as background information, mothers did not necessarily need to elicit further contributions from their children, and thus no difference was observed in maternal requests for actions. I therefore argue that these commonalities across the three groups are inherent to the nature of general developmental patterns in narrative (i.e. a universal or quasi-universal route of development).

In terms of maternal requests for evaluations, what appeared to be a difference between North American English-speaking children and Japanese children at age four, however, is no longer present at age five. Recall that in the monologic narrative context no differences were observed between five-year-olds and adults, although four-year-olds gave proportionately less evaluation than adults, and that, therefore, compared to four-year-olds, five-year-olds seem to begin to evaluate at a rate equivalent to the Japanese mothers (see Chapter 4). Although monologic narratives produced by Japanese five-year-olds living in the United States and North American five-year-olds are not available in this study, it seems reasonable to assume that five-year-olds also provided what seemed to mothers to be relatively sufficient evaluative accounts in mother–child interactions. Therefore, Japanese mothers did not need to insist that their children provide more evaluative comments. Overall, the similarities found in this study seem to indicate common developmental patterns across languages and cultures (i.e. universality); that is, what five-year-olds can include in their narratives are similar cross-linguistically as well as cross-culturally.

The assumption linking maternal narrative elicitation strategies with children's developing narrative skill alone, however, cannot adequately explain some of the similarities and differences that have emerged in this study. Rather, maternal elicitation strategies in part seem to reflect mothers' concerns/wishes or even folk psychology (i.e. culturally-based assumptions) to develop their children's particular narrative skills. That is, it has been claimed that in North America an individual should be verbally explicit, whereas in Japanese group-oriented society, an individual is allowed to be verbally implicit but should be empathic.

Not only in language skills but also in other areas, mothers' expectations concerning the development of their preschool children differ greatly between the United States and Japan (i.e. relativity). According to Hess *et al.* (1980), Japanese mothers expect earlier mastery of skills related to emotional maturity (e.g. 'does not cry easily'), discipline (e.g. 'comes or answers when called') and social courtesy (e.g. 'waits for turn in games'). Mothers in the United States, on the other hand, expect earlier mastery of verbal assertiveness (e.g. 'states own preference when asked') and social skills with peers (e.g. 'gets his way by persuading friends'). Japanese preference for verbal restraint rather than effusiveness is further reflected in child care settings, where there is correspondingly less emphasis on encouraging verbalization from children (Shigaki, 1987). These explanations may account for why North American mothers emphasize mastery of verbal skills and, in contrast, why Japanese mothers provide fewer evaluative comments in favor of a more implicit appraisal (Doi, 1973; Lebra, 1976). Following this line of interpretation, therefore, from early childhood on, children are accustomed to using these culturally valued narrative discourse skills due to interactions with their mothers. Furthermore, we are also impressed by the profundity of ethnopsychology in which alternative explanations are possible, from culture to culture, of why children behave in different ways and how adults contribute to such differences.

The complexity in the relationship between maternal narrative elicitation strategies and children's developing narrative skill is seen in the two studies reported in this chapter, particularly Study 2. Recall, for instance, that in the micro-level narrative discourse analysis, although both Japanese parental groups used *huun* ('well') as a discourse device, Japanese mothers living in the United States were more likely to use this device to preface topic-extension. Similarly, in the macro-level narrative discourse analysis, Japanese mothers in the United States were found to behave more like North American mothers, who requested a substantial amount of description from their children. These results seem to reflect the mothers' concern, which has been influenced by the culture. That is, these results imply that Japanese mothers living in the United States seem to be influenced by living in a loquacious environment and to have acquired a taste for descriptive elaboration. [Note: These results, which indicate the strong influence of environmental factors on the individual's behavior, become even more interesting when comparing them with Caudill and Frost's (1974) finding that Japanese-American infants behaved more like the American infants in Chapter 2.]

We should keep in mind, however, that even if Japanese mothers living in the United States behaved like North American mothers in some respects, those Japanese mothers behaved quite differently from North American mothers in other respects. That is, while North American mothers allow their children to take long monologic turns, and give many evaluative comments, Japanese mothers, whether living in Japan or the United States, simultaneously pay considerable attention to their children's narratives and facilitate frequent turn exchanges. The mothers in these two groups (i.e. English-speaking North American mothers and both subgroups of Japanese-speaking mothers) therefore differed considerably in the style and strategies that they used to elicit narratives from their children.

As a cautionary note, however, I do not simply argue that independence training in Americans produces longer turns, whereas *omoiyari* (empathy) training in Japanese produces the opposite. Rather, based on *omoiyari* (empathy), the Japanese language allows interlocutors to co-construct narrative tellings through specific mechanisms – the narrator's habitual use of attention-getting devices such as *ne* and the listener's verbal acknowledgment (e.g. *un*) to them. Moreover, Japanese mothers' frequent verbal acknowledgment contributed to their children's saying less per turn (i.e. lower utterances over turns) than those of North American children of the same age. I therefore assume that some typical Japanese habits are kept by Japanese mothers living in the United States, due not only to the nature of the language itself, but also to underlying cultural beliefs.

As another cautionary note, we should not simply conceptualize that because they are socially directed, children passively internalize the values of society. As stated previously, to explain these differences and similarities in maternal patterns of narrative elicitation, environmental factors, such as the social interaction paradigm in the larger framework of culture, should be considered (see Chapter 2). As Holloway and Minami (1996) suggest, children's active processing of information results in not only the reproduction of culture but also the production of new elements of culture. Because all the subject Japanese five-year-olds living in the United States were in local preschools, they were in a different social environment from that of the Japanese five-year-olds living in Japan. Recall, for instance, that the Japanese children living in the United States used the informal/plain verb-ending form *da* more frequently than did the Japanese children living in Japan. Through interaction with American mothers, moreover, the Japanese mothers were likely to be influenced with regards to how to interact with young children, such as behaving like authoritative parents, to borrow Baumrind's (1971) terminology (i.e. the 'authoritative' child-rearing style, which emphasizes respect for a child's individuality blended with an effort to instill social values in the child). Influenced by the behavioral patterns of the new group of people (i.e. middle-class American mothers), these Japanese mothers living in the United States might have developed greater tolerance of extended verbalization. In addition to other environmental factors, possible attitudinal differences between the two Japanese children's groups might have caused parents' attitude to change.

The attitudinal differences of parents are in turn reflected in their language practices, such as the more frequent use of *huun* to preface topic extension and the more frequent requests for topic description from their children. Thus, children and their environments should be viewed as a dynamic system in which they actively interact with and influence each other. Individuals – children and adults alike – should therefore be considered active sense makers, who view alternatives and exercise choice, participating in the creation of their social circumstances (Mehan, 1992). Both psychological and social interactional dimensions should not be ignored or slighted in order to understand not only the continuation of certain cultural patterns but also the dynamics of change that an individual experiences when living in a non-native culture.

This chapter, overall, suggests that the differences and similarities among these three groups can be explained in terms of a larger framework of culture based on the social interaction paradigm. Kağıtçıbaşı (1989) argues that non-Western urban families often evolve a hybrid structure in which certain values and practices consonant with Western views coexist with traditional non-Western values. This explanation seems to hold true of Japanese mothers, particularly those living in the United States. While inducting their children into a communicative style that is reflective of their native culture, Japanese mothers living in the United States, at the same time, are subject to the influence of Western culture.

Notes

1. I would like to thank Carole Peterson, Memorial University of Newfoundland, and Allyssa McCabe for providing the data that were collected as part of a research project supported by Natural Sciences and Engineering Research Council of Canada grant OGP0000513.
2. Piano Ranger appears in a TV children's show similar to 'Mighty Morphin Power Rangers,' which is originally a product of Japan.
3. A significant effect on initiation seems to be an artifact of the difference in the frequency of coded utterances between the Japanese mothers and the North American mothers. As reported previously, to establish a comparable data base, the initial three narrative productions were used; thus the number of narrative productions was controlled. However, because Harriet's mother prompted very little, the proportional frequency for initiation was much higher (9.68%) than any other mothers. In fact, when frequencies were analyzed, the difference in this category between these two groups did not approach statistical significance.
4. The information unit roughly corresponds to what Stein and Glenn (1979) call the propositional/informational unit. According to these researchers, 'A proposition is defined as a predicator or relational word, usually the verb, and one or more arguments which stand in some specific relation to the predicator, e.g. the actor of a verb' (Stein & Glenn, 1979, p. 55). Thus, a proposition roughly corresponds to a simple sentence/clause including a subject and/or predicate (Hudson & Shapiro, 1991; Reilly, 1992). In addition, unlike the terminable unit (T-unit) (Scott, 1988), which possibly contains a main clause with all subordinate clauses or nonclausal structure attached to or embedded within, the information unit does not contain more than one clause.

5. Using a two-sample t statistic, where the variance of each group is estimated separately, is appropriate whenever the population variances are not assumed to be equal, as is the case here.

6. Additionally, there was a significant interaction of group and gender on the connective, *dakara* ('so,' 'therefore'), $F(1, 14) = 9.06$, $p < 0.01$. However, because the frequencies were so low, this result was not reported in the text.

7. According to Brown (1996), a familiar example to illustrate this gender difference would be that women share and exchange confidences, whereas men try not to reveal secrets to others because doing so might put them at a great disadvantage. Brown, in fact, utilizes conceptual frameworks provided by Gilligan (1982) and Tannen (1990). Following Gilligan, for example, women develop identity differently from men; women, more often than men, focus on the interpersonal aspects. To take this one step further, Brown concludes his essay with implications that the Eastern self – the Japanese self in particular – is relational, whereas the Western self is independent and individualistic. Brown is probably right when he claims that the structure of the Japanese language itself offers the evidence that the Japanese self is relational. Yet there is a danger of stereotyping inherent in the inclusion of gender and culture. Moreover, we must dare to pit ourselves against the formidable task of proving the hypothesis. Although personal anecdotes may give credence to Brown's hypothesis, there still remains a need for further investigation, as Brown himself admits. Nevertheless, Brown's insight into the constellation of gender and culture is a fruitful line of inquiry to develop, one which might enable us to conclude that on a scale with the relational self at one end and the independent self at the other end of the scale, the men's self in the East and the women's self in the West are located closely whereas the women's self in the East is nearer the relational self end of the scale.

8. All transcripts were coded by an individual who is bilingual in Japanese and English. Two full transcripts of Japanese and two full transcripts of English were independently coded by individuals fluent in each of those languages, respectively. Cohen's kappa was 0.98 for the first level (topic-initiation, topic-extension and statements showing attention) of the Japanese coding; it was 0.83 for the second level (descriptive statements, statements about actions, mother's evaluative comments and mother's request for child's evaluative comments). Likewise, Cohen's kappa for the first level of the English coding was 1.00, and 0.90 for the second level.

9. The Japanese mothers in Japan and the Japanese mothers in the United States gave verbal acknowledgment 27.10 times $(SD = 20.85)$ and 17.50 times $(SD = 6.80)$, respectively, whereas the North American mothers gave verbal acknowledgment 7.50 times on average $(SD = 7.27)$. The box-plots shown in Figure 7.6 present the distributions of the three groups for the number of verbal acknowledgments. While the Japanese mothers living in Japan varied widely from 4 to 67 $(SD = 20.85)$ and thus had a large amount of within-culture variation, neither the Japanese mothers living in the United States $(SD = 6.80$, range $= 8$ to 29) nor the North American mothers $(SD = 7.27$, range $= 3$ to 24) showed such great variation. (As can be seen in this case, the box-plots in the figure are intended to make the patterns easier to follow; they provide a good deal of information on the distribution of subjects: the

mean [plotted with a dot in the box], the median [the horizontal line across the box], the middle half of the data between the 25th and 75th percentiles [the outlined central box], the range of the main body of the data [the whiskers extending above and below the box], and outliers [plotted with dots].)

10. Maternal evaluation accounts for 14.69% (SD = 6.62) for the Japanese mothers living in Japan and 8.85% (SD = 7.39) for the Japanese mothers living in the United States, whereas it accounts for 28.01% (SD = 12.41) for the North American mothers.

11. The category of statements showing attention accounts for 26.18% (SD = 19.16) for the Japanese mothers living in Japan and 28.31% (SD = 9.03) for the Japanese mothers living in the United States, whereas the same category accounts for 8.46% (SD = 4.17) for the North American mothers. The box-plots shown in Figure 7.18 present the distributions of the three groups for the proportion of verbal acknowledgment. The Japanese mothers living in Japan varied most widely (SD = 19.16, range = 5.44 to 58.77), followed by the Japanese mothers living in the United States (SD = 9.03, range = 16.67 to 42.55), and by the North American mothers (SD = 4.17, range = 2.33 to 14.47). Thus, while the Japanese mothers in Japan had a large amount of within-culture variation, neither the Japanese mothers in the United States nor the North American mothers had such great variation.

12. The category of maternal requests for descriptions accounts for 14.72% (SD = 4.83) for the Japanese mothers living in Japan, whereas the same category accounts for 20.81% (SD = 4.46) for the Japanese mothers living in the United States and 18.90% (SD = 5.38) for the North American mothers.

Chapter 8

Styles of Parent–Child Book-Reading in Japanese Families

Narrative serves a variety of important functions, such as mediating interpersonal relationships, self-presentation, making sense of experiences and a transition into literacy. The preschool and early elementary school years are a period of extremely rapid development in the acquisition of literacy-related skills; in the early elementary school years, narrative is a frequent writing assignment, as well as a bridge to stories read in school.

Chapters 4, 5 and 6 presented personal narratives collected from Japanese preschool children in two ways, once with an adult interviewer with minimal scaffolding, second by the mother with her usual scaffolding. In these chapters, the stories were analyzed basically in terms of the Labovian methodology (Labov, 1972; Peterson & McCabe, 1983) for elicited narratives and comparisons were made across age (four years old and five years old), between genders and between children. As far as the Japanese data collected in Japan are concerned, it turned out that the elements specifically elicited by the mothers were minimal in the unscaffolded stories of each individual child. To study culturally preferred narrative elicitation patterns, furthermore, Chapter 7 analyzed narrative discourse interactions between mothers and their preschool children from three different cultural groups.

In this chapter, changing the focus slightly, I once again concentrate on Japanese mother–child pairs living in Japan and examine preschoolers' readiness for school. By exploring book-reading interactions, I address two important transitions in child development: (1) from orality (narrative) to literacy (book-reading), and (2) from home to school.

Shared book-reading is similar to the dialogic mode of narrative telling, in which, as we have seen, narration proceeds through a question–answer format (e.g. mothers try to extend topics by providing requests for actions, descriptions and evaluations, to which children respond). This is the mode in which children come to tell stories from the early stages of language acquisition, and it specifically takes the form of co-construction. The mothers' echoing, back-channeling, latching or completing the child's utterance in dialogic narratives reveals that they share the same thinking patterns or take the same perspective toward a certain object or event. Similar types of interaction take place in shared book-reading activities.

In Chapter 8, to examine possible links between maternal styles of book-reading and children's book-reading, both quantitative and qualitative analyses are performed. As can be seen in the positive relationships between monologic and dialogic narratives, the quantitative analysis in the context of book-reading activities reveals that maternal utterances and child utterances are positively related in many ways. The qualitative analysis reveals a ubiquitous pattern of the three-part sequence among Japanese mothers during book-reading activities, the sequence that typically appears in classroom interactions: the mother initiates (usually in question form), the child responds, and the mother supplies feedback. Discussing the results of the analyses, this chapter suggests: (1) there is a continuity between oral and written language; (2) there is another continuum running between school language use and home language use (which we will see in greater detail in Chapter 9).

Emergent Literacy

Ever since Chomsky (1965) began to develop the theory of linguistic universals, researchers have been interested in the human biological endowment that enables us to discover the framework of principles and elements common to attainable human languages. To support his argument, Chomsky (1959) claimed: (1) human beings are distinct from all other animal species in the processing of language; (2) language is acquired quite rapidly (e.g. the speech of four-year-olds already resembles that of adults); (3) the language environment of the child does not provide sufficient data. As we saw in detail in Chapter 2, however, the process of language acquisition could not be explained without considering the significant influence of environmental or parental interactions (e.g. mothers modifying their speech to their children by simplifying, repeating and paraphrasing). Thus, the role of socialization should be recognized as important here; socialization, in other words, indicates the process whereby the biological is transformed into a specific cultural being.

The impact of environmental factors on child development is critical in the development of literacy-related skills including narration as well. To begin with, storytelling is a social act; prior research (e.g. Dickinson

& McCabe, 1991; Ninio & Snow, 1996; Reese & Cox, 1999; Snow & Ninio, 1986) indicates that storytelling offers an appropriate lens through which to study not only language but also social development. Second, orality and literacy interpenetrate and form a continuum in everyday language use. Individuals of all ages and cultural backgrounds need to narrate in order to communicate; children need storytelling ability in order to become accomplished readers and writers (Halliday, 1994; McCabe, 1996). Particularly, preschool children construct considerable literacy-related knowledge through mother–child interactions, as they acquire language (Reese & Cox, 1999). Furthermore, we might be able to assume that what mothers choose to add to the text during book-reading is influenced by their beliefs and understandings of the purpose of the book-reading activity and, more generally, by their culture in general. Obviously, this assumption, at the same time, implies that we might observe variation in interaction styles during book-reading activities across cultures.

In this chapter, I adopt Sulzby and Zecker's (1991) definition of emergent literacy, young children's 'everyday encounters with the print in their environments' (p. 175). Here, however, I define literacy as both spoken and written language. This is a much broader definition of literacy than is generally accepted, but I justify it by my belief that a strong connection exists between learning to talk (particularly learning to narrate) and learning to read and write. In other words, oral language development (narrative development in particular) is directly related to the later development of written language.

Furthermore, because literacy learning is fundamentally a sociocultural process, examining literacy practices holds significant meaning in deepening our understanding of cross-cultural differences. In actual observations, one will certainly find individual differences. Reese and Cox (1999), for instance, examined the relative benefits of three different styles of adult book-reading for four-year-old children's emergent literacy: (1) a describer style that focuses on describing pictures during book-reading activities, (2) a comprehensive style that emphasizes the meaning of the story and (3) a performance-oriented style that introduces the book and discusses story meaning on completion. While paying attention to within-culture variation, therefore, this chapter tries to identify culturally salient styles of book-reading. The chapter specifically tries to identify factors that predict the different pathways leading to successful literacy skills expected in Japanese settings. The chapter: (1) explores the relationship between mothers' book-reading styles and their preschool children's emergent literacy skills, and (2) identifies the relationship between sociocultural background and young children's literacy development. Specific research questions are as follows:

(1) Is there any association with a particular type of talk between the mother and her child while reading a book? [This question specifically relates to the quantitative data analysis in the results section.]
(2) What kind of verbal interaction takes place between the mother and her child during book-reading? [This question specifically relates to the qualitative data analysis in the results section.]

Method

Participants

Book-reading interactions in the homes of 20 middle-class mother–child dyads who appeared in previous chapters (i.e. the Japanese mother–child pairs living in Japan) were examined. As previously noted, the 20 mothers and their children in this sample are all native Japanese speakers; half of the children were four years old and half were five. Unlike previous chapters, the primary objective of this chapter is not to study gender differences or age differences. Note that five-year-old children were in five-year-old children's classrooms in preschool at the time of data collection (five boys and five girls, $M = 5;3$ years), whereas four-year-old children were in four-year-old children's classrooms in preschool at the time of data collection (five boys and five girls, $M = 4;3$ years).

Procedure

The mothers were asked to look at a book brought by the experimenter, *The Very Hungry Caterpillar* by Eric Carle (1969) and translated by Hisashi Mori into Japanese (Carle, 1976). The book is a simple narrative telling, following the life cycle of a butterfly. On a warm Sunday morning, a hungry caterpillar hatches out of an egg and eats through increasing numbers of pieces of fruit on each day of the week, until the next Saturday when it eats through ten different types of food (i.e. chocolate cake, ice cream, pickle, cheese, salami, lollipop, cherry pie, sausage, cupcake and watermelon). On Saturday night it has a stomach ache. On the next day, which is Sunday, the caterpillar eats through a green leaf. Having become full and big, it builds a cocoon and stays inside for more than two weeks. It finally emerges as a beautiful butterfly. Although *The Very Hungry Caterpillar* was unfamiliar to most of the mothers, most of the children said that they had already had exposure to it in their preschool classrooms.

Transcribing

All data were transcribed verbatim. Specifically, the data were transcribed using utterances as the unit of analyses. Transcripts were prepared using the transcribing conventions delineated by the Child Language Data Exchange System (MacWhinney & Snow, 1985). As a protocol designed for language research, Codes for Human Analyses Transcripts (CHAT) were utilized when transcribing (MacWhinney & Snow, 1990).

Coding

Subsequently, all transcripts were coded using coding systems. Note, however, that only the utterances other than reading were coded; it would be possible for a mother who does a 'straight read' to have no codes at all. The only print that is read and which gets coded is the title, the author's name, the translator's name and the dedication. The shared book-reading between mothers and children were coded using a modified version of *The Coding System for Home Bookreading*[1] (De Temple, 1993).

Results

Quantitative analysis

Using the previously mentioned coding rules, several principal characteristics of book-reading practices in Japanese homes were quantitatively analyzed. In this section, I first report the overall distributions and frequencies. I then focus on the distribution of immediate and non-immediate talk (Beals *et al.*, 1994; De Temple, 1993; De Temple & Beals, 1991; De Temple & Snow, 1996; Dickinson *et al.*, 1992).

The total number of utterances ranged from 26 to 182 ($M = 91.75$, $SD = 48.74$). For the preschoolers, the total number of utterances ranged from 21 to 137 ($M = 63.15$, $SD = 31.10$). Comparisons of mean scores by a t test showed that the total number of maternal utterances, $t(38) = -2.21$, $p < 0.05$, was significantly higher than that of child utterances. That is, the mothers asked more questions and provided more comments than their children.

The distinction between immediate and non-immediate talk is whether or not the book-reading interaction provides opportunities for improving decontextualized language skills. Immediate talk, which includes activities such as labeling pictures, counting and paraphrasing, tends to focus on information obtainable from each individual page of the book. On the other hand, non-immediate talk, which includes activities such as recall, real world connections and decontextualized analysis (e.g. explanations, inferences, predictions), is more global and often considered to be the kinds of skills necessary in school settings. In this way, to examine the roles that mothers and children played, each utterance was coded for the function of immediate or non-immediate talk.

For the mothers, the number of immediate talk ranged widely from 8 to 85 ($M = 31.00$, $SD = 20.17$), whereas for the children the amount of immediate talk ranged from 7 to 71 ($M = 25.1$, $SD = 16.59$). Likewise, the number of non-immediate talk by the mothers ranged from 4 to 82 ($M = 27.05$, $SD = 22.35$), whereas the number of non-immediate talk by the children ranged from 1 to 62 ($M = 19.25$, $SD = 16.71$). Overall, therefore, book-reading performance exhibited by the mothers and the children varied greatly, showing great individual differences.

The analysis further examined the relationships between the mothers' total number of utterances, immediate talk, non-immediate talk, and the children's total number of utterances, immediate talk and non-immediate talk. Table 8.1 displays correlations between these measures. A pattern of correlations that has emerged between these measures indicates that maternal utterances and child utterances are positively related in many ways. For example, the mothers were well matched to their children in terms of the amount of talk, $r(18) = 0.89$, $p < 0.0001$. This result indicates that those mothers who ask a great number of questions and provide a great number of comments are likely to those children who frequently respond to their mothers' questions and comments. Likewise, those mothers who do not ask questions very frequently or do not give many comments are likely to have reticent children.

Furthermore, the mother's total number of utterances was found to be associated with her own non-immediate talk, $r(18) = 0.77$, $p < 0.0001$, and immediate talk, $r(18) = 0.59$, $p < 0.01$. The mother's total number of utterances was also associated with her child's non-immediate talk, $r(18) = 0.67$, $p < 0.01$, and immediate talk, $r(18) = 0.48$, $p < 0.05$. These results seem to indicate that the more the mother talks, the more immediate and non-immediate talk not only the mother herself but also her child provides; likewise, the less the mother talks, the less talkative her child becomes in terms of providing immediate and non-immediate talk. There also exists a positive relationship between the mother's immediate talk and the child's immediate talk, $r(18) = 0.71$, $p < 0.001$, indicating that the child is likely to respond with immediate talk to his or her mother's

Table 8.1 Correlations between mother and child's utterances in book-reading activities

	Mother's utterances	Mother's immediate	Mother's non-Immediate	Child's utterances	Child's immediate
Mother's immediate	0.59**				
Mother's non-Immediate	0.77****	0.05			
Child's utterances	0.89****	0.42	0.66**		
Child's immediate	0.48*	0.71***	0.07	0.56**	
Child's non-Immediate	0.67**	−0.12	0.87****	0.70***	−0.06

Note: $*p < 0.05$; $**p < 0.01$; $***p < 0.001$; $****p < 0.0001$

immediate talk. Similarly, a positive correlation between the mother's non-immediate talk and the child's non-immediate talk, $r(18) = .87$, $p < 0.0001$, implies that the child is likely to respond with non-immediate talk to his or her mother's non-immediate talk.

Qualitative analysis

In this section I consider samples of several stylistic aspects of book-reading interactions. I also place a great deal of emphasis on discourse analysis, which considers both the mother's and the preschool child's contribution to book-reading activities. This analysis, in other words, does not simply describe the function of the mother's or the child's utterances; rather, it examines how the mother's and the child's utterances combine to form larger discursive units.

A fill-in-the-blank style

As can be seen in the following five examples, a fill-in-the-blank style of questioning has turned out to be very typical of Japanese mothers. In Example 8.1a, for instance, the mother reads a question 'On Saturday what did the caterpillar eat?', which is part of the text in the book and expects an answer from the child.

When I introduced the Sapir–Whorf hypothesis (Whorf, 1956) in Chapter 7, I stated that culture has a pervasive influence on language (Miura & Okamoto, 1989). Counting systems are often used as a good example of cultural influence on language. The nature of the book, 'The Very Hungry Caterpillar,' which emphasizes counting numbers of certain objects, results in mothers' initiating topics, which, in many cases, lead to children's counting numbers. Note that there are two separate number systems in Japanese up to number ten, one originally of Japanese and the other of Chinese origin. Sachi's *yottsu* ('four') In Example 8.1c is of Japanese origin, whereas Miki's *ni, san, shi, go* ('two, three, four, five') in Example 8.1d and Akihisa's *ichi, ni, san* ('one, two, three') in Example 8.1e are of Chinese origin. Compared to the number system of Japanese origin, that of Chinese origin is not only more complicated, but it is also more extensively used. Akihisa's response *san-ko* ('three') has a number in combination with a counter (or classifier), which is used for a broad category of small and compact objects, such as round fruit. As can be seen in this case, a set of counters (or classifiers) are used for a set of group items and attached immediately following the number. Children need to acquire a set of counters (or classifiers). In this sense, Akira's answer is cognitively advanced.

Example 8.1a Tamotsu (four years old) and his mother

Mother:	*chokoreeto keeki to . . .*	[Initiation]
	'And chocolate cake . . .'	
Tamotsu:	*aisu kuriimu to,*	[Response]
	'And ice cream,'	
	pikurusu to . . .	
	'And a pickle . . .'	
Mother:	*pikurusu to . . .*	[Echoing]
	'And a pickle . . .'	

Example 8.1b Shoichi (four years old) and his mother

Mother:	*nen'ne shiteru aida ni . . .*	[Initiation]
	'While (it's) sleeping . . .'	
Shoichi:	*choocho.*	[Response]
	'A butterfly.'	
Mother:	*choocho ni natchaun da kara.*	[Sentence Completion]
	'(It) becomes a butterfly.'	

Example 8.1c Sachi (five years old) and her mother

Mother:	*mokuyoobi, ichigo o . . .*	[Initiation]
	'On Thursday, (how many) strawberries . . .'	
Sachi:	*yottsu,*	[Response]
	'Four,'	
Mother:	*yottsu tabe mashita.*	[Sentence Completion]
	'(It) ate four strawberries.'	

Example 8.1d   Miki (five years old) and her mother
Mother: *kin'yoobi orenji o itsutsu tabe mashita.*
'On Friday (it) ate five oranges.'
ichi, ni . . . (the mother starts counting)   [Initiation]
'One, two . . .'
Miki: *ni, san, shi, go.*   [Response]
'Two, three, four, five.'
Mother: *un ana ga itsutsu aite ru wa.*   [Evaluation]
'Yes, there are five holes (in the oranges).'

Example 8.1e   Akihisa (four years old) and his mother
Mother: *suiyoobi, sumomo o . . .*   [Initiation]
'On Wednesday, (how many) plums . . .'
Akihisa: *ichi, ni, san,* (the child starts counting)
'One, two, three,'
san-ko.   [Response]
'three.'
Mother: *soo.*   [Evaluation]
'That's right.'
sumomo o mittsu tabe mashita.
'(It) ate three plums.'

A three-part sequence pattern

Many fill-in-the-blank interactions, as a matter of fact, can be included in the so-called three-part sequence (Cazden, 1988), in which the mother initiates (usually in question form), the child responds and the mother supplies feedback (i.e. Initiation–Response–Evaluation). In Example 8.2a, for instance, this three-phase discourse pattern even appears twice successively. In Example 8.2c, the pattern is further complicated by the mother's move from a general cue to a more specific one.

Example 8.2a   Shoichi (four years old) and his mother (looking at a picture book)
Mother: *dore otsuki sama?*   [Initiation]
'Which one is the moon?'
Shoichi: *kore.*   [Response]
'This one.'
Mother: *ah soo da ne.*   [Evaluation]
'That's right.'
happa no ue ni chitchana tamago tte dore kana?   [Initiation]
'Point at the little egg on a leaf for me?'
Shoichi: *kore.*   [Response]
'This one.'
Mother: *ah kitto soo da ne.*   [Evaluation]
'That's absolutely right.'

Example 8.2b   Sae (four years old) and her mother

Mother:	*kore wa?*	[Initiation]
	'What is this?'	
Sae:	*hamu.*	[Response]
	'Ham.	
Mother:	*un.*	[Evaluation]
	'That's right.'	

Example 8.2c   Sachi (five years old) and her mother

Mother:	*umareta bakkari no aomushi wa nani tabeta?*	[Initiation: general]
	'What did the caterpillar eat right after (it) was born?'	
	mazu saisho ni . . .	[Initiation: specific]
	'First of all . . .'	
Sachi:	*eh ringo.*	[Response]
	'Um, an apple.'	
Mother:	*un.*	[Evaluation]
	'Right.'	

Western researchers (e.g. Cazden, 1988; McCabe & Peterson, 1991) claim that exchanges of the three-part sequence typically occur in classroom interactions. In their study of North American mother–child interactions, McCabe and Peterson (1991) argue that what those mothers who display the three-phase discourse pattern (including the fill-in-the-blank style of questioning described previously) are adopting is a get-the-facts-straight, confrontational style of discourse, which might be associated with the 'transmission mode of education' pattern.

It would be an oversimplified idea, however, if we assume that the three-part sequence mainly occurs in classrooms. It would also be too simplistic if we assume that the specific features of the known-answer mother question and the immediate evaluation of the child response give a detached impression. To the contrary, from the observation of Japanese mother–child interactions, the three-part sequence does not give an impression that it is conducted in a corrective or detached fashion. Rather, Japanese mothers interact with their children in an affectionate and friendly manner. Although the Initiation–Response–Evaluation (IRE) structure might be typical of the teacher-talk register, because both teacher talk and child-directed speech (CDS) are employed for scaffolding, it should come as no surprise if mothers' CDS in some cultures is similar to the teacher-talk register.

Modified IRE patterns

Some mothers of five-year-old children use this pattern more extensively. In the first half of the following example, Wakao's mother asks the number and the name of objects. It is important to note that some sequences are not full IRE but just IR, although evaluation is likely to occur eventually at the end. What is more important, however, is that in the second half of the example, the mother does not simply give an evaluation but she also extends the discourse beyond the text – a move from immediate (which is directly connected with the text) to non-immediate (which has connections with the real world):

Example 8.3   Wakao (five years old) and his mother

Mother:	*kore wa nan da?*	[Initiation]
	'What is this?'	
Wakao:	*ringo.*	[Response]
	'An apple.'	
Mother:	*un.*	[Evaluation]
	'Yes.'	
	ringo ikutsu aru?	[Initiation]
	'How many apples are there?'	
Wakao:	*i kko.*	[Response]
	'One.'	
Mother:	*ringo o hitotsu mitsukete tabe mashita.*	
	'(It) found one apple and ate (it).'	
	pakupaku	
	'Crunch, crunch.' (an onomatopoeia of eating something)	

[...]

Mother:	*kore nan da?*	[Initiation]
	'What are these?'	
Wakao:	*ichigo.*	[Response]
	'Strawberries.'	
Mother:	*ikutsu aru?*	[Initiation]
	'How many are there?'	
Wakao:	*yon-ko.*	[Response]
	'Four.'	
Mother:	*Wa kkun no suki na ichigo da.*	[Evaluation]
	'Strawberries are your favorite.'	

Echoing as a variation of the three-part sequence pattern

Japanese mothers sometimes employ a modified pattern of the IRE structure by frequently using echoing (which, as explained earlier in Chapter 6, means the repetition of a word or word group immediately after hearing it produced by the interlocutor). In Example 8.4a, for instance, Shoichi's mother initially uses the standard three-part sequence; the second time, however, she incorporates echoing in the interaction. In other words, echoing plays a similar role to feedback or evaluation:

Example 8.4a   Shoichi (four years old) and his mother

Mother:	*kore wa nan de shoo?*	[Initiation]
	'What is this?'	
Shoichi:	*keeki.*	[Response]
	'Cake.'	
Mother:	*un.*	[Evaluation]
	'Yes.'	
	kore wa?	[Initiation]
	'How about this?'	
Shoichi:	*aisu.*	[Response]
	'Ice.'	
Mother:	*aisu.*	[Echoing]
	'Ice.'	
	kore wa?	[Initiation]
	'How about this?'	
Shoichi:	*kyuuri.*	[Response]
	'A cucumber.'	
Mother:	*kyuuri.*	[Echoing]
	'A cucumber.'	

Example 8.4b   Mari (four years old) and her mother

Mother:	*kore wa?*	[Initiation]
	'What is this?'	
Mari:	*hamu.*	[Response]
	'Ham.'	
Mother:	*hamu.*	[Echoing]
	'Ham.'	
	kore wa?	[Initiation]
	'What is this?'	
Mari:	*ame chan.*	[Response]
	'Candy.'	
Mother:	*ame chan.*	[Echoing]
	'Candy.'	

[. . .]

Mother:	*kore nan desho?*	[Initiation]
	'What is this?'	
Mari:	*choocho.*	[Response]
	'A butterfly.'	
Mother:	*choocho.*	[Echoing]
	'A butterfly.'	
	kirei na choocho ni nari mashita.	
	'(It) has become a beautiful butterfly.'	

Example 8.4c   Miki (five years old) and her mother

Mother:	*kore wa?*	[Initiation]
	'What is this?'	
Miki:	*uun, mushi.*	[Response]
	'Um, a bug.'	
Mother:	*mushi.*	[Echoing]
	'A bug.'	

Suspension as a variation of the three-part sequence pattern

In book-reading activities, not all answers provided by children are correct. In such cases, some mothers modify the three-part structure by using 'suspension.' In the example below, moreover, the modified three-part sequence pattern serves as a preparation for the talk to move from immediate talk to non-immediate talk.

Example 8.5   Takato (five years old) and his mother

Mother:	*aomushi ga hora choocho ni natta yo, Taka.*	
	'Look, Taka, the caterpillar has turned into a butterfly.'	
Takato:	*nan dee?*	
	'Why?'	
Mother:	*dooshite da roo?*	[Initiation]
	'What do (you) think?'	
Takato:	*sooka ippai tabeta kara.*	[Response]
	'Because (it) ate a lot.'	
Mother:	*ippai tabeta kara nattan?*	[Suspension]
	'Has (it) become a butterfly because (it) ate a lot?'	
	aomushi wa choocho no kodomo datta n da yo.	[Evaluation]
	'The caterpillar was a butterfly's child, in fact.'	

Onomatopoeias as a variation of the three-part sequence pattern

As previous research (e.g. Clancy, 1985) has revealed, Japanese mothers and children frequently use onomatopoeias. In the first half of the following example, the mother uses a simple three-part sequence pattern with an onomatopoeia as an evaluation. In the second half, she uses the fill-in-the-blank style of questioning, which is also a variation of the three-part sequence.

Example 8.6   Koji (five years old) and his mother

Mother:	*kore nani?*	[Initiation]
	'What is this?'	
Koji:	*ichigo.*	[Response]
	'A strawberry.'	
Mother:	*buubuubuu.*	[Evaluation]
	'booboo' (a sound signaling that the answer is wrong)	
	kayoobi nashi o ikutsu tabe mashita?	[Initiation]
	'On Tuesday how many pears did (it) eat?'	
Koji:	*futatsu.*	[Response]
	'Two.'	
Mother:	*pinpoon.*	[Evaluation]
	(a sound signaling that the answer is correct)	

Difficult vocabulary. Up to this point the main focus of the present study has been detailing stylistic aspects (i.e. a variety of IRE patterns). As previously mentioned, non-immediate talk is considered to be a type of decontextualized language skill. Non-immediate talk is more explicit and requires less reliance on shared physical context, such as the text in the book. Thus, non-immediate talk interactions beyond the text of the book may be more closely connected with the skills required in school settings, particularly for later successful literacy and school achievement. Whether the child can use a difficult vocabulary is one of the non-immediate related skills. Examples 7a and 7b indicate that preschool children have already obtained difficult vocabulary such as *yoochuu* ('larva'). The life-cycle discussion in Example 8.7c also reflects non-immediate talk; in this example, modified IRE structures are used because the child understands that his mother expects further responses.

Example 8.7a   Shoichi (four years old) and his mother
Mother: *choocho no aka chan wa nan nan da roo?*   [Initiation]
              'What is the baby of a butterfly?'
Shoichi: *yoochuu.*   [Response]
              'A larva.'
Mother: *yoochuu.*   [Echoing]
              'A larva.'

Example 8.7b   Koji (five years old) and his mother
Mother: *nani ni natta no kana kore?*   [Initiation]
              'What has (it) become, this one?'
Koji: *yoochuu.*   [Response]
              'A larva.'
Mother: *sanagi ni natta ne.*   [Evaluation]
              '(It) made a cocoon.'

Example 8.7c   Takanori (five years old) and his mother
Mother: *nan te yuu no?*   [Initiation]
              'What do (you) call (it)?'
Takanori: *sanagi.*   [Response]
              'A cocoon.'
Mother: *sanagi.*   [Echoing]
              'A cocoon.'
              de,   [Initiation]
              'and,'
Takanori: *choocho.*   [Response]
              'A butterfly.'
Mother: *un.*   [Evaluation]
              'Right.'

                            [. . .]

Mother: *ningen wa donna henshin suru no?*   [Initiation]
              'How does the human being change?'
Takanori: *otona.*   [Response]
              'An adult.'

Mother: *otona ni naru dake ka.*   [Suspension]
              '(The human being) simply becomes an adult.'
              un.   [Evaluation]
              'Yes.'

Co-construction as an underlying theme

In the case of book-reading between Japanese mothers and their preschool children, one culturally shared aspect is syntactic co-construction, i.e. a single turn-constructional unit that can be co-produced across the talk of two speakers (Lerner, 1991). Example 8.8a shows co-construction based on the fill-in-the-blank pattern. In Example 8.8b, although the first part is not a complete IRE pattern but just an IR pattern (as matter of fact, the IR pattern is omnipresent, as a variation of IRE), the mother supplies the object of the sentence, the child supplies the number of the object, and the mother then completes the sentence by adding the verb; therefore, the overall structure shows co-construction. Recall that Japanese is an SOV language, namely, a language in which the basic word order of the transitive sentence is subject-object-verb and that the samples of this type of co-construction reflect the syntactic structure of Japanese.

Example 8.8a   Kana (four years old) and her mother
Mother: *getsuyoobi, ringo o . . .*   [Initiation]
              'On Monday, (an) apple . . .'
Kana: *hitotsu . . .*   [Response]
              'One . . .'
Mother: *mitsukete tabe mashita.*   [Sentence Completion]
              '(It) found and ate (an apple).'
              mogumogumogu
              'Munch munch.' (an onomatopoeia of eating something)
              mada onaka wa pekko peko.
              '(It) was still hungry.'
              kayoobi, nashi o . . .   [Initiation]
              'On Tuesday, pears . . .'
Kana: *futatsu . . .*   [Response]
              'Two . . .'
Mother: *tabe mashita.*   [Sentence Completion]
              '(It) ate (them).'

Example 8.8b   Kimi (four years old) and her mother
Mother: *mokuyoobi,*
              'On Thursday,'
              kore nani?   [Initiation]
              'What are these?'
Kana: *eh tto, ichigo.*   [Response]
              'Um, strawberries.'

Mother:	*ichigo o . . .*	[Initiation]
	'Strawberries . . .'	
Kana:	*yottsu . . .*	[Response]
	'Four . . .'	
Mother:	*yottsu tabe mashita.*	[Sentence Completion]
	'(It) ate four.'	

Here, in a sense, we have returned where we started. As this co-construction becomes more advanced, the three-sequence style becomes less explicit but still exists. [Note: Recall that because of the difference in the sentence structure (i.e. unlike English, which has the subject-verb-object pattern, the basic word order of the Japanese sentence is subject-object-verb), when translated into English, the co-construction might become less obvious than it really is.]

Example 8.9a   Yuka (five years old) and her mother

Mother:	*kore nan no ana ka wakaru, Yuka chan?*	
	'Do you know what kinds of holes these are, Yuka?'	
	nan da to omou?	[Initiation]
	'What do (you) think?'	
Yuka:	*kore wa, ne,*	
	'These, uh,'	
Mother:	*un.*	
	'Go on.' (brief acknowledgment)	
Yuka:	*aomushi ga tabeta . . .*	[Response]
	'The caterpillar ate . . .'	
Mother:	*ana ka na.*	[Evaluation]
	'(and made these) holes.'	
	yappari soo omou?	[Initiation]
	'Do (you) think so, too?'	
Yuka:	*un.*	[Response]
	'Yes.'	
Mother:	*okaasan mo soo omotta.*	[Evaluation]
	'I think so, too.'	

Example 8.9b   Akihisa (four years old) and his mother

Mother:	*doko ga ichi-ban omoshiro katta?*	[Initiation]
	'What did (you) find most interesting?'	
Akihisa:	*eh tto, choocho ga ne choocho ni natta toki.*	[Response]
	'Um, when (it) turned into a butterfly.'	
Mother:	*choocho ni natta toki ga bikkuri shita?*	[Initiation]
	'Were (you) surprised when (it) became a butterfly?'	
Akihisa:	*un.*	[Response]
	'Yes.'	
Mother:	*honto.*	[Evaluation]
	'Really.'	

Discussion

Summary

In previous chapters, I focused on Japanese mothers' scaffolding of their preschool children's narratives, and I subsequently attempted to relate maternal behavior during joint production of narratives to the children's monologic production of narratives. More specifically, Chapters 4 and 5 reported monologic narratives; four- and five-year-olds were asked to produce narratives in conversation with an experimenter. Chapters 6 and 7 reported dialogic narratives; i.e. on a separate occasion, the children were asked to discuss past experiences with their mothers. In this way, I first tried to demonstrate development in children's monologic narratives, and then I tried to demonstrate that mothers' scaffolding strategies do not merely reflect their children's current level of narrative skills development but that they also reflect mothers' concerns/wishes or even folk psychology (i.e. culturally-based assumptions) to develop their children's particular narrative skills.

This chapter has continued to highlight the role of 'scaffolding,' the temporary support that the mother gives the child to perform a task (Bruner, 1977). Scaffolding encompasses a variety of parental supports for language development in the young child. Sometime in their first year of life, infants make sounds, trying to match what they hear from their environment, mostly from their mothers. Mothers also help children handle and construct (event) schemata – structures in semantic memory that specify the general arrangement of a body of information. To interpret the meaning of what the mother says, one-year-olds initially make use of the surrounding context such as particular settings. As they grow, however, schemata gradually become established and applicable to a wider range of contexts. This environmental shaping is largely attributable to mothers' scaffolding. More than that, the joint construction of stories by preschool children and mothers in later years is an important context in which mothers guide and support the children's preparation for literacy.

This chapter specifically examined 20 Japanese mothers paired with children of ages four and five. The chapter has reported the findings regarding the home language environments of middle-class Japanese preschool children. Both quantitative and qualitative analyses were performed to better understand the relationship between sociocultural background and young Japanese children's development of literacy.

The chapter first quantitatively analyzed book-reading practices and identified many patterns of correlations between maternal styles of book-reading and children's book-reading. Based on *The Coding System for*

Home Bookreading (De Temple, 1993), these mother–child book-reading activities were coded either as immediate talk (e.g. labeling pictures, counting, paraphrasing), non-immediate talk (e.g. recall, real world connections, explanations, inferences, predictions) or other types, such as providing feedback and requesting attention, evaluation and clarification. Non-immediate talk is particularly considered to be important because it is regarded as the type of skill necessary to be successful in school (in terms of literacy and later school achievement). Chapter 8 has revealed that maternal styles of book-reading were correlated with children's book-reading skills in diverse ways; specifically, there were positive correlations between the frequency of maternal verbalization and that of children. Generally, for example, the frequency of both the children's overall and non-immediate talk increased if their mothers spoke more to them during book-reading activities. Likewise, the magnitude of the correlation between the mother's non-immediate talk and the child's non-immediate talk was close to 0.90, indicating the existence of a strong, positive relationship.

The qualitative section of this chapter has revealed a ubiquitous pattern of a three-part sequence among Japanese mothers during book-reading activities, the sequence that typically appears in classroom interactions: i.e. the pattern that the mother initiates (usually in question form), the child responds and the mother supplies feedback closely resembles the teacher-fronted Initiation–Response–Evaluation (IRE) routine. The findings in this chapter seem to confirm many similarities between learning to talk (i.e. language acquisition) and learning to read and write (i.e. literacy). As I will describe in detail later in Chapter 9, according to Snow (1983), in US society the decontextualized and detached oral discourse style, which is employed by middle-class families at home, matches school language use including literacy; these children are more likely to succeed in school settings. Thus, early oral language development at home has a direct influence on the development of later language skills at school.

Certainly, the case in Japan may not completely fit the Western conceptualization of the home-school continuum. For example, some researchers (Peak, 1989, 1991) claim that early child-rearing at home and later schooling in Japan do not seem to parallel each other, but that rather, the two different socialization practices of home and school play complementary roles in helping an individual learn how to behave appropriately. Yet, this chapter confirms the existence of a certain type of continuity between home and school in Japan. The Western-type schooling emphasizes the three-sequence pattern (Cazden, 1988), and the Japanese-type of schooling, which is very Westernized, is no exception.

At the same time, however, the features of book-reading practices between Japanese mothers and their children should be explained in terms of a larger framework of culture based on the social interaction paradigm (Vygotsky, 1978). Japanese mothers and their preschool children's joint book-reading embodies the concept of co-construction in oral discourse, which we have observed in the previous two chapters and in *renga* ('linked verse') as a predecessor of *haiku* in Chapter 3. A Japanese mother typically asks her child in a one word format (e.g. when, where, who, what, how many) as opposed to full sentences. In contrast, an American mother reading the same story (i.e. *The Very Hungry Caterpillar*) to her child would be more likely to ask the child such questions as 'What animal is this?', 'What did the caterpillar do?' and 'What day of the week did he do this?' The mother will usually encourage the child to answer in a complete sentence. These features typically characterize the decontextualized, detached oral discourse style employed by US middle-class families at home.

The contrast between the United States and Japan reminds us of the contrast when children are much younger. In Chapter 2, I described Toda *et al.*'s work (1990) in which they found that Japanese mothers rarely used grammatically complete utterances, whereas US mothers used the grammatically complete sentences used in adult conversation. This contrast further implies that oral and written language form a continuum rather than a dichotomy; that is, a continued relationship exists between young children's oral language acquisition and the later years of their language skills development. But cultures differ in the way that they behave toward children acquiring language and language-related skills. Therefore, although a language-literacy continuum exists, it is culturally specific.

Also, recall that, at the end of Chapter 7, I referred to Kağıtçıbaşı's (1989) argument that urban families in non-Western societies develop a hybrid approach, retaining a focus on social relations but simultaneously emphasizing their individuality and means of self-expression. I stated that this child-oriented approach particularly applies to Japanese mothers living in the United States. As far as book-reading activities are concerned, however, Kağıtçıbaşı's explanation seems to hold true of Japanese mothers, as well. Maintaining a style reflective of their native culture (e.g. co-construction), Japanese mothers raised in today's westernized schooling are also subject to the influence of Western culture (e.g. the three-part sequence). In this sense, as Egan (1987) suggests, because the child's language development should be understood as developing from orality to a composite of orality and literacy, during the early school years children's orality should be used effectively, which would then lead to their later development of literacy.

From this chapter to the final chapter

Finally, to connect this chapter with the concluding chapter, which in part focuses on school success and failure in relation to cross-cultural misunderstanding, here I introduce the prevailing 'strong-text' view of literacy, in which one must be logical, literal, detached and message-focused, like an expository text. This view is deeply connected with Bernstein's (1971) theory of codes. As I described in detail in Chapter 2, according to his theory, students from middle-class families use an elaborated code, an explicit and decontextualized speech mode that generally matches school language use, whereas students from working-class families use a restricted code, an elliptical and context-dependent speech mode that generally does not correspond with school language. As Brandt (1990) puts it, 'In match-mismatch formulations, students are deemed to be at risk in school literacy performance to the extent to which their home language is at odds with the so-called explicit, decontextualized language of the school' (p. 106). Although the oral-literate dichotomy has often been confused with social class and is thus controversial, Bernstein's theory has been incorporated into strong-text accounts of literacy and has influenced studies of literacy particularly in the United States.

As seen in this chapter, literacy must be conceptualized as a context-making, involvement activity. Gee (1990), whom I introduced as a developer of stanza analysis, has made another contribution to language studies by rejecting the above view of literacy – an individual's ability to read and write to achieve an autonomous, higher-level cognitive skill, claiming that it is too naive to capture the sociocultural role of literacy. Rather, following the Brazilian educator, Freire's (1970a, 1970b) conceptualization of literacy as an emacipatory process, Gee argues that languages are always social possessions, and the notion of 'literacy' has been used in order to oppress nonliterate individuals and under-represented groups, and thus to consolidate the pre-established social hierarchy, especially in Western societies. Culture-related domains for the mastery of communicative competence have been mentioned, such as discourse, appropriateness, paralinguistics, pragmatics and cognitive-academic language proficiency (Ovando, 1993). Similarly, Gee's (1990) notion of discourse includes more than sequential speech or writing; it represents a sociocultural aggregate model that consists of 'words, acts, values, beliefs, attitudes, social identities, as well as gestures, glances, body positions and clothes' (p. 142). As can be inferred from this argument, diverse sociocultural variables are irrationally affecting children's school success and failure.

To conclude, discussing the results of the analyses, this chapter has suggested: (1) children gradually learn to internalize expectations of classroom life early in their homes; (2) the home-school continuum in language socialization seems to hold significant meaning for literacy skills acquisition, which may relate to later school achievement. Furthermore, an examination of studies of social interaction, socialization, and its resulting acquisition of communicative competence in different cultural contexts in previous chapters suggest the many complex relationships between oral language and literacy.

Note

1. I am grateful to Jeanne De Temple for her extremely helpful and detailed comments in the process of my developing the coding system for Japanese mothers and their preschool children's joint book-reading.

Chapter 9
Conclusions and Implications

The most fundamental characteristic of language acquisition and development is the change of the function of linguistic categories from the sentential level to the discursive one. In this sense, narrative serves as an important tool because the unit of its investigation extends over what phonology, syntax or semantics deals with. In this book, I have tried to identify cross-linguistically common – possibly universal or quasi-universal – characteristics in the area of narrative development and mother–child discourse interactions (both narrative and book-reading) as connected forms of discourse. At the same time, I have tried to distinguish linguistically or culturally specific traits, i.e. whether different discourse strategies are employed by children who are being raised in different societies, speaking different languages. Throughout the book, I have particularly emphasized that language is not only a window onto the microcosm of the individual mind, but that it also reflects the larger social world. In this concluding chapter, I discuss the educational significance and implications of the results obtained from the current research and apply them to various fields, such as continuities and discontinuities between home and school, children's imagination and creativity, implications to US classrooms and second/foreign language learning; based on these implications, I finally suggest directions for future research.

How to View Child Development, Revisited

In one way or another, most developmental theorists address the question of how language, thought and social interaction are related in a child's life. Depending on the particular focus of each theory, these three aspects of development can be defined and connected differently. It is possible to characterize some theories as cognitive developmental and others as social interactional (or sociocognitive). The former theories, represented by Piaget (1959), regard individual cognitive processes as primary in development, whereas the latter theories, represented by Vygotsky (1978) and Bruner (1977, 1986, 1990), regard social interaction as primary for development.

It is important to see these two approaches to cognitive development, the one as relatively autonomous from language (Piaget) and the other as highly dependent on language (Vygotsky and Bruner), in the light of how the two theories also relate cognitive development and social interaction. Cognitive development is for Piaget relatively autonomous, not only independent of language but also of social interaction. As is the case with language, Piaget has at times acknowledged social interaction as a possible, albeit secondary, factor in development. In contrast, Vygotsky and Bruner view children's participation in social interaction as a privileged kind of interaction with the world, which is can be characterized as a primary factor for cognitive development. In this theory, patterns of cognitive activity and changes in such patterns cannot be understood independently of the social-interactive processes that shape them and from which they emerge. In this theoretical framework, parents guide children in the learning process as the more knowledgeable of the partners. As Cummins (1994) puts it, therefore,

> 'Both first language acquisition and cognitive development are active, constructive processes whereby children generate their knowledge of the world and their linguistic knowledge within a matrix of social interaction'. (p. 45)

Furthermore, the social interaction paradigm is based on the bi-directional interaction assumption; i.e. there must be mutual influence between parent and child in the construction of socially meaningful activities. In this sense, too, social interaction (or sociocognitive) theory and language socialization studies reviewed in Chapter 2 are highly compatible.[1]

Following the social interaction paradigm, the present work has analyzed language development, narrative discourse structure and joint book-reading activities, by looking at how language shapes and is shaped by culture-specific experiences. Specifically, the present study has examined 40 transcripts of monologic narratives and 40 transcripts of mother–child interactions (for narrative discourse and book-reading combined). To complement this work and to support generalizations about the culture-specific nature of both caregivers' practices and children's emerging narrative structure, the study has also examined 10 middle-class English-speaking North American mother–child pairs and eight middle-class Japanese mother–child pairs living in the United States.

In Chapter 9, I will answer the overall research questions posed in Chapter 1. The results obtained in the present study are then summarized, with a particular emphasis on why Japanese narrative resembles the basic characteristics of *haiku*, a commonly practiced literary form that often combines poetry and narrative. I will then suggest that, in some ways, Japanese children's habitual ways of communicating at home differ from the linguistic and communicative styles used outside the home. In some respects, therefore, the case in Japan does not seem to fit – in fact it even challenges – the so-called match-mismatch formulation of literacy and discourse patterns conceived in the United States (see the end of Chapter 8). At the risk of sounding self-contradictory, however, referring to emergent literacy practices at home, I will also argue that the earlier (home) and later (school) pattern of socialization are parallel in some other respects. That is, the home and school practices sometimes play complementary roles in helping an individual learn how to participate in verbal interactions and, moreover, how to behave in Japanese society. Drawing upon the research findings in this book, I will finally look at the educational significance and implications of this study.

Summary

Children's narrative structure

The first question examined the existence of culture-specific narrative style. Specifically, personal narratives of 20 middle-class Japanese preschool children, half aged four and half five, and their mothers were analyzed using verse/stanza analysis (Gee, 1985; Hymes, 1981) and high point analysis (Labov, 1972; Peterson & McCabe, 1983). The patterning in stanzas yielded the following: (1) With regard to the proportion of three-verse stanzas, there were no differences between the groups of four-year-olds, five-year-olds and adults (i.e. mothers). This suggests that the three-verse stanza is the canonical Japanese narrative form. (2) However, a smaller proportion of two-verse stanzas and, in contrast, a larger proportion of four- or more verse stanzas produced by five-year-olds, indicated that they produce slightly longer stanzas than do four-year-olds. (3) Furthermore, no statistically significant differences were observed between five-year-olds and adults in any type of stanza, although four- or more verse stanzas are the most common form produced by adults. We can thus conclude that compared to four-year-olds, five-year-olds begin to use the form of adult-like narratives.

Furthermore, high point analysis indicated the following: (1) Compared to adults, young children emphasized a temporal sequence of action with less emphasis on non-sequential information, especially orientation. (2) Although four-year-olds gave proportionately less evaluation than adults, no differences were observed between five-year-olds and adults. Therefore, while both four-year-olds and five-year-olds emphasize simple description of successive events, compared to four-year-olds, five-year-olds begin to evaluate in adult-like ways.

The results thus indicate that with age, children change and develop in their capacity to provide non-sequential information in order to accomplish narrative tellability, which is the central aim of most adult narrators. Also, preschool children seem to understand culturally nurtured canonical narrative discourse patterns, and gradually try to tell narratives in culture-specific ways. The study thus reveals a steady developmental picture, that is, the steady increase with age in both the length of stanzas produced and their emphasis on evaluative components. From early childhood on, therefore, children have a well-developed sense of what the canonical narrative form is like, and gradually master narrative discourse skills expected in Japanese society.

The present study has shown that children's and adults' narratives are similar in terms of structure in that they both tend to have three-verse stanzas, and, moreover, children and adults alike tend to tell about multiple experiences. Particularly in children's narratives, each experience is summarized briefly, often in a scant three-verse elaboration. These findings confirm previous research findings by Minami (1990) and Minami and McCabe (1991). In many ways, Japanese children's stories of real experiences are reminiscent of *haiku*, a three-line form of poetry that often gives location, event and time in such a way that it functions as a compact one-event narrative.

By contrast, there are some clear differences in terms of content and delivery between children and adults; children tend to tell their stories in a sequential style whereas adults emphasize non-sequential information. Furthermore, adults deploy a variety of expressive options and rhetorical/linguistic devices to encode the narrator's perspective, such as the effective use of proper verb-ending forms; children, in contrast, do not distinguish these subtleties. Moreover, individual differences in narrative among Japanese mothers are not necessarily reflected in differences among their children's narratives at this single point in time.

As children become accustomed to the transition from home to school, a move from the *amae*-based inside world to some kind of outside world, where the meaning of life in a group and a social hierarchy are emphasized, they develop a more facile command of encodable perspectives (e.g. narrative external/internal perspective taking). Preschool and elementary school teachers have expectations that children will become adept at the use of certain narrative discourse skills. Overall, although children seem to be developing a sense of their voice and learning how to take audience into account when narrating, they have not yet learned how to manipulate linguistic devices for the best effect. As Berman and Slobin (1994) put it, 'One of the major tasks of childhood is to master and flexibly use the range of perspective-taking devices in the language' (p. 516). Children thus need to acquire a variety of expressive options across time and through experience. The present study, therefore, suggests that mastery of a full range of linguistic devices and manipulative strategies that encode the narrator's emotion has a fairly long developmental history.

The study also indicates the existence of complex interrelationships between development of language and cognition as well as sociocultural factors. As stated previously, one of the objectives of this book is to examine Japanese preschool children's acquisition of narrative capacity as evidence of their cognitive skills as well as linguistic competence. Children's narrative development is a strongly interactive process, one which relies not only on specific cognitive and linguistic mechanisms, but also on the child's active participation in a narrative discourse environment attuned to the sociocultural expectations of the parent for the child.

Mother–child interactions and children's narratives

While the first question addressed young children's free-standing personal narratives, the second looked at their narratives in the context of mother–child interactions. This intricate relationship is seen in the frequent use of the rapport particle *ne* (which facilitates narrator-listener rapport). What mothers provided in their narrative turns, while scaffolding their children's narratives (i.e. frequent use of *ne*), relates to the use of the linguistic items that children provided when telling narratives on their own.

Age differences in mothers' narrative elicitation strategies also emerged: (1) Compared to the mothers of five-year-olds, the mothers of four-year-olds were more likely to give their children topic-extension prompts right after uttering '*huun*' ('well'). (2) In comparison to the mothers of five-year-olds, moreover, the mothers of four-year-olds also requested more evaluation from their children. When a researcher elicited narratives from the children without providing any scaffolding, four-year-olds gave proportionately less evaluation than adults, while no differences were observed between five-year-olds and adults. The results thus seem to indicate that in mother–child interactions, unless the mother considers that her child gives sufficient evaluative statements, she guides her child by providing requests for evaluation. Furthermore, the results nicely support the hypothesized relationship between patterns of maternal narrative elicitation and children's developing narrative skill. Maternal narrative elicitation styles are associated with children's talking about past events on their own, although previous research (e.g. McCabe & Peterson, 1991; Peterson & McCabe, 1992) has tended to focus on the time-lagged relationship, i.e. that the kinds of questions parents ask during children's narratives predict the aspects of the narrative children elaborate a couple of years later. In the present study, it has been found that, by scaffolding children's narratives in ways that are consistent with the social interactionist paradigm (Bruner, 1977; Vygotsky, 1978), Japanese mothers support their children's progressive contributions to the narrative task.

This research was then extended within a cross-linguistic/cross-cultural approach comparing narrative elicitation patterns in different language/cultural groups. That is, to complement this work and to support generalizations about the *culture-specific* nature of both caregivers' practices and children's emerging narrative structure, the present study further compared conversations between mothers and children from three different groups: (1) Japanese-speaking mother–child pairs living in Japan, (2) Japanese-speaking mother–child pairs living in the United States and (3) English-speaking North American mother–child pairs.

As we saw in great detail in Chapter 7, mother–child behavior in narrative discourse interactions showed evidence of significant effects of culture. The Japanese four- and five-year-olds produced approximately 1.2 utterances per turn on average (including the Japanese five-year-olds living in the United States), whereas the English-speaking North American four- and five-year-olds produced about 1.8 and 2.1 utterances per turn, respectively. Thus, whereas English-speaking mothers allow their children to take long monologic turns and they give many evaluative comments, Japanese mothers – regardless of their child's age (i.e. whether the child is four or five) and regardless of where they live (i.e. whether living in Japan or the United States) – simultaneously pay considerable attention to their children's narratives and facilitate frequent turn exchanges. In this sense, we might be able to claim that compared to North American mothers, Japanese mothers are less directive but more subtle or even ambiguous (which is one of the important cultural aspects in Japan discussed in Chapter 2) when interacting with their children.

As mentioned previously, in connecting narrative elicitation with children's developing narrative skill, we can account for some results obtained from the cross-cultural comparison of maternal styles of narrative elicitation. For instance, the similarity in providing proportionate amounts of foreground/sequential information (i.e. action statements) between the Japanese mothers of four-year-olds and the North American mothers of four-year-olds seems to indicate that compared to non-sequential information, providing foregrounded/sequential accounts develops early both cross-culturally and cross-linguistically (Berman & Slobin, 1994). We could thus assume that because both Japanese and North American four-year-old groups provided relatively sufficient foreground information (i.e. actions), as far as this narrative element was concerned, in neither group did mothers support their children's further contributions.

In some cases, however, the assumption connecting maternal narrative elicitation strategies with children's developing narrative skill could not adequately explain cross-cultural differences. When comparisons are made across cultures or across linguistic systems, mothers' scaffolding strategies do not reflect children's mere failure to provide particular information. Rather, while both Japanese and English-speaking North American mothers support their four-year-olds' talk about the past by extending topics in a variety of ways, they ensure that it begins to take the shape of narration valued by their culture. Take, for example, the following: In comparison to the North American mothers of four-year-olds, the Japanese mothers of four-year-olds (1) requested proportionately less description from their children; (2) gave proportionately less evaluation; (3) requested proportionately more evaluation from their children; and (4) showed proportionately more verbal attention. It then seems that different cultural expectations are reflected in maternal narrative elicitation strategies; that is, whereas in North America an individual should be verbally explicit, in Japan an individual is allowed to be verbally implicit but should be empathic (e.g. Lebra, 1976).

The examination of the mothers of five-year-olds from the three different groups has provided results that further support the proposition that cognitive, linguistic and social-interactional factors affect one another in a complex fashion in narrative development, and, moreover, that mothers' elicitation strategies reflect these complexities. The comparison of the two different Japanese groups suggests that the Japanese mothers in the United States were more likely to give their children topic-extension prompts right after uttering '*huun*' ('well'). Further, the three-group comparison has suggested rather complicated differences: (1) In comparison to the English-speaking North American mothers, mothers of both Japanese groups gave proportionately less evaluation. (2) Both in terms of frequency and proportion, mothers of both Japanese groups gave more verbal acknowledgment than did the English-speaking mothers. (3) However, the Japanese mothers in the United States requested proportionately more description from their children than did the Japanese mothers in Japan.

As seen in the similarities in elicitation strategies between the Japanese mothers of four-year-olds and the North American mothers of four-year-olds, it can be assumed that because the five-year-olds from the three different groups alike provided relatively sufficient foreground information (i.e. actions), none of the three maternal groups needed to elicit further contributions from their children. In other words, the assumtion is that because of the quasi-universal tendency in cognitive development, compared to other components such as background information (i.e. orientations and evaluations), the three different groups of mothers of five-year-olds showed no differences in the elicitation of foreground information.

With respect to evaluation, moreover, what appeared to be a difference between North American English-speaking children and Japanese children at age four no longer holds true at age five. This difference seems attributable to five-year-olds' emergent capability of evaluating as much as adults do. That is, because five-year-olds could provide relatively sufficient evaluative accounts in mother–child interactions, mothers did not need to insist that their children provide evaluative comments. In this respect too, similar tendencies across the culturally different groups seem attributable to the general pattern of cognitive development.

Mothers' scaffolding strategies, however, sometimes fail to provide what is missing in children's monologic narratives. Rather, they may be reflective of mothers' concerns or folk psychology (i.e. culturally-based assumptions). Despite the fact that the Japanese mothers gave less evaluation than did the English-speaking North American mothers, this difference may not suggest that the Japanese children voluntarily gave more evaluation than did the North American children of the same age. As previously cautioned in Chapter 7, the assumption linking maternal narrative elicitation strategies with children's developing narrative skill alone cannot adequately explain maternal elicitation strategies deeply rooted in culture-specific beliefs. Differences in underlying cultural expectations may account for why North American mothers emphasize mastery of verbal skills and, in contrast, why Japanese mothers provide fewer evaluative comments in favor of a more implicit valuation (Doi, 1973; Lebra, 1976).

Parents' styles

Behavioral differences between the Japanese mothers (both living in Japan and the United States) and the North American mothers seem to relate to differences in strategies for controlling children's behavior. In the United States a widely accepted view about parenting has been that firm control by parents, such as setting clear standards for conduct and valuing compliance with reasonable rules, promotes internalization of values by children (Baumrind, 1973). The positive effects of restrictiveness, when incorporated in the authoritative parenting style, as defined by Baumrind (1971), blends respect for a child's individuality with an effort to instill social values in the child, outweigh the negative effects (Grusec & Lytton, 1988). With regard to Japanese mothers' behavior, on the other hand, Lewis (1991) writes:

> Japanese mothers apparently do not make explicit demands on their children and do not enforce rules when children resist; yet, diverse accounts suggest that Japanese children strongly internalize parental, group, and institutional values. (p. 82)

The results obtained in the present study – i.e. the Japanese mothers, whether living in Japan or the United States, gave few evaluations, whereas the North American mothers gave a great amount of evaluations – seem to support Lewis's above remarks. That is, the narrative elicitation strategies taken by the Japanese mothers do not match or might even challenge the North American view of firm control.

In reality, however, the issue is further complicated. The differences observed between the Japanese mothers living in Japan and the Japanese mothers living in the United States account for the hypothesis that mothers' scaffolding strategies do not necessarily reflect children's failure to provide particular information. These differences rather reflect the mothers' concerns influenced by the culture in which they live. It then seems reasonable to assume that while inducting their children into a communicative style that is reflective of their native culture, Japanese mothers living in the United States are, at the same time, subject to the influence of Western culture. Because the Japanese mothers living in the United States and the North American mothers were found to be alike in terms of requesting more descriptions from their children than the Japanese mothers living in Japan, we can claim that learned differences are predominant. Therefore, we cannot ignore the complex influence of multiple cultural/interactional patterns to which an individual may be exposed.

Why Japanese narrative resembles haiku

As Minami (1990) and Minami and McCabe (1991, 1996) have found in Japanese elementary school children's narratives, the present study shows that Japanese preschool children's narratives are also reminiscent of *haiku*, a form of Japanese poetry with a distinctive three-line format. Because depicting an actual scene in detail is impossible in a *haiku*'s seventeen syllables, a prerequisite of *haiku* is communicative compression. To write good *haiku*, for instance, one must use allusion, suggesting moods by selecting symbolic aspects of some situation, telling a whole story poetically. Not only the previous research (e.g. Minami, 1990; Minami & McCabe, 1991) but also the present study has identified that: (1) Japanese children's narratives (even with all the stanzas taken together) are strikingly succinct; and (2) Japanese young children and adults alike tend to talk about a stack of isolated, similar events in their narrative production. Thus, *haiku* is illustrative of these characteristics of Japanese narrative discourse patterns.

As we saw in great detail in Chapter 3, the similarities between *haiku* and Japanese narrative, however, are not coincidence. Instead, the findings in the present study suggest certain keys to understanding why Japanese narrative resembles *haiku*. Because *haiku* historically developed in an oral comic dialogue (Minami, 1990; Minami & McCabe, 1991; Yamamoto, 1969), *haiku* has a close relationship to Japanese narrative discourse style in terms of co-construction. In the original form of *haiku*, one party/person composes the first three-line verse, to which another party/person adds an additional two-line verse; this co-constructive exchange of an initial three-line verse and a responding two-line verse continues like a chain. Example 9.1, which I have already presented in Chapter 3 (Example 3.4), shows an exchange between the famous *haiku* poet, Basho Matsuo, who was composing *haiku* about 300 years ago, and one of his disciples, Boncho (my translation).

Example 9.1
Opening verse (by Boncho)
In the city,   (Location)
The smell of things;   (Object of deleted copula)
The summer moon.   (Time)
Responding verse (by Basho)
"It's hot, it's hot"
Voices at entrance gates   (Object of deleted copula)

As can be seen in this exchange, one piece of *haiku* corresponds to a narrative segment that can be provided in one turn of talk in narrative discourse. The way in which a series of *haiku* are chained by two people/parties (sometimes more than two) thus represents frequent turn exchanges in narrative discourse, a typical Japanese way of co-construction.

As seen in adults' monologic narratives, each stanza roughly corresponds to one turn of talk. Recall that even if the adult narrator is taking a narrative internal position in the middle of a stanza, at the end of that stanza she resumes a narrative external position. In the narrative presented below, an adult narrator told an injury story from her young childhood: She went on a bicycle trip with her father. On their way back home, while she was sitting on a cushion that her older sister had made (she was riding behind her father), the tassel of the cushion started sliding. She was afraid that if the tassel got out of shape, she would feel sorry for her older sister. So she tried to change her sitting position, but when she did so, she was caught under a wheel by the leg. Blood gushed out, and the Achilles' tendon was exposed where her ankle was cut. Unfortunately, because it was Sunday that day, her father had difficulty in finding an emergency hospital. As this example illustrates, although the adult narrator uses the formal verb-ending style *des(u)* at the outset of Stanza F, when narrating her experience, she uses informal endings, signaling that she is taking a narrative internal position. At the end of the stanza (which also corresponds to the end of her narrative in this case), however, she resumes using the formal style *mas(u)*. In addition, nominalization – i.e. a clause ('*sugoi bikkuri shita*': '[I] was very surprised') and a noun (*inshoo*: 'an impression') are combined by the quotative marker *to yuu* in Line 32 – at the very end of the narrative indicates some distance between the event (i.e. the narrator's severe injury in her early childhood) and the narrator who is currently narrating the event (also recall Example 5.5. in Chapter 5). Thus, while taking an internal perspective on a situation in the middle of a stanza, toward the end of that stanza the narrator usually conceptualizes the situation from an external perspective, using some linguistic devices. Likewise, toward the end of the entire narrative, the narrator makes a shift from the narrative internal to external perspective. By making use of rhetorical devices, therefore, adults can fully express the shifting between the two different narrative perspectives.

Example 9.2   A Japanese adult's (Tamotsu's mother) monologic narrative

Stanza A

(a) ORT	*nanka, anoo, chichioya to,*	1
	'Well, with my father,'	
(b) ACT	*issho ni saikuringu ni itte.*	2
	'together, on a bicycle trip (I) went.'	

Stanza B

(c) ORT	*de, kaerishina,*
	'And on our way back home,'

ACT:ORT	*chichioya no ushiro ni nottetan **desu** kedo.*	3
	'(I) was riding behind my father, though.'	
(d) ORT	*de, sono hi tamatama oneechan ga tsukutta zabuton o,*	4
	'And on that day, just by chance, on a cushion my older sister made,'	
(e) ACT:ORT	*hiite,*	5
	'(I) was sitting and,'	
	notte te.	6
	'(I) was riding.'	

Stanza C

(f) ORT	*sono zabuton no nanka bonbori ga,*	7
	'The tassel of that cushion,'	
	anoo, chotto zurete kite.	8
	'well, was sliding a bit.'	
(g) EVL	*sore o, anoo, guchagucha ni nattara,*	9
	'If (the cushion) got out of shape,'	
	ike nai na,	10
	'I would feel sorry (for my older sister).'	
	omotte.	11
	'(I) was afraid, so,'	
(h) ACT	*suwari naoshita shunkan ni,*	12
	'the moment (I) changed my sitting position,'	
(i) ACT	*makikondan **desu** ne,*	13
	'(I) was caught, you know,'	
	ashi o.	14
	'by the leg.'	
(j) ACT:EVL	*sorede chi ga sugoi dete.*	15
	'And blood gushed out.'	

Stanza D

(k) ORT	*sono nichiyoobi dattan de,*	16
	'Um, it was Sunday.'	
(l) ACT	*de, ano byooin o mawatte,*	17
	'And, well, (we) went around (to find) a hospital.'	
(m) ORT:EVL	*yatto, chotto tooku dattan **desu** kedo,*	18
	'Finally, (the hospital we found) was a bit distant, though.'	
(n) ACT	*ikkasho ittemo,*	19
	'Although we went to one place,'	
(o) ORT	*soko wa kyoo, anoo, rentogen ga torenai,*	20
	'in that place that day (I) couldn't have an X-ray (examination),'	
(p) ORT	*sensei ga inai to yuu koto de,*	21
	'(they) said that the doctor was absent (on that day),'	
(q) ACT:EVL	*soshite tooku made hakobarete.*	22
	'And (I) was taken to (that) distant (one).'	

Stanza E

(r) ORT:EVL	*de, koo akiresu ken ga mieta jootai datta kara,*	23
	'And the condition was that the Achilles' tendon was exposed (where my ankle was cut).'	

| (s) ACT:EVL | *de, maa nutte morattan desu kedo.* | 24 |
| | 'And (I) had (the wound) closed with stitches, though.' | |

Stanza F

(t) EVL	*sono toki ni sono chichioya wa moo*	
	hahaoya ni sugoi okoraretan desu kedo,	25
	'At that time, well, my father was heavily scolded by my mother, though.'	
(u) EVL	*sono jibun to shite wa sonoo ne oneechan no sore o,*	26
	'Well, as far as I was concerned, well, you know, my older sister's (cushion),'	
	gucha gucha ni shite wa,	27
	'if (I) made the cushion get out of shape,'	
	ikenai naa,	28
	'(I) would feel sorry,'	
	omotte.	29
	'(that was what I) was afraid of.'	
(v) EVL	*yatta koto ga,*	30
	'(but) what (I) did,'	
	motto taihen na koto ni nattan de,	31
	'brought a serious consequence.'	
(w) EVL	*sugoi bikkuri shita to yuu no ga inshoo ni ari masu ne.*	32
	'(I) have an impression that (I) was very surprised (at the consequence).'	

The abundance of speech acts categories for monologic narrative included in the above example suggests the complexity of communicative acts that the child is expected to acquire and control in interpersonal communication in years to come. For instance, although Stanza F consists of four verses (and adult narratives, in general, might not well be characterized as verse), the way in which the narrator constructs her narrative in a short turn/stanza by using the narrative internal/external positioning is similar to the *haiku* composition. Moreover, a stanza roughly corresponds to a compact one-event narrative seen in *haiku*. *Haiku*, which is effective in expressing one's empathy in brevity, is thus representative of the underlying culturally valued narrative discourse style predicated upon frequent turn exchanges.

As seen in mother–child interactions, from early childhood on, Japanese children have been abundantly exposed to this *haiku*-like, succinct storytelling style, particularly through frequent turn exchanges. As a cautionary note, I do not imply that Japanese parents are coaching children in *haiku*. Mothers might frequently provide their young children with direct instruction regarding the correct use of particular linguistic patterns. In terms of *haiku*, however, it is inconceivable that direct coaching by adults occurs in such a way. Rather, it seems that the *haiku* (or quasi-*haiku*) style is so culturally embedded and, even before entering preschool, children are so abundantly exposed to this style in home/local discourse situations, their oral narrative reflects the features associated with *haiku*. In other words, the Japanese (narrative) discourse style is illustrated in the *haiku* form.

Kamishibai and karuta: Continuity between orality and literacy

Furthermore, one distinctive practice in Japanese society is a kamishibai picture-story show, a series of large cards each consisting of a picture on the front and the narrative lines to be read by the storyteller/narrator on the back. Kamishibai storytelling is often used in Japanese preschools – nursery schools as well as day-care centers – as a support for children's emergent literacy (Tobin et al., 1989), and kamishibai storytelling has traditionally been very influential for children in Japan (Norton, 1991; Pellowski, 1977)

Momotaro (*The Peach Boy*) and *Hanasaka Jii-San* (*The Old Man Who Made Trees Blossom*) are the best-known traditional folktales that are read to preschoolers using *kamishibai*. In both folktales the protagonists are a nameless, good-natured, childless old couple; both start with the same opening, 'Long, long ago, in a certain place,' which flavors storytelling in classrooms with some authenticity (Norton, 1991). Likewise, both stories end with Heaven's reward for the good. *Momotaro*, scripted by Saneto (1986), and *Hanasaka Jii-San*, scripted by Yoda (1986), begin as follows (both originally in Japanese):

Example 9.3a
The Peach Boy
(1)   Long, long ago, in a certain place there were an old man and an old woman.
(2)   The old man (went) to the mountain every day to cut brushwood.
(3)   And the old woman went to the river to wash some clothes.

Example 9.3b
The Old Man Who Made Trees Blossom
(1)   Long, long ago, in a certain place there were an old man and an old woman.
(2)   They had a little dog named Shiro.
(3)   They loved Shiro very much.

Because they are written narratives, both stories later include a series of 'complicating actions' (Labov, 1972; Peterson & McCabe, 1983). As can be seen above, however, the beginning parts of these Japanese folktales illustrate a culturally nurtured traditional storytelling style that includes three-line structures similar to those seen in *haiku* and Japanese narratives.

In many ways, Japanese children are exposed to three-line forms of discourse both orally and in writing from a very early age. As introduced in Chapter 3, the most common way children encounter three lines of discourse would be an ancient but still widespread game called *karuta*, played from preschool through adulthood. One person reads and displays a card that has a three-line poem, proverb, or story. Children sit around a set of cards, each of which has the first letter of three-line poem, proverb or story with a picture that depicts the content of three-line sayings. Children listen carefully and compete with each other to pick up the appropriate card. Thus, not only at home but also in preschool Japanese children have been accustomed to this *haiku*-like, succinct storytelling style. These examples may demonstrate that prior experience with literacy activities – listening to stories in an oral tradition, for instance – helps children understand culture-specific narrative discourse styles. Moreover, it seems natural that not only young children but also adults tend to provide succinct narratives because early interactional patterns seem to contribute to interactional differences in later years. Conversely, one might be able to claim that differences in individuals' narrative discourse skills in later years – or even differences in adult individuals building relationships with others – can be traced back to this early age period. In this sense, I support the idea that development is continuous, i.e. each individual is located at a single point along the developmental continuum, with important and lasting effects of childhood experiences during the early stages of development.

Implications

In this book, I have suggested that in different environments, different patterns of social interaction are being emphasized. This is especially true in maternal styles of narrative elicitation, an important area of language socialization to cultivate children's culture-specific communicative competence. This study has thus emphasized from a narrative point of view how language socialization serves to generate members who are competent in socioculturally specific ways.

Transition from home to preschool

Continuity between home and school

As I stated in Chapter 8, one of the implications in this study is the difference in transition from home to school between Japan and the United States. From babyhood on, an individual is socialized in culturally specific ways, with the primary agent of socialization being the family. However, once a child has started schooling, which is widespread in modern societies, the main agent of socialization changes from the primary speech community, namely, the family and local community where the child was raised, to the secondary speech community, namely, the school, in which the child's narrative discourse style and subsequent literacy practices are often reshaped. In other words, children must make smooth transitions in moving from the primary oral discourse of the home to the discursive, scholastic discourse of the school.

Regarding this point, Olson (1977) argues that meaning-making in language always necessitates an act of disambiguation. He maintains that, as far as Western societies are concerned, procedures for an act of disambiguation exists from the earliest speech; thus, oral language skills at home are necessary precursors to the skills later required in an educational context. That is, Olson emphasizes that parallel transitions are considered important, (1) from home to school and (2) from utterance (i.e. orality) to text (i.e. literacy); he states that the acquisition of literacy proceeds from the context-dependent, emotionally charged oral world of the household to the realm of the school, where the acquisition of context-free, logical, message-focused skills, such as reasoning and problem solving, are considered important (see Chapter 3).

Once again, however, I would like to conceptualize that development – not only an individual but also a society at large – is continuous in many respects, if not all. As can be seen in Chapter 8, we must acknowledge that orality and literacy should be treated as a continuum rather than a dichotomy and that orality and literacy interpenetrate in everyday language use. The historical priority of orality over literacy in human experience indicates that not only the history of human beings but also each individual human being develops (in the course of his or her life) from context-bound orality to context-free literacy. Snow (1983), for example, suggests many similarities between learning to talk (i.e. language acquisition) and learning to read and write (i.e. literacy) in the early stages of the child's development. According to Snow, the specific oral discourse style employed by middle-class families at home, which has the characteristic features of being decontextualized and detached, closely matches school language use, a factor that accounts for the later literacy success of children from these homes. In other words, because Snow regards early oral language development as having direct influence on the development of later language skills, her emphasis is naturally placed on the importance of the continuity between oral language and literacy.

Possible discontinuity between home and school: Application to diverse societies

The above hypothesis suggests that oral language skills at home are necessary precursors to later literacy skills in an educational context. Conversely, it can be seen that if the nature of conversational interactions in children's homes and in school do not parallel each other, those children's academic success may be jeopardized. The above assumption, at the same time, implies that if the continuum from contextualized orality to decontextualized (or self-contextualized) literacy is missing in children's homes, they might face problems in school settings (Snow, 1983). Studies on the relationship between sociocultural background and minority children's literacy development (e.g. Cook-Gumperz & Gumperz, 1982) in the United States have indicated such a possible discontinuity. Some studies (e.g. Spener, 1988) have even argued that: (1) minority students do not prosper academically because the language practices of their homes do not match the language practices of the school environment; (2) in turn, such a mismatch tends to limit minority students' access to and participation in higher educational and occupational opportunities. As far as US society is concerned, therefore, it is critical to examine possible differences between discourse practices of the primary speech community (home) and those of the secondary speech community (school).

Some researchers, however, have opposed the literacy-as-development view and its resulting match–mismatch formulation of literacy. Based on their research, Scribner and Cole (1978, 1981) have challenged Olson's (1977) view, in which literacy, in combination with schooling, is supposed to equip children with the skills necessary for the transition from context-dependent thought (characteristic of oral language used in everyday life) to decontextualized abstract thinking (characteristic of literacy). Scribner and Cole studied the unschooled but literate Vai people of Liberia, who invented a syllabic writing system to represent their language. They suggest that in the case of the Vai, literacy is not associated with decontextualized thought. Scribner and Cole's argument is supported by other studies, such as research on the Cree-speaking people's syllabic script in northern Canada (Bennett & Berry, 1991). These research findings conclude that the relationship between higher-order intellectual skills and literacy practices is very complex, as is the relationship between literacy and schooling. Research conducted in other cultures thus warns that various modes of learning usually considered to be related to one another in Western societies may function differently in different cultures and societies.

Orality-literacy continuity in Japan

In the case of Japan, continuity and discontinuity exist simultaneously. To begin with, the present study seem to confirm that some types of continuity do exist between home and school, such as (1) *haiku*-like narrative discourse style based on frequent turn exchanges, (2) frequent use of the rapport particle *ne* ('you know') and (3) the three-part sequence during book-reading activities. The use of *ne*, for example, is strongly recommended in Japanese elementary school settings (Okubo, 1959; Uchida, 1986) because a certain type of *ne* helps the child pause and search for what to say next.

Another continuity between oral language skills developed in children's homes and literacy skills targeted in school settings can be identified in school textbooks. In contrast to American elementary school textbooks, which tend to instruct the child to take an objective and analytical view of the story, the situation, and the actions of the characters in order to evaluate the effectiveness of their actions, Japanese elementary school language textbooks tend to encourage 'the child to imagine the feelings of another and merge his or her identity with that of the character, even if that character should happen to be an animal[2]' (Gerbert, 1993, p. 161). Japanese teachers as well as textbooks ask their students to do some empathic reading, such as 'What do you think Character X really felt like at this point?' Throughout all grade levels, therefore, Japanese education encourages children to empathize with others (and personification is sometimes used for this empathy training). The school's emphasis parallels the strategy taken by Japanese mothers who, providing their young children with explicit training in empathy, appeal to the feelings of animals and even inanimate objects (Clancy, 1985, 1986). [Recall that the Japanese mothers of four-year-olds requested more evaluation from their children than did the North American mothers of four-year-olds.] In these respects, therefore, professional theories are in line with the folk psychology reflected in Japanese mothers' concerns.

Discontinuity in Japan

In some respects, however, Japanese children's habitual ways of communicating at home differ from the linguistic and communicative styles used outside the home. Discontinuity does exist in certain areas. For instance, generally speaking, by an early age Japanese children are already socialized in the use of polite language at home. When mothers verbally interacted with their young children during narrative elicitation, however, both mothers and children rarely used the formal *des(u)/mas(u)* styles. In US middle-class homes, on the other hand, using polite language to a family member may carry great weight (e.g. Berko Gleason & Weintraub, 1976). The role of the home and that of the school thus seem different in terms of language socialization between Japan and the United States. Although Japanese children rarely use the formal *des(u)/mas(u)* styles at home in their early childhood, they eventually learn to use these styles; as can be seen in Chapter 5, moreover, by deploying the proper verb-ending forms, they come to effectively encode the narrator's perspective. It seems then that Japanese children learn to use the formal styles and other linguistic/discursive forms later during school years. Recall that in Chapter 2, I referred to C. Chomsky's (1972) work that found that children's syntactic development continues into their elementary school years (although her study neither pays attention to sociocultural differences nor emphasizes conversational or social interactions). Based on the findings of the present study, I argue that, at the level of pragmatic development, too, children's language development – particularly socially accepted language patterns – continues actively into their elementary school years.

To understand the discontinuity between home and school in Japan, we need to stress the distinction between *uchi* ('inside') and *soto* ('outside') introduced in Chapter 5. If a person with whom the child interacts belongs to the child's circle, that person is an insider for the child. On the other hand, if a person is outside of the child's circle, then, that person is an outsider. Obviously, the child's inside circle is the family, and the outside circle that the child first experiences is the preschool. Although children may initially consider their preschool teacher as an insider to them and use the home-style in preschool at first, the gradual transition from home to preschool is from the *amae*-based inside world to the outside world where the meaning of group life is emphasized to some extent.

In the Japanese context, in spite of the apparent paradox that *amae*-based early child-rearing at home and later schooling do not seem parallel each other, Japanese children make the transition smoothly; furthermore, the two different socialization practices play complementary roles in helping an individual learn how to behave in Japanese society (Peak, 1989, 1991). The case in Japan, therefore, does not seem to fit the Western notion of the home-school continuum in socialization. In fact, the Japanese case even challenges the Western notion. Because of the differences in social structure and practices between the United States and Japan – US heterogeneous society as opposed to Japanese relatively homogeneous society[3] – direct comparison may not be possible. When we take previous studies into consideration (Peak, 1989, 1991), however, the findings presented here seem to suggest that regardless of home behaviors, children can learn to internalize new expectations of classroom life.

Imagination and creativity in narrative

In mother–child interactions, regardless of the context (i.e. whether joint book-reading activities or narrative discourse interactions), the mother always provides the child with many questions and prompts in order to facilitate the child's language development. As this book has revealed, however, both Japanese and North mothers prompt, question, encourage and capture their children's attention, but they seem to take these actions in different ways. Ninio and Snow (1996), for instance, claim that 'North American mothers ask for and help with clarification of orienting information, ask for and help with clarification of the events, and, in addition, clarify model, reinforce and demand information about the child's perspective on the story, making clear to the child that one cannot presuppose the interlocutor automatically understands the teller's point of view' (p. 186). As is clear now, the Japanese mothers in my data did not necessarily act like North American mothers.

One of the major differences in narrative discourse styles between Japanese and North Americans seems to lie in imagination and, moreover, creativity. Japanese children tend to just state facts (or they are encouraged to state facts) presumably because in group-oriented Japanese culture, explicit/logical articulation leans toward too much individual focus and is thus generally discouraged. On the other hand, North American children tend to go beyond simply stating facts (or they are encouraged to go beyond simply stating facts); in a society in which individualism prevails, individual topic delivery or simply being verbally assertive – including an individual's imagination and creativity – is understood and, moreover, respected. This difference might support Markus and Kitayama's (1991) claim that Japanese sociocultural patterns highlight interpersonal connectedness, whereas American patterns tend to accentuate individual autonomy.

We need to be careful, however, that theories based on a Western point of view might unnecessarily portray Japanese interactions in unfavorable ways. Recall the contrast between Sho's mother (Example 7.1) who discouraged her son's imaginative train-boarding story with repeated '*notte nai yo*' ('[You] have never ridden [on a red train], really [I tell you]') and Cara's mother (Example 7.2) who encouraged her daughter to continue her imaginative bear hunt story. Although Sho's mother seems to be adopting what Baumrind (1971) calls the authoritarian parenting style, when you listen to the audio tape, you can easily tell that she does not sound harsh or detached. Categorizing her style as the authoritarian parenting style, thus, might be based on cultural stereotypes (i.e. fixed ideas and opinions about people who are members of cultures other than one's own).

Similarly, following Bernstein's (1971) theory of codes, Sho's mother's interaction style might be categorized as a restricted code, whereas Cara's mother's style is regarded as an elaborated code. In Bernstein's original ideas, however, a restricted code, which is the communication style adopted by working-class families, would make their children disadvantaged in school settings where an elaborated code is prevalent. The restricted-elaborated distinction thus does not seem to apply to Sho's mother or, more generally, cross-culturally. If we blindly followed theories formulated in Western societies, we would tend to be caught up with the optimality assumption in which we see 'what is most desirable' in terms of Western society. It is based on the Western norm to consider that because children of authoritative parents tend to become self-reliant, self-controlled and self-assertive, they are better than children of authoritarian and permissive parents. By the same token, it is based on the Western norm to consider families with an elaborated code better than families with a restricted code. Ignoring the cultural implications, therefore, the optimality assumption puts a negative connotation on the behavior of parents who do not exhibit the optimal behavior according to the norm cherished by Western society.

Certainly, a word of caution is that culture is never a static entity. My interpretation of group-oriented Japanese culture versus individual-oriented North American culture, for instance, might be influenced by my stereotypes, i.e. overgeneralizations about the culture of each group of people that we tend to impose on the individuals within that group. Nonetheless, stating facts is a prevalently observed pattern among Japanese children.

Returning to the issue of imagination and creativity, as Okubo (1958) mentioned a long time ago, one of the features that is frequently observed among primary graders' oral narratives in Japan is reported speech (reported speech in Japanese is completed by simply adding the quotation-final particle *tte*; see Chapter 5). The use of reported speech is, in a sense, related to factual representation (although reported speech, which, as Tannen (1989) argues, reports not only the speaker's but also others' inner speech/thoughts, certainly retains the nature of constructed dialogue). In Japanese classrooms, moreover, such factual representation has traditionally been strongly recommended lest children should tell made-up stories (Okubo, 1959) (and thus, in this respect, a certain type of continuity exists between home and school).

Unlike the Western notion of individualism, the Japanese counterpart connotes that an individual can only claim his or her own will and personality within the framework of social relativism (Lebra, 1976), as reviewed in Chapter 2. According to Markus and Kitayama (1991), the Western self is characterized as independent, self-contained and autonomous, whereas the non-Western – mostly Asian – self is characterized as interdependent, relational and collectivistic. Note, however, that in this book I have intentionally avoided emphasizing the dichotomy between individualistic and collectivistic cultures, because (1) non-individualistic cultures do not necessarily fall under the category of collectivistic culture, and (2) whereas the word 'individualism' connotes positively, the word 'collectivism' does not (Azuma, 1996). As revealed in Chapter 5, social relativism, which I have preferred to use, is the norm in Japanese society, and this is reflected in certain linguistic devices and strategies. Under social relativism, an individual is defined in terms of the referential groups to which he or she belongs. One derives one's primary identity from the school one attends when one is young; when one is older, one identifies with the company for which one works. Being unique (too creative/imaginative) is often equivalent to being weird and, consequently, unacceptable. Under such social relativism, therefore, individualism and creativity are vulnerable to suppression.

Although not in Japan, Gardner (1989) reports that in China a prescribed series of basic skills lessons are valued highly, whereas American children are more imaginative and, moreover, creative in storytelling. As Gardner (1989) puts it, 'China and the United States turn out to embrace two radically different solutions to the dilemma of creativity versus basic skills' (p. 7). As mentioned in Chapter 2, the Confucian paradigm (e.g. malleability of human behavior) that has supported East Asian cultures still underlies contemporary Japanese culture (Feiler, 1991; Lebra, 1976, Miyanaga, 1991).

Certainly, Japan and China may differ greatly in their standards of early childhood education (Tobin et al., 1989), although they are both Asian societies in which group-oriented norms prevail and they might both be categorized as high context cultures, to borrow Hall's (1976, 1989) term. When comparing mathematics learning, for example, in Japanese, Chinese (Taiwan) and US elementary school classrooms, Stigler and Perry (1988) concluded that whereas Western educators tend to rely on nativism (children's inherently unique limitations), Asian educators are more comfortable with the principle of empiricism (all children's potential, with proper efforts to attain almost anything). In spite of such similarities between Japan and China (emphasizing effort as opposed to emphasizing ability), these researchers warn about the danger of lumping these Asians together. They state that 'Chinese classrooms are more performance oriented and Japanese classrooms more reflective' (Stigler & Perry, 1988, p. 40). Thus, not only in Japan but generally in other Asian cultures as well, less emphasis is placed on creativity and/or imagination; at the same time, however, Asian cultures, which are often considered to fall under the category of high context cultures (Hall, 1976, 1989) and/or collectivism in terms of describing beliefs about child rearing and education, should not be lumped together in one category.

Implications for US classrooms

In Chapter 7, we observed the encoding and decoding process. A message is encoded in a certain form of expression by means of the system of linguistic rules with which the speaker is equipped. In order to determine the meaning of the expressions, the listener mentally processes sentences that reflect complex structural properties of human language, which is universal. At the same time, however, this process is culturally determined; that is, encoding and decoding rules form the basis of the filters (or culturally specific schemata in some sense) that we deploy when we see the world. The more enculturated we become, the more layers we add to those filters. These filters are like lenses that allow us to perceive the world in a certain way. This process is one aspect of enculturation. By the time we become adults, therefore, we share more or less the same set of filters with other individuals in our culture. This aspect of enculturation at the same time implies that negative stereotypes can easily develop. Because our cultural filters and ethnocentrism create a set of expectations about others, observing individuals whose behavioral patterns, such as linguistic or, more specifically, narrative patterns, do not match our expectations often leads to negative reactions (or negative attributions).

The contrast between the West and the East presented above implies that habitual ways of communicating in one cultural setting may not necessarily work in another. To encourage and stimulate children from a different culture, therefore, one has to know something of the communicative style of that culture (Hymes, 1982). Particularly in the school setting, teachers need to understand children from different cultures. Otherwise, they are likely to judge other cultures through their own cultural lens and thus develop negative stereotypes.

This implication has a significant meaning in US educational settings where because of rapid social diversification, understanding other cultures is playing an increasingly important role. Minami (1990) found that American teachers from mainstream backgrounds responded merely as gatekeepers when shown Japanese children's personal narratives (the narratives were translated into English, and the teachers did not know that the stories were told by Japanese children), although schools have the social mission to prepare students to be able to function in society. That is, paying attention to the fact that the child talks in a different way (even in grammatically correct English), they stated the following: 'These children need help. They need more encouragement. They should be in a different type of program, not only because they themselves need to learn communicative skills, but also because if children who are more advanced are put in the same program, they would get bored. It is important to assess each child's skills, and to really help them improve upon what they have. That is education.' This type of approach taken by American educators thus illustrates their belief that learning settings should be sensitive to the needs of individual children.

This line of argument may ostensibly sound valid and convincing. It illustrates, however, that North American mainstream literacy practices are, in effect, playing a gatekeeping role, which fails to recognize and build on the literacy skills and cultures that minority students bring from their homes and local communities to school. Instead, it misinterprets cultural differences in narrative discourse structure as deficits, and, moreover, imposes mainstream norms on these children. We need then to keep in mind that 'what has often been viewed as a deficiency in imagination within schoolrooms turns out on close examination to arise because of cultural differences in its deployment,' and that 'what we tend to think of as imaginative is a highly culturally relative picture' (Sutton-Smith, 1988, p. 19).

In another study that analyzed in-depth interviews with thirty Asian adolescents in US schools (Minami, 2000), I found that: (1) Asian students want to be understood on their own terms; (2) teachers and policy makers need to be sensitive to cultural differences and create classrooms that maximize participation by students who might have different classroom behaviors. For example, a high school student from a Chinese background proudly claimed that Asians consider being quiet and listening intently in the classroom to be active, not passive, participation. Unfortunately, the current situation is that in order for children to be accepted by their teachers (and peers as well), they must demonstrate communicative competence (Hymes, 1972), which is, unfortunately, determined by the dominant culture in this case. Miscommunications certainly occur, because people are likely to continue to see other cultures through their own cultural lens as a result of enculturation and rely on stereotypical misconceptions. To break the stereotyped misconceptions, mainstream teachers need to take 'steps toward creating a composite classroom culture, one that meets school goals for literacy learning but is also responsive to students' cultural backgrounds' (Au, 1993, p. 104).

As Ogbu (1992) puts it, 'To understand what it is about minority groups, their cultures and languages that makes crossing cultural boundaries and school learning difficult for some but not for others, we must recognize that there are different types of minorities' (p. 8). According to Ogbu (1990, 1992), minority groups consist of different types, such as (1) immigrant or voluntary minorities, and (2) castelike or involuntary minorities. Asians, such as Chinese, Koreans and Japanese, are representative of voluntary or immigrant minorities. Ogbu argues that involuntary minorities try to preserve linguistic and cultural differences as symbolic of their ethnic identity and their separation from the oppressive mainstream culture.[4] In contrast, following Ogbu's discussion, voluntary minorities generally believe that their lives in the United States are better than their lives in their native countries. For instance, patterns of positive educational adaptation have been identified among Asian immigrants in the United States (De Vos, 1996). Voluntary minorities are therefore more likely to succeed than involuntary minorities, particularly in academic achievement. Voluntary minorities' positive appraisal of their situation is thus likely to have a positive influence on their overall performance.

Yet, the present study has revealed that voluntary minorities also try to maintain some of their original cultural characteristics (Chapter 7). That is, Japanese mothers living in the United States were influenced by American culture in some limited aspects (e.g. more topic-extension prompts right after uttering '*huun*' ('well') and more requests for description in eliciting narratives), while they retained other features that are considered to belong to Japanese culture. It is thus important to highlight the finding that people from other cultures are influenced by American culture in some ways but maintain certain original cultural traits.

Sociologists have long described the United States as a melting pot in which a variety of cultural experiences and backgrounds merge into something entirely new. While this trend has continued throughout the history of the United States, the last two decades in particular have witnessed a rapid influx of immigrants from Asian and Latin American countries. On the West Coast of the United States, for instance, because of rising immigration from Asian countries such as China, Korea, Taiwan and Japan, educational settings are becoming increasingly multicultural. According to a report on demographic changes summarized by the *San Francisco Examiner* (McCormick, 2000), for instance, a survey conducted by the US Census Bureau projects that San Francisco will soon join Honolulu as a major US city in which Asians outnumber whites. With increased immigration, the number of second- and third-generation Americans are also on the increase. When we turn our attention to school settings, students from minority backgrounds, like their parents and grandparents before them, maintain many of their ancestral culture's values and behaviors. Such minority students constitute a large proportion of the university student population that can be considered as engaged in intercultural communication on campus today.

The American public as a whole is becoming more sensitive to and aware of cultural and ethnic differences; yet, cross-cultural miscommunications and misunderstandings still lead to confusion and even anger. As McCabe (1991b) puts it, 'People should be encouraged to engage in a little more structural analysis before coming to a conclusion about the quality of some narratives' (p. xiv). When applied to educational environments in the United States, therefore, one of the implications of the present study is that educators need to nurture language-minority children by developing classroom activities that are congruent with those children's home/local community experiences.

Conclusions

The present work has described and analyzed how young Japanese children develop narrative structure; it has also illustrated how Japanese parents guide their children in the acquisition of culture-specific styles of narrative discourse and literacy. Moreover, the study has revealed that a variety of lexical items and discursive devices used by Japanese mothers and children reflect Japanese cultural norms represented by interdependence or, more precisely, the reciprocal nature of *amae*, the feeling of warmth, dependence and informality or the desire to be loved and cared for that typically characterizes mother–child relations. As seen in the encoding of the narrator's external/internal positioning in a narrative event through the set of verb-ending options, for instance, such Japanese cultural norms shape language use, and narrative discourse style in particular. Thus, I again emphasize that narrative can be viewed as a microcosm of the individual mind, but more than that, it reflects the larger social world.

The Application of the findings to other issues

Language acquisition

In addition to language acquisition, the cultural implications in the present work can further be applied to other issues, such as language learning and cross-cultural communication. As discussed in Chapter 5, studies on child language acquisition (e.g. Clancy, 1985) suggest that Japanese children begin to use connectives such as *dakara* ('so,' 'therefore,' 'that's why') at about three years of age and the formal *des(u)/mas(u)* verb-ending forms (i.e. suffixes) even earlier at about two years. However, even if Japanese young children have these lexical items, and even if they begin to talk about the past and thus produce narratives, they do not seem to have acquired the social pragmatic functions or interactional dimensions of these words occurring in narrative discourse. In other words, while they might have learned to use these words in restricted contexts (e.g. the here-and-now), they might not yet have reached the stage where they can manipulate more complicated functions of these words. Specifically, they do not seem to have fully grasped the societal concept of 'inside' and 'outside,' particularly how the *des(u)/mas(u)* styles function in relation to this societal concept. Cognitive and linguistic dimensions and sociocultural dimensions thus seem to take very different courses in the process of language acquisition.

Language learning

Likewise, for foreign/second language teachers and learners, as seen in the collaborative nature of narrative discourse, the present work lends support to intuitions about successful communications in a target language (e.g. learning when and how to take a turn). At the same time, however, learning culture-specific narrative styles (or more generally discourse style as observed in mother–child book-reading practices) along with lexical items and discursive devices is very difficult for those who are learning Japanese as a second language. To begin with, mastery of a full range of linguistic devices and manipulative strategies has a fairly long developmental history, and this development gradually takes place along with transitions from oral discourse to literacy. For example, it is a formidable task to master the proper use of the formal *des(u)/mas(u)* styles and the informal *da* style in oral narratives (i.e. the verb style choice in relation to the narrator's external/internal positioning in a narrative event); to make matters more complicated, the difference is sometimes related to the narrator's emotion. Furthermore, the interactional particles such as *ne* ('you know') and *yo* ('I tell you') are context dependent. Unless second-language learners have mastered these devices and manipulative strategies, their narratives may not sound natural to native speakers of Japanese.

Moreover, the importance of a culture-specific schema accompanied by linguistic devices with multiple functions is not necessarily emphasized in second or foreign-language classrooms. Being fluent speakers of a certain language does not simply mean that they can speak the language without a foreign accent and/or without syntactic errors; it also means that they can construct sentences and stories in accordance with a certain cultural schema. In other words, whether a second or foreign language learner can speak the target language naturally, to a certain extent, depends on whether he or she can present a series of events in culturally expected ways, using appropriate discourse markers.

Unfortunately, the ordinary classroom setting, where the need to teach sociocultural aspects is not necessarily a priority, may not be an ideal place for second-language learners to practice the use of these lexical items and discursive devices appropriately, effectively and – moreover – naturally in Japanese. For instance, According to Ohta (1994), affective particles (e.g. *ne* and *yo*), which modulate everyday interaction in Japanese, are used far less frequently in the Japanese-as-a-foreign-language classroom than in ordinary conversation. Ohta (1999, 2001) emphasizes the role of interactional routines in the socialization of second-language interactional competence. In an interview conducted by Mishima (1994), Sachiko Ide also suggests: 'Language teachers should emphasize the fact that the Japanese language is a direct reflection of the culture, and that to acquire the language one has to understand the culture behind it and take it as is' (p. 433).

The present study suggests the possibility of incorporating multiple functions of linguistic markers into classroom instruction. By doing so, language instructors may help prevent learners from making subtle but potentially critical mistakes associated with the culturally specific schema, such as misinterpreting turn-taking signals in conversational narrative discourse. Intermediate and advanced learners would particularly benefit from such incorporation.

Overall, in most foreign-language classrooms, students are explicitly taught grammar and vocabulary. Language learners' difficulties in conveying their messages in the target language, however, may relate closely to their way of structuring oral discourse. Unfortunately, the importance of discourse style is not emphasized in such classrooms. Instead, in such language classrooms, a greater awareness of the importance of oral and written personal narratives should be emphasized, because each individual has stories to tell, whether about something trivial that occurred just yesterday or something that happened a long time ago and still holds a significant meaning to his or her life. By telling or writing personal narratives [or even making *haiku* (Furukawa & Kitamura, 2001)], a foreign-language learner comes to display an array of his or her life experiences and learns how to express emotion naturally in the target language. Thus, the results of this study have significant implications for second or foreign language teaching.

Cross-cultural communication

By cross-cultural communication, I have meant the interaction between people of two or more different cultures. In cross-cultural interactions, interlocutors must be sensitive to subtle nuances that are easily overlooked. As Maynard (1993) puts it, 'Projecting oneself cross-culturally requires a special kind of awareness because when doing so, the dimensions of the projection become altered,' and 'more problematically, the very means of self-projection, the language itself, also takes a different personality' (p. 273). Notice, for example, that in the English translations of the adults' narrative examples in this book, the verb style choice in Japanese has obviously disappeared, and so has the narrator's external/internal positioning in a narrative event. Translated narratives, however sophisticated they are, may lose their subtlety and intricacy – which are deeply rooted in the original language and culture – and thus individuals may be unable to communicate culturally shared emotion to those who are from different cultures.

Furthermore, a series of important implications have been addressed in this book, in relation to US education, particularly in the sense that cross-cultural studies greatly help teachers working with students from other cultures. Because of rapid social diversification, due particularly to changes in immigration trends, early childhood education is playing an increasingly important role in the schools in the United States. In spite of the fact that educational settings are becoming increasingly multicultural, particularly in urban areas in the United States, people often assess other cultures through their own cultural lens and thus can fall back on stereotyped misconceptions. Most educational discourse and learning environments to date have tended to reflect primarily the discourse practices of mainstream society (i.e. European North American culture), often with unfortunate results for non-mainstream students, including many language-minority students (Cazden *et al.*, 1985; Gee, 1990, 1991b; Michaels & Collins, 1984; Philips, 1972). For instance, teachers who have been accustomed to a discourse with a clearly identifiable topic (i.e. topic-centered) tend to misunderstand children whose culture allows them to use a narrative discourse consisting of a series of implicitly associated personal anecdotes (i.e. topic-associating), and, what is worse, such teachers tend to terminate the discourse prematurely (Michaels, 1981, 1991).

Similarly, this chapter has disclosed how a middle-class European American teacher from a mainstream background evaluated Japanese elementary school children's narratives as being immature with little imagination because those children chose to string together anecdotes rather than discuss one incident in depth, while the same narratives were evaluated by Japanese adults as being typical or better than the average (Minami, 1990).

To conclude, I have emphasized that to study narratives, we cannot make light of the influence of sociocultural factors because narratives – oral personal narratives in particular – are always reflective of human interactions taking place in a specific culture and society. The study has also emphasized that cross-cultural studies are educationally important. For example, the more the political and economic relationship strengthens between the United States and Japan, the more opportunities the peoples of the these two nations have for contact and interaction. Consequently, misunderstandings based on cultural difference are likely to take place. We need to be aware that the basis for cultural difference originates in early stages of interaction at home and education. To analyze children's attainment of communicative competence in relation to education, other aspects, such as book-reading interactions with adults dealt with in Chapter 8, should be considered as well.

Obviously, in order to analyze children's attainment of communicative competence in relation to education, future research may need to include other aspects, such as narrative and explanatory sequences of talk during mealtimes. As I have emphasized repeatedly, narrative is a superordinate term that includes a variety of discourse genres – not only personal anecdote (i.e. autobiographical experience), but also fictional storytelling (i.e. pretend or replica play) and script (i.e. the typical series of events that takes place in a particular activity). The significance of narrative development, furthermore, goes far beyond mother–child interactions at home. Children's narrative skills continue to develop throughout the preschool and elementary school years. Related to the issue of continuity in narrative discourse development are possible differences between the narrative discourse practices of the primary speech community (generally the narrative discourse style used at home) and those of the secondary speech community (school). Thus, examining the relationship between home background and young children's transitions in narrative discourse development – shedding light on such transitions occurring during children's narrative performance across different genres in different domains of activity – holds promise.

Similarly, future research may need to examine 'within culture' differences (i.e. social class differences) through mother–child interactions. Exploring diversity within Japan is critical, particularly in terms of child rearing (e.g. literacy practices at home) and education because, in many societies, social class differences in child rearing and in education are profound (e.g. Heath, 1983). As a matter of fact, Azuma (1996) claims that, in his longitudinal study examining the relationship between maternal verbalization and children's cognitive attainment, he found greater social-class variation in Japan than the United States. His finding is contrary to the general belief that there would be little social class variation because Japanese society is often regarded as a single class, i.e. middle-class society. In this book, this study is only a beginning. However, it is my hope that this study can provide the basis to break through cultural stereotypes and improve cross-cultural education methods.

Notes

1. Recall that in Chapter 2, I referred to the recent emergentist paradigm (MacWhinney, 1999), which, unlike the Chomskyan linguistically based (or domain-specific) paradigm of the nature of language acquisition, explains language acquisition by domain-general leaning mechanisms, such as attentional processes, working memory, auditory processing and sequence learning skills (i.e. pattern detection). Therefore, the emergentist approach, which differs from the nativist approach that emphasizes rule-based knowledge representations, claims that the interplay between domain-general cognitive/learning mechanisms and the environment accounts for language development, particularly in the area of personal affect.
2. As Gerbert (1993) aptly points out, in the story 'Gon the Fox' (Ishimori *et al.*, 1992), children are encouraged to empathize with not only a human character (a farmer) but also an animal character (a fox). While personification is also prevalent in Western tales for children, Japanese textbooks differ greatly from their Western counterparts to the extent to which they emphasize the importance of the reader's affective responses to and inferences of the protagonists' inner states.
3. The distinction of homogeneous and heterogeneous society is considered to form a continuum rather than a dichotomy. Specifically, similarities in language, culture, value system and family structure are considered to compose this continuum.
4. Similar situations – diglossic situations (co-existence of languages of high prestige and low prestige) in particular – are found in other societies as well. For instance, Korean Japanese, descendants of Koreans who were brought into Japanese society through colonization, are discouraged from speaking the Korean language (and consequently lose their native tongue as if the eventual replacement of Korean by Japanese was necessary step in Japanization), whereas a great number of Korean Americans in the United States believe that they can speak the Korean language fluently (Kim, 1990).

References

Akatsuka, N. and Clancy, P. (1993) Conditionality and deontic modality in Japanese and Korean: Evidence from the emergence of conditionals. In P.M. Clancy (ed.) *Japanese/Korean Linguistics*: Vol. 2 (pp. 177–192). Stanford, CA: Stanford University.

Akmajian, A. and Heny, F.W. (1980) *An Introduction to the Principles of Transformational Syntax*. Cambridge, MA: MIT Press.

Aksu-Koç, A. (1996) Frames of mind through narrative discourse. In D.I. Slobin, J. Gerhardt, A. Kyratzis and J. Guo (eds) *Social Interaction, Social Context, and Language: Essays in Honor of Susan Ervin-Tripp* (pp. 309–328). Mahwah, NJ: Lawrence Erlbaum Associates.

Aksu-Koç, A. and von Stutterheim, C. (1994) Temporal relations in narrative: Simultaneity. In R.A. Berman and D. I. Slobin, *Relating Events in Narrative: A Crosslinguistic Developmental Study* (pp. 393–455). Hillsdale, NJ: Lawrence Erlbaum Associates.

Applebee, A.N. (1978) *The Child's Concept of Story: Ages Two to Seventeen*. Chicago: University of Chicago Press.

Asano, N. (1976) *Haikai no Goi to Bunpoo* [Vocabulary and Grammar of *Haikai*]. Tokyo: Ofusha.

Aso, I. (1959) *Chuukooki* [The Restoration period]. In M. Fumiiri (ed.) *Haiku Kooza* [Haiku Lectures] 4. Tokyo: Meiji Shoin.

Association for Japanese-Language Teaching (1984) *Japanese for Busy People* 1. Tokyo: Kodansha International.

Astington, J.D. (1990) Canonicality and consciousness in child narrative. In B.B. Britton and A.D. Pellegrini (eds) *Narrative Thought and Narrative Language* (pp. 151–171). Hillsdale, NJ: Lawrence Erlbaum Associates.

Au, K.H. (1993) *Literacy Instruction in Multicultural Settings*. Fort Worth, TX: Harcourt Brace Jovanovich.

Auerbach, E.R. (1989) Toward a social-contextual approach to family literacy. *Harvard Educational Review* 59 (2), 165–181.

Azuma, H. (1986) Why study child development in Japan? In H. Stevenson, H. Azuma and K. Hakuta (eds) *Child Development and Education in Japan* (pp. 3–12). New York: Freeman.

Azuma, H. (1996) Cross-national research on child development: The Hess–Azuma collaboration in retrospect. In D. Shwalb and B. Shwalb (eds) *Japanese Child Development: Classics Studies, Responses, and Prospects* (pp. 220–240). New York: Guilford Press.

Bachnik, J.M. (1994) Introduction: *Uchi/soto:* Challenging our conceptualizations of self, social order, and language. In J.M. Bachnik and C.J. Quinn, Jr. (eds)

Situated Meaning (pp. 3–37). Princeton: Princeton University Press.

Bakeman, R. and Gottman, J.M. (1986) *Observing Interaction: An Introduction to Sequential Analysis*. New York: Cambridge University Press.

Bamberg, M.G.W. (1997a) Positioning between structure and performance. *Journal of Narrative and Life History* 7 (1–4), 335–342.

Bamberg, M. (1997b) Language, concepts and emotions: The role of language in the construction of emotions. *Language Sciences* 19, 309–340.

Bamberg, M. (1997c) A constructivist approach to narrative development. In M. Bamberg (ed.) *Narrative Development: Six Approaches* (pp. 89–132). Mahwah, NJ: Lawrence Erlbaum Associates.

Bartlett, F.C. (1932) *Remembering*. New York: Cambridge University Press.

Baumrind, D. (1971) Harmonious parents and their preschool children. *Developmental Psychology* 41 (1), 92–102.

Baumrind, D. (1973) The development of instrumental competence through socialization. In A. Pick (ed.) *Minnesota Symposia on Child Psychology* Vol. 7 (pp. 3–46). Minneapolis: University of Minnesota Press.

Beals, D.E., De Temple, J.M. and Dickinson, D.K. (1994) Talking and listening that support early literacy development of children from low-income families. In D.K. Dickinson (ed.) *Bridges to Literacy: Children, Families, and Schools* (pp. 19–40). Cambridge, MA: Blackwell.

Benedict, R. (1946) *The Chrysanthemum and the Sword: Patterns of Japanese Culture*. Boston: Houghton Mifflin.

Bennett, J.A. and Berry, J.W (1991) Cree literacy in the syllabic script. In D.R. Olson and N. Torrance (eds) *Literacy and Orality* (pp. 90–104). New York: Cambridge University Press.

Berko Gleason, J. and Weintraub, M. (1976) The acquisition of routines in child language. *Language in Society* 5 (2), 129–136.

Berman, R.A. (1994, January) *Narrative Theory and Narrative Development*. Paper presented at the 18th Annual Boston University Conference on Language Development, Boston, MA.

Berman, R.A. (1995) Narrative competence and storytelling performance: How children tell stories in different contexts. *Journal of Narrative and Life History* 5 (4), 285–313.

Berman, R.A. and Neeman, Y. (1994) Development of linguistic forms: Hebrew. In R.A. Berman and D.I. Slobin, *Relating Events in Narrative: A Crosslinguistic Developmental Study* (pp. 285–328). Hillsdale, NJ: Lawrence Erlbaum Associates.

Berman, R.A. and Slobin, D.I. (1994) *Relating Events in Narrative: A Crosslinguistic Developmental Study*. Hillsdale, NJ: Lawrence Erlbaum Associates.

Bernstein, B. (1971) *Class, Codes and Control*: Vol. 1. *Theoretical Studies Towards a Sociology of Language*. London: Routledge & Kegan Paul.

Bloom, P. (2000) *How Children Learn the Meanings of Words*. Cambridge, MA: MIT Press.

Blum-Kulka, S. (1997) *Dinner Talk: Cultural Patterns of Sociability and Socialization in Family Discourse*. Mahwah, NJ: Lawrence Erlbaum.

Boocock, S. S. (1989) Controlled diversity: An overview of the Japanese preschool system. *Journal of Japanese Studies* 15 (1), 41–65.

Borker, R. (1980) Anthropology. In S. McConnell-Ginet, R. Borker and N. Furman (eds) *Women and Language in Literature and Society* (pp. 26–44). New York: Praeger.

Bornstein, M.C., Azuma, H., Tamis-LeMonda, C. and Ogino, M. (1990) Mother and infant activity and interaction in Japan and in the United States: I. A comparative macroanalysis of naturalistic exchanges. *International Journal of Behavioral Development* 13, 267–287.

Bornstein, M.H., Toda, S., Azuma, H., Tamis-LeMonda, C. and Ogino, M. (1990) Mother and infant activity and interaction in Japan and in the United States: II. A comparative microanalysis of naturalistic exchanges focused on the organisation of infant attention. *International Journal of Behavioral Development* 13, 289–308.

Bornstein, M.H., Tal, J., Rahn, C., Galperín, C.Z., Pêcheux, M.G., Lamour, M., Toda, S., Azuma, H., Ogino, M. and Tamis-LeMonda, C.S. (1992) Functional analysis of the contents of maternal speech to infants of 5 and 13 months in four cultures: Argentina, France, Japan, and the United States. *Developmental Psychology* 28 (4), 593–603.

Bornstein, M.H., Tamis-LeMonda, C.S., Tal, J., Ludemann, P., Toda, S., Rahn, C.W., Pêcheux, M.G., Azuma, H. and Vardi, D. (1992) Maternal responsiveness to infants in three societies: The United States, France, and Japan. *Child Development* 63 (4), 808–821.

Botvin, G.J. and Sutton-Smith, B. (1977) The development of structural complexity in children's fantasy narratives. *Developmental Psychology* 13 (4), 377–388.

Bowerman, M. (1991) Mapping thematic roles onto syntactic functions: Are children helped by innate linking rules? *Linguistics* 28, 1253–1289.

Brandt, D. (1990) *Literacy as Involvement: The Acts of Writer, Reader, and Texts.* Carbondale: Southern Illinois University Press.

Brown, R. (1996) The language of social relationship. In D.I. Slobin, J. Gerhardt, A. Kyratzis and J. Guo (eds) *Social Interaction, Social Context, and Language: Essays in Honor of Susan Ervin-Tripp* (pp. 39–52). Mahwah, NJ: Lawrence Erlbaum Associates.

Brown, R. and Bellugi, U. (1964) Three processes in the child's acquisition of syntax. *Harvard Educational Review* 34 (2), 133–151.

Brown, P. and Levinson, S.C. (1987) *Politeness: Some Universals in Language Usage.* Cambridge, England: Cambridge University Press.

Bruner, J. (1977) Early social interaction and language development. In H.R. Schaffer (ed.) *Studies in Mother–Child Interaction* (pp. 271–289). London: Academic Press.

Bruner, J. (1983) *Child's Talk: Learning to Use Language.* New York: Norton.

Bruner, J. (1986) *Actual Minds, Possible Worlds.* Cambridge, MA: Harvard University Press.

Bruner, J. (1990) *Acts of Meaning.* Cambridge, MA: Harvard University Press.

Bruner, J. and Lucariello, J. (1989) Monologue as narrative recreation of the world. In K. Nelson (ed.) *Narratives from the Crib* (pp. 73–97). Cambridge, MA: Harvard University Press.

Caffi, C. and Janney, R.W. (1994) Towards a pragmatics of emotive communication. *Journal of Pragmatics* 22, 325–373.

Carle, E. (1969) *The Very Hungry Caterpillar.* New York: Philomel Books.

Carle, E. (1976) *Harapeko Aomushi* (H. Mori, trans). Tokyo: Kaiseisha. (Original work published 1969.)

Caudill, W. and Frost, L. (1974) A comparison of maternal care and infant behavior in Japanese-American and American families. In W. Lebra (ed.)

Mental Health Research in Asia and the Pacific Vol. 2 (pp. 25–48) Honolulu: East–West Center Press.

Caudill, W. and Schooler, C. (1973) Child behavior and child rearing in Japan and the United States: An interim report. *Journal of Nervous and Mental Disease* 157 (5), 323–338.

Caudill, W. and Weinstein, H. (1969) Maternal care and infant behavior in Japan and America. *Psychiatry* 32, 12–43.

Cazden, C.B. (1988) *Classroom discourse*. Portsmouth, NH: Heinemann.

Cazden, C.B., Michaels, S. and Tabors, P. (1985) Spontaneous repair in sharing time narratives: The interaction of metalinguistic awareness, speech event, and narrative style. In: S.W. Freedman (ed.) *The Acquisition of Written Language* (pp. 51–64). Norwood, NJ: Ablex.

Chafe, W.L. (1977) Creativity in verbalization and its implications for the nature of stored knowledge. In R.O. Freedle (ed.) *Discourse Production and Comprehension* (pp. 41–55). Norwood, NJ: Ablex.

Chafe, W.L. (1980) The deployment of consciousness in the production of a narrative. In: W.L. Chafe (ed.) *The Pear Stories* (pp. 9–50). Norwood, NJ: Ablex.

Chafe, W.L. (1990) Some things that narratives tell us about the mind. In B.K. Britton and A.D. Pellegrini (eds) *Narrative Thought and Narrative Language* (pp. 79–98). Hillsdale, NJ: Lawrence Erlbaum Associates.

Chafe, W.L. (1993) Prosodic and functional units of language. In J.A. Edwards and M.D. Lampert (eds) *Talking data: Transcription and Coding in Discourse Research* (pp. 33–44). Hillsdale, NJ: Lawrence Erlbaum Associates.

Chomsky, C. (1969) *The Acquisition of Syntax in Children from 5 to 10*. Cambridge, MA: MIT Press.

Chomsky, C. (1972) Stages in language development and reading exposure. *Harvard Educational Review* 42 (1), 1–33.

Chomsky, N. (1957) *Syntactic Structures*. The Hague: Mouton.

Chomsky, N. (1959) Review of *Verbal Behavior* by B.F. Skinner. *Language* 35 (1), 26–58.

Chomsky, N. (1965) *Aspects of the Theory of Syntax*. Cambridge, MA: MIT Press.

Chomsky, N. (1985) *Knowledge of Language: Its Nature, Origin, and Use*. New York: Praeger.

Clancy, P.M. (1980) Referential choice in English and Japanese narrative discourse. In W.L. Chafe (ed.) *The Pear Stories: Cognitive, Cultural, and Linguistic Aspects of Narrative Production* 3 (pp. 127–201). Norwood, NJ: Ablex.

Clancy, P.M. (1985) The acquisition of Japanese. In D.I. Slobin (ed.) *The Crosslinguistic Study of Language Acquisition* Vol. 1: *The Data* (pp. 373–524). Hillsdale, NJ: Lawrence Erlbaum Associates.

Clancy, P.M. (1986) The acquisition of communicative style in Japanese. In B.B. Schieffelin and E. Ochs (eds) *Language Socialization Across Cultures* (pp. 373–524). New York: Cambridge University Press.

Clancy, P.M. (1992) Referential strategies in the narratives of Japanese children. *Discourse Processes* 15 (4), 441–467.

Clancy, P.M. (1999) The socialization of affect in Japanese mother–child conversation. *Journal of Pragmatics* 31, 1937–1421.

Clark, E.C. (1994) Reconstructing history: The epitomizing image. In E.M. McMahan and K.L. Rogers (eds) *Interactive Oral History Interviewing* (pp. 19–30). Hillsdale, NJ: Lawrence Erlbaum Associates.

Cook, H.M. (1997) The role of Japanese *masu* form in caregiver-child conversation. *Journal of Pragmatics* 28, 695–718.

Cook, H.M. (2000) The acquisition of social meaning: The case of the Japanese honorific *masu* form. In H. Sirai, S. Miyata, H. Nisisawa, H. Terada, K. Nakamura and N. Naka (eds) *Proceedings of the Second Annual Conference of the Japanese Society for Language Sciences* (pp. 9–14). Nagoya, Japan: JSLS Main Office.

Cook-Gumperz, J. (1992) Gendered talk and gendered lives: Little girls being women before becoming (big) girls. In K. Hall, M. Bucholtz and B. Moonwomon (eds) *Locating Power: Proceedings of the 1992 Berkeley Women and Language Conference* Vol. 1 (pp. 68–79). Berkeley, CA: Berkeley Women and Language Group, University of California.

Cook-Gumperz, J. and Green, J.L. (1984) A sense of story: Influences on children's storytelling ability. In D. Tannen (ed.) *Coherence in Spoken and Written Discourse* (pp. 201–218). Norwood, NJ: Ablex.

Cook-Gumperz, J. and Gumperz, J.J. (1982) Communicative competence in educational perspective. In L.C. Wilkinson (ed.) *Communicating in the Classroom* (pp. 13–24). New York: Academic Press.

Cummings, W.K. (1980) *Education and Equality in Japan*. Princeton, NJ: Princeton University Press.

Cummins, J. (1994) Knowledge, power, and identity in teaching English as a second language. In F. Genesee (ed.) *Educating Second Language Children* (pp. 33–58). New York: Cambridge University Press.

De Temple, J.M. (1993) *Coding System for Home Bookreading*. Unpublished Manual, Harvard University.

De Temple, J.M. and Beals, D.E. (1991) Family talk: Sources of support for the development of decontextualized language skills. *Journal of Research in Childhood Education* 6(1), 11–19.

De Temple, J.M. and Snow, C.E. (1996) Styles of parent–child book-reading as related to mothers' views of literacy and children's literacy outcomes. In J. Shimron (ed.) *Literacy and Education: Essays in Memory of Dina Feitelson* (pp. 49–68). Cresskill, NJ: Hampton Press.

De Vos, G. (1996) Psychocultural continuities in Japanese social motivation. In D. Shwalb and B. Shwalb (eds) *Japanese Child Development: Classics Studies, Responses, and Prospects* (pp. 44–84). New York: Guilford Press.

Deese, J. (1984) *Thought into Speech: The Psychology of a Language*. Englewood Cliffs, NJ: Prentice-Hall.

Dickinson, D.K. (1991) Teacher agenda and setting: Constraints on conversation in preschools. In A. McCabe and C. Peterson (eds) *Developing Narrative Structure* (pp. 255–302). Hillsdale, NJ: Lawrence Erlbaum Associates.

Dickinson, D.K., De Temple, J.M., Hirschler, J.A. and Smith, M.A. (1992) Book-reading with preschoolers: Coconstruction of text at home and at school. *Early Childhood Research Quarterly* 7, 323–346.

Dickinson, D. and McCabe, A. (1991) The acquisition and development of language: A social interactionist account of language and literacy development. In J.F. Kavanagh (ed.) *The language Continuum: From Infancy to Literacy* (pp. 1–40). Parkton, MD: York Press.

Doi, T. (1973) *The Anatomy of Dependence* (J. Bester, trans). Tokyo: Kodansha International. (Original work published 1971)

Donahue, R.T. (1998) *Japanese Culture and Communication: Critical Cultural Analysis*. Lanham, MD: University Press of America.

Downing, P. (1980) Factors influencing lexical choice in narrative. In W.L. Chafe (ed.) *The Pear Stories: Cognitive, Cultural, and Linguistic Aspects of Narrative Production* 3 (pp. 89–126). Norwood, NJ: Ablex.

Economic Planning Agency (1990) *Keizai Yooran* [Economic Survey]. Tokyo: Economic Planning Agency.

Egan, K. (1987) Literacy and the oral foundation of education. *Harvard Educational Review* 57 (4), 445–472.

Eisenberg, A.R. (1985) Learning to describe past experiences in conversation. *Discourse Processes* 8 (2), 177–204.

Ely, R. and McCabe, A. (1993) Remembered voices. *Journal of Child Language* 20 (3), 671–696.

Ervin-Tripp, S. M. and Küntay, A. (1997) The occasioning and structure of conversational stories. In T. Givón (ed.) *Conversation* (pp. 133–166). Amsterdam, The Netherlands: John Benjamins.

Faas, E. (1978) *Towards a New American Poetics*. Santa Barbara, CA: Black Sparrow Press.

Feiler, B.S. (1991) *Learning to Bow: An American Teacher in a Japanese School*. New York: Ticknor & Fields.

Feldman, C.F., Bruner, J., Renderer, B. and Spitzer, S. (1990) Narrative comprehension. In B.K. Britton and A.D. Pellegrini (eds) *Narrative Thought and Narrative Language* (pp. 1–78). Hillsdale, NJ: Lawrence Erlbaum Associates.

Fernald, A. and Morikawa, H. (1993) Common themes and cultural variations in Japanese and American mothers' speech to infants. *Child Development* 64 (3), 637–656.

Fischer, K.W. and Lazerson, A. (1984) *Human Development: From Conception Through Adolescence*. New York: Freeman.

Fivush, R. (1991) The social construction of parental narratives. *Merrill-Palmer Quarterly* 37 (1), 59–82.

Fivush, R. and Fromhoff, F.A. (1988) Style and structure in mother–child conversations about the past. *Discourse Processes* 11 (3), 337–355.

Fludernik, M. (1996) *Towards a 'Natural' Narratology*. London: Routledge.

Freire, P. (1970a) *Pedagogy of the Oppressed*. New York: Seabury Press.

Freire, P. (1970b) The adult literacy process as cultural action for freedom. *Harvard Educational Review* 40 (2), 205–225.

Fujimura-Fanselow, K. (1985) Women's participation in higher education in Japan. *Comparative Education Review* 29, 471–489.

Furukawa, Y. and Kitamura, T. (2001) Haiku o tsukurimasho (Let's make *haiku*) *Nihongo Kyoiku Tsushin* (Japanese language education correspondence) 39.

Gakken (1989) *Yonen no Gakushuu* [Fourth-Grader's Study] 11. Tokyo: Gakushu Kenkyusha.

Gal, S. (1992) Language, gender, and power: An anthropological view. In K. Hall, M. Bucholtz and B. Moonwomon (eds) *Locating Power: Proceedings of the 1992 Berkeley Women and Language Conference* Vol. 1 (pp. 153–161). Berkeley, CA: Berkeley Women and Language Group, University of California.

Gardner, H. (1989) *To Open Minds: Chinese Clues to the Dilemma of Contemporary Education*. New York: Basic Books.

Gee, J.P. (1985) The narrativization of experience in the oral style. *Journal of Education* 167, 9–35.

Gee, J.P. (1986a) Units in the production of narrative discourse. *Discourse Processes* 9 (4), 391–422.

Gee, J.P. (1986b) Orality and literacy: From the savage mind to ways with words. *TESOL Quarterly* 20, 719–746.

Gee, J.P. (1989a) Two styles of narrative construction and their linguistic and educational implications. *Discourse Processes* 12 (3), 287–307.

Gee, J.P. (1989b, October) *Stanzas: The Intersection of Psycho and Socio Linguistics.* Paper presented at the 14th Annual Boston University Conference on Language Development, Boston, MA.

Gee, J.P. (1990) *Social Linguistics and Literacies: Ideology in Discourses.* Bristol, PA: The Falmer Press.

Gee, J.P. (1991a) A linguistic approach to narrative. *Journal of Narrative and Life History* 1 (1), 15–39.

Gee, J.P. (1991b) Memory and myth. In A. McCabe and C. Peterson (eds) *Developing Narrative Structure* (pp. 1–25). Hillsdale, NJ: Lawrence Erlbaum Associates.

Gerbert, E. (1993) Lessons from the *kokugo* (national language) readers. *Comparative Education Review* 37 (2), 152–180.

Gilligan, C. (1982) *In a Different Voice: Psychological Theory and Women's Development.* Cambridge, MA: Harvard University Press.

Goldfield, B.A. and Snow, C.E. (1989) Individual differences in language acquisition. In J.B. Gleason (ed.) *The Development of Language* (2nd edn) (pp. 303–325). Columbus, OH: Merrill.

Goodwin, C. (1981) *Conversational Organization: Interaction Between Speakers and Hearers.* New York: Academic Press.

Grice, H.P. (1975) Logic and conversation. In P. Cole and J.L. Morgan (eds) *Syntax and Semantics* Vol. 3: *Speech Acts* (pp. 41–58). New York: Academic Press.

Grusec, J.E. and Lytton, H. (1988) *Social Development: History, Theory, and Research.* New York: Springer-Verlag.

Gumperz, J.J. (1981) The linguistic bases of communicative competence. In D. Tannen (ed.) *Analyzing Discourse: Text and Talk* (pp. 323–334). Washington, DC: Georgetown University Press.

Haley-James, S., Stewig, J.W., Ballenger, M.T., Chaparro, J.L., Millett, N.C., Terry, C.N. and Shane, J.G. (1988) *English: Teacher's Edition, Level 5.* Boston, MA: Houghton Mifflin.

Hall, E.T. (1976) *Beyond Culture.* New York: Anchor.

Hall, E.T. (1989) Unstated features of the cultural context of learning. *The Educational Forum* 54, 21–34.

Halliday, M.A.K. (1994) The place of dialogue in children's construction of meaning. In R. Ruddell, M.R. Ruddell and H. Singer (eds) *Theoretical Models and Processes of Reading* (4th edn) (pp. 70–82). Newark, Deleware: International Reading Association.

Harris, R.J., Lee, D.J., Hensley, D.L. and Schoen, L.M. (1988) The effect of cultural script knowledge on memory for stories over time. *Discourse Processes* 11 (4), 413–431.

Hayashi, N. (1986) *Hyakunin-Isshu no Sekai* [The World of One Hundred *Waka* Poems]. Tokyo: Aoki Shoten.

Hayashi, R. (1988) Simultaneous talk – from the perspective of floor management of English and Japanese speakers. *World Englishes* 7 (3), 269–288.

Heath, S.B. (1982) What no bedtime story means: Narrative skills at home and school. *Language in Society* 11 (1), 49–76.

Heath, S.B. (1983) *Ways with Words: Language, Life and Work in Communities and Classrooms*. New York: Cambridge University Press.

Heath, S.B. (1986) Taking a cross-cultural look at narratives. *Topics in Language Disorders* 7 (1), 84–94.

Hebb, D.O. (1953) Heredity and environment in mammalian behavior. *British Journal of Animal Behavior* 1, 43–47.

Hemphill, L. (1989) Topic development, syntax, and social class. *Discourse Processes* 12 (3), 267–286.

Henderson, H.G. (1958) *An Introduction to Haiku: An Anthology of Poems and Poets from Basho to Shiki*. New York: Doubleday Anchor Books.

Hendry, J. (1993) *Wrapping Culture: Politeness, Presentation, and Power in Japan and Other Societies*. Oxford: Clarendon Press.

Hess, R.D. and Shipman, V.C. (1965) Early experiences and socialization of cognitive models in children. *Child Development* 36, 860–888.

Hess, R., Kashiwagi, K., Azuma, H., Price, G.G. and Dickson, W. (1980) Maternal expectations for early mastery of developmental tasks and cognitive and social competence of preschool children in Japan and the United States. *International Journal of Psychology* 15, 259–272.

Hicks, D. (1990) Narrative skills and literacy learning. In J. Hardman, T. Hickey and J. Newman (eds) *Working Papers in Educational Linguistics* 6 (1), University of Pennsylvania Graduate School of Education.

Hicks, D. (1994) Individual and social meanings. *Journal of Narrative and Life History* 4 (3), 215–240.

Hinds, J. (1984) Topic maintenance in Japanese narratives and Japanese conversational interaction. *Discourse Processes* 7 (4), 465–482.

Hoff-Ginsberg, E. (1992) How should frequency in input be measured? *First Language* 12 (3), 233–244.

Holloway, S.D. (2000) *Contested Childhood: Diversity and Change in Japanese Preschools*. New York: Routledge.

Holloway, S.D. and Minami, M. (1996) Japanese childrearing: Two generations of scholarship. In D. Shwalb and B. Shwalb (eds) *Japanese Child Development: Classics Studies, Responses, and Prospects* (pp. 164–176). New York: Guilford Press.

Hopper, P. (1979) Some observations on the typology of focus and aspect in narrative language. *Studies in Language* 3, 37–64.

Hopper, P. and Thompson, S. (1980) Transitivity in grammar and discourse. *Language* 56 (2), 251–299.

Houghton Mifflin (1988) *English: Teacher's Edition, Level 5*. Boston, MA: Houghton Mifflin. Author.

Hudelson, S. (1994) Literacy development of second language children. In F. Genesee (ed.) *Educating Second Language Children* (pp. 129–158). New York: Cambridge University Press.

Hudson, J. A. (1990) The emergence of autobiographical memory in mother–child conversation. In R. Fivush and J.A. Hudson (eds) *Knowing and Remembering in Young Children* (pp. 166–196). New York: Cambridge University Press.

Hudson, J. A. (1993) Reminiscing with mothers and others: Autobiographical memory in young two-year-olds. *Journal of Narrative and Life History* 3 (1), 1–32.

Hudson, J.A. and Shapiro, L.R. (1991) From knowing to telling: The development of children's scripts, stories, and personal narratives. In A. McCabe and C. Peterson (eds) *Developing Narrative Structure* (pp. 89–136). Hillsdale, NJ: Lawrence Erlbaum Associates.

Hymes, D. (1964) Toward ethnographies of communication: The analysis of communicative events. In P.P. Giglioli (ed.) *Language and Social Context* (pp. 21–44). Harmondsworth, England: Penguin Books.

Hymes, D. (1972) Models of the interaction of language and social life. In J. Gumperz and D. Hymes (eds) *Directions in Sociolinguistics: The Ethnography of Communication* (pp. 35–71). New York: Holt, Rinehart and Winston.

Hymes, D. (1974a) *Foundations in Sociolinguistics: An Ethnographic Approach.* Philadelphia, PA: University of Pennsylvania Press.

Hymes, D. (1974b) Speech and language: On the origins and foundations of inequity among speakers. In E. Haugen and M. Bloomfield (eds) *Language as a Human Problem* (pp. 45–71). New York: Norton.

Hymes, D. (1981) *'In Vain I Tried to Tell You': Studies in Native American Ethnopoetics.* Philadelphia, PA: University of Pennsylvania Press.

Hymes, D. (1982) Narrative form as a 'grammar' of experience: Native Americans and a glimpse of English. *Journal of Education* 2, 121–142.

Hymes, D. (1985) Language, memory, and selective performance: Cultee's 'Salmon's myth' as twice told to Boas. *Journal of American Folklore* 98, 391–434.

Hymes, D. (1990) Thomas Paul's Sametl: Verse analysis of a (Saanich) Chinook jargon text. *Journal of Pidgin and Creole Languages* 5 (1), 71–106.

Hymes, D. (1996) Oral patterns as a resource in children's writing: An ethnopoetic note. In D.I. Slobin, J. Gerhardt, A. Kyratzis and J. Guo (eds) *Social Interaction, Social Context, and Language: Essays in Honor of Susan Ervin-Tripp* (pp. 99–111). Mahwah, NJ: Lawrence Erlbaum Associates.

Isawa, M. (1984) *Wabi, sabi* [Loneliness]. In K. Murayama and K. Yamashita (eds) *Haiku-yoogo no Kiso-Chishiki* [Basic Knowledge of *Haiku* Terms] (pp. 301–304). Tokyo: Kadokawa.

Ishida, Y. (1984) *Teika Fukugen: Hyakunin-Isshu* [Restoration to the Original State of *Teika*: One Hundred *Waka* Poems]. Tokyo: Ofusha.

Ishimori, N., Inoue, Y., Kurihara, K. and Hida, T. (eds) (1992) *Kokugo Yon Ge: Habataki* [National Language Grade Four, Vol. 2, Flapping of the Wings]. Tokyo: Mitsumura Tosho.

Iwata, J. (1992) Metaphor no kakutoku [Acquisition of metaphor]. *Gengo* [Language] 21 (4), 52–57.

Jensen, A. R. (1969) How much can we boost IQ and scholastic achievement? *Harvard Educational Review* 39 (1), 1–123.

Kağıtçıbaşı, Ç. (1989) Family and socialization in cross-cultural perspective: A model of change. In J.J. Berman (ed.) *Cross-Cultural Perspectives: Nebraska Symposium on Motivation* (pp. 135–200). Lincoln, NE: University of Nebraska Press.

Kaplan, R.B. (1966) Cultural thought patterns in intercultural communication. *Language Learning* 16, 1–20.

Kasper, G. (2000) Four perspectives on L2 pragmatic development. In H. Sirai, S. Miyata, H. Nisisawa, H. Terada, K. Nakamura and N. Naka (eds) *Proceedings of the Second Annual Conference of the Japanese Society for Language Sciences* (pp. 3–8). Nagoya, Japan: JSLS Main Office.

Kim, Y.D. (1990) *Zainichi Choosenjin no Kika* [Naturalization of Korean Japanese]. Tokyo: Akashi Shuppan.

Kimura, K. (1994) The multiple function of *sumimasen*. *Issues in Applied Linguistics* 5 (2), 279–302.

Kintsch, W. and Greene, E. (1978) Recalling and summarizing stories. *Language* 40, 98–116.

Kumon Education Institute (1988) Kongetsu no *haiku* [*Haiku* of this month]. *Tanoshii Yoochien: Sukusuku Ruumu* [Happy Preschool: Growing-up Room] 12 (2).

Kumon Education Institute (1989) *Kodama* [Echoes] 174.

Kuno, S. (1973) *The Structure of the Japanese Language*. Cambridge, MA: MIT Press.

Kuno, S. (1987) *Functional Syntax: Anaphora, Discourse and Empathy*. Chicago: University of Chicago Press.

Labov, W. (1972) *Language in the Inner City*. Philadelphia, PA: University of Pennsylvania Press.

Labov, W. (1981) Speech actions and reactions in personal narrative. In D. Tannen (ed.) *Analyzing Discourse: Text and Talk* (pp. 219–247). Washington, DC: Georgetown University Press.

Labov, W. and Waletzky, J. (1967) Narrative analysis: Oral versions of personal experience. In J. Helm (ed.) *Essays on the Verbal and Visual Arts* (pp. 12–44). Seattle, WA: University of Washington Press.

Labov, W., Cohen, P., Robins, C. and Lewis, J. (1968) *A study of Nonstandard English of Negro and Puerto Rican Speakers in New York City* Vol. 2 (Cooperative Research Project No. 3288) Washington, DC: US Office of Education.

Landis, J.R. and Koch, G.G. (1977) The measurement of observer agreement for categorical data. *Biometrics* 33, 159–174.

Lanham, B.B. and Garrick, R.J. (1996) Adult to child in Japan: Interaction and relations. In: D. Shwalb and B. Shwalb (eds) *Japanese Child Development: Classics Studies, Responses, and Prospects* (pp. 97–124). New York: Guilford Press.

Lave, J. (1991) Situating learning in communities of practice. In L.B. Resnick, J.M. Levine and S.D. Teasley (eds) *Perspectives on Socially Shared Cognition* (pp. 63–82). Washington, DC: American Psychological Association.

Lave, J. and Wenger, E. (1991) *Situated Learning: Legitimate Peripheral Participation*. New York: Cambridge University Press.

Lebra, T.S. (1976) *Japanese Patterns of Behavior*. Honolulu: University of Hawaii Press.

Lee, O-Y. (1983) *Haiku de Nihon o Yomu: Naze 'Furuike no Kawazu' Nanoka – Nihonjin no Bi-Ishiki, Koodoo-Yooshiki o Saguru* [Reading Japan with *Haiku*: Why 'A Frog in an Old Pond' – An Analysis of Sense of Beauty and Behaviors of the Japanese]. Kyoto: The PHP Institute.

Lerner, G.H. (1991) On the syntax of sentences-in-progress. *Language in Society* 20 (4), 441–458.

LeVine, R.A. (1990) Enculturation: A biosocial perspective on the development of self. In D. Cicchetti and M. Beeghly (eds) *The Self in Transition* (pp. 99–117). Chicago: University of Chicago Press.

Levinson, S.C. (1983) *Pragmatics*. New York: Cambridge University Press.

Lewis, C. (1984) Cooperation and control in a Japanese nursery school. *Comparative Education Review* 28, 69–84.

Lewis, C. (1991) Nursery schools: The transition from home to school. In B. Finkelstein, A.E. Imamura and J.J. Tobin (eds) *Transcending Stereotypes:*

Discovering Japanese Culture and Education (pp. 81–95). Yarmouth, ME: Intercultural Press.

Lewis, C.C. (1995) *Educating Hearts and Minds: Reflections on Japanese Preschool and Elementary Education.* New York: Cambridge University Press.

LoCastro, V. (1987) *Aizuchi*: A Japanese conversational routine. In L.E. Smith (ed.) *Discourse Across Cultures* (pp. 101–113) New York: Prentice Hall.

MacWhinney, B. (ed.) (1999) *The Emergence of Language.* Mahwah, NJ: Lawrence Erlbaum Associates.

MacWhinney, B. and Snow, C.E. (1985) The Child Language Data Exchange System. *Journal of Child Language* 12 (2), 271–296.

MacWhinney, B. and Snow, C.E. (1990) The Child Language Data Exchange System: An update. *Journal of Child Language* 17 (3), 457–472.

Makimura, K. (1989) *Haiku*, hyakka-ryooran [*Haiku*, alive like all sorts of bright flowers]. *Asahi Shinbun Newspaper Extra Report and Analysis* 2 (26), 32–36.

Mannari, H. and Befu, H. (1991) Inside and outside. In B. Finkelstein, A.E. Imamura and J.J. Tobin (eds) *Transcending Stereotypes: Discovering Japanese Culture and Education* (pp. 32–39). Yarmouth, ME: Intercultural Press.

Markus, H. and Kitayama, S. (1991) Culture and the self: Implications for cognition, emotion, and motivation. *Psychological Review* 98, 224–253.

Masuda, H. (1995) Versification and reiteration in Hawai'i Creole English: 'If nomo paila mœn, awarai!'. *World Englishes* 14, 317–342.

Masuda, H. (1999) *Disukoosu koozoo, sono unoosei to fuhensei: Creole-go kara no chiken* [Discourse structure and its right-cerebral linguistic computations and universals: What Creole languages tell us]. *Gengo* [Language] 28 (10), 90–100.

Matsui, T. (1967) *Masaoka Shiki.* Tokyo: Ofusha.

Matsumoto, D. (2000) *Culture and Psychology: People Around the World* (2nd edn). Belmont, CA: Wadsworth.

Matsumoto, Y. (1993) Linguistic politeness and cultural style: Observations from Japanese. In P.M. Clancy (ed.) *Japanese/Korean Linguistics*: Vol. 2 (pp. 55–67). Stanford, CA: Stanford University.

Mayer, M. (1969) *Frog, Where Are You?* New York: Dial Press.

Mayes, P. and Ono, T. (1993) The acquisition of the Japanese subject marker *ga* and its theoretical Implications. In P. M. Clancy (ed.) *Japanese/Korean Linguistics*: Vol. 2 (pp. 239–247). Stanford, CA: Stanford University.

Maynard, S.K. (1989) *Japanese Conversation: Self-Contextualization Through Structure and Interactional Management.* Norwood, NJ: Ablex.

Maynard, S.K. (1990) *An Introduction to Japanese Grammar and Communication Strategies.* Tokyo: The Japan Times.

Maynard, S.K. (1993) *Discourse Modality: Subjectivity, Emotion and Voice in the Japanese Language.* Amsterdam, The Netherlands: John Benjamins.

Maynard, S.K. (1997) *Danwa Bunseki no Kanoosei: Riron, Hoohoo, Nihongo no Hyoogensei* [Possibilities of Discourse Analysis: Theories, Methods, and Japanese Expressions]. Tokyo: Kurosio.

Maynard, S.K. (2000) *Jooi no Gengogaku: 'Ba-kooshoo-ron' to Nihongo Hyoogen no Pathos* [Emotive Linguistics: Place-Negotiation Theory and Pathos in Japanese Expressions]. Tokyo: Kurosio.

Mazuka, R. (1999) *The Development of Language Processing Strategies: A Cross-Linguistic Study Between Japanese and English.* Mahwah, NJ: Lawrence Erlbaum Associates.

McCabe, A. (1991a) Editorial. *Journal of Narrative and Life History* 1 (1), 1–2.

McCabe, A. (1991b) Preface: Structure as a way of understanding. In A. McCabe and C. Peterson (eds) *Developing Narrative Structure* (pp. ix–xvii). Hillsdale, NJ: Lawrence Erlbaum Associates.

McCabe, A. (1996) *Chameleon Readers: Some Problems Cultural Differences in Narrative Structure Pose for Multicultural Literacy Programs*. New York: McGraw-Hill.

McCabe, A. (1997) Developmental and cross-cultural aspects of children's narration. In M. Bamberg (ed.) *Narrative Development: Six Approaches* (pp. 137–174). Mahwah, NJ: Lawrence Erlbaum Associates.

McCabe, A. and Peterson, C. (1990, July) *Keep them Talking: Parental Styles of Interviewing and Subsequent Child Narrative Skill*. Paper presented at the 5th International Congress of Child Language, Budapest, Hungary.

McCabe, A. and Peterson, C. (1991) Getting the story: Parental styles of narrative elicitation and developing narrative skill. In A. McCabe and C. Peterson (eds) *Developing Narrative Structure* (pp. 217–253). Hillsdale, NJ: Lawrence Erlbaum Associates.

McCabe, A. and Peterson, C. (2000, July) *An Effort After Meaning: Parental Influences on Children's Evaluations in Narratives of Past Personal Experiences*. Paper presented at the 7th International Pragmatics Conference, Budapest, Hungary.

McConaughy, S.H., Fitzhenry-Coor, I. and Howell, D.C. (1983) Developmental differences in schemata for story comprehension. In K.E. Nelson (ed.) *Children's language* Vol. 4 (pp. 385–421). Hillsdale, NJ: Lawrence Erlbaum Associates.

McCormick, E. (2000, 3 September) Asians will soon be biggest S.F. group. *The San Francisco Examiner* A1, A12.

Mehan, H. (1992) Understanding inequality in schools: The contribution of interpretive studies. *Sociology of Education* 65, 1–20.

Merriam, S.B. (1988) *Case Study Research in Education: A Qualitative Approach*. San Francisco, CA: Jossey-Bass.

Michaels, S. (1981) 'Sharing time': Children's narrative styles and differential access to literacy. *Language in Society* 10 (3), 423–442.

Michaels, S. (1991) The dismantling of narrative. In A. McCabe and C. Peterson (eds) *Developing Narrative Structure* (pp. 303–351). Hillsdale, NJ: Lawrence Erlbaum Associates.

Michaels, S. and Collins, J. (1984) Oral discourse styles: Classroom interaction and the acquisition of literacy. In D. Tannen (ed.) *Coherence in Spoken and Written Discourse* (pp. 219–244). Norwood, NJ: Ablex.

Miller, P. (1982) *Amy, Wendy, and Beth: Language Acquisition in South Baltimore*. Austin: University of Texas Press.

Minami, M. (1990) *Children's Narrative Structure: How Do Japanese Children Talk About Their Own Stories*. Unpublished qualifying paper, Harvard Graduate School of Education, Cambridge, MA.

Minami, M. (1994) English and Japanese: Cross-cultural comparison of parental styles of narrative elicitation. *Issues in Applied Linguistics* 5 (2), 383–407.

Minami, M. (1995) Long conversational turns or frequent turn exchanges: Cross-cultural comparison of parental narrative elicitation. *Journal of Asian Pacific Communication* 6 (4), 213–230.

Minami, M. (1996a) Japanese preschool children's personal narratives. *First Language* 16 (3), 339–363.

Minami, M. (1996b) Japanese preschool children's and adults' narrative discourse competence and narrative structure. *Journal of Narrative and Life History* 6 (4), 349–373.

Minami, M. (1997) Cultural constructions of meaning: Cross-cultural comparisons of mother–child conversations about the past. In C. Mandell and A. McCabe (eds) *The Problem of Meaning: Cognitive and Behavioral Approaches* (pp. 297–345). Amsterdam: North-Holland.

Minami, M. (1998) Politeness markers and psychological complements: Wrapping-up devices in Japanese oral personal narratives. *Narrative Inquiry* 8 (2), 351–371.

Minami, M. (2000) Crossing borders: The politics of schooling Asian students. In C.J. Ovando and P. McLaren (eds) *The Politics of Multiculturalism and Bilingual Education: Students and Teachers Caught in the Cross-Fire* (pp. 188–207). New York: McGraw-Hill.

Minami, M. and McCabe, A. (1991) *Haiku* as a discourse regulation device: A stanza analysis of Japanese children's personal narratives. *Language in Society* 20 (4), 577–600.

Minami, M. and McCabe, A. (1993, July) *Social Interaction and Discourse Style: Culture-Specific Parental Styles of Interviewing and Children's Narrative Structure.* Paper presented at the 4th International Pragmatics Conference, Kobe, Japan.

Minami, M. and McCabe, A. (1995) Rice balls and bear hunts: Japanese and North American family narrative patterns. *Journal of Child Language* 22 (3), 423–445.

Minami, M. and McCabe, A. (1996) Compressed collections of experiences. In A. McCabe (ed.) *Chameleon Readers: Some Problems Cultural Differences in Narrative Structure Pose for Multicultural Literacy Programs* (pp. 72–97). New York: McGraw-Hill.

Mishima, S. (1994) A new perspective on women's language in Japanese: An interview with Sachiko Ide. *Issues in Applied Linguistics* 5 (2), 425–435.

Mishler, E. G. (1990) Validation in inquiry-guided research: The role of exemplars in narrative studies. *Harvard Educational Review* 60 (4), 415–442.

Mishler, E. G. (1991) Representing discourse: The rhetoric of transcription. *Journal of Narrative and Life History* 1 (4), 255–280.

Mishler, E.G. (1995) Models of narrative analysis: A typology. *Journal of Narrative and Life History* 5 (2), 87–123.

Miura, I.T. and Okamoto, Y. (1989) Comparisons of U.S. and Japanese first graders' cognitive representation of number and understanding of place value. *Journal of Educational Psychology* 81 (1), 109–113.

Miyanaga, K. (1991) *The Creative Edge: Emerging Individualism in Japan.* New Brunswick, NJ: Transaction Publishers.

Modell, J. and Brodsky, C. (1994) Envisioning homestead: Using photographs in interviewing (Homestead, Pennsylvania) In E.M. McMahan and K.L. Rogers (eds) *Interactive Oral History Interviewing* (pp. 141–161). Hillsdale, NJ: Lawrence Erlbaum Associates.

Morgan, J.L. and Demuth, K. (1996) *Signal to Syntax: Bootstrapping from Speech to Grammar in Early Acquisition.* Mahwah, NJ: Lawrence Erlbaum Associates.

Morigami, S. (1993) *Saishin Hoiku Shiryoo-Shuu* [Current Child-Care Materials]. Kyoto: Minerva.

Morikawa, H., Shand, N. and Kosawa, Y. (1988) Maternal speech to prelingual infants in Japan and the United States: Relationships among functions, forms and referents. *Journal of Child Language* 15 (2), 237–256.

Morioka, K. (1986) Privatization of family life in Japan. In H. Stevenson, H. Azuma and K. Hakuta (eds) *Child Development and Education in Japan* (pp. 63–74). New York: W. H. Freeman.

Murasawa, K. (1984) *Renjuu* [Linked people]. In K. Murayama and K. Yamashita (eds) *Haiku-yoogo no Kiso-Chishiki* [Basic Knowledge of *Haiku* Terms]. Tokyo: Kadokawa, 297–300.

Murayama, K. (1984) *Ryooyoo haiku* (Convalescence *haiku*) In K. Murayama and K. Yamashita (eds) *Haiku-Yoogo no Kiso-Chishiki* [Basic Knowledge of *Haiku* Terms] (pp. 286–291). Tokyo: Kadokawa.

Nakamura, K. (1996) The use of polite language by Japanese preschool children. In D.I. Slobin, J. Gerhardt, A. Kyratzis and J. Guo (eds) *Social Interaction, Social Context, and Language: Essays in Honor of Susan Ervin-Tripp* (pp. 235–250). Mahwah, NJ: Lawrence Erlbaum Associates.

Nakamura, K. (2000) Polite language usage in mother-infant interactions: A look at language socialization. In H. Sirai, S. Miyata, H. Nisisawa, H. Terada, K. Nakamura and N. Naka (eds) *Proceedings of the Second Annual Conference of the Japanese Society for Language Sciences* (pp. 43–48). Nagoya, Japan: JSLS Main Office.

Nelson, K. (1981) Individual differences in a language development: Implications for development and language. *Psychological Bulletin* 17, 170–187.

Nelson, K. (1986) *Event Knowledge: Structure and Function in Development.* Hillsdale, NJ: Lawrence Erlbaum Associates.

Nelson, K. (1989) Introduction. In K. Nelson (ed.) *Narratives from the Crib* (pp. 1–23). Cambridge, MA: Harvard University Press.

Nelson, K. (1991) Remembering and telling: A developmental story. *Journal of Narrative and Life History* 1 (2 & 3), 109–127.

Nezworski, T., Stein, N.L. and Trabasso, T. (1982) Story structure versus content in children's recall. *Journal of Verbal Learning and Verbal Behavior* 21, 196–206.

Nicolopoulou, A., Scales, B. and Weintraub, J. (1994) Gender differences and symbolic imagination in the stories of four-year-olds. In A.H. Dyson and C. Genishi (eds) *The Need for Story: Cultural Diversity in Classroom and Community* (pp. 102–123). Urbana, IL: National Council of Teachers of English.

Ninio, A. and Snow, C.E. (1996) *Pragmatic Development.* Boulder, CO: Westview Press.

Nittetsu Human Development (1993) *Nippon: The Land and Its People* (4th edn). Tokyo: Gakuseisha.

Niwa, T. and Matsuda, M. (1964) *Basic Japanese for College Students* (revised). Seattle, WA: University of Washington Press.

Norton, D.E. (1991) *Through the Eyes of a Child: An Introduction to Children's Literature* (3rd edn). New York: Macmillan.

Ochs, E. (1979) Transcription as theory. In E. Ochs and B.B. Schieffelin (eds) *Developmental Pragmatics* (pp. 43–72). New York: Academic.

Ochs, E. (1986) Introduction. In B.B. Schieffelin and E. Ochs (eds) *Language Socialization Across Cultures* (pp. 1–13). New York: Cambridge University Press.

Ochs, E. (1996) Linguistic resources for socializing humanity. In J.J. Gumperz and S.C. Levinson (eds) *Rethinking Linguistic Relativity* (pp. 407–437). New York: Cambridge University Press.

Ochs, E. and Schieffelin, B.B. (1984) Language acquisition and socialization: Three developmental stories. In R. Schweder and R. LeVine (eds) *Culture Theory: Essays on Mind, Self and Emotion* (pp. 276–320). New York: Cambridge University Press.

Ochs, E. and Schieffelin, B.B. (1989) Language has a heart. *TEXT* 9, 7–25.

Ogbu, J.U. (1990) Cultural model, identity, and literacy. In J.W. Stigler, R.A. Shweder and G. Herdt (eds) *Cultural Psychology: Essays on Comparative Human Development* (pp. 520–541). New York: Cambridge University Press.

Ogbu, J.U. (1992) Understanding cultural diversity and learning. *Educational Researcher* November 21 (8), 5–14.

Ohta, A.S. (1994) Socializing the expression of affect: An overview of affective particle use in the Japanese as a foreign language classroom. *Issues in Applied Linguistics* 5 (2), 303–325.

Ohta, A.S. (1999) Interactional routines and the socialization of interactional style in adult learners of Japanese. *Journal of Pragmatics* 31, 1493–1512.

Ohta, A.S. (2001) *Second Language Acquisition Processes in the Classroom: Learning Japanese*. Mahwah, NJ: Lawrence Erlbaum Associates.

Okubo, T. (1958) *Shoogakusei no Kotoba* [Elementary-School Children's Language]. Tokyo: Shunjusha.

Okubo, T. (1959) *Shikoo-Ryoku o Sodateru Hanashi-Kotoba Kyoiku* [Spoken-Language Education to Raise Thinking Power]. Tokyo: Shunjusha.

Olson, D.R. (1977) From utterance to text: The bias of language in speech and writing. *Harvard Educational Review* 47 (3), 257–281.

Ovando, C.J. (1993) Language diversity and Education. In J.A. Banks and C.A.M. Banks (eds) *Multicultural Education: Issues and Perspectives* (2nd edn) (pp. 215–235). Boston, MA: Allyn & Bacon.

Peak, L. (1989) Learning to become part of the group: The Japanese child's transition to preschool life. *Journal of Japanese Studies* 15, 93–123.

Peak, L. (1991) *Learning to Go to School in Japan: The Transition from Home to Preschool Life*. Berkeley: University of California Press.

Pellowski, A. (1977) *The World of Storytelling*. New York: Bowker.

Peterson, C. (1990) The who, when and where of early narratives. *Journal of Child Language* 17 (3), 433–455.

Peterson, C. and McCabe, A. (1983) *Developmental Psycholinguistics: Three Ways of Looking at a Child's Narrative*. New York: Plenum.

Peterson, C. and McCabe, A. (1991) On the threshold of storyrealm: Semantic versus pragmatic use of connectives in narratives. *Merrill-Palmer Quarterly* 37 (3), 445–464.

Peterson, C. and McCabe, A. (1992) Parental styles of narrative elicitation: Effect on children's narrative structure and content. *First Language* 12 (3), 299–321.

Philips, S.U. (1972) Participant structures and communicative competence: Warm Springs children in community and classroom. In C.B. Cazden, V.P. John and D. Hymes (eds) *Functions of Language in the Classroom* (pp. 370–394). Prospect Heights, IL: Waveland Press.

Philips, S.U. (1982) *The Invisible Culture: Communication in Classroom and Community on the Warm Springs Indian Reservation*. New York: Longman.

Phillips, J.R. (1973) Syntax and vocabulary in mothers' speech to young children: Age and sex comparisons. *Child Development* 44 (1), 182–185.

Piaget, J. (1952) *The Origins of Intelligence in Children* (M. Cook, trans). New York: International Universities Press. (Original work published 1936.)

Piaget, J. (1959) *The Language and Thought of the Child*. London: Routledge & Kegan Paul. (Original work published 1926.)

Pinker, S. (1984) *Language Learnability and Language Development*. Cambridge, MA: Harvard University Press.

Preece, A. (1987) The range of narrative forms conversationally produced by young children. *Journal of Child Language* 14 (2), 353–373.

Reese, E. and Cox, A. (1999) Quality of adult book-reading affect children's emergent literacy. *Developmental Psychology* 35 (1), 20–28.

Reese, E. and Fivush, R. (1993) Parental styles of talking about the past. *Developmental Psychology* 29 (3), 596–606.

Reese, E., Haden C.A. and Fivush, R. (1992) *Mother–Child Conversations About the Past: Relationships of Style and Memory Over Time*. Atlanta, GA: Emory Cognition Project.

Reilly, J.S. (1992) How to tell a good story: The intersection of language and affect in children's narratives. *Journal of Narrative and Life History* 2 (4), 355–377.

Rogoff, B. (1990) *Apprenticeship in Thinking: Cognitive Development in Social Context*. New York: Oxford University Press.

Rogoff, B., Mistry, J., Göncü, A. and Mosier, C. (1993) *Guided Participation in Cultural Activity by Toddlers and Caregivers*. Chicago: University of Chicago Press.

Sachs, J. (1979) Topic selection in parent–child discourse. *Discourse Processes* 2 (2), 145–153.

Sachs, J. (1982) Talking about the there and then: The emergence of displaced reference in parent–child discourse. In K.E. Nelson (ed.) *Children's Language* (pp. 1–28). Hillsdale, NJ: Lawrence Erlbaum Associates.

Sacks, H., Schegloff, E.A., Jefferson, G. (1978) A simplest systematics for the organization of turn taking for conversation. In J. Schenkein (ed.) *Studies in the Organization of Conversational Interaction* (pp. 7–56). New York: Academic Press.

Saito, Y. (1979) *Chuusei Renga no Kenkyuu* [Study of *Renga* in the Middle Ages]. Tokyo: Yuseido.

Sakata, M. (1991) The acquisition of Japanese 'gender' particles. *Language and Communication* 11 (3), 117–125.

Sakurai, M. (ed.) (1976) *Hikkei Manyooshuu Yooran* [Survey Handbook of the *Manyoshu*]. Tokyo: Ofusha.

Saneto, A. (1986) *Momotaro* [The Peach Boy]. Tokyo: Doshinsha.

Saussure, F. de. (1959) *Course in General Linguistics* (W. Baskin, trans). New York: McGraw-Hill. (Original work published 1915)

Schank, R. and Abelson, R. (1977) *Scripts, Plans, Goals, and Understanding: An Inquiry into Human Knowledge Structures*. Hillsdale, NJ: Lawrence Erlbaum Associates.

Schieffelin, B.B. (1986) Teasing and shaming in Kaluli children's interactions. In B.B. Schieffelin and E. Ochs (eds) *Language Socialization Across Cultures* (pp. 165–181). New York: Cambridge University Press.

Schieffelin, B.B. (1990) *The Give and Take of Everyday Life: Language Socialization of Kaluli Children*. New York: Cambridge University Press.

Schieffelin, B.B. and Eisenberg, A.R. (1984) Cultural variation in children's conversations. In B.B. Schieffelin and J. Picker (eds) *The Acquisition of Communicative Competence* (pp. 378–420). Baltimore, MD: University Park Press.

Schieffelin, B.B. and Ochs, E. (1996) The microgenesis of competence: Methodology in language socialization. In D.I. Slobin, J. Gerhardt, A. Kyratzis and J. Guo (eds) *Social Interaction, Social Context, and Language: Essays in Honor of Susan Ervin-Tripp* (pp. 251–263). Mahwah, NJ: Lawrence Erlbaum Associates.

Schieffelin, B.B. and Ochs, E. (eds) (1986) *Language Socialization Across Cultures.* New York: Cambridge University Press.

Schooler, C. (1996) William Caudill and the reproduction of culture: Infant, child, and maternal behavior in Japan and the United States. In D. Shwalb and B. Shwalb (eds) *Japanese Child Development: Classics Studies, Responses, and Prospects* (pp. 139–163). New York: Guilford Press.

Schoolland, K. (1990) *Shogun's Ghost: The Dark Side of Japanese Education.* New York: Bergin and Garvey.

Scollon, R. and Scollon, S. (1981) *Narrative, Literacy and Face in Interethnic Communications.* Norwood, NJ: Ablex.

Scott, C.M. (1988) Spoken and written syntax. In M.A. Nippold (ed.) *Later Language Development: Ages Nine to Nineteen* (pp. 49–95). Austin, TX: Pro-Ed.

Scribner, S. and Cole, M. (1978) Literacy without schooling: Testing for intellectual effects. *Harvard Educational Review* 48 (4), 448–461.

Scribner, S. and Cole, M. (1981) *The psychology of Literacy.* Cambridge, MA: Harvard University Press.

Shapiro, L.J. and Fernald, A. (1998, August) *Enculturation Through Mother–Child Play in the United States and Japan.* Paper presented at the 106th Annual Convention of the American Psychological Association, San Francisco, CA.

Shapiro, L.R. and Hudson, J.A. (1991) Tell me a make-believe story: Coherence and cohesion in young children's picture-elicited narratives. *Developmental Psychology* 27 (6), 960–974.

Shibata, H. (1984) *Daidokoro haiku* (Kitchen *haiku*) In K. Murayama and K. Yamashita (eds) *Haiku-Yoogo no Kiso-Chishiki* [Basic Knowledge of *Haiku* Terms] (pp. 185–189). Tokyo: Kadokawa.

Shibatani, M. (1990) *The Languages of Japan.* New York: Cambridge University Press.

Shigaki, I.S. (1987) Language and the transmission of values: Implications from Japanese day care. In B. Fillion, C.N. Hedley and E.C. DiMartino (eds) *Home and School: Early Language and Reading* (pp. 111–121). Norwood, NJ: Ablex.

Shimizu, M. (1978) *Haikai-Shi Basho* [*Haikai* Poet *Basho*]. Tokyo: Gakubunsha.

Skinner, B.F. (1957) *Verbal Behavior.* Englewood Cliffs, NJ: Prentice-Hall.

Slobin, D.I. (1985) Introduction: Why study acquisition crosslinguistically. In D.I. Slobin (ed.) *The Crosslinguistic Study of Language Acquisition* Vol. 1: *The Data* (pp. 3–24). Hillsdale, NJ: Lawrence Erlbaum Associates.

Snow, C.E. (1972) Mothers' speech to children learning. *Child Development* 43 (2), 549–565.

Snow, C.E. (1977) Mother's speech research: From input to interaction. In C.E. Snow and C. Ferguson (eds) *Talking to Children: Language Input and Acquisition* (pp. 31–49). New York: Cambridge University Press.

Snow, C.E. (1983) Literacy and language: Relationships during the preschool years. *Harvard Educational Review* 53 (2), 165–189.

Snow, C.E. (1986) Conversation with children. In P. Fletcher and M. Garman (eds) *Language Acquisition* (pp. 69–89). New York: Cambridge University Press.

Snow, C. E. (1989a) Imitativeness: A trait or a skill? In G. Spiedel and K. Nelson (eds) *The Many Faces of Imitation in Language Learning* (pp. 73–90). New York: Springer-Verlag.

Snow, C.E. (1989b) Understanding social interaction and language acquisition: Sentences are not enough. In M.H. Bornstein and J.S. Bruner (eds) *Interaction in Human Development* (pp. 83–103). Hillsdale, NJ: Lawrence Erlbaum Associates.

Snow, C.E. and Ferguson, C. (eds) (1977) *Talking to Children: Language Input and Acquisition*. New York: Cambridge University Press.

Snow, C.E. and Goldfield, B.A. (1981) Building stories: The emergence of information structures from conversation. In D. Tannen (ed.) *Analyzing Discourse: Text and Talk* (pp. 127–141). Washington, DC: Georgetown University Press.

Snow, C.E. and Ninio, A. (1986) The contracts of literacy: What children learn from learning to read books. In W. Teale and E. Sultzby (eds) *Emergent Literacy: Written and Reading* (pp. 116–138). Norwood, NJ: Ablex.

Snow, C.E., De Temple, J., Tabors, P.O. and Kurland, B. (1994, August) *Literacy Across Two Generations*. Paper presented at the 102nd Annual Convention of the American Psychological Association, Los Angeles, CA.

Soga, M. (1983) *Tense and Aspect in Modern Colloquial Japanese*. Vancouver: University of British Columbia Press.

Spener, D. (1988) Transitional bilingual education and the socialization of immigrants. *Harvard Educational Review* 58 (2), 133–153.

Sperber, D. and Wilson, D. (1986) *Relevance: Communication and Cognition*. Cambridge, MA: Harvard University Press.

Staats, C.K. and Staats, A.W. (1957) Meaning established by classical conditioning. *Journal of Experimental Psychology* 54, 74–80.

Stanzel, F.K. (1984) *A theory of Narrative* (C. Goedsche, trans.) Cambridge, England: Cambridge University Press.

Stavans, A. (1996) Development of parental narrative input. *Journal of Narrative and Life History* 6 (3), 253–280.

Stein, N.L. (1988) The development of children's storytelling skill. In M.B. Franklin and S. Barten (eds) *Child Language: A Reader*. New York: Oxford University Press.

Stein, N.L. and Glenn, C.G. (1979) An analysis of story comprehension in elementary school children. In R.O. Freedle (ed.) *New Directions in Discourse Processes* (pp. 53–120). Norwood, NJ: Ablex.

Stevenson, H.W., Lee, S., Chen, C., Stigler, J.W., Hsu, C. and Kitahara, S. (1990) *Context of Achievement: A Study of American, Chinese, and Japanese Children*. Chicago: University of Chicago Press.

Stevenson, H.W., Stigler, J.W. and Lee, S. (1986) Achievement in mathematics. In H. Stevenson, H. Azuma and K. Hakuta (eds) *Child Development and Education in Japan* (pp. 201–216). New York: Freeman.

Stigler, J. and Perry, M. (1988) Mathematics learning in Japanese, Chinese and American classrooms. In G. Saxe and M. Gearhart (eds) *Children's Mathematics: New Directions for Child Development* 41 (pp. 27–54). San Francisco: Jossey-Bass.

Strauss, S. and Stavy, R. (eds) (1982) *U-Shaped Behavioral Growth*. New York: Academic Press.

Sulzby, E. (1986) Writing and reading: Signs of oral and written language organization in the young child. In W.H. Teale and Sulzby, E. (eds) *Emergent Literacy: Writing and Reading* (pp. 50–89). Norwood, NJ: Ablex.

Sulzby, E. and Zecker, L.B. (1991) The oral monologue as a form of emergent reading. In A. McCabe and C. Peterson (eds) *Developing Narrative Structure* (pp. 175–213). Hillsdale, NJ: Lawrence Erlbaum Associates.

Super, C.M. and Harkness, S. (eds) (1980) *Anthropological Perspectives on Child Development* (*New Directions for Child Development*, No. 8). San Francisco: Jossey-Bass.

Sutton-Smith, B. (1988) In search of the imagination. In K. Egan and D. Nadaner (eds) *Imagination and Education* (pp. 3–29). New York: Teachers College Press.

Sypher, H.E., Hummert, M.L. and Williams, S.L. (1994) Social psychological aspects of the oral history interview. In E.M. McMahan and K.L. Rogers (eds) *Interactive Oral History Interviewing* (pp. 47–61). Hillsdale, NJ: Lawrence Erlbaum Associates.

Tamis-LeMonda, C.S., Bornstein, M.H., Cyphers, L., Toda, S. and Ogino, M. (1992) Language and play at one year: A comparison of toddlers and mothers in the United States and Japan. *International Journal of Behavioral Development* 15 (1), 19–42.

Tannen, D. (1985) Relative focus on involvement in oral and written discourse. In D.R. Olson, N. Torrance and A. Hildyard (eds) *Literacy, Language and Learning: The Nature and Consequence of Reading and Writing* (pp. 124–147). New York: Cambridge University Press.

Tannen, D. (1986) Introducing constructed dialogue in Greek and American conversational and literary narrative. In F. Coulmas (ed.) *Direct and Indirect Speech* (pp. 311–332). Berlin: Mouton.

Tannen, D. (1989) *Talking Voices: Repetition, Dialogue, and Imagery in Conversational Discourse*. New York: Cambridge University Press.

Tannen, D. (1990) *You Just Don't Understand: Women and Men in Conversation*. New York: William Morrow.

Teale, W.H. and Sulzby, E. (eds) (1986) *Emergent Literacy: Writing and Reading*. Norwood, NJ: Ablex.

Templin, M. (1957) *Certain Language Skills in Children*. Minneapolis: University of Minnesota Press.

Tobin, J.J., Wu, D.T.H. and Davidson, D.H. (1989) *Preschool in Three Cultures: Japan, China, and the United States*. New Haven: Yale University Press.

Toda, S., Fogel, A. and Kawai, M. (1990) Maternal speech to three-month-old infants in the United States and Japan. *Journal of Child Language* 17 (2), 279–294.

Toolan, M.J. (1988) *Narrative: A Critical Linguistic Introduction*. London: Routledge.

Torrance, N. and Olson, D.R. (1985) Oral and literate competencies in the early school years. In D.R. Olson, N. Torrance and A. Hildyard (eds) *Literacy, Language, and Learning: The Nature of Consequences of Reading and Writing* (pp. 256–284). New York: Cambridge University Press.

Tsubouchi, T. (1985) *Yooji ni koso haiku o* [It is young children who should learn *haiku*]. In K. Kumon (ed.) *Haiku Cards*. Tokyo: Kumon.

Tulving, E. (1972) Episodic and semantic memory. In E. Tulving and W. Donaldson (eds) *Organization in Memory* (pp. 381—403). New York: Academic Press.

Uchida, N. (1986) *Gokko kara Fantajii e: Kodomo no Soozoo Sekai* [From Play to Fantasy: Children's Imaginary World]. Tokyo: Shinyosha.

Uchida, N. (1990) *Kodomo no Bunshoo: Kaku Koto to Kangaeru Koto* [Children's Sentences: Writing and Thinking]. Tokyo: Tokyo University Press.

Vogel, E. (1979) *Japan as Number One*. Cambridge, MA: Harvard University Press.

Vygotsky, L.S. (1978) *Mind in Society: The Development of Higher Psychological Processes*. Cambridge, MA: Harvard University Press.

Wanner, E. and Gleitman, L.R. (eds) (1982) *Language Acquisition: The State of the Art*. New York: Cambridge University Press.

Weist, R.M. (1986) Tense and aspect. In P. Fletcher and M. Garman (eds) *Language Acquisition: Studies in First Language Development* (pp. 356–374). Cambridge, England: Cambridge University Press.

White, S. (1989) Back-channels across cultures: A study of Americans and Japanese. *Language in Society* 18 (1), 59–76.

Whiting, B.B. and Edwards, C.P. (1988) *Children of Different Worlds: The Formation of Social Behavior*. Cambridge, MA: Harvard University Press.

Whorf, B.L. (1956) *Language, Thought, and Reality: Selected Writings* (J.B. Carroll, ed.). Cambridge, MA: MIT Press.

Winner, E. (1988) *The Point of Words: Children's Understanding of Metaphor and Irony*. Cambridge, MA: Harvard University Press.

Yamada, H. (1992) *American and Japanese Business Discourse: A Comparison of Interactional Styles*. Norwood, NJ: Ablex.

Yamada, Y. (1956) *Manyooshuu to Nihon-Bungei* (The Manyoshu and Japanese Literature). Tokyo: Chuokoron.

Yamamoto, K. (1969) *Haiku no Sekai* [The World of *Haiku*]. Tokyo: Kodansha.

Yamashita, H., Stowe, L. and Nakayama, M. (1993) Processing of Japanese relative clause constructions. In P.M. Clancy (ed.) *Japanese/Korean Linguistics*: Vol. 2 (pp. 248–263). Stanford, CA: Stanford University.

Yamashita, K. (1984) *Ageku* (Raising verse). In K. Murayama and K. Yamashita (eds) *Haiku-Yoogo no Kiso-Chishiki* [Basic Knowledge of *Haiku* Terms]. Tokyo: Kadokawa, 13–18.

Yasuda, A. (1962) *Nihon no Shiika* [Japanese Poems]. Osaka: Sogensha.

Yngve, V. H. (1970) On getting a word in edgewise. *Papers from the sixth regional meeting of the Chicago Linguistics Society*. Chicago: Chicago Linguistics Society.

Yoda, J. (1986) *Hanasaka jii-san* [Old man Flower Blower]. Tokyo: Doshinsha.

Index

Subjects

African American Vernacular English (AAVE) 17, 82

Amae (psychological and emotional dependence) 55, 67, 133, 139, 144, 147, 167, 203, 262, 277, 284

Ambiguous communication 27-32, Ch.2 Note 6, 73

Back-channel (*aizuchi*) 4, 170, 212

Basho (*haiku* poet) 67-68, 268

Behaviorism
— behaviorist (Skinnerian) approach 14, 76, 194
— empiricism 24, 280
— stimulus-response-reinforcement system 15
— verbal behavior 14

Bootstrapping 155

Case markers
— object marker *ga* 156
— subject marker *ga* 30, 117, 124, 133, 141, 156
— *ga* for a staging effect 117
— *wa* (contrastive) 121, Ch.5 Note 5, 204
— *wa* (thematic/topic marker) 30, 116, 135, 141

Causal relationship (connectives and adverbs) 129, 164, 188, 285

Characteristics of the Japanese language
— Altaic language 30
— postpositional 30
— SOV language 30, 252
— subject-prominent Ch.5 Note 3
— topic-prominent Ch.5 Note 3

Child Language Data Exchange System
— CHAT 65, 242
— CHILDES 65, 82
— CLAN 65, 89, 182

Child-directed speech (CDS or motherese) 22, 247

Chomskyan linguistics
— competence 16

— nativism as view of language acquisition 239
— parameter 14-15
— performance 16
— universal grammar (UG) 14
— universalism 13, 76

Co-construction 52, 61, 252, 256

Codes
— elaborated code 19, 195, 279
— restricted code 19, 195, 279

Collectivism 29, 280

Communicative competence 2, 13, 16, 258

Constructivism 20

Contrastive narrative discourse analysis 197

Conversation analysis 158

Cultural transmission model 25

Culturally canonical forms of narrative 2, 95, 105, 148, 261

Culture
— definition of culture 1, 20

Decoding process 202, 213, 281

Decontextualization/self-contextualization 63, 73, 256, 274

Dual landscape of narrative
— landscape of action 37, 55
— landscape of consciousness 37, 55

Emergentist approach Ch.2 Note 11, Ch.9 Note 1

Empathy 111, 139, 146

Empiricism (*also see* Behaviorism) 24

Encoding process 202, 213, 281, 284

Enculturation 26

Episodic analysis 45

Ethnography of communication 16

Foreign/second language learning 285

Frame theory (framing) 41, 110

Gender differences 101, 104, Ch.4 Note 7, 176, 189, 213, 215, 219

Authors

Feldman, C.F. 37, 295
Fernald, A. Ch.2 Note 5, 295
Fischer, K.W. 1, 295
Fivush, R. 38, 92, 157, 295
Fludernik, M. 145, 295
Freire, P. 257, 295
Fujimura-Fanselow, K. 57, 295
Furukawa, Y. 286, 295

Gal, S. 36, 295
Gardner, H. 280, 295
Gee, J.P. 3, 5, 28, 40, 42, 48, 64, 80, 109, 113, 146, 154, 220, 257, 261, 287, 295, 296
Gerbert, E. Ch.5 Note 3, 276, Ch.9 Note 2, 296
Gilligan, C. Ch.7 Note 7, 296
Goldfield, B.A. 102, 296
Goodwin, C. 61, 296
Grice, H.P. 203, 204, 214, 296
Grusec, J.E. 267, 296
Gumperz, J.J. 13, 17, 296

Haley-James, S. 72, 296
Hall, E.T. 28, 280, 281, 296
Halliday, M.A.K. 240, 296
Harris, R.J. 45, 296
Hayashi, N. 71, 296
Hayashi, R. 4, 212, 296
Heath, S.B. 2, 21, 28, 63, 289, 297
Hebb, D.O. Ch.2 Note 1, 297
Hemphill, L. 19, 73, 297
Henderson, H.G. 68, 297
Hendry, J. 130, 297
Hess, R.D. 27, 155, 232, 297
Hicks, D. Ch.1 Note 2, 43, 77, 297
Hinds, J. 32, 110, 117, 297
Hoff-Ginsberg, E. 183, 226, 297
Holloway, S.D. 23, 25, 53, 234, 297
Hopper, P. 85, 98, 104, Ch.5 Note 7, 213, 297
Hudelson, S. 38, 156, 157, Ch.7 Note 4, 297
Hudson, J.A. 39, 77, 78, Ch.4 Note 3, 297, 298
Hymes, D. 2, 6, 13, 16, 20, 21, 28, 40, 41, 42, 44, 64, 80, 109, 113, 146, 154, 220, 261, 281, 282, 298

Isawa, M. 68, 298
Ishida, Y. 71, 298
Ishimori, N. Ch.9 Note 2, 298
Iwata, J. 55, 298

Jensen, A.R. 19, 298

Kağıtçıbaşı, Ç. 235, 256, 298

Kaplan, R.B. 45, 298
Kasper, G. 36, 298
Kim, Y.D. Ch.4 Note 4, 299
Kimura, K. Ch.4 Note 13, 299
Kintsch, W. 45, Ch.2 Note 10, 299
Kitayam, S. 278, 280, 300
Kuno, S. 30, 31, Ch.4 Note 2, 111, 117, 119, Ch.5 Note 5, 299

Labov, W. Ch.1 Note 1, 13, 17, 18, 19, 43, 58, 64, 69, 77, 80, 82, 83, 84, 85, 98, 100, 104, 109, 114, 145, 154, 182, 187, 188, 220, 238, 261, 272, 299
Landis, J.R. 87, 176, 206, 299
Lanham, B.B. 26, 299
Lave, J. 35, Ch.2 Note 7, 299
Lebra, T.S. 23, 24, 26, Ch.4 Note 2, 139, 233, 265, 266, 280, 299
Lee, O-Y. 69, 299
Lerner, G.H. 252, 299
LeVine, R.A. 26, 32, 299
Levinson, S.C. 158, 299
Lewis, C. 26, 55, Ch.5 Note 34, 205, 267, 299, 300
LoCastro, V. 4, 212, 300

MacWhinney, B. Ch.2 Notes 2 & 11, 65, 82, 160, 242, Ch.9 Note 1, 300
Makimura, K. 72, 74, 300
Mannari, H. 130, 300
Markus, H. 278, 280, 300
Masuda, H. 40, 43, 60, 81, 300
Matsui, T. 68, Ch.3 Note 4, 300
Matsumoto, D. 1, 20, 300
Matsumoto, Y. 27, Ch.5 Note 15, Ch.6 Note 2, 300
Mayer, M. Ch.5 Note 32, 300
Mayes, P. 156, 300
Maynard, S.K. 4, 23, 60, 83, Ch.4 Note 12, 110, 117, 118, 130, 131, 132, 144, 146, Ch.5 Notes 5, 8, 25 & 30, 166, 167, 169, 170, 212, 287, 300
Mazuka, R. 15, 300
McCabe, A. x, 5, 7, 8, Ch.1 Note 1, 13, 38, 39, 40, 43, 54, 59, 61, 62, 64, 77, 79, 80, 92, 102, 110, 144, 156, 157, 159, 179, 183, 197, 199, 226, 240, 247, 264, 284, 301
McConaughy, S.H. Ch.4 Note 4, 301
McCormick, E. 283, 301
Mehan, H. 235, 301
Merriam, S.B. 62, 301
Michaels, S. 3, 73, 78, 146, 301
Miller, P. 20, 21, 301
Minami, M. 5, 7, 8, 11, 13, 41, 45, 46, 47, 54,

78, 157, 189, 190, 256, 260, 264, 308

Wanner, E. 15, 308
Weist, R.M. 111, 131, 308
White, S. 4, 212, 309
Whiting, B.B. 32, 309
Whorf, B.L. 194, 245, 309
Winner, E. 55, 309

Yamada, H. 4, 30, 170, 212, 309
Yamada, Y. 66, 309
Yamamoto, K. 67, 68, 70, 268, 309
Yamashita, H. 31, 309
Yamashita, K. 70, 309
Yasuda, A. 66, 67, 309
Yngve, V.H. 170, 309
Yoda, J. 272, 309